CLARENDON LAW SERIES

Edited by

H. L. A. HART

CLARENDON LAW SERIES

———

ADMINISTRATIVE LAW

BY

H. W. R. WADE, Q.C., LL.D., D.C.L.

HONORARY BENCHER OF LINCOLN'S INN
PROFESSOR OF ENGLISH LAW IN THE
UNIVERSITY OF OXFORD

THIRD EDITION

CLARENDON PRESS · OXFORD

Oxford University Press, Ely House, London W.1

GLASGOW NEW YORK TORONTO MELBOURNE WELLINGTON
CAPE TOWN IBADAN NAIROBI DAR ES SALAAM LUSAKA ADDIS ABABA
DELHI BOMBAY CALCUTTA MADRAS KARACHI LAHORE DACCA
KUALA LUMPUR SINGAPORE HONG KONG TOKYO

ISBN 0 19 876016 7

FIRST EDITION 1961
SECOND EDITION 1967
THIRD EDITION 1971
REPRINTED 1974

Printed and bound in Great Britain by
REDWOOD BURN LIMITED
Trowbridge & Esher

PREFACE

In this new edition I have attempted to deal with many notable new events which bear on the two main themes of the book: the keeping of the powers of government under legal control; and the enforcement of fair administrative procedure.

I am not one of those who think that we have no real system of administrative law, or that almost every part of the subject is a jumble of contradictions and loose ends. To the student it may well seem that the case-law is excessively erratic in places. But he will find from the textbooks that their authors are just as much at variance about fundamentals as some of the judges. My own belief is that the main framework of rules has more logical, historical and constitutional validity than is sometimes supposed. This book is an attempt to present the subject as a system, stripped so far as possible of encumbering detail in order that the framework itself may appear clearly.

Since the previous edition was published in 1967 the courts have clarified and strengthened the law significantly. In retrospect one can see that they have been shaking off a mood of defeatism when they underrated their own resources. I have listed at p. 52 some of the more remarkable reversals of judicial policy which now give the subject a very different flavour from that of twenty years ago. The decision in *Ridge v. Baldwin* (1963) alone has opened the way to an apparently ceaseless stream of decisions on natural justice which are rapidly producing a detailed law of administrative due process.

A helping hand might now be given by Parliament. A Bill of Rights would strengthen the position of the courts and make the citizen more actively conscious of what the law can do for him. At the more technical level it is to be hoped that legislative reform of the law of remedies will result from the studies now under way in the Law Commission. For myself I welcome the decision of the Lord Chancellor against a Royal Commission with wide terms of reference, which would have had to spend much time considering a separate system of administrative courts of the continental type—a system in which I see little advantage and considerable disadvantage.

Above all, if the courts are to hold the scales fairly between government and governed, the bench and bar must be as familiar with administrative law as they are, say, with landlord and tenant. Many of the anomalies which I venture to criticize in this book arise because this happy state has not yet been attained. But at least it can be said that it now looks more attainable. The improvements which the courts have recently succeeded in effecting have been embodied in striking decisions which have mostly been based on law long-established but temporarily forgotten. This revival, combined with the current spate of administrative litigation, should in time solve the problem. But an administrative division of the High Court, as was established in New Zealand in 1968, might also have a healthy effect.

In order to accommodate as much as possible of the latest material I have removed or shortened a number of passages which had begun to look dated. Since it seems that the courts may be drawn into problems of university discipline, I have added a note to the Appendix on that topical subject.

While the book was in the press the courts have further developed the idea of a duty to act fairly and in accordance with natural justice even where there is no duty to act judicially. The cases cited at pp. 203, note 1, and 218, note 3, therefore deserve more prominence.

I have the pleasure of thanking not only the Clarendon Press but also the Italian house of Giuffrè, which in 1969 published an Italian translation (of the second edition) by C. Geraci under the title *Diritto amministrativo inglese*. The Italian version is honoured by an introductory essay by Professor M. S. Giannini which is of great comparative interest.

November, 1970   H.W.R.W.

CONTENTS

TABLE OF CASES

TABLE OF STATUTES

IN CHRONOLOGICAL ORDER

1

INTRODUCTION

THE NATURE OF ADMINISTRATIVE LAW

ADMINISTRATIVE law deals with one aspect of the problem of power. During the last hundred years the conception of the true sphere of governmental activity has been transformed. Instead of confining itself to defence, public order, the criminal law, and a few other general matters, the modern state also provides elaborate social services and undertakes the regulation of much of the daily business of mankind. The state has seized the initiative, and has put upon itself all kinds of new duties. Hand in hand with these new duties must go new powers. In order to carry out so many schemes of social service and control, powerful engines of authority have to be set in motion. To prevent them running amok there must be constant control, political control through Parliament and legal control through the courts.

This legal control provides much of the substance of administrative law. In essence it is the practical enforcement of the rule of law, meaning that the government must have legal warrant for what it does and that if it acts unlawfully the citizen has an effective remedy. As a necessary corollary, the government's powers must be limited. Wide as are the powers which Parliament grants, they are always subject to numerous restrictions, both express and implied. The implied restrictions which the courts have devised are what give this branch of the law its special flavour. Parliament may enact that a minister may make such order as he thinks fit, but the court may still invalidate the order if it breaks one of the many judge-made rules.

The protection of the citizen against abuse of power by the government is therefore the primary objective. 'The government' includes all kinds of public authorities, so that a docker wrongfully suspended by a Dock Labour Board may as easily be the subject of a leading case as a farmer whose claim is mishandled by the Minister of Agriculture. But this litigious aspect is by no means everything. Lawyers are much concerned with promoting fairness in administrative procedure, for example where a licence may be refused or where there is a formal tribunal or inquiry. Legal principles can do much to help the system of administration to work equitably and efficiently.

The party system gives the government of the day such a powerful hold over Parliament that Parliament's traditional control over the executive has been progressively weakened. As the constitutional balance of power has shifted, the importance of administrative law has grown. It is now all the more necessary for the courts to maintain and develop the legal restraints which make drastic governmental power tolerable. The more power the government wields, the more sensitive is public opinion to any kind of abuse or unfairness. Among the notable results of this mentality in recent times are the legislation about tribunals and inquiries, the establishment of the Parliamentary Commissioner for Administration, and a series of vigorous decisions by the courts.

It is more important to understand the broad objectives than to attempt to define administrative law scientifically. It should suffice to say that it is concerned with the nature of the powers of public authorities and, especially, with the manner of their exercise. Can a compulsory purchase order be quashed by the court? Can a minister's decision be set aside as unreasonable? Can an objector at a public inquiry demand to know the reasons for the proposed scheme? In answering such questions we are more concerned with the working of the administration than with its structure. Most of all, we are concerned with general principles which apply to public authorities of every kind, and which equally come into play whether a minister is confirming a slum clearance scheme or a chief constable is dismissed from the police force.

There is no need, therefore, to anatomize the system of government in extensive detail. We do not have to inquire how a town clerk is appointed, or what are the qualifications of borough councillors. A great deal must be taken for granted in order to clear the field. In just the same way constitutional law concentrates on the most important aspects of the organs of government, but leaves out much detail. The status of judges, for example, is of the greatest importance; but the precise structure of the courts is not. Nor, similarly, need we set out all the particular powers of administrative authorities. An account of them could fill several volumes, but it would distract attention from the general rules for their control.

Since it deals with the exercise of governmental power, administrative law is itself part of constitutional law. We are here on the most lively sector of the front in the constant legal warfare between government and governed. Whole new empires of executive power have been created. For the citizen it is vital that all power should be used in a way conformable to his ideas of liberty, fair dealing, and good administration. This is a matter of great consequence and of some difficulty, for social needs and traditional liberties are frequently hard to reconcile. The courts have, on the whole, evolved a body of sound and valuable rules for effecting this reconciliation. But they have sometimes failed to recognize their own achievements. There is a special need for presenting the subject in simplified form, so that its principles may stand out clearly.

A synopsis

A short epitome of the topics treated in this book will probably be of more help in explaining the nature of the subject-matter than any further preliminary discussion. The list is as follows.

1. *Constitutional principles.* The remainder of this chapter will be given to brief discussion of some of the main constitutional principles, such as the rule of law and parliamentary sovereignty, which have a formative effect on administrative law.

2. *Administrative authorities.* This chapter will discuss the constitutional and legal position of the more important types of authority, in particular ministers, the civil service, local government, the police, nationalized industries, and other public corporations. Some parts of their structure will be sketched, not with a view to presenting a picture of the administrative system as a whole, but in order to illustrate a few important aspects which will help in understanding the examples to come later.

3. *Judicial control of powers.* Here we reach the pith of administrative law proper: how far can the law control the exercise of the innumerable discretionary powers which Parliament has conferred on the various authorities? What happens if a minister or a city council acts unlawfully or carelessly or unreasonably? And what are the varieties of unlawful action? What will count in law as an abuse of power? Setting out from the simple proposition that the power granted must not be exceeded, the courts have devised numerous limits to the idea of discretionary power, so that public authorities often have less extensive power than might be thought.

4. *Remedies.* In theory this should be merely supplementary to the previous chapter, explaining the various remedies (damages, injunctions, certiorari, &c.) available against excess and abuse of power. But it is impossible to separate the two subjects cleanly, because some of the technical rules for particular remedies react in a confusing way on the principles of judicial control. Problems encountered in the previous chapter therefore tend to break out afresh. This is the most difficult part of the subject.

5. *Natural justice.* This is one special aspect of judicial control which can be treated separately. The rules of natural justice require that no one should be judge in his own cause, and that no one should suffer without being heard in his own defence. How far these rules can apply to administrative acts, such as authorizing housing schemes, granting planning applications, or cancelling licences, is both an important and a difficult question. How far the work of administration can be 'judicialized' by such rules, and how far the courts ought to assist the process, is one of the central problems of the whole subject.

6. *Statutory inquiries.* Parliament's favourite device for attempting to reconcile acts of administrative power (such as planning or housing schemes) with judicial consideration of objections is the statutory public inquiry. Here the administrative and judicial techniques meet in an awkward amalgam, and their incompatibility has caused trouble. The Report of the Franks Committee (1957) is

an important milestone on the road of reform. The same problems as to 'judicializing' administration arise again here, but in a more formal setting.

7. *Special tribunals.* Under many Acts of Parliament, especially those providing for social services, special tribunals have been set up to decide disputes which would otherwise go to the ordinary courts of law—disputes about national insurance payments, for example, go to national insurance tribunals. So many statutory tribunals had been set up, and so little system was there in some aspects of their work, that a thorough review had to be undertaken by the Franks Committee. Here we meet the highest possible degree of 'judicialization' of administration. Legislation now attempts to ensure that the fundamentals of proper procedure—'openness, fairness, and impartiality'—are observed, and that uniform standards are applied to all the numerous different tribunals.

8. *Crown proceedings.* Enforcing the law against the Crown and its servants is a topic which stands alone because of its special history, culminating in the Crown Proceedings Act 1947. In principle it is part of the law of remedies, but it is so specialized that it is best treated separately. We can then include two other important matters: the law of Crown service, i.e. the terms of employment of civil servants and others; and Crown privilege, by which evidence can be withheld from a court if its disclosure would be against the public interest. These have been two particularly weak spots of our legal system.

9. *Delegated legislation.* The outpouring of rules and regulations by government departments and other authorities is the source of various difficulties, some legal and some political. Judicial control must be exercised by the courts on the same principles as in Chapter 3, but in a specialized environment. There must be a proper system of publication. The remarkable extent of delegated legislative power means that the political machinery for supervising it is under constant strain, and something must be said of Parliament's counter-measures.

It will be observed that under some of these rubrics, especially

Nos. 6, 7, and 9, we will be concerned with questions of legal
and political organization rather than with problems of
positive law. But a single unifying thread will run throughout,
for in each case we are faced with the same question: how can
the legal ideals of fair procedure and just decision be infused
into the administrative powers of the state? How can the profession of the law contribute to the improvement of the technique of government? It is because all these topics offer scope
for this missionary spirit that they form a harmonious subject.
The quest for administrative justice is what gives direction to
our whole study.

SOME CONSTITUTIONAL PRINCIPLES

The rule of law

Everyone knows that the British Constitution is founded on
the rule of law, but the more closely we inspect this sacred
conception the more elusive we find it. Its simplest meaning is
that everything must be done according to law, but in that sense
it gives little comfort unless it also means that the law must not
give the government too much power. The rule of law is
opposed to the rule of arbitrary power. Coke, in picturesque
Jacobean language, spoke of 'the golden and straight metwand'
of law, as opposed to 'the uncertain and crooked cord of discretion'.[1] It is easy to appreciate the general drift: the rule of law
requires that the government should be subject to the law
rather than the law subject to the government. This broad ideal
is to be seen especially in administrative law, where the main
question is how executive power can be controlled by law and
also, so to speak, colonized by legal principles of fair and proper
procedure.

But, easy though it is to distinguish the rule of law from the
rule of arbitrary power, the difference comes down to no more
than one of degree. In our constitution there is now an enor-
mous amount of discretionary power—indeed, if there were
not, the subject of administrative law would fall to pieces. All
this power is subject to legal control, the courts can restrain
excesses, and the courts are independent of the executive. So
long as there are legal limits enforced by independent judges,

[1] 4 Inst. 41.

we say that the rule of law is upheld. But if the government or public authorities are exempted from the general law, as in the case of the Crown's former immunity in tort,[1] or where the decisions of a tribunal are made unchallengeable,[2] we say that the rule of law is broken. It comes to no more, in the last analysis, than striking a balance between power and responsibility at a point which commends itself to public opinion. But, nevertheless, there is no more genuine and necessary element in our law.

Theories and fallacies

This is no place to repeat the famous formulation of the rule of law in Dicey's *Law of the Constitution*. But Dicey's work for long threw a chilly shadow over administrative law, and this demands a few words. The paradox partly arises out of a verbal misunderstanding. Dicey maintained that 'administrative law' was utterly foreign to our constitution, that it was incompatible with the rule of law, with the common law, and with constitutional liberty as we understand it. But Dicey's 'administrative law' was a translation of the French *droit administratif*, and it was this, rather than any British conception, that Dicey denounced. He regarded it as a prime virtue of our rule of law that all cases came before the ordinary courts, and that the same general rules applied to an action against a government official as applied to an action against a private individual. Under the French system there were (and still are) special administrative courts, so that actions against officials or the state are in many cases subject to a separate system of judicature. What Dicey meant by 'administrative law' was a special system of courts for administrative cases. Even in Dicey's generation this was an unusual sense of the expression. But once that sense is appreciated, the paradox disappears.

Dicey's denunciation of the French system was based on his mistaken conclusion that the administrative courts of France, culminating in the Conseil d'État, must exist for the purpose of giving to officials 'a whole body of special rights, privileges, or prerogatives as against private citizens', so as to make them a law unto themselves. It has long been realized that this picture

[1] Below, p. 279.   [2] Below, p. 150.

was wrong, but it has become a traditional caricature. English judges can still speak as if *droit administratif* was a system for putting the executive above the law.[1] In reality the French administrative courts (which have served as a model for a number of other countries) have striven effectively to impose control on officials and to raise the standard of administration. The Conseil d'État, in its judicial and controlling functions, has achieved a high degree of objectivity, and its principal problem has been to prevent itself being overwhelmed with the number of cases brought to it. An administrative court such as the Conseil d'État, forming a wing of an administrative college of great power and prestige, can develop its own principles of law and keep them in step with the prevailing philosophy of the respective rights of government and governed. An English judge, trained basically in private law and administering a legalistic control, may feel less free to break new ground where new problems of public law call for new solutions.

The interesting aspect of the French system is that the administration has succeeded in developing, from within itself, its own machinery of self-discipline, administrative in its origins but yet fully imbued with legal technique. In Britain, on the other hand, the civil service works in an atmosphere far removed from legal influence, and legal control lies with entirely different organs, which by nature are unaccustomed to administrative work.[2] This exaggerates the cleavage between the legal and administrative worlds, and impedes the great objective—the improvement of administration by transfusion of the legal standards of justice. Both countries can claim great advantages for their methods. In Britain the standing of the courts is extremely high, and few would wish to see them abandon their historic function of protecting the subject against unlawful acts of government. But no one should suppose that administrative courts necessarily weaken administrative law. The natural result ought to be the opposite.

Parliamentary sovereignty

This peculiar feature of the British Constitution exerts a constant and powerful influence. In particular, it is an ever-present

---

[1] See [1965] Ch. at p. 1261; [1970] 2 W.L.R. at pp. 813, 821.
[2] See below, p. 22.

threat to the position of the courts, and it makes the judges cautious in controlling the executive.

The sovereign legal power in the United Kingdom is the Queen in Parliament, acting by Act of Parliament. An Act of Parliament requires the assent of Queen, Lords, and Commons, and the ordinary form of Act (assented to, in practice, by simple majorities in both Houses) is the only form of sovereign legislation. It is true that there are special procedures under the Parliament Acts 1911 and 1949 for overriding the House of Lords, but the true view of these is, probably, that they confer delegated, not sovereign, powers. Any previous Act of Parliament can always be repealed by a later Act. The Habeas Corpus Act, the Bill of Rights, the Act of Settlement, and so forth, are (legally speaking) just as easy to repeal as the Protection of Birds Act. No special majorities or procedure are needed. The ordinary, every-day form of Act of Parliament is sovereign, and can effect any legal consequences whatsoever. Once an Act of Parliament is shown, the court cannot question it: it can only apply it. The courts give their entire obedience to the Parliament for the time being.

The practical result is that this country has no constitutional guarantees. We have nothing like the Constitution of the United States (including the so-called Bill of Rights) or the 'entrenched clauses' in South Africa, which can be changed only by special procedures. In other countries the normal thing is to have a written constitution, embodied in a formal document, and protected, as a kind of fundamental law, against amendment by simple majorities in the legislature. In Britain, however, we have never made a fresh start with a new constitution, although in the seventeenth century the courts bowed to several revolutionary changes of sovereign. Not only do we have no constitutional guarantees: we cannot, it seems, create them. Since an ordinary Act of Parliament can repeal any law whatever, it is impossible for Parliament to render any statute unrepealable, or repealable only subject to conditions. Parliament cannot, in other words, modify or destroy its own sovereignty, for the courts will always obey its commands. This situation could, indeed, be changed by a revolution of some kind. But while it lasts, the whole of our law and our liberties are at the mercy of the parliamentary majority of the moment.

The position of the courts

The sovereignty of Parliament profoundly affects the position of the judges. They are not the appointed guardians of constitutional rights, with power to declare statutes unconstitutional, like the Supreme Court of the United States. They cannot insist, for example, that power should be subject to 'due process of law' and similar guarantees, if a statute should attempt to infringe them. They can only obey the latest expression of the will of Parliament. If they go too far in interfering with administrative affairs, Parliament may retaliate by legislation. Since the government is supported by the majority party in Parliament, it is relatively easy for a minister, prompted perhaps by his department which dislikes some legal decision, to procure an Act to overrule it. Under these influences the courts are bound to tread delicately.

Accordingly, the principles of administrative law cannot be derived from any sacrosanct constitution: they can only be found by studying the ways in which the courts interpret many different statutes, and looking for the logical connexions between different types of cases. For the most part, the courts show a strong desire for consistency, combined with an equally strong desire to give the citizen legal protection. Many general principles thus emerge. Although some writers criticize analytical study as 'conceptualism', this seems to be meaningless jargon. All law is 'conceptual' in that it demands synthesis of concepts and inductive logic. Administrative law, in particular, is in especial need of clear analysis in some of its most important parts, as later chapters will make plain. Its fundamental ideas are often by-products of the process of statutory interpretation, and it is only by comparison and analysis of numerous cases, often arising under very different statutes, that a coherent picture of the law can be drawn.

Administrative law has been seriously retarded by the neglect of such study in the past. As long ago as 1888 Maitland perceptively remarked that about half the cases in the Queen's Bench reports had to do with rules of administrative law.[1] But instead of studying these rules as a system, generations of lawyers were brought up on the fashionable fallacy that

[1] *Constitutional History*, 505.

administrative law was repugnant to the British Constitution. They deserved Tennyson's reproach that they treated the decisions as 'a wilderness of single instances'.[1] This neglect of general principles made it possible for an eminent judge to say in 1963 that 'we do not have a developed system of administrative law'.[2] One of the objects of this book is to disprove that statement.

Ministerial responsibility

The collective responsibility of the Cabinet to Parliament has most important effects of many kinds, for example on the organization and methods of the civil service, as explained in the following chapter. The courts, also, often take judicial notice of this link between the legislature and the executive. It inevitably makes the character of public administration very different from what it is in America under the presidential system, where Congress does not have ministers daily appearing before it to answer for their actions. But these are general constitutional differences, and their effects in the narrower field of administrative law will be best noticed from time to time as we proceed.

Ministerial responsibility is rightly praised as a means of making the government sensitive to the feelings of the electors, or at least of the elected. At the same time, on a lower and more practical plane of constitutional theory, it tends to be an impediment to the development of administrative law. The doctrine that a minister is responsible in Parliament for all his and his department's acts is easily turned into an argument that he ought not to be responsible in any other way—unless, of course, he incurs legal liability. But other kinds of political responsibility are needed also. For Parliament cannot possibly control the ordinary run of daily governmental acts except by taking up occasional cases which have political appeal. Administrative justice demands some regular, efficient and non-political system of investigating individual complaints against governmental action of all kinds, including the action of subordinate officials. Ministerial responsibility is an erratic and defective instrument for this purpose. Every so often a Member

[1] Aylmer's Field. See (1968) 21 Current Legal Problems, 75 at 84.
[2] Below, p. 203.

of Parliament achieves spectacular success with a constituent's grievance by a parliamentary question or a motion on the adjournment. But this is the safety-valve, not the control mechanism, of the administrative system. Parliament works in a highly-charged atmosphere, in which the doctrine of ministerial responsibility may make it politically suicidal for a minister to admit a mistake. This is exactly what is not required.

Control of administration

The feeling that the constitution in its classical form gives inadequate protection against the ever-growing powers of government has stimulated interest in the systems of other democratic countries. Some, like France, Italy, and Western Germany, have special administrative courts for actions against ministers and officials. These courts can develop extensive doctrines of legal liability, and can thus bring under legal control many acts of bad administration. They also have the advantage of their specialized administrative training. The courts in Britain, on the other hand, have no such advantage, and they have to be concerned with the technical legality of the action rather than with its merits. But public opinion sets great store by the right to take the government to law before the ordinary courts, which command high confidence; and there is a general distrust of governmental jurisdictions. There is also a feeling that it is in political rather than legal control that the real deficiency lies.

Attention has therefore turned to the Scandinavian device of the 'Ombudsman'. An ombudsman (the word means 'officer') is an official whose duty it is to investigate and report to Parliament on citizens' complaints against civil servants, the police, and other authorities. It is the Ombudsman's business to operate beyond the frontier where the law stops, and to take up complaints about action which, while perhaps legal, is unfair or inconsiderate. He has no legal powers, except to inquire, and he cannot reverse a decision. But his ability to investigate grievances and report them to Parliament, with consequent publicity, is a powerful lever. Thus he may often be able to persuade a department to modify a decision or to pay compensation; and the consciousness of his vigilance has a healthy effect on the whole administration.

The office of ombudsman has existed in Sweden for more than a century and a half. But it is as established in Denmark since 1954 that it has captured the attention of other countries. It has the advantage that it can be added to almost any parliamentary constitution. The first British country to adopt it was New Zealand, where an Ombudsman was established (under that name) in 1962. His reports showed the success of the experiment, and the United Kingdom followed suit.[1] Under the Parliamentary Commissioner Act 1967 the first Parliamentary Commissioner for Administration now investigates complaints of 'injustice in consequence of maladministration'.

Needless to say, it was objected that the sacred principle of ministerial responsibility would be violated. But in reality there seems to be no likelihood of incompatibility. The Council on Tribunals already acts as an ombudsman for some purposes.[2] The Comptroller and Auditor-General, who reports to the House of Commons on wasteful government expenditure, has been a kind of financial ombudsman for a century. It is significant that a former Comptroller and Auditor-General has now become the first Commissioner, as if to emphasize this point. The problems of his office arise not from constitutional theory but from the size of his task, since the United Kingdom is much larger than any other country which has adopted an ombudsman. His existence may also be unwelcome to a strongly entrenched civil service. But, since the great majority of his investigations result in justifying the government, he is in fact proving a valuable ally to the departments by explaining their ways to aggrieved citizens.

The Parliamentary Commissioner Act contains various restrictions. The Commissioner may receive complaints only from members of the House of Commons. This questionable provision is designed to preserve the traditional channel for the redress of grievances, in appearance at least. Once he has taken charge of the complaint the Commissioner may investigate it in any way he thinks fit. But he must make his report to the member of Parliament from whom the complaint came. He cannot be denied information by any claim of Crown privilege, but he is

---

[1] As recommended in *The Citizen and the Administration* (a report by 'Justice', 1961).
[2] See below, pp. 230, 276.

3—A.L.

subject to the Official Secrets Acts and ministers have power to prevent him disclosing specified information.

The Commissioner's powers extend only to the central government departments specified in the Act. But he may criticise the acts of ministers, which the New Zealand Ombudsman may not do. He cannot investigate local government or the police, except in cases where the central government is responsible. He is also excluded from some important areas of central government. These include action taken overseas, action under the Extradition and Fugitive Offenders Acts (but not the Commonwealth Immigrants Act 1962), action for investigating crime or protecting the security of the state, legal proceedings and the prerogative of mercy, the hospital service, contractual or commercial dealings and the treatment of servants of the Crown, both civil and military. Hospitals are excluded because the remainder of the national health service, being administered by executive councils and local authorities rather than by the central government, is excluded in any case. Nor may the Commissioner investigate cases where there is a remedy in a court of law or tribunal, unless he is satisfied that it is not reasonable to expect the legal remedy to be used.

In a large country there are sound reasons for limiting the Ombudsman's responsibilities in the initial period. But in principle he should cover every branch of administration. The government has announced that ombudsman arrangements for local government and for the national health service are under study with a view to legislation. Similar arrangements may eventually prove necessary for the police also.[1]

The annual reports of the Parliamentary Commissioner contain numerous case histories and statistics. His first reports showed that he upheld the complaint in about ten per cent of the cases fully investigated.[2] In 1968 he received 1,120 complaints, rejected 727 as outside his jurisdiction, completed 374 investigations and upheld 38 complaints. In 1969 the corresponding figures were 761, 445, 302 and 48. The increased percentage of complaints upheld (16%) was largely due to a period of abnormal strain on the Inland Revenue Department, which accounted for over half of them. The Parliamentary

---

[1] See below, p. 36.
[2] In New Zealand the figure is about fifteen per cent.

Commissioner has also issued special reports on important cases, such as the handling by the Foreign Office of the claims of the Sachsenhausen prisoners.[1] In several such cases the government have paid compensation to the complainants. Reports are also issued by the House of Commons Select Committee on the Parliamentary Commissioner, which plays an important part in supervising his work.

The Parliamentary Commissioner, who strangely is not a qualified lawyer, at first took a narrow view of 'maladministration', and supposed himself restricted to questions of procedure as opposed to matters of discretion. The Act provides that he is not to question the merits of discretionary decisions taken without maladministration;[2] but since he is concerned only with maladministration, the provision seems redundant. Under pressure from the Select Committee he has now undertaken to deal with bad discretionary decisions and bad departmental rules, and also with the administrative aspects of delegated legislation.[3] 'Maladministration' is a new legal term, but clearly it requires to be interpreted generously.

Examples of the Commissioner's ability to obtain a remedy where the law provides none include cases of people misled by official advice. Thus £167 of purchase tax was refunded by the Customs on a car imported into Scotland, since the owner had been wrongly advised that it would be free of tax. £950 was paid to compensate a company which had been misled into supposing that its new plant would qualify for investment grant.[4] In a bad case of delay, where the department had failed to deal with correspondence about a wife's claim to maintenance payments from New Zealand, she was paid £250 ex gratia.[5]

There is some overlap between the Commissioner and the Council on Tribunals, as explained later.[6]

[1] H.C. 54 of 1967–68.
[2] S. 12 (3).
[3] H.C. 350 of 1967–68; H.C. 385 of 1968–69; H.C. 13 of 1969–70.
[4] Commissioner's Annual Report for 1969, pp. 18, 141.
[5] Ibid. p. 50.
[6] Below, p. 276.

ADMINISTRATIVE AUTHORITIES

THE aim of this chapter is not to describe the whole structure of public administration, but to supply information about some of the types of authority which will play leading parts in later examples, or are otherwise of special interest. For our purposes these authorities tend to demand increasing attention as we descend the scale of constitutional importance. There is greater need to explain the status of the police, for example, than that of the Crown and ministers.

THE CROWN AND MINISTERS

Convention requires—and convention in this case is probably an even surer safeguard than law—that the Crown should act as its ministers advise in all constitutional affairs. The one case where the Crown still acts of its own volition is in the appointment of a prime minister, the initial act of impetus which sets the machinery of cabinet government in motion; but even that is governed by settled conventions. The Crown, therefore, has no political will of its own. The Crown's legal powers, which are manifold, are exercised by ministers who must answer for themselves in Parliament.

The Crown's powers are either prerogative or statutory. There is little left of the prerogative in our domestic administrative law. In the seventeenth century the Crown lost most of its powers of oppressing the subject; the residual prerogative is now confined to such matters as summoning and dissolving Parliament, declaring war and peace, regulating the armed forces in some respects, governing certain colonial territories, making treaties (though as such they cannot affect the rights of subjects), and conferring honours. The one drastic internal power of an administrative kind is the power to intern enemy aliens in time of war. We will investigate 'Crown Privilege' in Chapter 8; the right way to regard it, probably, is not as a branch of the prerogative but as a rule of the law of evidence based on public policy and controlled by the courts.

Innumerable statutes confer powers on the Crown and its servants. To-day the practice is usually to empower a designated minister or Crown agency. But sometimes the Crown itself is given power to act, often by Order in Council. A quaint feature of the statute book is its reluctance to mention the Prime Minister, so that for matters within his department the power is usually conferred upon Her Majesty in Council.[1] Where this taboo does not operate, the Act will confer it upon the appropriate minister or agency, e.g. the Home Secretary or the Treasury.

Until quite recently the great difference between the Crown, on the one hand, and its ministers and servants, on the other, was that the Crown was not, but its ministers and servants were, personally liable for wrongs in the nature of torts, such as negligence, nuisance, and trespass. The Crown Proceedings Act 1947 put an end to this anomaly, as Chapter 8 will explain. Even now, the central government is not subject to the compulsory processes of law enforcement, and has certain remaining privileges; but these are not very serious. It may be said today that the Crown and its ministers fit quite harmoniously into the pattern of legal duties and liabilities of which administrative law consists. The old obstacles, based historically on the doctrine that the Crown could not be subject to the jurisdiction of its own courts, have now been overcome. Even before the Act of 1947 much had been done to mitigate them in practice, for otherwise of course the rule of law would have failed just where the needs of the times were most insistent.

THE CIVIL SERVICE

General aspects

A rough definition of the civil service would include all non-political offices and employment held under the Crown with the exception of the armed forces. If all clerical and industrial employees are included, the grand total is in the order of 700,000. But the number of civil servants holding positions of any constitutional importance is very much smaller. The governors of the great administrative machine are the 'adminis-

---

[1] E.g. Parliamentary Commissioner Act 1967, s. 4 (2).

trative class', numbering about 4,500, who are assisted by the
'executive class', numbering some 90,000. It is to this small
élite that the term 'civil servant', in a political or constitutional
context, usually refers. The great numbers in the clerical and
industrial grades, though equally servants of the Crown and
subject to the same laws and principles, mostly do work which
is similar to other civilian work outside the Crown's service.
An additional quarter of a million or thereabouts used to be
accounted for by the Post Office, which could in a sense be
regarded as the first of the nationalized industries, although
formerly organized as a government department and subject to
the full measure of ministerial control and responsibility. Now
that the Post Office has been reorganized as a public corporation it ceases to count as part of the civil service.

To a political scientist's eye the most striking aspects of the
civil service are no doubt its political impartiality, its relations
with ministers, its methods of recruitment, and its centralized
administration. To a lawyer's eye a different but very remarkable characteristic presents itself: the extra-legal nature of
service of the Crown. The civil service is a world with which the
courts of law have little to do, except of course when civil
servants transgress their legal powers and provoke other people
to seek legal remedies. Matters of that kind are the subjects of
later chapters on 'Crown Proceedings', 'Judicial Control', and
'Natural Justice'. In that wider sense, administrative law is
throughout concerned with the activities of civil servants. But
as to their relations with the Crown and with one another the
law is strangely silent—or, if it speaks, it speaks with confusion.
The law of Crown service, such as it is, will be treated in the
chapter on 'Crown Proceedings'. Meanwhile we can notice
some general features of the civil service.

Detachment and anonymity
The British civil servant's remarkable detachment from politics and publicity is in a large degree due to the rigid constitutional doctrine of ministerial responsibility to Parliament.
Ministers must be answerable to Parliament for all that is done
in their departments, and, except in cases where orders have
been disobeyed or some mistake has been made, they cannot
throw the blame onto their officials. The cabinet system with

its parliamentary majority provides a firm front against which the tides of public criticism surge and break, and behind which the civil service shelters. The whole shock of any political attack is taken by political office-holders, and convention forbids any inquiry as to who has advised ministers or what advice has been given. By corresponding rules it is improper for civil servants in the higher ranks to take part in political controversies, to write letters to the newspapers on political topics, or to publish their replies to attacks made on them or their departments—although the practice of employing departmental public relations officers has led to some relaxation of the rule against self-defence in recent years. As a general rule, it is in Parliament that any defence must be made, and attacks made in other quarters are ignored. The civil servant thus achieves a very high degree of self-effacement, and although he is bound to be much concerned with questions of policy as well as with administration, he is insulated from the effects of political controversy. Working in this atmosphere of detachment, he can give his services to a government of any complexion with impartiality—or at least with the greatest degree of impartiality that it is reasonable to ask of a human being.

These interdependent qualities of impartiality and anonymity, being counterparts of fundamental constitutional principles, are indispensable benefits of our governmental system. But they encourage, naturally, another trait on which critics often dwell, the civil service's occupational tendency to secrecy. It is impossible to have the best of all worlds, and the secretiveness which sometimes becomes a vice is the price paid for the anonymity which must be counted as a virtue. The official instinct of hiding all kinds of departmental papers from the public gaze had important consequences for the law as to production of documents in court,[1] and it retarded the valuable reform of publishing the reports of inspectors who hold inquiries.[2] It is only on most exceptional occasions that the public is allowed to see the full details of the handling of some matter by government departments. One such occasion was the Crichel Down affair of 1954 (mentioned more explicitly below),[3] when

---

[1] Below, p. 306.   [2] Below, p. 235.   [3] P. 265.

the working of the administrative machine was made the subject of a detailed public inquiry and report. But an inquiry of that kind, involving the disclosure of departmental files and the pinning of responsibility upon particular officials, must make every civil servant all the more determined to avoid provoking such an event again. Certainly it would be impossible to hold such inquiries frequently without causing big changes in the machinery of government. A compromise has now been found, however, in the investigations of the Parliamentary Commissioner for Administration,[1] whose reports contain detailed accounts of cases giving rise to complaints of maladministration but do not identify the officials or the complainants.

The Fulton Committee's criticisms of departmental secrecy led the government to publish a white paper explaining how much information is already provided and encouraging the provision of more.[2] But it is complacent about the Official Secrets Acts 1911–39, which are a serious impediment to openness in government.[3] The principal Act of 1911 was a hasty piece of catch-all legislation which passed through the House of Commons in one day at the time of the Agadir crisis. It makes a criminal offence of all unauthorized disclosure of information from official sources, regardless of the question whether the public interest demands secrecy. Prosecutions require the consent of the Attorney-General, and it is only by executive control that the law has been rendered tolerable. An indiscriminate law of this kind is a breeding-ground of abuse, as was so clearly shown by the former law about Crown privilege under which the government could refuse to produce official documents in court.[4] In the United States, by contrast, the Freedom of Information Act of 1967 entitles any one to have access to any identifiable document of the federal government, subject only to specific exceptions relating to national defence, foreign policy, commercial secrets, etc. The American citizen interested in the government of the country is thus given a legal right to a great deal of information which it would be a

---

[1] See above, p. 13.
[2] Information and the Public Interest, 1969, Cmnd. 4089.
[3] For their history and defects see David Williams, *Not in the Public Interest*.
[4] See below, p. 308.

crime to disclose or receive in Britain.[1] In Sweden also governmental papers are largely open to public inspection.[2]

Control, recruitment and character

As regards internal administration, the ideals of the modern
civil service were proclaimed by the Northcote–Trevelyan
Report of 1853[3], much of which was put into force by Order in
Council in 1870. The Report called for entry by competitive
examination instead of patronage, promotion by merit rather
than by seniority, clear distinction between intellectual and
manual work, and unified control of the service as a single
organization. This last principle was until recently carried out
through Treasury control. The Treasury was accustomed to
dealing with all government departments in its supervision of
their expenditure, and thus it came to control 'personnel administration' throughout the civil service, regulating pay and
conditions of service, and issuing instructions to other departments in Treasury circulars and minutes. In his capacity as
head of the civil service the Permanent Secretary to the Treasury
used to advise the Prime Minister (who is also First Lord of the
Treasury) rather than the Chancellor of the Exchequer. A
radical reorganization was made in 1968, when general control
of the service was transferred to the new Civil Service Department. The Prime Minister has become also the Minister for the
Civil Service and day-to-day business is the responsibility of the
Paymaster-General. The Civil Service Commission, an independent body established in 1855, continues to have charge of the
standards of entry into the service and the holding of examinations. It is now part of the Civil Service Department, but its
independence is preserved.

The method of recruitment to the administrative class has
constitutional results of some significance. The entrance examinations are based on general education, not on technical or
professional knowledge, and they attract entrants of the highest
intellectual calibre. There are, of course, many civil servants

---

[1] See e.g. *Consumers Union of U.S. v. Veterans Administration* 301 F. Supp. 796
(1969) (government department required to disclose records).
[2] See Herlitz, Publicity of Official Documents in Sweden, [1958] Public Law
50.
[3] Reprinted in the Fulton Report, 1968, Cmnd. 3638, Appendix B.

with special technical and professional qualifications, obtained from outside professional bodies and demanded as prerequisites for civil service posts requiring expert knowledge. But the general principle on which the highest class of administrators is recruited is that they should have distinguished themselves in the ability to learn rather than in expertise. Legal qualifications, in particular, are relatively rare except among those recruited for legal posts, such as the office of the Treasury Solicitor and the Lord Chancellor's Department. The training and outlook of our leading administrators, therefore, offer a marked contrast with those of their counterparts in many European countries, where the passport to an official career is a degree in law or a highly specialized training. It is surprising to foreigners that under the British system so many eminent public servants have been first appointed on the strength of their skill in dead languages, history or mathematics. A major survey of the civil service by an independent committee has made this 'philosophy of the amateur' its primary point of criticism: 'The ideal administrator is still too often seen as the gifted layman who, moving frequently from job to job within the service, can take a practical view of any problem, irrespective of its subject-matter, in the light of his knowledge and experience of the government machine.'[1]

This contrast helps to explain the relative insignificance of the civil service as a topic in our administrative law. It also accentuates a feature of our system of government which is of deeper importance: the antagonism between the legal and official worlds. Perhaps antagonism is too strong a word. Nevertheless, the non-legal character of the civil service and its internal management tends to create habits of mind which are distinctly different from those of the legal profession. That profession, on the other hand, is exceptionally independent compared with the legal professions of other countries, especially in the fact that judges are recruited from the practising bar; there is no distinct judicial career in which a man's promotion may depend throughout his working life on a minister of justice.

The two professions of the public service and the law are thus inclined towards opposite poles of thought. This creates a gulf

[1] Report of the Committee on the Civil Service, 1968, Cmnd. 3638 (the Fulton Report), para. 15.

between the legal and administrative professions, and an exaggerated concept of the separation of powers. That is one reason why Britain has not favoured administrative courts, councils of state, and other such expedients which have helped to bridge the gulf in other countries. In later chapters we shall see how this dichotomy gives a stiff and formal character, in appearance at least, to our law of judicial control,[1] and produces two radically different views of the nature of special tribunals[2]. There can be no doubt that it is an impediment to the development of administrative law which is one of the needs of the times. On the other hand, it helps to preserve the fundamentals of the rule of law in as undefiled a form as the facts of modern life permit. It has also helped to produce a public service in which much pride is rightly taken. The balance-sheet is not an easy one to settle.

When the new methods of recruitment were first advocated by the reformers of 1854 it was said that such high qualifications were unnecessary for administrative staff, and that they would produce 'statesmen in disguise'. Experience has proved exactly the opposite, for the British system has produced in a high degree the combination of executive ability with political neutrality. If men such as John Milton, Matthew Prior, Matthew Arnold, and Anthony Trollope are no longer found in government offices, it is because of the professionalization of the service rather than because of any fall in the level of ability. The conventions and the rigours of government employment today mean that its Miltons are relatively mute and inglorious.

Restrictions on the political activities of civil servants were precisely formulated in 1954 as the result of the report of a committee in 1949. These are stringent for the administrative and professional classes, and for many of the executive and clerical grades who work with them and come into contact with the public. These classes may not take part in national politics, but may take part in local politics with the permission of their own departments. The rest of the executive and clerical grades may take part both in national and in local politics, subject to departmental permission, and subject also to a code of rules

---

[1] Below, p. 51.   [2] Below, p. 266.

enjoining discretion on matters of government policy. The other minor grades are free from restriction except when on duty or on official premises or when wearing uniform. But it is an over-riding rule for all classes that they must resign office if they stand for election to Parliament; this was ordained by Order in Council in 1927 and again in 1950.

The legal power of control over the civil service is nothing more than the power to employ and dismiss servants. This is probably not even 'prerogative' power, since it is shared by everyone under the ordinary law; but the Crown cannot, of course, pay its servants out of public money without authority from Parliament. In the background is a power which is, how-ever, prerogative: the Crown can dismiss its servants at pleasure. Civil servants enjoy no legal security of tenure whatever; thus all Orders in Council, Treasury regulations, and other directions as to conditions of service are effectively enforceable by dis-missal. The civil service, though it has grown into an enor-mous industry, still retains a kind of legal extraterritoriality in its internal affairs, in marked contrast to the liability of officials to obey the ordinary law of the land in their dealings with other people. These differing aspects of the legal status of civil servants need detailed discussion, which will be found in the chapter on Crown Proceedings.

Since 1919 there has been special consultative machinery for settling questions affecting the lower grades of the service, analogous to the machinery of industrial negotiation: there is a National Whitley Council (so called from the Report of the Whitley Committee of 1917) composed of representatives of the official and staff sides, and there are departmental Whitley councils also. But, like all the regulations of the service, these are its own domestic arrangements rather than matters of con-cern to lawyers.

LOCAL GOVERNMENT
Local authorities

Although many examples of the powers of local authorities will be found in the chapter on judicial control, the structure of the system of local government is not normally considered to be part of administrative law. Local government organization is a subject by itself, and all that need be done here is to draw attention to its general features. The numerous elected local authorities are grouped in a hierarchy known as the 'two-tier structure'. The upper tier is formed by the county councils, created by the Local Government Act 1888 to take over most of the administrative work which used to be done for each county by the justices of the peace. The lower tier is made up of urban districts, rural districts, and boroughs. But in many large cities there is a special unit, the county borough, which combines both tiers in one single authority. Thus any given place will be within the area of two authorities, a county council and a district or borough council, unless it is within a county borough. There is a division of powers and functions between the county and the district or borough authorities. In a county borough there is only the one authority for all purposes. London, however, has a two-tier system, which was radically revised and extended by the London Government Act 1963: the Greater London Council forms the upper tier and the London borough councils the lower. The City of London, a very small area, is in a special position, though it counts as a part of Greater London under the Act of 1963.

Urban and rural districts were established by the Local Government Act 1894. Boroughs were of ancient origin, and were originally created by royal charter. Their old and usually oligarchic constitutions were reformed by the Municipal Corporations Act 1835. But the City of London was spared, and subject to various statutes its ancient constitution still continues. Boroughs and district councils have much the same powers, but different constitutions. Boroughs have a mayor and aldermen as well as elected members of the council. District councils have a chairman. County councils have a chairman and aldermen. County borough councils have a mayor (called the Lord Mayor in a few special cases) and aldermen. Mayors and chairmen are elected annually by their councils. Aldermen, limited in number to a third of the elected councillors, are elected by their councils every three years and hold office for six years, half the number being elected at any one time. Borough councillors are elected annually by the voters and serve for three years, one-third being replaced each year. This arrangement secures continuity of experience on these councils. But county councillors all retire together every three years, though some

continuity is preserved through their aldermen. District councillors also serve for three years, but sometimes retire annually in
rotation and sometimes simultaneously, since there is power to
substitute the latter for the former system if the district council
wishes and the county council approves.

The division of powers between county councils, on the one
hand, and borough and district councils, on the other, is
roughly as follows. County councils are responsible for education, the fire service, town and country planning, and a number
of miscellaneous services connected with welfare and health—
though the central government administers the primary system
of social security, including the national health service (the
hospital service directly and the remainder indirectly through
local executive councils), national insurance and 'supplementary benefit', i.e. the former 'national assistance' which
replaced the old locally-administered poor law. County councils also play an important part in administering the police.[1]
Borough and district councils are primarily sanitary authorities, though in addition to this they have the important
function of being housing authorities. Urban district councils
also have powers to provide libraries, parks, and other amenities.
Responsibility for roads lies in many different quarters: trunk
roads are maintained by the central government; other main
roads, and in rural districts all roads, are under the county
council; the residue of urban roads belong to the borough or
urban district council, though the county council is also concerned with them for some purposes. In some matters, for
example roads and planning, powers may be delegated by
county councils to borough and district councils. A very important function of borough and district councils is to levy rates.
County councils do not collect rates directly, but address their
demands (precepts) to the local councils which must then levy
rates to meet both their own needs and those of the county.

An extensive review by a Royal Commission has resulted in
proposals for a radical reorganization of local government,
under which some 1,200 local authorities would be reduced in
number to under 100.[2] The main authorities would thus be

[1] Below, p. 30.
[2] Reform of Local Government in England, 1970, Cmnd. 4276; Report of the
Royal Commission on Local Government, 1969, Cmnd. 4040.

formed into much fewer and much more powerful units, with a much greater concentration of functions than at present.

Central control

The powers of local authorities are far from being exclusive, for these authorities form part of the general administrative hierarchy and are subject to much central control, as well as to control by one another. Thus county councils' powers over education and highways are subject to restrictions and directions given by the Department of Education and Science and the Ministry of Transport. Services such as housing, education, and police are often dependent on grants from the central government, which can, if dissatisfied, reduce its grants (though subject in some cases to approval by the House of Commons) and so exert a powerful influence. Its inspectors can keep a close watch on the police and on the schools. By-laws must be confirmed by the minister; so must housing, planning, and highway schemes; so must the raising of loans; so must appointments of chief constables. Sometimes ministers have power to compel county councils to delegate their powers to other councils. In many matters local authorities have little independence, and have become virtually organs of the central government. Nevertheless, much of the central control is merely regulatory, and is designed to secure the necessary uniformity of administration throughout the country. Within these limits local authorities still have initiative, and can act in accordance with local opinion.

An important instrument of central supervision is the district audit. It does not apply to certain parts of the accounts of many boroughs outside London, but with this exception it is a general system for the auditing of local government accounts by central government auditors, called district auditors. Thus the Ministry of Housing and Local Government keeps its finger on the pulse of local finance, and local authorities feel a powerful deterrent. The certainty that extravagances will be exposed in the audit is a more effective restraint than the more vague responsibility of councils to their ratepayers. It is also reinforced by personal liability. It is the auditor's duty to disallow any wrongful expenditure, provided it has not been approved by the Minister, and to surcharge the amount upon the persons responsible—who will usually be the councillors who voted for the expenditure. Similarly, the auditor must surcharge any one whose negligence or misconduct has caused a loss or deficiency in the accounts. Any such sum becomes a debt legally due from the person surcharged, so that councillors have a strong personal interest in taking due care of ratepayers' money. But if surcharged they may both appeal and apply for relief. Appeal lies to the High Court if the surcharge relates to an amount exceeding £500; in any other case there is a choice of appealing either to the High Court or to the Minister of Housing and Local Government; and on any appeal the Court or the Minister may confirm, quash, or vary the auditor's decision, or remit the case to him. Whether or not there is an appeal, the Court and the Minister further have power to remit the surcharge in whole or in part, if satisfied that the person surcharged ought fairly to be excused. A surcharge of more than £500 disqualifies from membership of any local authority for five years, but the Court or the Minister may grant relief from this penalty also.

It will already be obvious that district audit imposes a legal rather than a political control of the accounts. The auditor is only able to disallow expenditure which is not authorized by law, except in cases of negligence or misconduct. The auditor in fact exercises a judicial function, in much the same way as a statutory tribunal. Local electors may appear or be represented before him at the audit in order to object to any particular item, and he may be required to give a reasoned decision in writing either for rejecting objections or for making any disallowance or surcharge. District auditors thus carry out their statutory duties in a judicial and independent spirit, concerned rather to protect the ratepayer than to please the Ministry. Indeed, the Ministry has no power to interfere with their work except that it may approve irregular expenditure and so protect it from disallowance, and that it may make regulations as to the preparation and audit of the accounts. Some examples showing the part played by district auditors in keeping local authorities within their legal bounds will occur in the chapter on judicial control.

Local divergencies

It must not be supposed from this brief account that the powers and duties of the various local authorities are uniform throughout the country. Many of the more important authorities have obtained special powers by local Acts of Parliament, and although government departments have exerted themselves to advocate certain common principles, the patchwork of local legislation shows considerable diversity. There are also general statutes which leave the local authority with the option whether to adopt the statute or not. And Parliament has provided several special legislative procedures for certain purposes: Provisional Orders may be made by a minister after a public inquiry into any objections, but do not take effect until Parliament has passed legislation confirming them; and Special Procedure Orders under the Statutory Orders (Special Procedure) Act 1945 begin in a similar way, but are scrutinized by Parliament under a more expeditious procedure, which nevertheless provides for matters of general principle to be debated. These devices are attempts to improve on the slow and costly process of obtaining local Acts of Parliament, while at the same time allowing local and national interests to be weighed fairly in the balance. By these various means local authorities may enlarge their powers and functions.

THE POLICE

Local police forces

The outstanding fact about the British police is that, except in London, they are not under the direct control of the central government: they are organized in local forces maintained by local authorities. The central government has effective regulatory power, reinforced by financial control, which ensures that, for example, the pay, dress, allowances, and other conditions of service in the police force are uniform throughout the country. But it has no power to give orders directly to local forces, and local chief constables have a high degree of independence from any kind of political control. This is an important facet of the constitution, and a prime safeguard against the evils of the police state. A Royal Commission has discounted the idea that a centralized police force would endanger liberty,[1] but the aversion to such a force in this country is deep-seated.

[1] Final Report of the Royal Commission on the Police, 1962, Cmnd. 1728, para. 147.

The reason for this independence is that the modern police system, replacing the inefficient system of constables inherited from the middle ages, was devised in the golden age of political liberty in the nineteenth century. In London the Metropolitan Police were established in 1829 and were put under the Home Secretary's control—where they remain to this day. The next step was to establish borough police forces as part of the general reform of the boroughs, but so lively was the fear of creating a government-controlled *gendarmerie* that each borough was made responsible for its own force by the Municipal Corporations Act 1835. The City of London, untouched by that Act, obtained its police in 1839 and kept control of them itself within its small enclave in the metropolitan area. The county justices were empowered to form county police forces in 1839, and were obliged to do so in 1856.

The weakness of this scheme of things lay in the numerous small borough police forces, and there has accordingly been an inevitable tendency for borough forces to be merged in county forces. A drastic step was taken by the Police Act 1946, which merged nearly all borough police with the county police. The new basis, under the Police Act 1964, is that the police forces outside London belong to counties and county boroughs. But since these authorities may themselves be too small, there are powers for both voluntary and compulsory amalgamation of forces, subject to the control of the Home Secretary. Large composite forces have been formed, and many smaller authorities have been exterminated. Yet the number of separate forces in Great Britain still exceeds 60. It cannot therefore be said that there is yet any prospect of a single state police force.

Local councils do not themselves administer their police forces directly, but must act through statutory police authorities, which are called police committees in counties and watch committees in boroughs. These committees are composed as to two thirds of councillors and as to one third of magistrates. It is only under the Act of 1964 that magistrates have begun to sit on watch committees. But magistrates have always played an important part in the government of the county police. Originally the county justices were the sole county police authorities, under the Act of 1839. But when most of their administrative work was transferred to the new county councils in 1888, they continued to provide half the members of the police committee (then called the Standing Joint Committee). In Scotland magisterial participation has been abolished since 1929. But England has preserved the link with the justices, and has now extended it from the counties to the boroughs, though reducing the share of membership to one third.

The powers of appointment and dismissal of chief constables and of deputy and assistant chief constables belong to the police authority, but appointments require the Home Secretary's approval. Lower ranks are appointed and dismissed by the Chief Constable. Disciplinary powers are exercised similarly, but dismissals and other punishments are subject to appeal to the Home Secretary.

Central control

Along with this local autonomy there is much central control, although it always falls short of direct control of executive action. Under the Police Act 1964 the Home Secretary may make regulations 'as to the government, administration and conditions of service of police forces', and the regulations may cover (*inter alia*) qualifications, discipline, hours of duty, leave, pay and clothing. Parliament has thus conferred very wide regulatory power, which has been freely used. Regulations on such matters as hours of duty, pay and clothing must be submitted in draft to the Police Council, a statutory body representing the interests both of members of the police forces and of police authorities, and their representations must be considered. Regulations on certain other matters must similarly be submitted to a Police Advisory Board. Regulations have imposed a uniform code for the administration of the numerous forces, and have made great inroads on local independence. The Home Secretary is also armed with other powers, such as to require the police authority to retire a chief constable in the interests of efficiency. His power to withhold consent to the appointment of a chief constable is frequently used to compel the police authority to fill the post from outside rather than promote the next man in the local force, in order to prevent 'inbreeding'.

The other instrument of control, perhaps even more efficient, is finance. The central government has for over a century made a grant in aid of the cost of police services, which since 1918 has been 50 per cent. No local authority can afford to dispense with this assistance. But, as the price of it, its force must be certified as efficient by an inspector of constabulary, who is an officer of the Crown; and the government may withhold the grant wholly or partially unless satisfied that the force is efficient and that the regulations are being duly observed. These arrangements apply equally to the City of London Police. The Metropolitan Police in London, though partly financed out of local rates, are under the Home Secretary's direct orders. The central government can thus keep all police forces under close inspection and control. In particular, the size of each local force is effectively decided in Whitehall.

Nevertheless, a clear distinction is made between general regulation of conditions of service and interference with the daily duties of the police in enforcing the law. Ministers expressly recognize the principle that the police are independent in their task of preserving law and order. No ministerial responsibility is acknowledged for specific things that the police do, except in the case of the Metropolitan Police in London. This puts obstacles in the way of Members of Parliament wishing to criticize or discuss the conduct of provincial police forces. The Royal Commission which reported on the whole question of police status and accountability in 1962 recommended that ministers should be given statutory responsibility for the efficiency of the police, though not for their day-to-day actions.[1] The Act of 1964 accordingly requires the Home Secretary 'to promote the efficiency of the police,'[2] but this hardly alters the previous state of affairs.

The status of police officers

The position of the police in their ordinary activities is equally independent of the local police authority. It is a mistake to suppose that because they do not take orders from the central government, therefore they must take orders from the police authority. The truth is that a police officer holds a public

---

[1] 1962, Cmnd. 1728, para. 230.   [2] S.28.

position, that of peace officer, in which he owes obedience to no executive power outside the police force. The chain of command therefore terminates at the chief constable, who is in effect an independent authority,[1] and must act free from all political influence, whether national or local. Despite all the regulatory powers which the central and local authorities share between them, the responsibility for deciding whether (for example) the police shall arrest or prosecute some particular person cannot rest upon any one but the police themselves. As it was put in an Australian case:

The powers of a constable *quâ* peace officer, whether conferred by common or statute law, are exercised by him by virtue of his office and cannot be exercised on the responsibility of any person but himself.[2]

In the leading English case, where the police had by mistake arrested the wrong man on a criminal charge, an action for damages against the local police authority met with no success because the police, in making such an arrest, were acting on their own responsibility and not as servants of the local authority.[3] The legal link which could make the local authority liable was therefore missing. The position of a police officer was thus described:

He is a servant of the State, a ministerial officer of the central power, though subject, in some respects, to local supervision and local regulation.

And again:

The police, in effecting that arrest and detention, were not acting as the servants or agents of the defendants. They were fulfilling their duties as public servants and officers of the Crown sworn to 'preserve the peace by day and by night, to prevent robberies and other felonies and misdemeanours and to apprehend offenders against the peace'.

---

[1] See 1962, Cmnd. 1728, paras. 106 seq. Both the local and the central authorities may call for reports under the Police Act 1964, ss. 12, 30.
[2] Griffith C.J. in *Enever v. The King* (1906) 3 C.L.R. 969, an Australian case cited in *Fisher v. Oldham Corporation* (below).
[3] *Fisher v. Oldham Corporation* [1930] 2 K.B. 364.

And, to show the position still more graphically, the learned judge said:

> Suppose that a police officer arrested a man for a serious felony. Suppose, too, that the watch committee of the borough at once passed a resolution directing that the felon should be released. Of what value would such a resolution be? Not only would it be the plain duty of the police officer to disregard the resolution, but it would also be the duty of the chief constable to consider whether an information should not at once be laid against the members of the watch committee for a conspiracy to obstruct the course of criminal justice.

The Privy Council approved these passages in an Australian case, and added:

> To-day, as in the past, he (the police officer) is in common parlance described in terms which aptly define his legal position as 'a police officer', 'an officer of justice', 'an officer of the peace'. If ever he is called a servant, it is in the same sense in which any holder of a public office may be called a servant of the Crown or of the State.[1]

The State of New South Wales here attempted unsuccessfully to show that a police officer was their servant, but the Privy Council made it clear that their contention was just as fallacious as the contention that the police are servants of local authorities. They do indeed hold office under the Crown: when appointed they swear that they will well and truly serve the sovereign in the office of constable. And a policeman has, to the surprise of some critics, been held to be 'a person holding office under His Majesty' so as to make information obtained from him subject to the Official Secrets Acts.[2] But the oath no more makes him a servant of the Crown, in the sense of the relationship of master and servant, than does the oath taken by a judge.[3] The position, therefore, is that for purposes of legal liability the constable is the servant of no one, neither of the Crown nor of the local authority nor of the chief constable.

There must, however, be some way of charging to public funds the liability for wrongs committed by individual police

---

[1] *Attorney-General for New South Wales v. Perpetual Trustee Co. Ltd.* [1955] A.C. 457 at 480.

[2] *Lewis v. Cattle* [1938] 2 K.B. 454.   [3] See below, p. 286.

officers; for otherwise there might be no defendant worth suing. It was therefore the practice for the police authority to stand behind its police officers and pay the damages, much as the Crown used to do for its servants in the days before the Crown Proceedings Act 1947.[1] The Police Act 1964[2] now makes a subordinate police officer the notional servant of the chief constable for this purpose (but this purpose only), and provides that any damages and costs thus awarded against the chief constable shall be paid out of the police fund. This gives a legal basis to the former practice.

It should be remembered that the legal independence of a police officer at common law is due to the special nature of his duties as a peace officer. It is possible that constables performing other duties might be held to be acting on behalf of other persons. Cases of that kind have occurred in South Africa, where the government have been held liable for careless driving by a constable ordered to take charge of a vehicle, and for negligent custody by a constable of an arrested person's motor-car.[3]

Public relations and complaints

It is impossible to examine the cases on the status of the police without marvelling at how few they are, and in how many respects their position and powers are still not clearly defined. The police have had remarkable success in avoiding challenge in the courts of law. Yet the law does not give them wide discretionary powers: they must, for example, depose as to facts on oath before they can obtain a warrant for arrest; and in the cases where they may arrest a man without warrant, they must be prepared to prove at least reasonable grounds for suspicion.[4] Their independent position has no doubt greatly contributed to their ability to avoid legal disputes. Cases of malpractice inevitably occur, and a succession of these led to the appointment of the Royal Commission which reported in 1962. The Commission's recommendations were based on its general approval of the present system, despite powerful advocacy of a centrally controlled police force.[5]

---

[1] See below, p. 281. [2] S. 48.
[3] *Union Government v. Thorne* (1930) A.D. 47; *Lawrie v. Union Government* (1930), T.P.D. 402.
[4] See Criminal Law Act 1967, s. 2.
[5] By Professor A. L. Goodhart, Q.C. (dissenting memorandum in 1962 Cmnd. 1728, p. 157).

One problem which is likely to be a continuing source of difficulty is that of complaints against the police. The investigation of complaints is the responsibility of the chief constable, but it is obvious that he may find difficulty in judging the actions of members of his own force impartially. The Police Act 1964 now allows him (and allows the Home Secretary to direct him) to call in an officer from another force to conduct the investigation.[1] It also emphasizes that the handling of complaints is an important aspect of police efficiency. But the problem remains, and it caused a minority of the Royal Commission to recommend that a Commissioner of Rights (a kind of police ombudsman) should be appointed.

PUBLIC CORPORATIONS

Their uses

The public corporation is a hybrid organism, showing some of the features of a government department and some of the features of a business company, and standing outside the ordinary framework of central and local government. As an administrative device it has been in use for over a century, but it has leapt into particular prominence since it became the instrument of extensive nationalization of industry by the Labour government elected in 1945. It is by no means the only device for government control of industry. The government is a shareholder, and sometimes a controlling shareholder, in many large concerns.[2] But the public corporation has achieved a special constitutional position of its own.

The purpose of setting up a special corporation is to enable some industry or service to be operated for the benefit of the public rather than for the benefit of shareholders, but without the constant parliamentary investigation and criticism to which it would be subjected if it were merely a government department, as the Post Office has been for the past three centuries. Even the Post Office has now been turned into a public corporation in order to give it more commercial liberty and to free it from over-centralized civil service management.

An industry needs to be master in its own house and it needs

---

[1] S.49.

[2] e.g. Cable and Wireless Ltd. (wholly owned); British Petroleum Ltd. (49% shareholding, two government directors with powers of veto); Short Bros. & Harland Ltd. (70% shareholding).

enough independence to encourage bold and far-sighted decisions, subject only to the public interest. Thus there is an indefinite distinction between 'broad policy' and 'day-to-day administration', the former being the sphere in which ministers have power to intervene, and the latter being the sphere of independent self-management. In the case of social services such as the National Health Service or the creation of new towns, responsibility is devolved onto corporate bodies (regional hospital boards and new town corporations) so that there may be some degree of local independence combined with the necessary central control. Sometimes departmental functions are taken over by semi-independent corporations, as happened with the British Airports Authority and with the Post Office. Whenever Parliament is willing to grant a measure of autonomy, the public corporation is commonly employed. It has a legal existence of its own, and can be given statutory duties and powers which will fall outside the normal organization of the service of the Crown. It offers scope for many kinds of governmental experiment, under which central control, local control and independence can be blended in any desired proportions. We need not here pay special attention to bodies which are virtually part of the ordinary departmental machinery, and covered by full ministerial responsibility, such as the Forestry Commission, or to local government corporations, such as boroughs.

Two different techniques of nationalization were followed in the period 1945–9. One was to set up a corporate body, such as the National Coal Board, and to transfer to it, by force of statute, all the assets belonging to the industry. This was the method followed for the nationalization of coal-mining, electricity, gas, railways, airlines, and road transport. The statute then gave special powers of control to the appropriate minister, empowering him to give general directions which the corporation was required to obey. The other technique was the compulsory acquisition of shares. The shares might then either be vested by the statute in a public corporation, as the shares in iron and steel companies were vested in the Iron and Steel Corporation, or else they might simply be held by the government, as was the case with the nationalization of the Bank of England; in either event, the control of the undertaking was then secured through the operation of the ordinary rules of company law as well as by giving the minister special powers. The chronological list of the nationalizing statutes and the corporations created by them is as follows.

Bank of England Act 1946. No new corporation.

Coal Industry Nationalisation Act 1946. The National Coal Board.

Civil Aviation Act 1946. British Overseas Airways Corporation (which existed previously); British European Airways Corporation; British South American Airways Corporation (merged in B.O.A.C. in 1949 and later dissolved).

Transport Act 1947. The British Transport Commission (in which all assets were vested). Various corporate Executives were also created, including the Railway Executive and the Road Transport Executive. All these bodies have now been replaced by the British Railways Board and three other Boards (London Transport Board, British Transport Docks Board and British Waterways Board) under the Transport Act 1962. The Transport Act 1968 makes further changes, establishing the National Freight Corporation, the National Bus Company and other bodies.

Electricity Act 1947. The Central Electricity Authority (succeeded in 1957 by the Central Electricity Generating Board and the Electricity Council); Area Electricity Boards.

Gas Act 1948. Area Gas Boards; the Gas Council.

Iron and Steel Act 1949. The Iron and Steel Corporation. This was replaced by the Iron and Steel Board on the denationalization of the industry in 1953, and by the National Steel Corporation on renationalization under the Iron and Steel Act 1967.

Ministerial control

These statutes all contain different provisions, but a common pattern can be seen throughout. The key provisions are that the power of appointment and removal of members of the corporations is vested in the Crown or in a minister, and that the minister may give to the corporation 'directions of a general character'. This formula, vague though it is, indicates the distinction between the government's general powers of control in the public interest, for which some minister is responsible to Parliament, and the ordinary business management of the industry, in which the corporation is supposed to be free from ministerial and parliamentary interference. Any directions given under this power must be published in the corporation's annual report, which has to be laid before Parliament; but the minister is also given power to suppress publication if in his opinion it is contrary to the national interest.

These powers are enough to put the minister in a commanding position; but he also has important financial powers which by themselves give him a stranglehold. Programmes of reorganization or development, if they involve substantial capital expenditure, are subject to his approval. He may give directions, particular as well as general, as to the use of surplus revenues. He has control of the corporation's borrowing powers. For commercial purposes these are powers of life and death. But the minister need not, of course, use them. In fact the statutory power to give general directions has so far been used with marked restraint, and few directions of importance are to be found in the corporations' annual reports.

On the other hand, the small number of directions issued formally under the Acts is not an accurate measure of the extent of ministerial abstinence. The important financial powers can be exercised informally; and in the background are the more general powers, which cast a deep shadow over the corporations' precarious independence. The corporations are in constant touch with their supervising ministries, and the ministries exert much influence merely by holding the trump cards, without having to play them. Select committees of the House of Commons have reported, for instance, that the Air Corporations were subject to a 'formidable collection' of unofficial powers and 'to a degree of control far in excess of that envisaged by the statutes'.[1] Thus commercial judgment is warped by departmental influence, as appears to have happened when B.O.A.C. ordered too many Super VC-10 aircraft.[2] Similarly attention has been drawn to a 'gentlemen's agreement' made by the Coal Board that the general price level should not be increased

[1] *Report from Select Committee on Nationalised Industries*, 14 May 1959, pp. li, lii.
[2] Report of 9 June 1964, p. 22.

without the minister's consent[1]; and to the ministerial control established over gas prices, although the Area Boards were by statute responsible for fixing their own prices and were advised that the minister had no legal power to control them.[2] The B.B.C. insisted on a formal direction being made about the 'fourteen day rule' in 1955,[3] when the government wished to avoid giving directions and were yet determined to exercise control.[4] But the government have contrived to establish control over the nationalized industries without resort to this power. This not only has the effect of 'blurring the lines of responsibility' by mixing political and commercial motives[5]: it also means that ministers are exercising more power than appears openly, so that Parliament loses its opportunity to criticize.

Paradoxically the most effective use so far made of the power to give general directions has been as a means of escaping responsibility. In 1961 the government were attempting to enforce a 'pay pause' to prevent the constant rise of wages. A large wage claim was then pending before the Electricity Council. But the government declined to intervene on the ground that they were advised that they had no power, apparently because a particular wage claim could not be the subject of a 'general' direction.[6] Thus, while constantly exercising informal control, the government can shelter behind a narrow interpretation of the formal powers when they do not wish to embroil themselves. This hardly seems to be what the nationalizing legislation intended.

Degrees of control

Corporations which form part of the administrative structure of social services are usually more closely controlled by their ministers than are corporations which manage industrial undertakings producing revenue. For example, Regional Hospital Boards under the National Health Service Act 1946 are sub-

---

[1] Report of 29 Apr. 1958, p. xvii; cf. Report of 20 Oct. 1965, Pt. I, p. 52.
[2] Report of 31 July 1961, pp. 18–20. Excessive ministerial interference with the London Transport Board is criticized in the Report of 3 August 1965, p. 27.
[3] See below, p. 41.   [4] See 546 *H.C. Deb.*, col. 2318.
[5] Reports of 14 May 1959, pp. li, lii; 9 June 1964, p. 91; 3 August 1965, p. 27.
[6] See 649 *H.C. Deb.*, cols. 1146–1147; 650 *H.C. Deb.*, cols. 238–239; 81 Law Quarterly Review at p. 363. Contrast the influence of the Ministry of Transport on wages paid by the London Transport Board: Report of 3 August 1965, p. 23.

ject to ministerial directions in all respects. So are New Town Development Corporations under the New Towns Act 1965 (replacing the original Act of 1946). So also is the Bank of England—though no directions have been given.

At the other extreme there are statutory corporations which enjoy a very substantial degree of autonomy. The British Broadcasting Corporation, first constituted by royal charter in 1926 and at present chartered until 1976, operates under a statutory licence granted by the Postmaster-General.[1] The licence contains numerous restrictive conditions, both technical and political. In particular, the Corporation's members are appointed by the Crown; it may be required to transmit government announcements; and it may be required by the Postmaster-General to refrain from transmitting any specified matter or class of matter—for example, the 'fourteen day rule' (imposed in 1955 and revoked in 1956) put a ban on broadcasts about matters to be debated in Parliament within the next fortnight. But as a matter of policy the Corporation is given almost complete independence, subject only to standing directions forbidding it to give its own comments on current affairs and restricting party political broadcasts. Despite his extensive powers, the Postmaster-General normally accepts responsibility only for the general framework within which the Corporation works. Similarly, the Independent Television Authority, established by the Television Act 1954, may be required by the Postmaster-General to transmit or refrain from transmitting particular items, and is subject to directions as to the hours of its programmes and the areas which it serves (it was also directed to obey the 'fourteen day rule' of 1955–6); but otherwise it is independent.

There are other public corporations of a more local character which likewise operate independently, such as the Port of London Authority (created in 1908) and the Mersey Docks and Harbour Board (created in 1857). There are government members of these boards, but they are in a minority among the other representatives elected by local interests. These mixed corporations have many of the traits of elected local authorities. The public corporation is a flexible device for the diffusion of responsibility, and it is often resorted to when the stereotyped

[1] Charter, 1964, Cmnd. 2385; Licence and Agreement, 1963, Cmnd. 2236.

organs of central or local government do not provide what is required.

The Post Office

The Post Office has a special position, having been a government department in the full sense until turned into a public corporation by the Post Office Act 1969. Here therefore the device of the public corporation has been employed to increase rather than reduce the independence of a major industry.

The Minister of Posts and Telecommunications has the usual powers to give directions of a general character in the national interest and to appoint the chairmen and members, as well as a number of special powers. Whether the Post Office will enjoy genuine commercial independence will therefore depend on ministerial restraint, as in the case of the nationalized industries.

It is expressly provided that the new corporation is not to be regarded as the servant or agent of the Crown or as entitled to any Crown status or to any general immunity from taxation.[1] But the Act has preserved, and indeed extended, a wide statutory immunity from liability for wrongful acts which government departments themselves do not enjoy. It is provided that neither the Post Office *nor any of its officers* shall be liable in tort for what happens to anything in the post or for any failure, mistake or delay in the telecommunications service.[2] This is a breach of the important principle that a public official is personally liable for wrongful injury.[3] A person who delivers a parcel to the Post Office and sees it damaged or destroyed before his eyes has, it seems, no civil remedy—though criminal proceedings will lie, and even carelessness is a statutory offence in such a case.[4] What justification there is for depriving the subject of his personal remedy does not appear. There is a limited liability for registered packets,[5] but even this is hedged about with illogical limitations. It extends only to inland packets, so that a packet addressed to a foreign country is not covered, even though lost or damaged in this country.[6] The amount recoverable is limited by the fee

---

[1] S. 6 (5). [2] S. 29, replacing Crown Proceedings Act 1947, s. 9.
[3] Below, pp. 280, 282. [4] Post Office Act 1953, s. 59.
[5] S. 30 (also dating from 1947).
[6] *Triefus & Co. Ltd. v. Post Office* [1957] 2 Q.B. 353.

paid, so that it is a form of statutory insurance rather than ordinary liability in tort.[1] The action must also be brought within twelve months, instead of the usual six years. Thus is the Post Office made a law unto itself, in a manner which seems difficult to justify.

Legal consequences

Where public corporations have any appreciable degree of independence, they and their employees are not legally servants of the Crown. This means that they are themselves vicariously liable for the torts (e.g. trespass or negligence) of their servants or agents, in the same way as any other employer. They are as subject to statute law (e.g. for purposes of taxation) as is any other corporate body, unless expressly exempted. The legal independence of the corporation, precarious though it may be in fact, breaks the chain of command leading down from the Crown. The legal relationship of master and servant demands that the master shall have complete control of what the servant does. This test is not satisfied, in the case of a public corporation, merely because the minister may appoint and dismiss the members, or give directions 'of a general character', or (probably) because he can give any kind of directions. In one decided case, the result of which has since been confirmed by statute,[2] the British Transport Commission claimed to be able to eject a tenant from a house on the ground that the legislation protecting tenants did not apply to the Crown. But the Court of Appeal rejected the Commission's claim to Crown immunity.[3] Lord Justice Denning considered the minister's various powers and said:

These are great powers but still we cannot regard the corporation as being his agent, any more than a company is the agent of the shareholders, or even of a sole shareholder. In the eye of the law, the corporation is its own master and is answerable as fully as any other person or corporation. It is not the Crown and has none of the immunities or privileges of the Crown. Its servants are not civil servants, and its property is not Crown property.

[1] See *Buildings and Civil Engineering Holidays Scheme Management Ltd. v. Post Office* [1966] 1 Q.B. 247.
[2] Transport Act 1962 s. 30.
[3] *Tamlin v. Hannaford* [1950] 1 K.B. 18.

Similarly the British Broadcasting Corporation is not an agency of the Crown, and is therefore not entitled to the Crown's immunity from taxation.[1] A Regional Hospital Board, on the other hand, is a statutory agent of the Minister of Health, though subject to special provisions,[2] and the National Health Service is in law part of the services of the Crown.[3] The liability of the Crown and its servants is explained in Chapter 8.[4]

Responsibility to Parliament

When it comes to political responsibility, ministers can naturally be called to account in Parliament in so far as they have exercised, or failed to exercise, their statutory powers of control. But, as has been mentioned, a large measure of indirect and informal control is exercised for which the minister in effect escapes responsibility. Parliament is naturally much concerned over the working of nationalized industries, and from the first there were complaints that ministers would answer only general questions about them. Perhaps the most effective weapon in the hand of the Member of Parliament is the parliamentary question, which may often raise a general principle out of a particular case; but if questions on matters of day-to-day administration are refused, a large and important area is screened from inquiry. This, no doubt, is what was intended— otherwise the industries might as well have been run by government departments like the Post Office (formerly), the naval dockyards, and the ordnance factories. But there is a persistent feeling in Parliament that the curtain should somehow be drawn aside with the object at least 'of informing Parliament about the aims, activities and problems of the corporations and not of controlling their work'.[5]

A distinction between information and responsibility was thus suggested, and a Select Committee of the House of Commons was proposed. A first attempt in 1955 came to nothing, since the Select Committee was debarred from considering (*inter alia*) matters which were clearly the responsibility of

---

[1] *British Broadcasting Corporation v. Johns* [1965] Ch. 32.
[2] National Health Service Act 1946 ss. 12, 13.
[3] *Pfizer Corporation v. Ministry of Health* [1965] A.C. 512; *Nottingham Hospital Management Committee v. Owen* [1958] 1 Q.B. 50.
[4] See in particular p. 261.
[5] *Report from Select Committee on Nationalised Industries*, 23 July 1953, p. xii.

ministers and also matters of day-to-day administration. Since hardly anything falls between these two stools, the Committee had to report that it was powerless. But in 1956 a new Select Committee was empowered simply 'to examine the Reports and Accounts of the Nationalised Industries', and in due course a comprehensive series of investigations was made.[1] The Committee's terms of reference were extended in 1969 to cover the Bank of England (subject to certain exceptions), the Independent Television Authority, Cable and Wireless Ltd. and the Horserace Totalisator Board. Although the Bank of England was the subject of the first of the nationalizing statutes, it was the last corporation to be investigated by the Committee, which reported upon it in 1970.

The Select Committee's reports are of great value. They have revealed, and also criticized, the development of informal ministerial control discussed above. So far from subjecting the nationalized industries to excessive parliamentary interference, they have attempted to rescue them from excessive domination by government departments. They have also greatly helped towards public understanding of the industries' difficulties. As the industries have become adjusted to the balance of forces in the constitution, it has become plain that the original schemes of nationalization were unrealistic, and that Parliament has an important part to play.

---

[1] The Committee also investigated the Post Office before it became a public corporation.

3

JUDICIAL CONTROL OF
ADMINISTRATIVE POWERS

The task of the courts

GOVERNMENT under the rule of law demands proper legal limits on the exercise of power. This does not mean merely that acts of authority must be justified by law, for if the law is wide enough it can justify a dictatorship based on the tyrannical but perfectly legal principle *quod principi placuit legis habet vigorem*. The rule of law requires something further. Powers must first be approved by Parliament, and must then be granted by Parliament within definable limits. These limits must be consistent with certain principles—for instance, with the principles of natural justice—so that a standard is imposed on the administration which commends itself to the public conscience. The instinct for justice must be allowed to infuse the work of executive government, just as it must infuse the work of Parliament and the work of the courts.

How are these standards to be enforced? In France, and in other countries which have followed her example in developing special administrative courts, it is thought to be logical, and in accordance with the true separation of powers, to prevent the judiciary from interfering with the executive, and therefore to equip the executive with its own tribunals to deal with the legal control of its activities. Such a system of administrative self-discipline has some undoubted advantages, and in particular it softens the contrast between 'law' and 'policy', with their rigid demarcations, which occasionally inhibits the working of judicial control in England. But the English method is more logical still, for it distinguishes powers by their nature rather than by the persons who wield them, and regards judicial decisions of all kinds as the province of the ordinary courts of law. Today a great many new statutory tribunals share in this work, but their place in the scheme of things is considered elsewhere. The important point is that it is the ordinary courts of law which pass judgment on the legality of acts of government.

In doing this the judges are keenly conscious of their historic function of protecting the rights of the citizen against the executive. Working within a unitary legal system, they have devised principles of wide scope and considerable subtlety, and out of their somewhat antiquated legal armoury they have produced a battery of effective remedies. These two topics—the substantive law and the remedies for enforcing it—must to some extent be treated separately. Even from a brief account it will be seen that the material is abundant. If the high quality of the case-law is sometimes marred by erratic application, that is perhaps the price to be paid for the confusion of public and private law in one wide jurisdiction, where particular public-law principles do not stand out as clearly as they should from the general mêlée. If some of the remedies have the defects of their antiquity, that again is part of the price. The English courts of law are held in great respect by the public, and the satisfaction of being able to challenge the legality of the government's acts in the ordinary courts by ordinary procedure is a real one, not to be decried. That the courts can still play their traditional role of protector is something of more than sentimental importance.

Rights and remedies

Rights and remedies can never, in fact, be kept in separate compartments, and at the outset the 'ordinariness' of the law of judicial control is best illustrated by the remedies used. If a man is wrongfully arrested by the police, he may bring an ordinary action in tort for damages for assault and false imprisonment against any police officer who arrested or detained him, or on whose orders this was done, just as if the police were private individuals. Habeas corpus is available for his release, if necessary, without any distinction as to who is the person responsible. In one of the most famous of eighteenth-century cases, where a publisher's house and papers were ransacked by king's messengers sent by the Secretary of State, Lord Halifax, the remedy was an ordinary action of trespass, in which £300 damages were awarded.[1] In just the same way, if a man's land is compulsorily acquired under an order which for some reason

---

[1] *Entick v. Carrington* (1765) 19 St. Tr. 1030.

is illegal, he can bring an action of trespass against any person who disturbs his possession in attempting to execute the order. Or, if execution is merely threatened, he can obtain an injunction to forbid it.

When acting outside their powers, therefore, public authorities are as liable for injury that they do as is any one else. So, as a general rule, are the Crown and its servants, though the law as to remedies against the Crown is a separate subject.[1] The liability of statutory bodies for the misdeeds of their servants was settled by the House of Lords in a case of 1866, in which the Mersey Docks and Harbour Board were held liable for not removing a mud-bank at the entrance to one of their docks, on which a ship was damaged.[2] The House refused to extend to bodies of this kind the rule that applied to ministers of the Crown, namely, that they and their subordinates were all alike holders of public offices, and that the relationship of master and servant did not exist between them. That principle may well apply to relieve one subordinate from liability for another's wrongful act. But it does not protect the body which is the employer of them all. Thus statutory authorities such as the National Coal Board, the British Railways Board and the British Airports Authority have the same legal liabilities as commercial companies, subject only to the provisions of their constituent statutes.

Some immunity is given to persons executing the orders of courts of law, such as sheriffs and prison warders[3]; and the police have a narrow statutory immunity in executing warrants for arrest.[4] But administrative authorities have virtually no immunity. A few statutes exempt the members and servants of local authorities from personal liability for things done bona fide, but in those cases the authority itself can be made liable.[5] In any case, of course, a plaintiff is more likely to sue the authority who gave the orders than the servant who executed them, because the authority will be best able to pay the damages. All who participate in a wrongful act are jointly and

[1] Below, Chapter 8.
[2] *Mersey Docks & Harbour Board Trustees v. Gibbs* (1866) L.R. 1 H.L. 93.
[3] *The Case of the Marshalsea* (1613) 10 Co. Rep. 76a.
[4] Constables Protection Act 1751.
[5] E.g. Public Health Act 1875 s. 265, extended by National Health Service Act 1946 s. 72.

equally liable, and there is no defence of superior orders. 'English law does not allow a public officer to shelter behind a *droit administratif*.'[1]

But in many cases a public authority can act unlawfully without committing any actionable tort, for example where a claim for national insurance benefit or an application for a licence is wrongfully refused. The only remedy of private law which is then of use is the action for a declaration, in which the court can declare the claimant's rights. But this remedy has only recently come to the fore. Long before it did so, the courts had developed the nucleus of a system of public law out of the special 'prerogative' remedies of certiorari, prohibition and mandamus, together also with habeas corpus. These remedies are still of the greatest importance for the purpose of compelling ministers, tribunals and other governmental bodies to act lawfully and to perform their duties. They cover the area where the remedies of private law are weak or ineffective. But this in no way alters the fact that legality is enforced through the ordinary courts, applying principles of ordinary law.

Statutory power

The heart of the whole matter is statutory construction. Almost all the important powers of government derive from Acts of Parliament. There is little executive power to be found in the royal prerogative, for that has been whittled down to a handful of powers such as the declaring of war and peace, and the prerogative of mercy, which are not potential instruments of oppression. A few common law powers are also exercised by the police, but they are not extensive. So it is generally true to say that administrative powers derive from statute. There is no limit to the power which Parliament *can* confer, and in wartime it may be very wide indeed. In the Second World War, for example, ministers were given power to detain people without trial, and to impose certain kinds of taxation.[2] There are no constitutional safeguards to restrain the delegation of power by Parliament in any way whatever. What limits there are, therefore,

---

[1] *Ministry of Housing and Local Government v. Sharp* [1970] 2 Q.B. 223 (Lord Denning, M.R.).
[2] Below, pp. 321, 324.

are those which Parliament intended, or is deemed by the court to have intended. Under this system the law of judicial control depends entirely upon the presumptions which the court will make as to Parliament's intentions, reading between the lines of the statutes. The rules of natural justice, for example, are generalized presumptions of this kind. They have never been expressly enacted, but they result from the general assumption made by the judges that when Parliament confers certain kinds of powers it is intended that they should only be exercised in accordance with the rules of fair play.

The doctrine of ULTRA VIRES

The general theory of judicial control is correspondingly simple. It is commonly called the doctrine of *ultra vires*. Administrative power derives from statute. The statute gives power for certain purposes only, or subject to some special procedure, or with some other kind of limits. The limits are to be found not only in the statute itself, but in the general principles of construction which the courts apply, provided, of course, that the statute has not expressly or impliedly modified them—for every statute is an act of sovereign legislation and can abrogate all principles of administrative law if Parliament so wishes. But in practice all statutory powers have statutory limits; and where the expressed limits are indefinite, the courts are all the more inclined to find that limits are implied. The notion of unlimited power has no place in the system.[1]

It then follows that any act outside the defined limits (*ultra vires*) is an act unjustified by law, which can have no legal validity. The court will accordingly declare it to be quashed or to be a nullity. If it is also a wrongful act by the ordinary law (such as a trespass to person or property), damages may also be awarded; and in a suitable case the court may prohibit the wrongful act in advance. In granting these remedies the court is enforcing the rule of law, which requires that public authorities of all kinds should be able to show legal warrant for what they do, and that if legal warrant is lacking their action should be condemned. As a general rule the legality of their acts is

[1] Below, p. 78.

always open to attack, and there is no presumption in their favour.[1]

It will be evident that this system of judicial control of the executive, though concerned almost exclusively with statutory powers, itself rests primarily on the inherent jurisdiction of the courts. The fundamental principle of administrative law is the doctrine of *ultra vires*, and the source of this principle is the common law as laid down in decided cases by the judges. Administrative law has therefore ultimately a common law basis, which indeed is merely the application of the rule of law in the form of detailed legal doctrine.

When Parliament grants *power* to authorities, it inevitably also gives them *discretion*. The authority has to decide for itself whether to act or not to act, and how it wishes to act. If this discretion is not conferred, the authority has not a *power* but a *duty*. Many of the most difficult problems of judicial control are concerned with the question where power stops and duty begins. Even if the authority has undoubted power to do something, there may be duties as to *how* it is to be done. The *ultra vires* doctrine is therefore not confined to cases of plain excess of power; it also governs abuse of power, as where something is done for the wrong reasons, or by the wrong procedure. In law the consequences are exactly the same: an improper motive, or a false step in procedure, make an administrative act just as illegal as does a flagrant excess of authority.

It is hardly necessary to emphasize the strictly 'legal' character of this supervision which the ordinary courts of law exercise. No complaint will succeed unless the plaintiff proves a distinct breach of the law.[2] The courts have no concern with the conduct of government provided that it proceeds within its legal powers. Any misuse of power within the law is a political matter, and for discussion in Parliament or reference to the ombudsman. The courts of law are not general courts of administrative justice. Nor have we any general administrative appeal courts. The whole basis of control is 'legality' rather than 'merits'.

That, at least, is the theory. But there are many situations in which 'merits' may govern 'legality'. Most powers are exercisable for certain purposes but not for others, and are required

---

[1] See cases cited below, pp. 79, 145.
[2] But see Appendix, B.

to be exercised reasonably. The courts have been deeply drawn into this field, so that they frequently have to pass judgment on the motives and propriety of government action in order to determine whether it is legal. Thus they are accustomed to operating in the borderland which in some other countries is the province of special administrative courts. It would be a great mistake to suppose from the legalistic appearance of the doctrine of *ultra vires* that it need prevent the development of wide-ranging judicial review. Several recent decisions of the House of Lords illustrate this truth vividly.[1]

Judicial vacillations

The vigour and effectiveness of judicial review are particularly subject to fluctuations of judicial philosophy. These fluctuations can never have been more striking than in the last thirty years. In the decade that followed the Second World War the courts seemed to be in danger of losing faith in their function. This was the period which moved a distinguished judge to offer a 'death certificate' for a system of law which had lost the power to control the executive.[2] The mood of defeatism has now been thrown off, and the courts have reasserted their powers in a succession of invigorating decisions. As will be seen in this and later chapters, they have revived the old jurisdiction to quash decisions which are wrong on their face; they have re-established the principles of natural justice as a broad foundation for fair administrative procedure; they have not been daunted by 'blank cheque' powers saying that a minister may act as he thinks fit, and so forth; they have refused to be disarmed by statutes purporting to make decisions unchallengeable in the courts; and they have recovered control of the suppression of evidence by 'Crown privilege'. All these doctrines rest on well established authority, much of it going back for centuries. All of them were denied by the courts during and after the Second World War. All of them are now back in force.

These abrupt changes of front represent the price that has been paid for neglect of general principles, and for the failure

---

[1] Below, pp. 78, 151.
[2] (1956) 8 Current Legal Problems at p. 14 (Lord Devlin).

of the legal profession to understand what had been achieved by the courts in the past.[1] The present renaissance has resulted more from the rediscovery of old doctrine than from the invention of new. Its spirit is well expressed by a learned judge:

Indeed I consider that one of the most important functions of our courts is vigilantly to protect the rights of the individual against unlawful encroachment by public officers and by the administration. The courts' powers to this end might well, in my view, be enlarged. Certainly such powers as we possess should be vigorously exercised.[2]

Review and appeal contrasted

The system of judicial review is radically different from a system of appeals—though it is easy to confuse them, and sometimes they appear to overlap. An *appeal* means that some superior court or tribunal has power to reconsider the decision of a lower tribunal on its merits. Sometimes any aspect of the lower decision is open to appeal, but sometimes there is only an appeal on a point of law (as opposed to a question of fact). Rights of appeal are given by statute, and unless some statute confers the right, it does not exist. Appeals from the High Court to the Court of Appeal, for instance, are authorized by the Judicature Act 1925. In later chapters we will meet cases where appeals lie from administrative authorities or tribunals to higher authorities or tribunals. Statutes have created many special appeal tribunals, e.g. the National Insurance Commissioner, the Lands Tribunal, and Rent Assessment Committees; and sometimes appeals lie to a minister, as, for example, from the Air Transport Licensing Board. The world of special tribunals and statutory authorities has its own network of appeals, to which we will turn in Chapter 7. But the courts of law have no inherent jurisdiction to act as courts of appeal from administrative authorities and tribunals.[3]

Review, on the other hand, is based not on the merits but on the legality of the lower authority's proceedings. At the root of

---

[1] Above, p. 10.

[2] *Ministry of Housing and Local Government v. Sharp* [1970] 2 Q.B. 223 (Salmon, L.J.).

[3] See *Healey v. Minister of Health* [1955] 1 Q.B. 221.

the matter is *jurisdiction*, or, more simply, power. The principle is that if an administrative authority is acting within its jurisdiction, or *intra vires*, and no appeal from it is provided by statute, then it is immune from control by a court of law.[1] If there is a right of appeal, and the appeal succeeds, the appellate court substitutes its own decision for that of the tribunal below, and disposes of the case conclusively. But if an unlawful act or decision is quashed on judicial review, the result is merely to establish that it is a nullity.[2] Fresh proceedings can then be started in order to obtain a lawful act or decision in place of the unlawful one. If a compulsory purchase order is quashed as being *ultra vires*, there is nothing to prevent a fresh order being made in respect of the same land, provided that it is done lawfully. Thus a public authority or tribunal is often given *locus poenitentiae* and is able to correct an error by starting afresh.

It is an inevitable consequence of our concept of the separation of powers, and of our lack of administrative courts, that there is this sharp distinction between appeal and review. It means that fine points of law, alleged to 'go to jurisdiction', are sometimes put forward in support of what is a thinly disguised appeal on the merits.[3] We will find, also, that the courts themselves have in effect abandoned the principle in one type of case, where they will review for 'error on the face of the record'—for, where this doctrine applies, they will quash a decision which they admit to be *intra vires*.[4]

Judicial control, therefore, primarily means review, and is based on the fundamental principle, inherent throughout the legal system, that powers can be validly exercised only within their true limits. The doctrines by which those limits are ascertained and enforced form the very marrow of administrative law. Rights of appeal, on the other hand, have no such central

---

[1] See the quotation at the foot of p. 92, below.

[2] The effect is 'not to substitute another order in its place, but to remove that order out of the way, as one which should not be used to the detriment of any of the subjects of Her Majesty': see [1952] 1 K.B. at p. 344.

[3] Examples are *Woollett v. Minister of Agriculture and Fisheries* [1955] 1 Q.B. 103, below, p. 65 and *Anisminic Ltd. v. Foreign Compensation Commission* [1969] 2 A.C. 147 (below, p. 151).

[4] Below, p. 94.

place. They may or may not exist, and though it is often most desirable that they should exist, this is a question of policy which can be reserved for the chapter on 'Special Tribunals'.

The anatomy of judicial control is best approached by classifying examples according to the nature of the fault—excess of power, abuse of power, and so on. Abuse of power can be found in many guises, and the illustrations will proceed from the simpler to the more refined.

DOING THE WRONG THING

This is the most obvious category of error, although the cases may involve difficult points of statutory construction. For instance, a local authority had power under the Housing Act 1936 to acquire land compulsorily for housing provided that it was not part of any 'park, garden or pleasure ground', and the owner of land affected by an order succeeded in invalidating it by showing that the land was in fact parkland, although the order had been confirmed by the Minister of Health after a public inquiry.[1] In such a case the court will quash the compulsory purchase order, which is tantamount to declaring that in law it is a nullity because of non-compliance with the Act. Similarly there have been decisions, on particular statutes, that a power to run tramways does not authorize the running of omnibuses,[2] that a power to provide 'wash-houses' does not authorize a municipal laundry,[3] and that a power to set up one electricity authority does not authorize two authorities.[4] In these cases the courts are discharging their ordinary task of applying the language of the statute to the facts of the case. The fact that an administrative act is in issue, and that one of the parties to the case is a public authority, does not affect the decision in any way.

ACTING IN THE WRONG MANNER

There have been many cases where the thing done is ostensibly within the statutory power, but, nevertheless,

---

[1] *White and Collins v. Minister of Health* [1939] 2 K.B. 838.
[2] *London County Council v. Attorney-General* [1902] A.C. 165; below, p. 126.
[3] *Attorney-General v. Fulham Corporation* [1921] 1 Ch. 440.
[4] *The King v. Electricity Commissioners* [1924] 1 K.B. 171; below, p. 133.

contravenes it because some false step is taken or some condition is ignored. Several different types of case may be instanced.

Breach of mandatory conditions

Very often the empowering statute will require some procedure to be followed. The court will then normally conclude that the power is to be exercised in accordance with that procedure but not otherwise, so that any departure from it will invalidate the action. For example, a local education authority was prohibited by injunction from proceeding with a scheme for comprehensive schools, since this involved ceasing to maintain some of their former schools and they had not first given public notice and opportunity for objection as required by the Education Act 1944.[1] In another case, after receiving a report from an Agricultural Land Tribunal recommending that a farmer be dispossessed from 151 acres, the Minister of Agriculture made a dispossession order covering 155 acres. This was held wholly invalid, since part of the land comprised in it had never been referred to the tribunal under the statutory procedure.[2] Similarly where a police officer was dismissed by a watch committee without being given a hearing as required by the disciplinary regulations, the dismissal was void.[3] Where a deportation order had to be made in a certain form, an order made merely orally was insufficient.[4] And where an assessment notice was required to state how the recipient might appeal its failure to do so rendered it ineffective.[5] More examples of procedural *ultra vires* will be found in cases where authorities have acted irregularly by delegating their powers, or by failing to give reasons for their decisions.[6]

Normally the court requires every statutory condition to be properly fulfilled, since where the law requires such-and-such steps to be taken it is to be implied that the action is valid only if they are duly taken. The steps are then said to be 'mandatory'. But occasionally it is held that procedural requirements are

---

[1] *Bradbury v. Enfield L.B.C.* [1967] 1 W.L.R. 1311.
[2] *R. v. Agricultural Land Tribunal* [1955] 2 Q.B. 140.
[3] *Ridge v. Baldwin* [1964] A.C. 40.   [4] *Musson v. Rodriguez* [1953] A.C. 530.
[5] *Agricultural Training Board v. Kent* [1970] 2 Q.B. 19.
[6] Below, pp. 63, 236, 271.

merely 'directory' or 'regulatory', that is to say, that it is not intended by Parliament that their observance should be a legal condition of validity. In one case, where statutory regulations required local planning authorities to decide applications within two months, it was held that this condition was directory only, so that permission given after the two months was valid, at least in some circumstances.[1] In another case, where a statutory notice was required to contain reasons, failure to give reasons was held not to invalidate the notice.[2] Such decisions are exceptional; but further examples of merely 'regulatory' conditions will be found in the chapter on delegated legislation.[3] And Parliament itself may grant some latitude, as it has done in many modern statutes under which orders failing to comply with some requirement of the Act are to be quashed only where 'the interests of the applicant have been substantially prejudiced'.[4]

The rule against negligence

Powers must be exercised with reasonable care. A statutory power to do something is not a charter of exemption from all ordinary law, and in particular it does not justify negligence. In one case a local council built an air-raid shelter in a road and left it unlit at night, so that a motorist collided with it and was injured. The council had power to build shelters on highways, but it was held that this did not absolve it from the general duty of taking reasonable steps to make such erections as safe as possible.[5] During the war, therefore, when normal street-lighting was prohibited, the shelter should have been lit with small red lamps so as to make it as safe as conditions permitted. The shelter was, in fact, provided with such lamps, but on the night in question no one had turned them on. The council were accordingly liable in damages. Lord Blackburn had said in an earlier case:

. . . it is now thoroughly well established that no action will lie for doing that which the legislature has authorised, if it be done

---

[1] *James v. Minister of Housing and Local Government* [1966] 1 W.L.R. 135, not reversed on this point, [1967] 1 W.L.R. 171.

[2] *Brayhead (Ascot) Ltd. v. Berkshire C.C.* [1964] 2 Q.B. 303.   [3] Below, pp. 327, 334.

[4] See *Re Bowman* [1932] 2 K.B. 621; *De Rothschild v. Wing U.D.C.* [1967] 1 W.L.R. 470.

[5] *Fisher v. Ruislip-Northwood U.D.C.* [1945] K.B. 584.

without negligence, although it does occasion damage to anyone; but an action does lie for doing what the legislature has authorised, if it be done negligently.[1]

This was a case where a reservoir company had statutory power to make use of a certain stream, but neglected to clean it out, so that their use of it caused flooding and made them liable. Road accidents naturally give rise to numerous actions for negligence against public authorities—as for example where a schoolchild was allowed to run out onto the road and a lorry-driver was killed in trying to avoid her.[2]

This liability for negligence extends to all the categories covered by the principles of negligence in the law of tort. One category which particularly concerns the government is liability for the negligent custody of dangerous prisoners. The prison authorities may be liable for damage done by escaped prisoners if in all the circumstances their arrangements were unduly careless or unreasonable in relation to the risk. The Home Office were accordingly held liable where the assumed facts were that boys with records of crimes and escapes were negligently left unguarded at night in an 'open borstal' and escaped and did damage to a yacht.[3]

The courts seem reluctant, however, to extend to public authorities the rule in *Rylands* v. *Fletcher*[4] which imposes strict liability for specially hazardous activities even in the absence of negligence. In one case, where a gas board was held not liable for an exploding gas main which had been laid with due care, it was said that the rule did not apply to operations undertaken for public purposes.[5] But in such cases especially justice surely requires that the loss should be borne by the public, for whose benefit the service is provided, rather than by the injured party alone. This is at least recognized in the case of the central government, since the Crown has been made liable by legislation.[6] It is clearly necessary to extend the same liability to other public authorities.

---

[1] *Geddis v. Proprietors of Bann Reservoir* (1873) 3 App. Cas. 430 at 455.

[2] *Carmarthenshire C.C. v. Lewis* [1955] A.C. 549.

[3] *Dorset Yacht Co. Ltd. v. Home Office* [1970] 2 W.L.R. 1140. Cf. *Ellis v. Home Office* [1953] 2 Q.B. 135, below, p. 309.

[4] (1868) L.R. 3 H.L. 330.

[5] *Dunne v. N.W. Gas Board* [1964] 2 Q.B. 806.

[6] See below, p. 283.

In cases based on negligence it may sometimes be far from easy to say whether the real cause of the damage is non-exercise or negligent exercise of the power—or, in more old-fashioned language, whether it is a case of non-feasance or misfeasance. The dilemma was presented to the House of Lords in a teasing form in a case where a gale made a breach in a river wall and the plaintiff's land was flooded.[1] The catchment board, in the exercise of their statutory power, then undertook the repair of the wall but did the work so slowly that a repair which should have taken 14 days in fact took 178 days. The plaintiff claimed damages for the excess time for which his land had been flooded and for the consequent injury to it. But was the damage caused by negligent exercise of the power? The majority of the House of Lords held that it was not. The board had merely a power to repair the bank. They had no duty to do anything, and had they been completely inactive they would not have been liable. Nor would they have been liable had they begun the work and then abandoned it. The complaint was that, having started the work, they had done it excessively slowly, which was really no more than a complaint of their inactivity. Putting it another way, the true cause of the damage was the flood and not the conduct of the board. The board came in at a later stage, and could be liable for inefficient reclamation only if they had a *duty* to the plaintiff to act efficiently. But in fact they had merely a *power* to act, coupled with the ordinary *duty* not to cause additional injury by their negligence.

Highway cases formerly exhibited a similar distinction, the distinction between non-feasance and misfeasance. This had, however, a rather different basis. Highway authorities had a statutory duty to repair their roads, but it was not a duty owed to individuals, and therefore individuals could not sue for its breach.[2] But they could always sue for active negligence. Thus if a local council merely neglected the road (non-feasance), so that a hole formed and some one was injured, they had no responsibility in law. Nor were they liable if a third party damaged the road and they failed to repair it. But if they made a hole and left it unlit (misfeasance), an injured party could

[1] *East Suffolk Catchment Board v. Kent* [1941] A.C. 74.
[2] *Cowley v. Newmarket Local Board* [1892] A.C. 345. For such duties see below, p. 157.

recover damages. The immunity for non-feasance was an un-justifiable anomaly. It has now been abolished by statute, so that highway authorities are liable in the same way as other authorities for negligent exercise of their powers and duties.[1]

Other injurious acts

Just as powers do not justify acts of negligence, so they do not justify other injuries such as nuisances, unless it seems that Parliament must have intended to authorize them. Thus where power was given to build hospitals in London for the benefit of the poor, it was held not to authorize a small-pox hospital in Hampstead where the hospital was a nuisance to the neighbour-hood.[2] Since the statutory power gave discretion as to the sites of the hospitals, it was presumed that Parliament did not in-tend to permit the violation of private rights. There is therefore a presumption that discretionary power shall, if possible, be exercised so as to respect the rights of other people. But often, of course, there is no such choice open, for the object of con-ferring power is commonly to legalize some invasion of other people's property or liberties. For example, where Parliament by a railway Act gave power to build and operate a railway along a certain line, the owner of a house beside the line had no remedy for the nuisance resulting from the running of the trains and for the diminution in the value of his property.[3] For no railway could have been run along the line sanctioned by the Act without causing a nuisance by smoke, vibration, and so forth. The Act gave no right to compensation to those who so suffered, although, of course, it gave compensation to those whose land was compulsorily acquired. And unless the Act gives a right to compensation, no compensation is payable. This follows inexorably from the proposition that what is done within the statutory powers is a lawful act of which no one can complain.[4]

These general principles apply to duties as well as to powers. If an authority is performing a statutory duty, it has no more

---

[1] Highways (Miscellaneous Provisions) Act 1961 s.1, taking effect in 1964 and providing a statutory defence of reasonable care.

[2] *Metropolitan Asylum District v. Hill* (1881) 6 App. Cas. 193.

[3] *Hammersmith Rly. Co. v. Brand* (1869) L.R. 4 H.L. 171. Another example is *Smeaton v. Ilford Corporation* [1954] Ch. 450.

[4] See also below, p. 169.

right to commit unnecessary acts of negligence, or to cause nuisances, than it has if exercising a discretionary power. The question in each case is whether Parliament must be taken to have authorized the act to be done in that particular way. A case arose at Derby where the Corporation ran the sewerage system in a way which polluted the river and injured the fishing in it. The owners of the fishing rights sued for an injunction to prohibit further pollution. The Corporation had a statutory duty to provide a sewerage system and had originally provided an adequate one, but the growth of the city had overloaded it. The urgent necessity of disposing of sewage was held not to justify the injury to the fishing, since there was nothing in the statutory powers which permitted such injury, and since it was clear from the statutes that Parliament never contemplated that it might be necessary to cause it. An injunction was accordingly granted, though the court suspended its operation so as to allow the Corporation reasonable time to make other arrangements.[1] An injunction was also granted against the British Electricity Authority in the same proceedings. This case is a good example of the truth that there is no defence of public necessity open to governmental authorities, even where the injury caused might be thought to be of secondary importance compared with the services rendered.

Breach of statutory duty

Although, as has been seen, there is no remedy for the non-exercise of a discretionary *power*, it might be thought that there must always be a remedy for the non-performance of a *duty*. But this is not so, for the courts may interpret the statutory duties of public authorities as owed to the public generally, and not to particular persons. Examples of this attitude will be found in the chapter on Remedies,[2] where they can more conveniently be discussed in the light of the various remedies available for enforcing public duties.

The rule against delegation

Duties and powers are inevitably much intermingled. An administrative body may have a duty to act, but a power to

---

[1] *Pride of Derby & Derbyshire Angling Association Ltd. v. British Celanese Ltd.* [1953] Ch. 149; below, p. 112.   [2] Below, p. 156.

6—A.L.

decide how it shall act—as, for example, where a statutory tribunal must decide a case, but has discretion to decide it as it thinks right. One way in which such functions can be abused is where the function is delegated to some one not entitled to exercise it. There is a maxim *delegatus non potest delegare*—the kind of tag which is so hard to eradicate, once it has secured a foothold in the law, but which really gives very little help. What does give help is to see how the judges interpret statutes, though the maxim perhaps justifies its existence by hinting that there is some judicial bias against allowing delegation. The central question, as always, is what Parliament intended to permit. Statutes confer power on persons or bodies by their proper styles and titles, using phrases such as 'The Minister may by order direct . . .', 'The local authority may require . . .', or 'The tribunal may decide . . . '. The simple reason why such powers cannot usually be delegated is that Parliament has provided that *the Minister* (&c.) may direct, and not that any one else may do so. The statute may, of course, itself permit delegation, either expressly, as where planning authorities are empowered to let their officers decide various planning applications,[1] or impliedly, as where it is obvious from the facts that the power will have to be exercised through some subordinate agency.[2] But as a general rule the courts are vigilant in preventing discretion of any kind being exercised by any one other than the persons to whom it is entrusted by Parliament.

In one case a county council had power to license the showing of films in cinemas on such terms and conditions as the council might determine. The council also had statutory power to delegate these functions to local justices of the peace. The council licensed a cinema on condition (*inter alia*) that no film should be shown which had not been certified by the British Board of Film Censors—an unofficial body established by the film industry. The proprietors of the cinema were prosecuted for showing an uncertified film, but were acquitted on the ground that the council had no power to impose this condition.[3] Lawrence C.J. said:

[1] Town and Country Planning Act 1968, s. 64. Another example is Exchange Control Act 1947, s. 37 (4).
[2] As, for example, servants of the Crown: below, p. 64.
[3] *Ellis v. Dubowski* [1921] 3 K.B. 621.

The effect is to transfer a power which belongs to the County Council and can be delegated to committees of the Council or to district councils or to justices sitting in petty sessions also. I think that such a condition is unreasonable, and that the committee had no power to impose it . . . a condition putting the matter into the hands of a third person or body not possessed of statutory or constitutional authority is ultra vires the committee.

But, by a fine distinction, a condition of this kind is valid if by inserting words such as 'without the consent of the Council' it preserves the council's discretion and does not dispose of it absolutely.[1]

More obvious cases of illegal delegation occur where the power is conferred upon some particular body, and without any statutory authority they allow some officer or employee to exercise it. Under the defence regulations, for instance, the Minister of Agriculture delegated to War Agricultural Executive Committees the power of directing what crops should be grown by farmers. This delegation was expressly authorized by statute. But the Bedfordshire Committee, having resolved that a farmer should grow 8 acres of sugar-beet, left it to their executive officer to specify on which field it should be grown. This he had no power to do, for the power belonged only to the Committee, and accordingly a prosecution for disobedience of the directions failed.[2] Similar objections have been successfully raised by dockers under the statutory dock labour schemes, where disciplinary bodies have powers of suspension and dismissal. In one case a whole series of suspensions and dismissals proved to be invalid because the initial suspensions had been made by the port manager, when in fact they should have been made by the dock labour board.[3] In another, a docker's dismissal was invalid because the local board had not decided on it themselves, as the scheme required, but had left it to their disciplinary committee.[4] In the latter case the House of Lords emphasized the judicial nature of the board's function: they had to hear and determine charges against the docker and decide whether or not to deprive him of his employment and of

---

[1] *Mills v. London County Council* [1925] 1 K.B. 213.
[2] *Allingham v. Minister of Agriculture and Fisheries* [1948] 1 All E.R. 780.
[3] *Barnard v. National Dock Labour Board* [1953] 2 Q.B. 18; below, p. 141. See also *Kanda v. Government of Malaya* [1962] A.C. 332.
[4] *Vine v. National Dock Labour Board* [1957] A.C. 488.

his livelihood. This made it all the less likely that Parliament should have contemplated delegation of the power. But, as Lord Somervell pointed out, there are plenty of examples of ordinary administrative powers, such as the power to appoint some one to an office, which cannot be delegated, and it should not be supposed that it is merely the judicial or disciplinary character of the power which brings the rule against delegation into play. The rule must always apply unless it is expressly excluded, or unless, on a true construction, the delegate is within the statutory description of the persons authorized to wield the power.

The rule cannot, however, be carried to the point of requiring a minister of the Crown to give his mind personally to all the things he is empowered to decide. In empowering ministers to act, Parliament well knows that in very many cases the effective work must be done by departmental officials. If an Act provides, as so many Acts do, that 'the Minister' may do this or that, if satisfied that it is desirable, the power may be exercisable by an official of the department for whom the minister is responsible to Parliament; it may suffice that the official is satisfied, and the minister may never have known of the matter at all. There was a war-time case where the Commissioners of Works had power to requisition land 'if it appears to that authority to be necessary or expedient to do so'.[1] The Commissioners were one of those bodies, like the Commissioners of the Treasury, which never met; formerly the First Commissioner of Works used to exercise their powers, and since 1942 they have been transferred to the Minister of Works. The Commissioners (now the Ministry of Public Building and Works) requisitioned a factory for use as a store, by a letter signed on their behalf by an assistant secretary of the department. The case was dealt with entirely by this official, and the factory owners contested the requisition on the ground that the Commissioners, in whom the power to requisition was legally vested, had never in fact considered the necessity or expediency of the requisition at all. Could the exercise of the discretion be delegated to someone quite different from the body specified by Parliament? (There was, incidentally, ample power under the war-time legislation to delegate powers, but it was not the

[1] *Carltona Ltd. v. Commissioners of Works* [1943] 2 All E.R. 560.

practice to make orders for delegation within the department—
that would have been at variance with the hypothesis that
officials should have no legal powers independently of their
ministers.) The Court of Appeal, in dismissing the objection,
furnished an example of a court of law expounding constitutional convention in order to justify its reading of an Act of
Parliament. Lord Greene M.R. said:

> It cannot be supposed that this regulation meant that, in each
> case, the minister in person should direct his mind to the matter.
> The duties imposed upon ministers and the powers given to ministers
> are normally exercised under the authority of the ministers by
> responsible officials of the department. Public business could not be
> carried on if that were not the case. Constitutionally, the decision
> of such an official is, of course, the decision of the minister. The
> minister is responsible. It is he who must answer before Parliament
> for anything that his officials have done under his authority. . . .

So where members of a tribunal have to be appointed by the
Minister of Agriculture, they can validly be appointed by an
official of the Ministry.[1] But he must act in that capacity, for
instance by writing a letter beginning with the common official
formula: 'I am directed by the Minister, &c.'

Although, therefore, the courts are strict in requiring that
statutory power shall be exercised by the persons on whom it is
conferred, and by no one else, they make liberal allowance for
the working of the official hierarchy, at least so far as it operates
within the sphere of responsibility of ministers of the Crown.[2]
Powers conferred upon special statutory bodies are more jealously watched, as we have noticed. Yet the maxim *delegatus non
potest delegare*, like so many of the other rules of administrative
law, turns out to be no more than a qualified rule for the interpretation of Parliament's intentions.

Surrender or abdication of discretion

A kindred method of vitiating the exercise of a discretion is
where the person entrusted with it, instead of delegating it,
exercises it at the dictation of some other person. For although
he is then acting himself, it is not his own discretion which

---

[1] *Woollett v. Minister of Agriculture and Fisheries* [1955] 1 Q.B. 103. See also *Lewisham Borough v. Roberts* [1949] 2 K.B. 608.
[2] For its limits see *Nelms v. Roe* [1970] 1 W.L.R. 4.

governs the act, as the legislature intended that it should be. On this ground the court quashed a minister's refusal of planning permission for gravel-working on top-class agricultural land, since the minister was acting on a rigid policy of refusing permission whenever the application was opposed by the Ministry of Agriculture.[1] The effective decision was thus made by the wrong minister, and the right minister had never genuinely considered the case or exercised a proper discretion. The courts are distinctly strict in invalidating decisions made in such a manner.

An authority may thus offend by adopting unduly rigid policies. The abdication of what Parliament intended to be a genuine discretion is just as objectionable in that case as it is where the discretion is entrusted to another. A local authority, for instance, has power to refer a furnished tenancy to a rent tribunal in order that the tribunal may decide whether the rent is too high. But if, as happened in one case, the local authority makes it a rule to refer to the tribunal all tenancies in any block of flats where two or more reductions of rent have already been ordered, whether or not the tenant has complained and without even making sure that all the lettings are furnished, the references are invalid.[2] For this is indiscriminate use of a power which was given in order to be used in proper cases after due investigation.

But it is not illegal, merely on this account, for an authority to adopt a general line of policy and adhere to it.[3] The Board of Trade may therefore make it a rule to refuse discretionary subsidies for new machinery in respect of any item costing less than £25, provided that any special case is still considered on its merits.[4] But however firm its policy may be, nothing can absolve a public authority from the duty of forming its judgment on the facts of each case, if that is what the statute intended. A tribunal which has to exercise discretion must

---

[1] *Lavender & Son Ltd. v. M.H.L.G.* [1970] 1 W.L.R. 1231; similarly *Simms Motor Units Ltd. v. Minister of Labour* [1946] 2 All E.R. 201 (order made on minister's directions invalid).

[2] *The King v. Paddington and St. Marylebone Rent Tribunal* [1949] 1 K.B. 666.

[3] See *R. v. Port of London Authority* [1919] 1 K.B. 176; *R. v. Torquay Licensing Justices* [1951] 2 K.B. 784; *Schmidt v. Home Secretary* [1969] 2 Ch. 149; *Stringer v. M.H.L.G.* [1970] 1 W.L.R. 1281.

[4] *British Oxygen Co. Ltd. v. Board of Trade* [1970] 3 W.L.R. 488.

therefore be careful not to treat itself as bound by its own previous decisions. Unlike a court of law, it must not 'pursue consistency at the expense of the merits of individual cases'.[1]

Fettering of powers by contract

This branch of the doctrine of *ultra vires* may impinge on private law where the statutory discretion conflicts with the terms of a contract. Just as a statutory authority has no power to abdicate the discretion entrusted to it by Parliament, so it has no power to fetter its discretion by contract. The leading case concerned the trustees of Ayr Harbour, who had power under their Act to acquire land and build upon it. The House of Lords decided that the trustees had no power, on acquiring land, to undertake not to obstruct the former owner's use of it for access to the harbour.[2] This would have been to fetter the power of building on the land in the future, so that the trustees would have been able to prevent their successors from exercising the power to build which the Act conferred for the public good. Another example occurred where barge-owners contracted with the London Corporation for the removal of refuse by water. During the period of the contract the Corporation altered their by-laws for barges carrying refuse, thereby making future performance of the contract a commercial impossibility. The contractors claimed that this was a breach of the terms of the contract. But the Court of Appeal held the contrary, since the duty to make new by-laws whenever the public interest so required was not capable of being fettered by any mere contract.[3] Similarly the court held void local authorities' contractual undertakings not to exercise its powers of compulsory purchase[4], and to discourage building near the Jodrell Bank Telescope.[5]

It is plain, however, that this rule cannot be applied rigidly, since otherwise it would be impossible for statutory authorities to make many contracts which are necessary in their ordinary course of business. The House of Lords escaped from it in a case where a statutory electricity company had made an

[1] *Merchandise Transport Ltd. v. B.T.C.* [1962] 2 Q.B. 173.
[2] *Ayr Harbour Trustees v. Oswald* (1883) 8 App. Cas. 623. Compare *Commissioners of Crown Lands v. Page* [1960] 2 Q.B. 274.
[3] *William Cory & Son Ltd. v. City of London Corporation* [1951] 2 K.B. 476.
[4] *Triggs v. Stains U.D.C.* [1969] 1 Ch. 10.
[5] *Stringer v. M.H.L.G.* [1970] 1 W.L.R. 1281.

agreement with the Southport Corporation not to increase its charges above those of the Corporation.[1] It is difficult to find any short ground of distinction except by saying that as a matter of construction the restrictions were or were not in conflict with the statutory powers. In the *Ayr* case the trustees were held to have renounced a part of their 'statutory birthright' by a covenant 'fraught with potential suicide for the covenantors'. But an authority's statutory birthright will often include power to make binding contracts, and therefore to commit itself for the future; these are 'mere contracts restricting the undertakers' future freedom of action in respect to the business management of their undertaking'.[2]

Estoppel and consent

The principle that statutory powers cannot be artificially fettered appears again in connection with estoppel. As a general rule, a man is estopped from denying facts which he has caused some one to believe are true, if reliance has been placed on the misrepresentation. He may not deny what he has asserted even though the assertion is wrong. But a public authority cannot abdicate its duty to exercise an unhindered discretion on the true facts in the public interest. This may produce hard results. In one notable case an officer of a planning authority told a firm that if they bought certain property they would not need planning permission to use it as a builder's yard since it had already been used for this purpose so that the purchaser would have the benefit of the 'existing use right'. In fact this proved to be wrong information, and planning permission was subsequently refused. It was held that the planning authority were not estopped from relying on the true facts, and could enforce their refusal of permission.[3]

Sympathy for persons misled in this way has tempted the courts to strain the law.[4] In one case a planning authority were held bound by their officer's erroneous statement that planning

---

[1] *Birkdale District Electric Supply Co. v. Southport Corporation* [1926] A.C. 355.

[2] The quotations are from Lord Sumner [1926] A.C. at 372.

[3] *Southend-on-Sea Corporation v. Hodgson (Wickford) Ltd.* [1962] 1 Q.B. 416. Contrast *N.W. Gas Board v. Manchester Corporation* [1964] 1 W.L.R. 64.

[4] In *Robertson v. Minister of Pensions* [1949] 1 K.B. 227 an official statement that a person was entitled to a pension was held binding. But the principle of this decision was criticized in *Howell* v. *Falmouth Boat Co.* [1951] A.C. 837.

permission was not required for substantial alterations in buildings.[1] But this result was partly attained by way of technicalities of planning law. There must be serious objections to giving the force of law to wrong advice from officials. Where the Parliamentary Commissioner for Administration has jurisdiction, a more suitable remedy is to seek financial compensation through him.[2]

For similar reasons a statutory authority cannot obtain power which does not belong to it merely because the parties consent. If a tenant successfully applies to a rent tribunal for a reduction of rent, but later discovers that the house was outside the tribunal's jurisdiction, the tenant may treat the tribunal's award as a nullity and pursue other remedies.[3] Thus the question of jurisdiction is not *res judicata* between the parties, as it would be if determined by the High Court. 'It is a fundamental principle that no consent can confer on a court or tribunal with limited statutory jurisdiction any power to act beyond that jurisdiction, or can estop the consenting party from subsequently maintaining that such court or tribunal has acted without jurisdiction.'[4] This principle extends equally to all administrative action. Even where a man has pleaded guilty in a prosecution for violation of an enforcement notice issued by a planning authority, he is not estopped from later asking the High Court to declare that the notice is invalid.[5]

But where there is no question of jurisdiction there may perhaps be an effective estoppel or waiver. The House of Lords has left this point open. But the Court of Appeal has held that the benefit of an existing planning permission may be waived if the recipient later obtains compensation on the footing of a refusal.[6]

Disregard of natural justice

Failure to give a proper hearing may also quite properly be regarded as one of the varieties of abuse of power. There are

[1] *Lever Finance Co. v. Westminster L.B.C.* [1970] 3 W.L.R. 732.

[2] Above, p. 15.

[3] *R. v. Judge Pugh* [1951] 2 K.B. 623.

[4] *Essex Incorporated Congregational Church Union v. Essex C.C.* [1963] A.C. 808 (Lord Reid).

[5] *Munnich v. Godstone U.D.C.* [1966] 1 W.L.R. 427.

[6] *Slough Estates Ltd. v. Slough B.C.* (No. 2) [1969] 2 Ch. 305; [1970] 2 W.L.R. 1187.

many cases where either common law or statute makes the exercise of a power illegal if the person who will suffer has not first been fairly heard in his own defence. But this opens the whole subject of natural justice, which needs a chapter to itself. It is, indeed, full of examples of the right thing being done in the wrong manner. But it also has wider aspects, and will be best treated independently.

MOTIVES. REASONABLENESS. GOOD FAITH

Discretionary power

In all the law of judicial control perhaps the central topic is the question how far the courts will go in investigating the motives and merits of government action. Abuse of power is not confined to cases where the wrong thing is done, or the right thing is done by the wrong procedure: the right thing may be done by the right procedure, but on the wrong grounds. Connected with this is the question of reasonableness: can the law prevent powers being exercised unreasonably? Here the courts meet many difficult conundrums. The doctrines of law are, once again, easy to state. The difficulty lies in applying them.

Two principles of statutory interpretation often come into conflict. First, it is to be presumed that powers, even though widely defined, have some ascertainable limits, and that Parliament is unlikely to intend the executive to be the judge of the extent of its own powers; therefore, if it can fairly be implied that the powers were given for some particular purpose, exercise for any other purpose will be illegal. Secondly, however, the court must take care not to usurp the discretion given to some other body. If the statute says that the minister, or the local authority, may decide something, it is not for the court to impose its own idea of what ought to have been decided, for the statute intended the power of decision to lie elsewhere. The court must not, in other words, concern itself with the politics of the case, or with the 'mere merits'. The court's only concern is with the *legality* of what is done. It is not every mistake or aberration which affects legality. It is of the essence of *discretion* that it involves the power to make mistakes. The court has therefore to draw the line between mistakes made *intra vires* and mistakes made *ultra vires*. Acting perversely is not necessarily acting *ultra vires*; but it is tempting to the court to interfere with the unreasonable exercise of a power on the ground that there is some implied statutory restriction which gives the offending act an aspect of irregularity.

Even the widest powers can thus be made subject to a measure of control. The typical example is where the Act of Parliament gives power to an authority to act in certain circumstances 'as it may think fit'. It might be supposed that, provided the circumstances existed and no procedural mistake was made, such a power would be quite 'judge-proof'; for plainly the 'thinking fit' is intended to be done by the authority, and not by a court of law trying to control it. Here, one might suppose, was the domain of pure policy which no legal control could touch. But in fact the courts have contrived to make a number of successful sorties into this territory, using as their passport some implied statutory restriction which they have been able to discover.

Legitimate discretion

It is well to look first at the boundary where the court feels bound to stop. In a leading case of 1948 an attack was made on conditions attached to a licence for Sunday showings at a cinema. The Cinematograph Act 1909 empowered the local council to license Sunday opening of cinemas 'subject to such conditions as the authority think fit to impose'. A licence was granted subject to the condition that no children under fifteen years of age should be admitted, whether accompanied by an adult or not. This total ban on children and indirectly (in effect) on parents was attacked as being unreasonable and therefore *ultra vires*. The attack failed, for the court held that the discretion belonged to the council and not to the court.[1] Lord Greene M.R. expounded the law with great lucidity, and explained that there was indeed a rule of law that 'powers must be exercised reasonably', but that it was true only if 'reasonably' was understood in a special way. A few extracts from his judgment will make this clear.

What, then, is the power of the courts? They can only interfere

[1] *Associated Provincial Picture Houses Ltd. v. Wednesbury Cpn.* [1948] 1 K.B. 223.

with an act of executive authority if it be shown that the authority has contravened the law.

When discretion of this kind is granted the law recognises certain principles on which that discretion must be exercised, but within the four corners of those principles the discretion, in my opinion, is an absolute one, and cannot be questioned in any court of law. What then are those principles?

Bad faith, dishonesty—those of course stand by themselves—unreasonableness, attention given to extraneous circumstances, disregard of public policy and things like that have all been referred to, according to the facts of individual cases, as being matters which are relevant to the question. If they cannot all be confined under one head, they at any rate overlap to a very great extent. For instance, we have heard in this case a great deal about the meaning of the word 'unreasonable'.

It is true that discretion must be exercised reasonably.[1] Now what does that mean? Lawyers familiar with the phraseology commonly used in relation to exercise of statutory discretions often use the word 'unreasonable' in a rather comprehensive sense. It has frequently been used and is frequently used as a general description of the things that must not be done. For instance, a person entrusted with a discretion must, so to speak, direct himself properly in law. He must call his own attention to the matters which he is bound to consider. He must exclude from his consideration matters which are irrelevant to what he has to consider. If he does not obey those rules, he may truly be said, and often is said, to be acting 'unreasonably'. Similarly, there may be something so absurd that no sensible person could ever dream that it lay within the powers of the authority. Warrington L.J. in *Short v. Poole Corporation*[2] gave the example of the red-haired teacher, dismissed because she had red hair. That is unreasonable in one sense. In another it is taking into consideration extraneous matters. It is so unreasonable that it might almost be described as being done in bad faith; and, in fact, all these things run into one another.

It appears to me quite clear that the matter dealt with by this condition was a matter which a reasonable authority would be justified in considering when they were making up their mind what condition should be attached to the grant of this licence. Nobody, at this time of day, could say that the well-being and the physical and moral health of children is not a matter which a local authority,

---

[1] Cf. Lord Macnaghten's statement in *Westminster Corporation v. London & North Western Railway Co.* [1905] A.C. 426 at 430.
[2] [1926] Ch. 66.

in exercising their powers, can properly have in mind when those questions are germane to what they have to consider.

I think [counsel] in the end agreed that his proposition that the decision of the local authority can be upset if it is proved to be unreasonable, really meant that it must be proved to be unreasonable in the sense that the court considers it to be a decision that no reasonable body could have come to. It is not what the court considers unreasonable, a different thing altogether.

This is a very clear statement of the principle that the courts of law cannot be used as courts of appeal to review the merits of administrative decisions. It has since been approved and applied by the appellate courts.[1] But it specifically reserves the jurisdiction to give protection against abuse of power on the simple and sound principle that Parliament cannot have intended powers to be stretched beyond the area where opinions may legitimately differ. Powers must be exercised reasonably, provided it is remembered that 'reasonable' has here a wider meaning than in most other legal contexts. It is in this sense that one must understand the words of Lord Halsbury, which derive from Lord Mansfield:

. . . 'discretion' means when it is said that something is to be done within the discretion of the authorities that that something is to be done according to the rules of reason and justice, not according to private opinion: . . . according to law, and not humour. It is to be, not arbitrary, vague and fanciful, but legal and regular.[2]

For Lord Halsbury himself also said:

Where the legislature has confided the power to a particular body, with a discretion how it is to be used, it is beyond the power of any court to contest that discretion.[3]

Abuse of discretion. The Poplar case

Outstanding among the earlier examples on the other side of the line, where unreasonableness was held to reach the point of abuse of power, was the famous decision of the House of Lords

---

[1] *Fawcett Properties Ltd. v. Bucks. C.C.* [1961] A.C. 636; *Hall & Co. Ltd. v. Shoreham-by-Sea U.D.C.* [1964] 1 W.L.R. 240; and by Lord Reid in *Smith v. East Elloe R.D.C.* [1956] A.C. 736.
[2] *Sharp v. Wakefield* [1891] A.C. 173, based on *R. v. Wilkes* (1770) 4 Burr. 2527.
[3] *Westminster Corporation v. London & North Western Railway Company* [1905] A.C. 426; below, p. 82.

in the *Poplar* case. In 1920 the Poplar Borough Council, wishing
to set an example as model socialist employers, instituted a
minimum weekly wage for all their employees of £4 for men
and women alike. The minimum wage had previously been
£3. 4s. for men and £2. 9s. 9d. for women. In 1921–2 there
was a sharp fall in the cost of living and in wages, but the minimum wage of £4 was left unchanged. The Council's statutory
power was to pay their servants 'such salaries and wages as
[they] may think fit'. It would be difficult for Parliament to
confer a wider discretion. But the House of Lords upheld a
complaint that the weekly minimum of £4 was so excessive,
in relation to the labour market, that it amounted to a gratui-
tous subsidy to the employees and contained an element which
was not 'wages' at all.[1] The legislature must have intended that
in fixing wages the Council should have regard to the labour
market. By acting without regard to it, and for extraneous
reasons which Lord Atkinson described as 'eccentric principles
of socialistic philanthropy' and 'feminist ambition', the Council
had abused their powers. The House of Lords unanimously
upheld an order of the district auditor (a central government
official who inspects local government accounts)[2] disallowing
a proportion of the wages, amounting in aggregate to £5,000,
as being an 'item of account contrary to law' and surcharging
it upon the councillors responsible, so that they were personally
liable to make it good. The Minister of Health later purported
to remit the surcharge, but this too was found to be *ultra vires*,[3]
and the district auditor's order withstood all attacks.

This decision was in its own period regarded as touching,
if not overreaching, the absolute high-water mark of legitimate
judicial control, and there were not wanting people who imputed motives of a political character to the highest court of
this country. To read the speeches in the House of Lords is the
best antidote to these criticisms. In an earlier case Farwell L.J.
had prophetically said[4]:

It is not easy to draw the line between policy and administration,
or to give a definition except by way of example, but in my opinion

---

[1] *Roberts v. Hopwood* [1925] A.C. 578. For the political background, a story of
great interest, see B. Keith-Lucas, 'Poplarism', [1962] Public Law 52.
[2] Above, p. 27.   [3] *The King v. Minister of Health* [1927] 1 K.B. 765.
[4] *The King v. Roberts* [1908] 1 K.B. 407 at 435.

the establishment of a works committee would be a question of policy into which the auditor could not go, but the payment of abnormally high wages to the workmen employed by such committee would be a matter of administration.

Just as this well expressed the auditor's jurisdiction, so it well expresses the court's, for both are concerned solely with acts of administration which overstep the law. The difficulty is not in understanding the doctrine which the courts apply, but in knowing when they are going to apply it. For instance, in 1944 the Court of Appeal quashed orders of disallowance and surcharge made by the district auditor at Birmingham in respect of children's allowances which the City Council had begun to pay to their staff.[1] The auditor supposed that he was correctly following the *Poplar* case, particularly where it had been said that payments for other reasons than for services actually rendered were mere gratuity and not 'wages' within the statutory power. He also contended that the Council were taking into account the irrelevant factor of the employee's family responsibilities. But the court rejected all these arguments on the ground that the wages paid at Birmingham were reasonable in themselves, and that unless they were really inordinate or indiscriminate the court had no concern with them. The danger is that the more precise the court attempts to be in formulating its reasons for control, the more misleading may be the result. It is the general impression made by all the facts and all the arguments combined which is decisive.

Some subsequent decisions

More recently there have been many decisions to keep the *Poplar* case company. One of them comes, again, from the progressive city of Birmingham. That city's scheme for allowing free travel to old-age pensioners was disallowed by the Court of Appeal in 1955.[2] The Birmingham City Council runs its own bus and tram services under statutes which empower them to charge 'such fares and charges as they may think fit'. In 1952 the Council resolved to allow free travel on their transport services to all men aged 70 and over and to all women aged 65 and over who were resident in the city. The estimated annual

---

[1] *In Re Decision of Walker* [1944] K.B. 644.
[2] *Prescott v. Birmingham Corporation* [1955] Ch. 210.

cost of this concession was £90,000—and it fell upon the rate-payers, since the transport services were in any case run at a loss. A ratepayer brought an action claiming a declaration that the scheme was *ultra vires* and illegal, and so it was judged to be. A local authority, it was held, owed a fiduciary duty (like that of a trustee) to their ratepayers; their statutory authority to run the transport services was authority to run them on com-mercial lines, even though at a loss, but did not entitle them to give subsidies to one class of the community at the expense of another merely for the sake of benevolence or philanthropy. Accordingly, the decision to grant the concession was not a proper exercise of the discretionary power. By way of contrast it was remarked that free or cheap travel for children might well be perfectly legal, for there were probably valid commercial reasons for such concessions, as the general practice of other transport businesses showed. What the Council were not at liberty to do was to use the ratepayers' money to inaugurate a new form of social subsidy under the cloak of their transport service. As a consequence of this decision an Act of Parliament was passed in 1955 to legitimate travel concessions already in force for certain classes of old people, disabled people, and children. This Act did nothing to authorize such concessions for the future. But by the Travel Concessions Act 1964 Parlia-ment has now done so and has thus removed the restrictions imposed by the *Birmingham* case.

A still stronger echo of the *Poplar* case comes from a case about rent subsidies.[1] The question was how far the St. Pancras Borough Council were justified in paying subsidies to the owners of derequisitioned houses occupied by protected tenants. The protected rent could not be increased 'except so far as the local authority may from time to time determine', and the statute required them to pay to the owner the difference between that rent and the higher rent which he could otherwise claim. When the Rent Act 1957 brought general increase of rents the Council decided as a matter of policy, and without looking at individual cases, to pay higher subsidies to the owners rather than fix higher rents. The Council were hostile both to any sort of means test for tenants, and also to the Rent Act generally; their

---

[1] *Taylor v. Munrow* [1960] 1 W.L.R. 151.

policy was 'to protect the tenants from the Rent Act'. The district auditor disallowed the additional subsidies, and the court upheld his decision. The Council were held to have acted arbitrarily and therefore illegally. Their duty to their ratepayers meant that their statutory discretion to determine rents was not an absolute one, but required due consideration of relevant factors. Looking simply at the statute, it would seem that the councillors were here condemned for mere inaction in failing to exercise a power. But in fact their transgression lay in their misapplication of ratepayers' money.

A planning authority may grant planning permission 'subject to such conditions as they think fit'; and a caravan site licensing authority may impose such conditions as it 'may think it necessary or desirable to impose'. The court will interpret such conditions benevolently if they can be given a reasonable meaning.[1] But they must fairly and reasonably relate to the permitted development and they must not go beyond the limited purposes of the legislation. Thus conditions were condemned as unreasonable which required caravan sites to be let at controlled rents and on terms giving social and economic protection to the tenants in various ways outside the scope of the law governing caravan sites.[2] Other comparable cases will be found under the next title.

Where a minister allowed only four days for objections to be made to a scheme for a comprehensive school, the court declared that the time allowed was wholly unreasonable and that the opportunity required by the statute had not been given.[3]

Statutory regulations and by-laws are also subject to the requirement of reasonableness, as is explained in the chapter on Delegated Legislation.[4]

The limits of discretion

The Crown and other public authorities frequently argue that a power to act as they think fit gives them unfettered discretion. But unfettered discretion is precisely what the courts

---

[1] *Fawcett Properties Ltd. v. Buckingham C.C.* [1961] A.C. 636 at 679.

[2] *Mixnam's Properties Ltd. v. Chertsey U.D.C.* [1965] A.C. 735 (esp. at 765).

[3] *Lee v. Department of Education and Science* (1967) 66 L.G.R. 211.

[4] Below, p. 325.

will not countenance, for it is incompatible with the overriding requirement of legality. Every discretion is capable of unlawful abuse, and the court must decide where this point is reached. Only within its lawful boundaries is discretion free. In order to discern the boundaries the court must consider the whole statutory framework within which the power lies. Action which conflicts with a statutory policy will be *ultra vires*, as were the Poplar Wages and St. Pancras rent subsidies discussed above. Sometimes the action is characterized as unreasonable, or as arbitrary and capricious, or as based on inadmissible grounds or irrelevant considerations. But the guiding principle is that public authorities, unlike private persons, are not free agents in the use of discretionary powers. They must act on proper and valid grounds of public interest. This was already recognized in 1598, when an order of the Commissioners of Sewers was held void:[1] 'notwithstanding the words of the commission give authority to the commissioners to do according to their discretions, yet their proceedings ought to be limited and bound with the rule of reason and law', which required them to do what was right, and 'not to do according to their wills and private affections'. The current of recent case-law leaves no doubt that the courts are exploring and generalizing this identical doctrine. In doing this they are responding to the challenge of the incessant growth of governmental power.

The House of Lords firmly rejected a minister's claim to unfettered discretion where a statute provided for complaints by milk producers against the Milk Marketing Board to be referred to a committee of investigation 'if the Minister in any case so directs'.[2] It was held that the Act intended that genuine complaints should be duly investigated, and that the apparently permissive language did not entitle the Minister to refuse to refer a complaint for inadequate reasons so as to thwart the objects of the Act. An order of mandamus was therefore granted, compelling the Minister to make the reference.[3] Lord Upjohn said that the Minister's claim that his discretion was 'unfettered' was an unauthorized gloss, and that, in any case,

---

[1] *Rook's Case* (1598) 5 Co. Rep. 99b.
[2] *Padfield v. Minister of Agriculture* [1968] A.C. 997. See similarly *Car Owners' Mutual Insurance Co. Ltd. v. Treasurer of Australia* [1970] A.C. 527.
[3] The Committee later reported in favour of the complainants but the Minister refused to take action.

the use of that adjective, even in an Act of Parliament, can do nothing to unfetter the control which the judiciary have over the executive, namely that in exercising their powers the latter must act lawfully and that is a matter to be determined by looking at the Act and its scope and object in conferring a discretion upon the Minister rather than by the use of adjectives.

This principle is in no way new[1] but here it is particularly clear. In holding the Minister's inaction unlawful the House of Lords thoroughly examined his reasons, as explained in correspondence, and exposed their inadequacy.

The House also laid down the important corollary that the minister could not take refuge in silence by giving no reasons at all. In that case, it was held, his reasons might be presumed to be bad. Although any one asserting the invalidity of a ministerial act or order must always bear the burden of proof initially, it is in effect shifted to the minister in these cases by the requirement that he should produce satisfactory reasons. This appears also in a case where the Privy Council set aside the order of a Canadian minister disallowing a taxpayer's expenses, the Act providing that 'the Minister may disallow any expense which he in his discretion may determine to be in excess of what is reasonable'. It was held that if the minister could not show that he had facts before him which could support his decision in law, his decision could only have been arbitrary and unlawful.[2] Once again the guiding principle is that a public authority must justify its acts on valid grounds of public interest. It has no power to act arbitrarily.[3]

Overlapping powers

Overlapping powers present interesting problems. Different statutes may appear to provide alternative ways of achieving

[1] See for example *Rook's Case* (1598) (above); *R. v. Boteler* (1864) 4 B. & S. 959; *R. v. St. Pancras Vestry* (1890) 24 Q.B.D. 371; *R. v. Minister of Transport* [1934] 1 K.B. 277; *Taylor v. Munrow* and its companion cases discussed above; *R. v. Metropolitan Police Commissioner* [1968] 2 Q.B. 118 (discretion of police to prosecute offenders). In [1968] Public Law 216 it is said that *Padfield's* case is 'very French in its approach' and 'only an isolated example'. It might rather be said that it is very English, and illustrates long established law.

[2] *Minister of National Revenue v. Wrights' Canadian Ropes Ltd.* [1947] A.C. 109.

[3] Corresponding principles play an important part in French law. See e.g. Vedel, *Droit Administratif*, 4th ed., 1968, pp. 529–530, and C.E. 28 Mai 1954, *Barel* (reasons refused: decision annulled).

the same purpose, but with different effects. Land required for road-widening may be acquired compulsorily, subject to compensation; but no compensation is normally payable for restrictive conditions imposed by a planning authority, which may be 'such conditions as they think fit'. In one case a planning authority granted permission on condition that a strip of land should be made available as a public roadway. This was held unreasonable and *ultra vires* as attempting to encroach on the province of another statute and so avoid paying the compensation intended by Parliament.[1] Similarly the House of Lords has invalidated a condition restricting a caravan site and cutting down the owner's 'existing use rights', which under the planning legislation are not to be taken away without compensation.[2] A discretionary power, however wide, may not therefore be used to deprive a citizen of specific statutory rights. This is an example of the principle *generalia specialibus non derogant*. In applying it the court will have to consider not only the statute granting the power, but other statutes as well.

This sound restriction has since been rejected by a sharply divided Court of Appeal in a case where planning permission had been refused for over twenty years on account of nebulous plans for road-widening, so that the land lay under prolonged 'planning blight'. Specific powers for reserving land for road-widening, subject to compensation, are given by the Highways Act 1959, and the question was whether payment of compensation could be avoided merely by persistent refusal of planning permission. But in the House of Lords it was discovered that the planning legislation provided expressly that in cases of overlap powers of planning control should be unaffected.[3] In cases not governed by this provision the principle of the earlier decisions should still prevail.

Ulterior objects and mixed motives

Many cases raise the question whether an authority is motivated by a proper or improper purpose. In one, which came to

---

[1] *Hall & Co. Ltd. v. Shoreham-by-Sea U.D.C.* [1964] 1 W.L.R. 240.

[2] *Hartnell v. M.H.L.G.* [1965] A.C. 1134. A similar case is *Allnatt London Properties Ltd. v. Middlesex C.C.* (1964) 62 L.G.R. 304. See also *Pyx Granite Co. v. M.H.L.G.* [1958] 1 Q.B. 554 at 573.

[3] *Westminster Bank Ltd. v. M.H.L.G.* [1970] 2 W.L.R. 645. See Town and Country Planning Act 1962, s. 220.

the Privy Council from New South Wales, the city of Sydney had acted under a power to acquire land compulsorily for making streets and also for 'carrying out improvements in or remodelling any portion of the city'. A landowner threatened with a compulsory purchase order succeeded in obtaining an injunction to prohibit it, since it appeared that the Municipal Council had in fact no plan for improving or remodelling that part of the city, but were merely trying to acquire as much as possible of an area which was due for a rise in site values owing to the extension of a street.[1] The Council was in fact making use of its power to carry out schemes of improvement for what was really quite a different purpose, namely, the expropriation of the 'betterment' which the new street would create. This is a straightforward example, since the purposes of the statutory power were expressed, and the purposes of the Council were manifestly different. It is comparable with the case, mentioned below, where land was acquired ostensibly for a scheme of coast protection works but in fact for other purposes which were not authorized.[2]

In a more difficult case the House of Lords upheld the action of the Central Land Board in acquiring land compulsorily in order to compel its owner to sell it at 'existing use value', although the planning statutes then in force give no power for this purpose expressly.[3] The objections to the use of power for ulterior objects are well expressed in a dissenting judgment of Lord Justice Denning.[4]

The mere fact that a scheme serves some other purpose in *addition* to its authorized purpose is not a legal objection provided that the authorized purpose is the genuine motive. A good example of this proposition is found in the case which concerned a subway built under the street at the foot of Whitehall. The Westminster Corporation had power under a Public Health Act to provide public conveniences and to build them under streets if necessary; but they had no power to build subways. They built conveniences under the middle of the street, with access from either side, so that a subway crossing was also

---

[1] *Municipal Council of Sydney v. Campbell* [1925] A.C. 338.
[2] Below, p. 83.
[3] *Earl Fitzwilliam's Wentworth Estates Co. v. M.T.C.P.* [1952] A.C. 362.
[4] [1951] 2 K.B. 284 at 300.

provided. This was held to be a reasonable and bona fide use of their power, since the scheme to provide access from both sides of the street was quite genuine and proper in itself, and the additional facility of the subway was immaterial.[1] But had the subway been the primary object of the scheme, it might not have been valid. Lord Halsbury said:

I quite agree that if the power to make one kind of building was fraudulently used for the purpose of making another kind of building, the power given by the Legislature for one purpose could not be used for another.

And similarly Lord Macnaghten said:

Then I come to the question of want of good faith. That is a very serious charge. . . . In order to make out a case of bad faith it must be shown that the corporation constructed this subway as a means of crossing the street under colour and pretence of providing public conveniences which were not really wanted at that particular place.

The Court of Appeal had in fact been persuaded that this was so, and had held the scheme invalid.[2] Vaughan Williams L.J. said, apostrophizing the Corporation:

You are acting mala fide if you are seeking to acquire land for a purpose not authorised by the Act. . . .

These remarks accord well with the views of Lord Greene M.R., already quoted, as to the close relationship between 'unreasonableness', 'bad faith', and similar charges.[3] Again and again it is laid down by the judges that powers must be exercised reasonably and in good faith. In their ordinary legal sense these terms have very different meanings, for reasonableness means the standard of conduct of a person of prudence and sense, whereas good faith is opposed to bad faith, meaning actual dishonesty. But in their application to the control of powers they overlap and merge together, for they are used almost indiscriminately to describe the exercise of powers for their proper purpose. An accusation of bad faith is, as Lord Macnaghten said, a very serious charge. But it is clear from the statements of Lord Halsbury and of Vaughan Williams L.J. that it may merely be a charge of acting *ultra vires*, which many

---

[1] *Westminster Corporation v. London & North Western Railway* [1905] A.C. 426.
[2] [1904] 1 Ch. 759.   [3] Above, p. 72.

authorities have done in their time in perfectly good faith—like, for example, the Birmingham Corporation in the case of the buses, and the Poplar Borough Council with their minimum weekly wage.[1] It is for this reason that Lord Greene's analysis of the terms is important. What is really required is that the authority should act 'statutably', and up to that point the reasonableness (in the normal sense) of their action is no affair for the court. On the other hand, the court will often intervene long before there is anything which would normally be called fraud.

Fraud

Ulterior objects and improper motives are sometimes linked in a confusing way with the more opprobrious sin of fraud. In the milder sense, as we have seen, "bad faith" may be applied to almost any abuse of power. In the *Paddington Rent Tribunal* case,[2] for example, it was held that the reference to the tribunal of tenancies *en masse*, without proper examination, was not 'a valid and bona fide exercise of the powers conferred by Parliament'. Here 'valid' and 'bona fide' are almost synonyms, so that 'invalid' and 'mala fide' may become synonyms also. In this sense there is no suggestion of real dishonesty, and *mala fide* means little more than *ultra vires*. It would be more satisfactory if fraud and bad faith were dropped from the vocabulary except in cases where some definite dishonesty is alleged. That would have the advantage that they would almost disappear from the subject, since almost all the errors which can be committed by those in authority are committed with honest motives.

Accusations of bad faith were put forward in a case in which an Urban District Council made a scheme for building a sea wall under their powers as coast protection authority. The scheme included the construction of a footway or promenade behind the wall, for which land was to be acquired compulsorily. Since this land was not genuinely required for coast protection, it could not be validly acquired under coast protection powers, and the compulsory purchase order was accordingly quashed (after it had in fact been confirmed by the

[1] A further example is *Hoggard v. Worsbrough U.D.C.* [1962] 2 Q.B. 677.
[2] Above, p. 66.

Minister).[1] The council had made certain untrue and misleading statements, but in the end the court thought that these were due to ineptitude rather than to bad faith of the more serious kind. The case is thus an ordinary example of *ultra vires*.

In one of the rare cases in which a serious charge of dishonesty was made, Lord Somervell said:[2]

Mala fides is a phrase often used in relation to the exercise of statutory powers. It has never been precisely defined as its effects have happily remained in the region of hypothetical cases. It covers fraud or corruption.

But even here the words carry two different senses. If they were confined to cases of fraud and corruption only, they would be much less often used. It may, of course, be taken for granted that Parliament intends powers to be exercised honestly, and that dishonesty or corruption will make the act *ultra vires*. As Lord Denning has said: 'No judgment of a court, no order of a Minister, can be allowed to stand if it has been obtained by fraud—fraud unravels everything.'[3] But in the only case where actual dishonesty was alleged, this principle came into conflict with an express provision in the Act that the order 'shall not be questioned in any legal proceedings whatsoever', and by a dubious decision the House of Lords held the order impregnable.[4] Exclusion clauses of this kind, where Parliament has itself created the impediment to the enforcement of its presumed wishes, will be considered later in connexion with certiorari and other remedies.[5]

Malice

Occasionally it is alleged that a public authority has withheld some permission or done some other act out of mere malice or spite. This is hardly distinguishable from a charge of bad faith, for if malice were proved it would obviously show that the power was not exercised reasonably and in good faith. Thus where building and drainage plans were rejected by a sanitary authority and they were alleged to have acted out of spite, because they had previously been in litigation with the appli-

---

[1] *Webb v. Minister of Housing and Local Government* [1965] 1 W.L.R. 755.
[2] *Smith v. East Elloe Rural District Council*, below, p. 150.
[3] *Lazarus Estates Ltd. v. Beasley* [1956] 1 Q.B. 702 at 712.
[4] *Smith v. East Elloe R.D.C.*, above.   [5] Below, p. 150.

cant, it was held that his proper remedy was to apply for a mandamus ordering the sanitary authority to determine the application properly.[1] Although in this case a claim for damages failed, the Privy Council has since indicated that damages might be awarded for malicious refusal of a licence, apparently on the ground that it might be an actionable breach of statutory duty.[2] This head of liability is explained below.[3]

Subjective powers

Sometimes Parliament confers power in terms so wide as to be almost incapable of abuse. Two favourite formulas are to the effect that action may be taken 'if the Minister is satisfied' or 'if it appears to the Minister' that some state of affairs exists. Here it is plainly intended that the power is to be exercisable only in some particular state of affairs; but it is equally plain that the judge of that fact is to be the minister and not the courts of law. The Act is so expressed that what it requires is not an objective state of fact, but a mere state of mind on the part of the minister. The overriding power of Parliament, when it wishes to use it, is well illustrated by provisions of this kind, which tie the hands of the courts. A case arose at Plymouth where the Minister made an order for the compulsory purchase of a large area of the city which had suffered severe war damage. The Act provided: 'Where the Minister . . . is satisfied that it is requisite, for the purpose of dealing satisfactorily with extensive war damage, in the area of a local planning authority, that a part or parts of their area . . . should be laid out afresh and redeveloped as a whole, an order . . . may be made by the Minister . . . .' The Minister's order was disputed by the owners of some land at the edge of the area because the plan was merely to restore and repair it, and not to lay it out afresh or redevelop it. But these objections failed, because once the Minister declared himself satisfied, according to the Act, the court could not control him.[4] The argument that he could not have been so

---

[1] *Davis v. Bromley Corporation* [1908] 1 K.B. 170. For the remedy of mandamus in such cases see below, p. 162.

[2] *David v. Abdul Cader* [1963] 1 W.L.R. 834 (refusal of licence for cinema in Ceylon).

[3] P. 156.

[4] *Robinson v. Minister of Town and Country Planning* [1947] K.B. 702. Powers of similar extent were in question in the *Stevenage* case (below, p. 182) and the *Kingston By-Pass* case (below, p. 197). Cf. below, p. 91.

satisfied as to the land in question, because he could have had no evidence before him that redevelopment was requisite, was firmly rejected. The Act had made the Minister the final arbiter of the existence of his own power, and the grounds on which he might be satisfied were matters of executive policy which were no concern of the court.

But even in this forbidding context the judges find scope for their natural inclination to set legal limits to sweeping powers. So where purchase tax regulations were inherently unreasonable and *ultra vires*, it did not avail the commissioners that they had power to make regulations for any matter 'for which provision appears to them to be necessary'.[1] Another loophole appears where the authority can be shown never to have given its mind to the question on which it is required to be satisfied.[2] On the same principle the action taken will be invalid if it can be established that the Minister was satisfied on the wrong question. In one case a minister imposed a manager on a school in Ceylon because of certain alleged defaults in its past management, whereas he was required to be satisfied that there was default in the present; since there was no evidence of present default, there was no ground on which the Minister could be satisfied at the time of making his order.[3] This reasoning runs counter to that of the Plymouth case, and it may be reinforced by the tendency to invalidate decisions based on 'no evidence', to be mentioned shortly.[4] The doctrine of reasonableness may also perhaps be invoked, thereby making a wide opening for judicial intervention where there are no reasonable grounds for the minister's satisfaction.[5]

A remarkable case

A war-time case of outstanding interest raised this question of subjective versus objective conditions. It owes its fame, such as it is, to the fact that a majority of the House of Lords held that, in the circumstances of the war, a power which most

[1] *Commissioners of Customs and Excise v. Cure and Deeley Ltd.* [1962] 1 Q.B. 340; see below, p. 326.

[2] *Webb v. Minister of Housing and Local Government* [1965] 1 W.L.R. 755. See also *R. v. Chief Immigration Officer, Lympne Airport* [1969] 2 Q.B. 333.

[3] *Maradana Mosque Trustees v. Mahmud* [1967] A.C. 13.

[4] Below, p. 99.

[5] *D.P.P. v. Head* [1959] A.C. 83 (Lord Denning).

lawyers would normally regard as objective must be regarded as subjective. This was the power of detention under Regulation 18B of the Defence (General) Regulations, 1939, which provided: 'If the Secretary of State has reasonable cause to believe any person to be of hostile origin or associations . . . he may make an order against that person directing that he be detained.' This, on the face of it, was objective language. The Act did not merely require a state of satisfaction: it required that there should be reasonable cause for the belief, and such a condition is ordinarily for the courts to judge, in case of dispute, according to the legal standard of reasonableness. Numerous precedents and analogies supported this interpretation. But all the courts, including the House of Lords, held that the Secretary of State could not be called upon to state and justify his grounds.[1] It was, they said, so much a matter for executive discretion, in the circumstances of the war, that courts of law could not sit in judgment on the Secretary of State. But Lord Atkin delivered a dissenting speech which is one of the *tours de force* of legal literature. After showing that the phrase used in the regulation had a settled legal meaning, he said:

I view with apprehension the attitude of judges who on a mere question of construction when face to face with claims involving the liberty of the subject show themselves more executive minded than the executive. . . . It has always been one of the pillars of freedom, one of the principles of liberty for which on recent authority we are now fighting, that the judges are no respecters of persons and stand between the subject and any attempted encroachments on his liberty by the executive, alert to see that any coercive action is justified in law. In this case I have listened to arguments which might have been addressed acceptably to the Court of King's Bench in the time of Charles I.

I protest, even if I do it alone, against a strained construction put on words with the effect of giving an uncontrolled power of imprisonment to the minister. To recapitulate: the words have only one meaning. They are used with that meaning in the common law and in statutes. They have never been used in the sense now imputed to them. . . . After all this long discussion the question is whether the words 'If a man has' can mean 'If a man thinks he has'. I am of opinion that they cannot . . .

[1] *Liversidge v. Anderson* [1942] A.C. 206.

This case, it may be said in retrospect, stands as an isolated example to show how strongly, in exceptional circumstances, the ordinary train of judicial reasoning may be deflected. It does not, fortunately, mean that the courts have abrogated their duty to ensure that those entrusted with power shall observe the conditions which Parliament imposes on them. This was shown in an appeal to the Privy Council from Ceylon in 1950. The authority concerned was a controller of textiles, who had power to cancel a dealer's licence 'where the Controller has reasonable grounds to believe that any dealer is unfit to be allowed to continue as a dealer'. It was held that these words imposed a condition that reasonable grounds must be shown to exist, to the court's satisfaction.[1] Lord Radcliffe said:

> Indeed, it would be a very unfortunate thing if the decision of *Liversidge's* case came to be regarded as laying down any general rule as to the construction of such phrases when they appear in statutory enactments. It is an authority for the proposition that the words 'if A.B. has reasonable cause to believe' are capable of meaning 'if A.B. honestly thinks that he has reasonable cause to believe. . . . However read, they must be intended to serve in some sense as a condition limiting the exercise of an otherwise arbitrary power. But if the question whether the condition has been satisfied is to be conclusively decided by the man who wields the power, the value of the intended restraint is in effect nothing.

This was a welcome restatement of the objective canon of construction upon which the whole fabric of judicial control must be based. A Lord of Appeal has since described *Liversidge's* case as a 'very peculiar decision of this House'.[2]

JURISDICTION OVER FACT AND LAW

Jurisdictional questions

There are indeed cases where, to repeat again the words of Lord Radcliffe, 'the question whether the condition has been satisfied is to be conclusively decided by the man who wields the power'. As we have seen, this is often the position when Parliament resorts to the formula 'If the Minister is satisfied . . . ,

---

[1] *Nakkuda Ali v. Jayaratne* [1951] A.C. 66. For another point in this case see below, p. 198.

[2] Lord Reid in *Ridge v. Baldwin* [1964] A.C. 40 at 73.

he may direct, &c.' In such cases Parliament's directions are categorical. But in other cases they may have to be guessed, and it may be difficult to tell whether facts and conditions which determine the existence or limits of a power are to be objectively controlled or not. The question then arises: has the authority the prerogative of determining the facts or questions upon which its own jurisdiction depends? This is sometimes called the problem of 'jurisdictional fact', though this is a misleading expression since the question on which the jurisdiction depends is often one of law rather than of fact. English courts prefer to speak of 'collateral' questions, meaning questions which the minister or other authority has no power to decide conclusively.[1] In any case, the principle at work is that of *ultra vires*, of which this topic is one branch.

For instance, in the case already cited where the Housing Act gave power to acquire land which was not part of any park, the argument for the Minister was that the court could not challenge his findings of fact.[2] It was for him, he said, to determine what was part of a park. Had the Court of Appeal accepted this argument, the result would have been exactly as described by Lord Radcliffe: the Minister would have been the judge of the limits of his own power. But the court held that the test was objective, that evidence must be heard on the question, that on the evidence the land was part of a park, and that the order was illegal. Here the question was really one of 'jurisdictional law', since the facts were agreed and the only question was what was a 'park' within the meaning of the Act.

The same principle applies not only to administrative acts but also to the findings of tribunals. As was said in one case,

it is a general rule that no court of limited jurisdiction can give itself jurisdiction by a wrong decision on a point collateral to the merits of the case upon which the limit to its jurisdiction depends.[3]

But the real difficulty is to tell where the limit to the jurisdiction lies. In a well-known judgment Lord Esher added the necessary correction:

---

[1] 'Jurisdictional' fact appears for the first time in [1969] 2 A.C. at 208 (Lord Wilberforce).

[2] *White and Collins v. Minister of Health*, above, p. 55.

[3] *Bunbury v. Fuller* (1853) 9 Ex. 111 at 140; and see *The King v. Fulham, Hammersmith and Kensington Rent Tribunal* [1951] 2 K.B. 1 at 6.

But there is another state of things which may exist. The legislature may intrust the tribunal or body with a jurisdiction, which includes the jurisdiction to determine whether the preliminary state of facts exists as well as the jurisdiction, on finding that it does exist, to proceed further or do something more.[1]

Everything therefore depends, as usual, upon the true construction of the particular Act; and on this question the Act is commonly silent, and so difficult to construe. Where justices of the peace were empowered to sit 'for the purpose of granting licences to persons keeping or being about to keep inns, alehouses and victualling houses', the majority of the Court of Appeal concluded that it was for the justices to decide whether any particular applicant fell within this description, and that if they decided the point wrongly this did not amount to excess of jurisdiction, despite the apparently objective language.[2] Similarly, where justices had power to make a bastardy order 'if the evidence of the mother be corroborated in some material particular by other evidence to the satisfaction of the said justices', it was held that it was for the justices to determine whether the other evidence was really corroborative or not, and that their order could not be challenged merely because it was not.[3] The words 'to the satisfaction of the said justices' naturally helped towards this interpretation.

There is also another consideration. Even where the court regards itself as competent to review jurisdictional facts, it may be reluctant to disturb the findings of a tribunal which heard and weighed conflicting testimony. The court will intervene if there is a clear deficiency of evidence to support the finding;[4] but where there is a conflict of evidence, the court will use its powers of control with restraint.[5]

Subjective conditions

A common condition for the exercise of a power is 'if it appears to the authority that, &c.', or 'if the authority is satis-

---

[1] *The Queen v. Special Commissioners of Income Tax* (1888) 21 Q.B.D. 313 at 319.
[2] *The King v. Woodhouse* [1906] 2 K.B. 501 (reversed on other grounds, *Leeds Corporation v. Ryder* [1907] A.C. 420).
[3] *The King v. Lincs. Justices* [1926] 2 K.B. 192.
[4] As in *R. v. Board of Control* [1956] 2 Q.B. 109.
[5] See *The King v. Fulham, Hammersmith and Kensington Rent Tribunal* [1951] 2 K.B. 1 at 11–14.

fied that, &c.'[1] Here the legislature seems plainly to have
stepped across the frontier which divides the objective from the
subjective and to have given the authority jurisdiction over the
facts. In one case a reinstatement committee had power to
make orders 'where the committee are satisfied that default has
been made by the former employer . . .', and it was held that
the question whether some person was truly the former employer or not was wholly for the committee to determine.[2] But
in other cases the courts have refused to be daunted by this kind
of formula. For example, a board had power to declare a house
insanitary 'whenever it appears to the Board' that a house was
unfit for human habitation, but the Privy Council invalidated
their order on the ground that they had applied the wrong
standard to a particular house.[3] A case of the same kind concerned a rent tribunal which was empowered to reduce a rent
'where . . . it appears to the tribunal that . . . a premium has
been paid'. Despite this language, the court quashed the tribunal's order because they had treated as a premium a sum
which the tenant had paid in respect of work done by the landlord and not in respect of the grant of the lease.[4] The Supreme
Court is, naturally, strongly tempted to control tribunals which
err in their decisions, and this is the explanation of cases which
may seem to strain the ordinary rule that excess of jurisdiction
invalidates an order, while error within the jurisdiction does not.
An extreme example is the *Anisminic* case, discussed below.[5]

Theory versus reality

It is sometimes said that the only logical way of escape from
the problem of deciding whether any given question is 'jurisdictional' is to be found in the 'theory of jurisdiction'. According
to this, an administrative authority or tribunal ought to have
jurisdiction to determine conclusively any question which is a

---

[1] Above, p. 85.
[2] *The King v. Ludlow* [1947] 1 K.B. 634. Cf. *Ashbridge Investments Ltd. v. Minister
of Housing and Local Government* [1965] 1 W.L.R. 1320 ('If the Minister is of
opinion . . . .'); see below, p. 102, note 2.
[3] *Estates and Trust Agencies Ltd. v. Singapore Improvement Trust* [1937] A.C. 898.
[4] *The King v. Fulham, Hammersmith and Kensington Rent Tribunal* [1950] 2 All E.R.
211.
[5] P. 151.

necessary element in its final decision.[1] Thus if a rent tribunal has power to fix the rents of furnished houses, the preliminary question whether the house is a furnished house must, if disputed, be decided by the tribunal before it can tell whether it has jurisdiction over the case. The decision on this point ought, it is argued, to be subject to no greater degree of control than the decision as to the proper rent, since the jurisdiction over the latter question impliedly requires an equal jurisdiction over the former.

Although the courts occasionally flirted with this theory in the nineteenth century,[2] before the heyday of administrative discretion, they have long abandoned it for good and self-evident reasons. For it opens the door to arbitrary power, by allowing administrative authorities to be the judges of the extent of their own jurisdiction. Therefore a rent tribunal's order can be quashed by showing to the court that the property is unfurnished or let for business purposes and so outside the jurisdiction of the tribunal.[3] Similarly a deportation order made by the Home Secretary, who has power to deport aliens, will be quashed if shown to be made against a British subject.[4] To allow the Home Secretary conclusive power to determine for this purpose that a British subject was an alien would plainly be intolerable.

The great objective of the courts is to prevent such abuses by keeping all powers within proper legal limits. As a learned judge well put it:

Subjection in this respect to the High Court is a necessary and inseparable incident to all tribunals of limited jurisdiction; for it is a contradiction in terms to create a tribunal with limited jurisdiction

---

[1] See de Smith, Judicial Review of Administrative Action, 2nd ed., 96; Rubinstein, Jurisdiction and Illegality, 212. Neither author advocates the theory.
[2] See e.g., Brittain v. Kinnaird (1819) 1 Br. v. B. 432; R. v. Bolton (1841) 1 Q.B. 66; and cf. Ashbridge Investments Ltd. v. Minister of Housing and Local Government [1965] 1 W.L.R. 1320 at 1326. Lord Reid's puzzling remarks in R. v. Governor of Brixton Prison ex parte Armah [1968] A.C. 192 at 234 (which contrast with Lord Upjohn's at 257) are explained in Anisminic Ltd. v. Foreign Compensation Commission [1969] 2 A.C. 147 at 171.
[3] R. v. City of London Rent Tribunal [1951] 1 K.B. 641; R. v. Fulham (&c.) Rent Tribunal [1951] 2 K.B. 1; R. v. Hackney (&c.) Rent Tribunal [1951] 2 K.B. 15, holding that 'a more dangerous usurpation of power by one of these tribunals it is impossible to imagine'.
[4] R. v. Home Secretary [1917] 1 K.B. 922 at 930.

and unlimited power to determine such limit at its own will and pleasure—such a tribunal would be autocratic, not limited. . . .'[1]

How faithfully the courts have clung to this principle, which indeed is a sheet anchor of the rule of law, can be seen from the examples already discussed. That the principle is often uncertain in its application is of small account by comparison with the importance of preserving it.

The power to err

In all the cases so far mentioned the court's claim to intervene has been based on some sort of excess of jurisdiction: the whole discussion has been an elaboration of the doctrine of *ultra vires*. But what if the ministry or statutory authority is acting within its powers? If it merely makes mistakes, will the court's arm be long enough to reach it?

The general answer, of course, is in the negative. A tribunal acting within its jurisdiction, or an official exercising the discretion committed to him, must be at liberty to go wrong. It is inherent in discretionary power that it includes the power to make mistakes. Authorities of all kinds are subject to the same principle, which has often been judicially approved in the following form.

Where the proceedings are regular on their face and the inferior tribunal had jurisdiction, the superior court will not grant the order of certiorari[2] on the ground that the inferior tribunal had misconceived a point of law. When the inferior tribunal has jurisdiction to decide a matter, it cannot (merely because it incidentally misconstrues a statute, or admits illegal evidence, or rejects legal evidence, or misdirects itself as to the weight of the evidence, or convicts without evidence) be deemed to exceed or abuse its jurisdiction.[3]

'The reason is,' added Lord Goddard, 'that if Parliament has chosen to make the lower tribunal or body the absolute judges of the matter before it and to give no appeal, this court cannot interfere in a matter regarding which the lower court has been clothed with jurisdiction by Parliament.'[4] Of course, an appeal may be available by statute. But many authorities and tribunals

---

[1] Farwell L.J. in *R. v. Shoreditch Assessment Committee* [1910] 2 K.B. 859 at 880. The House of Lords approved this passage in the *Anisminic* case (below, p. 151).

[2] That is to say, quash the decision. For certiorari see below, p. 128.

[3] Halsbury's *Laws of England*, 3rd ed., vol. 11, p. 62.

[4] *The King v. Ludlow* [1947] K.B. 634 at 639. For in this case see above, p. 91.

8—A.L.

have powers of final decision, and then the possibility of judicial review hinges on the question whether there can be said to be an excess of jurisdiction.

Error on the face of the record

There is, however, one important exception. There is only immunity from judicial review where, in the words of the above quotation, 'the proceedings are regular on their face'. If an inferior tribunal makes an order which on the face of it displays a mistake, this is (so to speak) an affront to the law which cannot be overlooked, and the order stands self-condemned even though it may be within jurisdiction. The power to make mistakes does not extend to mistakes which are self-evident on the record. Otherwise, to adopt the words of Lord Denning in another context, 'it would mean that the tribunal could disregard the law, which is a thing no one can do in this country'.[1] For a mistake displayed on the record will usually be a mistake of law, such as misconstruction of a statute or misapplication of a legal rule. Where such a mistake appears, the urge to intervene is more than judicial flesh and blood can resist.

It is not easy, on the standard theory of jurisdiction, to explain why tribunals are permitted to make mistakes of law, provided that they do not display them in the record of their proceedings. But history supplies the explanation. When in the seventeenth century the remedy of certiorari was first used to control statutory powers, its primary object was to call up the record of the proceedings into the Court of King's Bench[2]; and if the record displayed error, the decision was quashed. What is now an exception was then a primary rule, and it was not founded on any idea of jurisdiction or *ultra vires*. But if the applicant wanted to go outside the record, and bring other evidence to show some abuse of the power, the court would quash only where an excess of jurisdiction could be shown.[3] Here, of course, was the principle of *ultra vires*—which developed so fruitfully that it overshadowed the original jurisdiction over the record, and indeed almost led to its being forgotten.

This jurisdiction used to be one of the chief weapons by

---

[1] See below, p. 141.
[2] See below, p. 129.
[3] Rubinstein, Jurisdiction and Illegality, 78.

which the superior courts controlled the proceedings of justices of the peace. At one time justices were required to furnish elaborate written statements of evidence and reasoning, all of which were part of the record and which afforded ample opportunities for correction. But this era ended in 1848, when the Summary Jurisdiction Act introduced a short form of conviction which gave none of these details. This did not alter the law of judicial control as such. 'What it did was to disarm its exercise. The effect was not to make that which had been error, error no longer, but to remove nearly all opportunity for its detection.' Instead of providing what was called a 'speaking order', 'the face of the record "spoke" no longer: it was the inscrutable face of a sphinx.'[1]

It is only in recent years that the old principle of control has found a new application in the field of statutory tribunals. In 1944 the Court of Appeal held that it could intervene only where there was a true excess of jurisdiction.[2] But in 1951 it overruled itself, and thereby made an important extension of the field of judicial control.[3] The case turned upon the amount of compensation payable to the clerk to a hospital board in Northumberland who had lost his post in 1949 after the National Health Service was introduced. He claimed that not only his service with the hospital board, but also his earlier service with the local authority ought to be included in calculating his statutory compensation. The Compensation Appeal Tribunal were required to apply the regulations made under the Act, which as a matter of law required both periods of service to be taken into account. In their decision dismissing the appeal the tribunal stated that there had been these two periods of service, but that in their judgment it was only the second period which should count. The order therefore contained a manifest error of law, and on this ground it was declared void. Lord Denning said:

We have here a simple case of error of law by a tribunal, an error which they frankly acknowledge. It is an error which deprives Mr. Shaw of the compensation to which he is by law entitled. So long as the erroneous decision stands, the compensating authority dare not

---

[1] *The King v. Nat Bell Liquors Ltd.* [1922] 2 A.C. 128, at 159 (Lord Sumner).
[2] *Racecourse Betting Control Board v. Secretary for Air* [1944] Ch. 114.
[3] *The King v. Northumberland Compensation Appeal Tribunal* [1952] 1 K.B. 338.

pay Mr. Shaw the money to which he is entitled lest the auditor should surcharge them. It would be quite intolerable if in such a case there were no means of correcting the error.

This reasoning would be no less persuasive if the error had not appeared on the record. But the court's jurisdiction does not extend to errors which do not so appear, for those are the errors which the tribunal is as free to make as is any other court. Lord Denning did indeed suggest that the court could correct any admitted error of law, or bring an error onto the record by ordering the record to be supplemented. But this would be a further invasion of the tribunal's own jurisdiction, and it has been questioned in the House of Lords whether it is right to probe into speaking orders where 'the inscrutable face of a sphinx' is merely replaced by 'the ambiguous voice of the oracle'.[1] Only where there is a clear error 'on the face' will the court intervene.[2] But it will intervene where there is clear error of any kind, for example where the record shows that the tribunal refused to receive relevant evidence.[3]

It is established that 'the record' includes the documents in the case which are the basis of the decision as well as the statement of the decision itself. Thus in quashing a decision of the Patents Appeal Tribunal the court looked at the application and specification submitted by the applicant in order to detect the error of law.[4] It has even been held that an oral statement of reasons is part of 'the record'[5]—a decision which may surprise purists, but which accords well with the provision of the Tribunals and Inquiries Act discussed in the next paragraph.

This important head of jurisdiction seemed at first to have one serious weakness: tribunals were not in general legally obliged to make speaking orders. But subsequently the Tribunals and Inquiries Act 1958 provided that reasons must be given, if requested in accordance with the Act, for decisions by most tribunals and by ministers required to hold statutory inquiries; and that any reasons given under a statutory duty shall be

---

[1] *Baldwin & Francis Ltd. v. Patents Appeal Tribunal* [1959] A.C. 663 at 687 (Lord Tucker). In this case the error was held not to be apparent on the record.
[2] *R. v. Industrial Injuries Commissioner* [1966] 2 Q.B. 39.
[3] *R. v. Medical Appeal Tribunal* [1966] 1 W.L.R. 883.
[4] *R. v. Patents Appeal Tribunal* [1962] 2 Q.B. 647.
[5] *R. v. Chertsey Justices* [1961] 2 Q.B. 152.

taken to be incorporated in the record.[1] The obvious implication is that Parliament approves the control which the courts
have asserted, and has decided to remedy its one weakness by
enabling speaking orders to be obtained on demand. Even
when reasons are given orally, which the Act allows, they are
to be taken as part of the record; and thus Parliament anticipa-
ted the decision mentioned above, that the 'record' might be
partly oral.

The court's power to quash a decision for error of law on the
face of the record has thus become an efficient remedy, of
which much use has been made. In particular, it has enabled
the courts to pronounce on important questions in the law of
national and industrial injuries insurance.[2] But it has one
feature that is all too characteristic of our law: it is available only
under one particular procedure (that of certiorari), which does
not suit all situations. This awkward technicality must be explained in a later place.[3]

These developments show how the courts have extended their
control, and how far the pendulum has now swung in the direction indicated by Lord Denning. The result is that most decisions of tribunals may be challenged on a point of law, provided
only that the point enters into the stated grounds of decision.
Now that virtually any error of law can be dragged forth into
the light and exhibited as part of the record, statutory tribunals have in effect been stripped of all power to give final
decisions on points of law. The new system is further but-
tressed, as we shall see, by the provision of the Act of 1958
which protects it against statutory clauses which purport to
make various orders and decisions unchallengeable. The notion
that statutory tribunals can be the final arbiters on matters of
law has fallen far back from the high-water mark which it
attained not very long ago. It is interesting that Parliament has
done so much to speed this movement.

The movement has one aspect of special significance: it has
pushed judicial control beyond the boundary of the doctrine
of *ultra vires*. Throughout this chapter we have seen that the

---

[1] S. 12. See below, p. 271.
[2] See e.g. *R. v. Medical Appeal Tribunal* [1957] 1 Q.B. 574; *R. v. Deputy Industrial Injuries Commissioner* [1966] 2 Q.B. 1; *R. v. Deputy Industrial Injuries Commissioner* [1967] 1 A.C. 725; *R. v. National Insurance Commissioner* [1970] 2 W.L.R. 182.
[3] P. 123.

courts intervene against action which is beyond jurisdiction, and therefore unlawful, but will not intervene where the action is within jurisdiction, and therefore lawful. A mere mistake of law, however, often does not deprive a tribunal of jurisdiction.[1] Yet if the mistake appears on the record the court will strike down the decision. The action is *intra vires*, yet the court treats it as unlawful.[2] To this extent the judges have emancipated themselves from the jurisdictional theory which elsewhere is dominant.

Errors of fact. 'No evidence'

Questions of fact are a domain where statutory authorities still preserve much of their final jurisdiction. Just as the courts look jealously on decisions by other bodies on matters of law, so they look indulgently on their decisions on matters of fact, for here clearly they are on their own allotted ground. Without digressing into the question whether 'law' and 'fact' can be clearly distinguished,[3] we can adopt a working test. Where the facts of a case are agreed or established, any inference from them or application of the law to them is an inference or conclusion of law. But where the actual events or circumstances are disputed, the question is one of fact; and of course facts are often admitted or are otherwise undisputed.

The *locus classicus* is the celebrated opinion given by Lord Sumner in a Privy Council case from Canada, where a firm had been convicted before a magistrate for selling liquor contrary to the local Liquor Act.[4] The only evidence of the fact of sale was that of an *agent provocateur* of the police, which was the subject of a number of objections. Could the inferior court's decision be quashed as *ultra vires* (as opposed to being challenged on appeal) because they had no proper evidence before them? In rejecting the contention that 'want of evidence on which to convict is the same as want of jurisdiction to take evidence at all', Lord Sumner said:

This, clearly, is erroneous. A justice who convicts without evidence is doing something which he ought not to do, but he is doing it as

---

[1] It does so only if the question is one of 'jurisdictional law': above, p. 89.
[2] See *R. v. Agricultural Land Tribunal* [1960] 1 W.L.R. 911 at 914.
[3] For this see below, p. 260.
[4] *The King v. Nat Bell Liquors Ltd.* [1922] 2 A.C. 128; above, p. 95.

a judge, and if his jurisdiction to entertain the charge is not open to impeachment, his subsequent error, however grave, is a wrong exercise of a jurisdiction which he has, and not a usurpation of a jurisdiction which he has not. . . . To say that there is no jurisdiction to convict without evidence is the same thing as saying that there is jurisdiction if the decision is right, and none if it is wrong. . . .[1]

This principle applies to all inferior jurisdictions; and thus to tribunals, ministers and officials as well as to magistrates. Speaking of tribunals, Lord Goddard has said:

If it is acting within its jurisdiction, it is now settled law that absence of evidence does not affect the jurisdiction of the tribunal to try the case, nor does a misdirection by the tribunal to itself in considering the evidence nor what might be held on appeal to be a wrong decision in point of law.[2]

But this discussion inevitably leads back to the question whether the facts or law determined by the tribunal are 'jurisdictional', which we have already investigated.[3] If they are, a wrong finding will mean an excess of jurisdiction; if they are not, a wrong finding cannot be impugned except by way of appeal, if Parliament has provided for it.

New tendencies

That, at least, is the canonical doctrine. But change is now in the wind, for there are signs that the courts may be ready to assert control over findings of fact based on no evidence, just as they have done over mistakes of law apparent on the record. A finding based on no evidence, as opposed to a finding which is merely against the weight of the evidence, is an abuse of power which judges are naturally loath to tolerate. The remarks of Lord Sumner and Lord Goddard are founded upon the classical theory of jurisdictional control, in other words the principle of *ultra vires*. But that theory no longer reigns supreme: the doctrine of error on the face of the record infringes it, and there is really no reason why new doctrines as to findings of fact should not infringe it also. In particular, if it should be

---

[1] [1922] 2 A.C. at 151.
[2] [1947] K.B. at 639. But this 'settled law' may not be beyond question. It is flatly contradicted by the Court of Appeal in *Allison v. General Medical Council* [1894] 1 Q.B. 750, holding that absence of evidence goes to jurisdiction.
[3] Above, p. 89.

apparent on the record that a finding was based on no evidence, the courts could quash it, even under the present law, for error 'on its face'.[1] It is a recognised rule that 'whether or not there is evidence to support a particular decision is always a question of law'.[2] This rule is frequently applied by courts of appeal where statute gives a right of appeal on a point of law only, so that even then findings can be challenged on the ground of 'no evidence', as well as on the ground of wrong interpretation of evidence.[3]

A recent case in the House of Lords appears to show that this rule can be invoked successfully in cases of judicial review (as opposed to appeal) where the lack of evidence appears on the record.[4] There have also been wider judicial dicta to the effect that the court will quash decisions based on no evidence,[5] without reference to the record, and this has even been conceded by counsel for the Crown.[6] Another judicial suggestion is that some supporting evidence is required by the principles of natural justice.[7]

'No evidence' does not necessarily mean a complete absence of evidence. The question is whether the evidence, taken as a whole, is reasonably capable of supporting the finding.[8] In the United States the courts have made extensive use of a comparable rule, under which they will set aside decisions not found to be based on 'substantial evidence', looking at the record as a whole. With this example before them, the English courts may well take the analogous step of controlling decisions for

---

[1] See *Davies v. Price* [1958] 1 W.L.R. 434; *R. v. Agricultural Land Tribunal* [1960] 1 W.L.R. 911; *R. v. Governor of Brixton Prison ex parte Armah* [1968] A.C. 192, where the House of Lords held that the evidence in a 'fugitive offender' case formed part of the record, thus justifying the court in granting habeas corpus since the evidence for the committal was insufficient. There is plenty of support in older law for quashing on the ground of want of evidence in the record: see *R. v. Mahony* [1910] 2 I.R. 695 at 703, 710, 716.

[2] [1968] A.C. at 234 (Lord Reid).

[3] See below, p. 260.

[4] See note 1 (the *Armah* case).

[5] See, e.g., [1956] 2 Q.B. at 124; [1969] 2 Q.B. at 231; below, p. 102, note 2.

[6] *Ashbridge Investments Ltd. v. Ministry of Housing and Local Government* [1965] 1 W.L.R. 1320 at 1325. See also below, p. 102, note 2.

[7] Below, p. 213.

[8] *Allison v. General Medical Council* [1894] 1 Q.B. 750; *Lee v. The Showmen's Guild* [1952] 2 Q.B. 329 (showing that the court is more ready to intervene in cases based on contract).

which the evidence is totally inadequate. The respect which is rightly shown to a tribunal's findings of fact should stop at the point where they are patently baseless, for otherwise grave injustice may be done. Appellate jurisdiction has made the courts expert in applying this test.[1]

Present possibilities

Even under the law as it now stands, what is shut out at the front door may get in by the back. A decision based on no evidence is very likely capricious or unreasonable,[2] or given upon wrong legal grounds, or in breach of natural justice,[3] so that the court, if it wants to intervene, can do so.

A case arose in Flintshire where the licensing justices, who for over fifty years had licensed a theatre for the sale of liquor and tobacco, withdrew the licence because there were other licensed premises close at hand, and also because they had refused to license a new theatre in the neighbourhood and considered that for the sake of consistency they should license both theatres or neither. The justices had power to make 'suitable rules for ensuring order and decency' at the theatres, and it was admitted that there was no evidence before them of any disorder or indecency at the older theatre which the withdrawal of the licence could remedy. The Divisional Court held that they could not intervene, since the justices had acted within the limits of their discretion. But the Court of Appeal reversed them, holding that the justices had failed to consider each case separately on its own merits, and that their real motive was not to safeguard order or decency but to achieve consistency.[4] Lord Parker agreed with a remark in the court below that order and decency were not preserved or advanced by telling the patrons of the theatre that they could drink next door instead, and he added: 'In other words, as it seems to me, there was no evidence at all on which the committee could impose the prohibition on the sale of liquor.' This comment well shows how easily control

---

[1] In the *Armah* case (above) the House of Lords seems to have gone further and weighed conflicting evidence. But habeas corpus cases may be a special category.

[2] As suggested in *Osgood v. Nelson* (1872) L.R. 5 H.L. 636. Cf. *Lee v. Showmen's Guild* [1952] 2 Q.B. 329, holding the contractual jurisdiction of a 'domestic tribunal' to require findings reasonably supported by evidence.

[3] See below, p. 213.

[4] *The Queen v. Flintshire C.C. County Licensing Committee* [1957] 1 Q.B. 350.

may seem to be based on 'no evidence' when really it is based on 'wrong grounds', a familiar category of abuse of power,[1] which is part of the doctrine of *ultra vires*. The courts are so familiar with 'no evidence' as a ground of appeal that they are naturally tempted to press it into service as a ground of review.[2]

Wrongful rejection of evidence

If a tribunal wrongfully refuses to receive evidence on the ground that it is irrelevant or inadmissible, this error does not go to jurisdiction and the court cannot intervene unless the error appears on the face of the record. But there will be a jurisdictional error if the reason for rejecting the evidence is a mistaken belief by the tribunal that it has no business to investigate the question at all. In that case the tribunal is wrongfully refusing to exercise its jurisdiction. Its order can therefore be quashed[3] and it can be ordered to determine the question properly.[4] This distinction has nothing to do with the legal rules of evidence, which in general do not apply to statutory tribunals.[5] The question is simply whether the tribunal has failed to discharge its duty to inquire into the case before it.

EFFECT OF ILLEGALITY

Partial invalidity

An administrative act may be partially good and partially bad. If an invalid condition is attached to a licence or to planning permission, the question arises whether the whole permission is void, or whether the void condition alone can be struck out, leaving the permission in other respects valid. The answer will be of great importance to the licensee.

As a general rule the court is reluctant to sever the bad from the good, since the terms of the permission may then become such as the licensing authority would not have thought compatible with the public interest. In a recent case the House of

---

[1] Above, p. 78.

[2] Other examples are *R. v. Birmingham Compensation Appeal Tribunal* [1952] 2 All E.R. 100, note (error of statutory interpretation represented as 'no evidence'); *Ashbridge Investments Ltd. v. Minister of Housing and Local Government* [1965] 1 W.L.R. 1320 at 1327–8 (representing the case of *White and Collins*, discussed above, p. 89, as one of 'no evidence', whereas it was expressly decided on the ground of excess of jurisdiction).

[3] *Toronto Newspaper Guild v. Globe Printing Co.* [1953] 3 D.L.R. 561 (certiorari).

[4] *R. v. Marsham* [1892] 1 Q.B. 371 (mandamus).

[5] Below, p. 272.

Lords held by a narrow majority that they could not sever a planning condition requiring that the permission should lapse after three years unless in the meantime detailed plans were approved by the planning authority.[1] If this condition had been void, therefore, the whole planning permission would have been void likewise. Similarly planning permission was wholly void where an invalid condition required the applicant to provide a piece of roadway at his own expense.[2]

The House of Lords suggested that severance may be possible where the void condition is merely incidental or is directed to some quite extraneous purpose. But the only precedents mentioned were cases of cinema licensing, where cinema operators were unsuccessfully prosecuted for breach of specific conditions which the court held void, and no question of severance therefore arose.[3] As Lord Reid observed, there is a surprising dearth of authority on what ought to be a frequent problem. In one planning case, however, the court allowed severance of an invalid condition, so that the planning permission stood.[4]

Void or voidable?

Stress has already been laid on the fact that the courts are primarily concerned with administrative *illegality*.[5] This is the constitutional dividing line. The courts can interfere where administrative action is unauthorized by law: it is then *ultra vires* or, as it is often put, outside jurisdiction. If it is duly authorized, and so *intra vires*, the court has no concern with it. The one recognized exception is the power to quash for error on the face of the record, where even *intra vires* action may be quashed; but for this there are valid historical reasons.

All the cases discussed in this chapter may therefore be divided into two classes: cases where the action is *ultra vires* and void; and cases of error on the face of the record where the decision, assuming it to be *intra vires*, may be said to be voidable.[6]

---

[1] *Kingsway Investment Ltd. v. Kent C.C.* [1970] 2 W.L.R. 397 (condition held valid). See now Town and Country Planning Act 1968, s. 66).
[2] *Hall & Co. Ltd. v. Shoreham-by-Sea U.D.C.* [1964] 1 W.L.R. 240 (above, p. 80).
[3] E.g. *Ellis v. Dubowski* [1921] 3 K.B. 621 (above, p. 62).
[4] *Allnat London Properties Ltd. v. Middlesex C.C.* (1964) 62 L.G.R. 304 (condition restricting use right).
[5] Above, p. 51.
[6] See *D.P.P. v. Head* [1959] A.C. 83 (Lord Denning); but the majority of the House of Lords appeared to treat the order in question as *ultra vires* and void.

'Voidable' means that the action is legally valid in the first instance, and remains valid if the court does not intervene. It follows inexorably that voidable action is initially authorized by law, though the court is also authorized by law to avoid it. It follows no less inexorably that action which is not authorized by law at any time cannot be voidable: it is *ultra vires* and void. All the examples given earlier in this chapter are based on this approach, which is fundamental to the whole subject of judicial control, and to the distinction between appeal and review. A decision which is valid unless reversed on appeal is an example of a voidable decision, while a decision which is an excess of jurisdiction is obviously a void decision. The courts have extended their control by developing the notion of 'excess of jurisdiction' into a highly refined concept, so that it embraces (for example) decisions which are unreasonable or where the procedure is wrong or where wrong legal criteria are applied.[1]

This artificiality may have prompted the judicial suggestions, which have appeared recently, that action which is *ultra vires* may be merely voidable, at any rate where the illegality is not obvious on its face. In one case a ratepayer challenged the whole rating valuation list made by the local authority on the ground that.it was compiled on an entirely wrong basis, contrary to the directions in the statute.[2] The challenge failed on the facts, but differing opinions were expressed in the Court of Appeal on the law. One suggestion was that, even though it would be an excess of jurisdiction to make an invalid list, the list would be voidable and not void and would remain good until set aside. But the other view, based on sounder logic, was that if the challenge succeeded there could be no valid list in existence.[3] Soon afterwards it was also suggested that the decision of a planning authority, which is required by law to deal with an application within two months, was 'not void but at most voidable' if given after the permitted time[4]; but since at the same time it was held that the requirement was not mandatory but directory,[5] the question did not appear to arise.

---

[1] See especially the *Anisminic* case, below, p. 151.

[2] *R. v. Paddington Valuation Officer* [1966] 1 Q.B. 380.

[3] See below, p. 163.

[4] *James v. Minister of Housing and Local Government* [1966] 1 W.L.R. 135, reversed (without mention of this point) [1967] 1 W.L.R. 171.

[5] See above, p. 57.

The cases on natural justice, to be examined later, offer particularly strong proof that administrative action which is irregular and ultra vires is void, not voidable. The House of Lords decided the point expressly in *Ridge v. Baldwin*, although it had never been in doubt in any of the numerous cases of *ultra vires*. The authorities are discussed at two places in chapter 5.[1] It is there pointed out that the object of holding unlawful action to be voidable is to give the court discretion to uphold or condemn the action as it feels inclined, and that this policy is full of danger. The courts have never had discretion to decide whether governmental action is lawful or unlawful: the citizen is entitled to resist unlawful action as a matter of right, and to live under the rule of law, not the rule of discretion. 'To remit the maintenance of constitutional right to the region of judicial discretion is to shift the foundations of freedom from the rock to the sand.'[2] The true scope for discretion is in the law of remedies, where it operates within much narrower limits and is far less objectionable. If the courts were to undermine the principle of *ultra vires* by making it discretionary, no victim of an excess or abuse of power could be sure that the law would protect him.[3] Another serious consequence would be that the declaratory judgment, a very valuable remedy, would as the law now stands lose much of its efficacy, since it is of use only against action which can be declared to be *ultra vires*, i.e. void *ab inito*.[4]

Voidness, third parties and remedies

Although action which is adjudged to be *ultra vires* is properly described as void or a nullity, this voidness necessarily depends upon the right remedy being sought successfully by the right person. If for example a chief constable is illegally dismissed, he may have the dismissal declared void.[5] But if he does not dispute it, other people will have to accept it also. For as against third parties, whose rights are not infringed, a 'void'

---

[1] Below, pp. 185, 204.
[2] *Scott v. Scott* [1913] A.C. 417 (Lord Shaw).
[3] On the whole question of 'void or voidable' see 83 L.Q.R. 499, 84 L.Q.R. 95.
[4] Below, p. 123.
[5] Below, p. 201.

act may well be valid if they have no legal title to challenge it.[1] Even the injured party may be refused relief, e.g. by an exercise of discretion[2] or because of some waiver.[3] The meaning of 'void' is thus relative rather than absolute; and the court may in effect turn void acts into valid ones by refusing to grant remedies. There is no absurdity in this. The absurdity lies rather in supposing that 'void' has an absolute meaning independently of the court's willingness to intervene. As in all litigation, and as the next chapter emphasizes, everything depends upon the remedy.

This principle of relativity is also illustrated by the doctrine of officers *de facto*. There may be some legal defect in the appointment of a public officer, but if he is effectively in possession of his office he can sometimes validly exercise its powers.[4] Just as the wrongful possessor of land is protected by law against third parties,[5] so third parties may be prevented from taking advantage of a flaw in the title to an office. It may be more important that the duties of the office be effectively discharged than that the incumbent's legal title be impregnable.

---

[1] See below, pp. 123, 139. In *Durayappah v. Fernando* [1967] 2 A.C. 337 the Privy Council resolved a problem of this kind by holding the same act to be both void and voidable; but the reasoning defies analysis: see below, pp. 205, 217.

[2] Below, p. 144.

[3] *Ibid.*; and see 84 L.Q.R. at p. 109.

[4] *Scadding v. Lorant* (1851) 3 H.L.C. 418; *Re Aldridge* (1893) 15 N.Z.L.R. 361; Rubinstein, *Jurisdiction and Illegality*, 205; cf. *Adams v. Adams* [1970] 3 W.L.R. 934 at 951.

[5] Megarry and Wade, *Real Property*, 3rd ed., 997.

4

REMEDIES

RIGHTS AND REMEDIES

RIGHTS depend upon remedies. Our legal history is rich in examples of general rules of law which have been distilled from the system of remedies, as the remedies have been extended and adapted from one class of case to another. There is no better example than habeas corpus. This remedy, since the sixteenth century the chief cornerstone of personal liberty, grew out of a medieval writ which at first played an inconspicuous part in the law of procedure: it was used to secure the appearance of a party, in particular where he was in detention by some inferior court. It was later invoked to challenge detention by the king and by the Council; and finally it became the standard procedure by which the legality of any imprisonment could be tested. The right to personal freedom was almost a by-product of the procedural rules. A similar preoccupation with remedies is to be seen in many cases dealing with the control of administrative powers: the courts seem sometimes more at ease in considering 'whether certiorari will lie' than in revealing the general principles which ought to govern judicial intervention. The ideals which inspire the legal mind then become veiled in a mist of secondary technicalities.

This tendency has both good and bad effects. It is good in that the emphasis falls on the practical methods of enforcing any right. Efficient remedies are of the utmost importance. It is bad in that the remedy comes to be looked upon as a thing in itself, divorced from the legal policy to which it ought to give expression. This leads to gaps and anomalies, and to a confusion of doctrine to which the courts sometimes seem strangely indifferent. The law of habeas corpus itself contains unfortunate lacunae. No right of appeal used to exist against refusal of habeas corpus in cases of imprisonment on a charge of a criminal nature—a grave and irrational defect which is at last now cured by legislation.[1] There is no proper procedure for investigating questions of fact on which the legality of the imprisonment may depend. It has also come to light that the provisions of the Habeas Corpus Act 1679, for release of accused persons on bail, are inapplicable to modern criminal procedure and so ineffective.[2] This is the natural result of enacting legal reforms in terms of procedural technicalities instead of general rules. The remedy may be very efficient—habeas corpus has a well-deserved reputation for efficiency in protecting liberty—yet it may fail to reach cases which, on any general view of the matter, ought to be included.

Habeas corpus itself plays a larger part in general constitutional law than in administrative law. But it is one of a family of 'prerogative' remedies, the rest of which lie within our field: the remedies of certiorari, prohibition and mandamus. The family name 'prerogative' indicates that they share the same ancestry and that once they were more freely available to the Crown than to the subject. But now the emphasis is reversed, and they are of more importance to the subject than to the Crown. As remedies they have much the same sort of virtues and defects as has the writ of habeas corpus. Within their accustomed limits they work well, and they are well-tried instruments of judicial control. Yet they have also inherited a legacy of imperfections, mostly procedural, for which there were valid reasons in the distant past, but which are out of place in the new spheres that these remedies have won for themselves.

The account of remedies given in this chapter will necessarily cut across other chapters, since we are here largely concerned with the means of enforcing principles discussed elsewhere. Remedies against the Crown and its servants must be mentioned incidentally, but the main discussion of Crown liability must be reserved for Chapter 8. The prerogative remedies will not be taken as the starting-point, since they are the most highly specialized of all. It will be best to look first at the more commonplace remedies and see how far they go. It will then be easier to understand how the specialized remedies supplement them. Remedies for the control of powers will be followed by remedies for the enforcement of duties.

---

[1] Administration of Justice Act 1960, s. 15.
[2] *R. v. Campbell* [1959] 1 W.L.R. 646.

ACTIONS FOR DAMAGES

Recourse to private law

The fact that administrative law is 'ordinary law', enforced by the ordinary courts, becomes particularly plain from the large part played by the ordinary remedies of private law, such as actions for damages, injunctions, and declarations. If, for example, an authority exceeds its powers, the position is simply that it has no legal right to act. If its act, being without justification, constitutes a tort or a breach of contract or any other legal wrong, it is just as liable to an action for damages as is any private individual—save only that the Crown Proceedings Act somewhat modifies the procedure for suing the Crown, and gives the Crown a few special privileges.[1]

A good example of the ordinary remedy is furnished by a case which we will later meet in connexion with the right to be heard.[2] When the local authority at Wandsworth demolished a building because the person who built it had not given them the notice required by statute, they were held to have acted wrongly because, although the statute gave them a power of demolition, such a power could not be exercised without first giving the offender an opportunity to be heard in his own defence. Since damage had already been done, the owner simply brought an ordinary action for trespass against the local authority, just as he would have done against any private person if that person had come and done unlawful injury to his property. Since he showed the local authority to have acted illegally, he recovered full damages. The local authority would have been liable to the normal process of execution for enforcing the judgment. It is only against the Crown (meaning, in effect, central as opposed to local government) that the ordinary enforcement machinery gives place to the special procedure of the Crown Proceedings Act 1947.

Again, the famous cases which centred round John Wilkes in the eighteenth century, and which denied the power of ministers to issue warrants of arrest and search, took the form of actions for damages against the particular servants who did the deeds, who were sued in trespass just as if they were private individuals. The individual liability of Crown servants, which formed

---

[1] Below, Chapter 8.   [2] Below, p. 188.

the basis of our law of Crown proceedings before the Act of
1947,[1] is the direct result of this wide use of ordinary remedies—
a course fostered by the courts and tolerated by the government
for the sake of maintaining a genuine rule of law.

Another rule which emerged in the course of Wilkes' legal
adventures was that oppressive or unconstitutional action by
servants of the government could justify an award of exemplary
or punitive damages, i.e. damages which take into account the
outrageous conduct of the defendant and not merely the actual
loss to the plaintiff. Exemplary damages are only rarely allowed
in other cases, so the position here is that the law is sterner with
the government than with the citizen.[2]

The scope of the ordinary law

Many other leading cases could be given in illustration.
Actions for negligence are, of course, common, and the cases
mentioned in an earlier chapter show how public authorities
are liable to ordinary actions for damages for negligent exercise
of their powers.[3] Another example is an action for trespass
against a colonial governor, where the Governor of Jamaica
had seized a ship chartered to the plaintiff, and could plead no
legal justification.[4] In Canada there has even been a successful
action for damages against the Prime Minister of Quebec for
directing the cancellation of a liquor licence because the licensee
supported the sect called Jehovah's Witnesses—which he was
entitled to do, and which had nothing to do with his qualifications for his licence.[5] The law in Quebec, modelled on the
French principle of giving damages for any injury caused by
fault, treats wrongful cancellation of a licence as a actionable
wrong, as indeed it may be in England if malice can be shown.
But gaps in the categories of the law of tort are always likely to
reveal themselves in connexion with administrative powers, for
the old rules of common law do not touch some of the important
questions of modern life. Many decisions of ministers, tribunals,
or licensing bodies, which may be of the greatest importance to
a man's status or livelihood, inflict no recognized legal injury
if they are wrongly made. It is true that wrongful administrative

---

[1] Below, p. 280.   [2] See *Rookes v. Barnard* [1964] A.C. 1129 at 1226.
[3] Above, p. 57.   [4] *Musgrave v. Pulido* (1879) 5 App. Cas. 102.
[5] *Roncarelli v. Duplessis* (1959) 16 D.L.R. (2d) 689.

action is breach of statutory duty and that breach of statutory duty may be actionable.[1] But the law in this area is uncertain, and a more reliable remedy is required. The action for damages is therefore unsuitable for dealing with large classes of administrative acts. In practice it plays a relatively small role.

INJUNCTIONS

General

Much the same is true of the injunction. This is also one of the standard remedies of private law. It is an order requiring some person to refrain from breaking the law, e.g. by committing a tort or breach of contract, and is enforced if necessary by imprisonment or fine for contempt of court, or by attachment of property. It is an equitable remedy, meaning that it derives from the former Court of Chancery, and that it has a discretionary character. We shall find that most of the important remedies are discretionary—injunctions, declarations, certiorari, and prohibition, for example—but this does not greatly affect their nature since the discretion must be exercised judicially and according to settled principles. The only marked effect is that there is some tendency for the court to refuse the remedy where the plaintiff has some other equally good remedy, available or where he has been guilty of delay or in some other way has forfeited the court's sympathy.

It is also possible for the court to grant a mandatory injunction, i.e. a positive order to do some act rather than a negative order to refrain. Mandatory injunctions are rare, and in particular they play little part in public law because there is a special procedure for enforcing the performance of a public duty in the prerogative remedy of mandamus dealt with below.

Subject to certain mainly formal differences in the case of the Crown, injunctions are just as readily available against public authorities as they are against private persons, and they fulfil their usual function of providing a valuable alternative to actions for damages. There are many cases where prevention is better than cure, and where either a perpetual injunction or an interim injunction will be awarded to restrain a threatened wrong before it has taken place. And the cure itself is specific, so that a final injunction puts an end to the

[1] See below, p. 156.

wrong complained of instead of merely assessing it in money. This remedy, therefore, provides a means both of testing the legal validity of some act which still lies in the future, and also of preventing the continuance of some wrong which has already begun.

The courts are not deterred by the fact that an injunction against a public authority is a particularly drastic step, bringing the machinery of government to a halt. They do not lend a ready ear to pleas of administrative inconvenience. 'Even if chaos should result, still the law must be obeyed.'[1]

Examples of injunctions

One of the commonest uses of an injunction is to prevent the commission or continuance of nuisances. At Derby, for example, this remedy was invoked to deal with pollution of the rivers Trent and Derwent caused by municipal and industrial effluents which damaged the fishing. The owners of the fishing rights brought their action against three separate bodies—an industrial company which was discharging chemicals and over-heated water, the Derby Corporation which was fouling the rivers with its sewage, and the British Electricity Authority which was over-heating the water. Injunctions to prohibit this invasion of private rights were granted against all three defendants, and it made no difference in principle that one was a commercial firm, one a local government authority, and one a nationalized industry.[2] But in the case of the Derby Corporation the court suspended the injunction for a period of sixteen months in order to give the Corporation time to make new arrangements for sewage disposal. The Corporation had statutory authority for their sewage scheme which when first installed had been quite satisfactory. But it had been overloaded by the great growth of Derby, and the Corporation had been driven to use the river for discharge at certain times. The court rejected their argument that, since they had in the first place done what the statute authorized, they could not be blamed for maintaining the system as best they could subsequently. The point was rather that, unless anything could be found in the

---

[1] *Bradbury v. Enfield L.B.C.* [1967] 1 W.L.R. 1311 (Lord Denning, M.R.).
[2] *Pride of Derby & Derbyshire Angling Association, Ltd. v. British Celanese, Ltd.* [1953] Ch. 149; above, p. 61.

Act to allow such interference with private rights, the powers
should never be exercised so as to commit the tort of nuisance.
Unless Parliament provided otherwise, the authority must obey
the ordinary law. Nor was the Corporation more successful in
its claim that it should not be subjected to an injunction but
should be liable (if at all) only in damages. If this had been
right, then the Corporation could in effect have compulsorily
expropriated the owners of the fishing subject to payment of
damages by way of compensation. To say that the sewage-
disposal arrangements were an urgent necessity for public
health, while the fishing rights were relatively of minor importance, did not alter the case at all: for it still remains true that
private rights can be expropriated only by statutory authority,
and no such authority could be found in the statutes under
which the Corporation operated. Accordingly, the Corporation
was ordered to cease from polluting the rivers within the specified time, and they were thus compelled to make new arrangements. Needless to say, a public authority will fully respect the
court's order. But it is not unknown, where an authority has
been tardy in its obedience, for the courts to threaten to fine or
imprison its members or officers for contempt.

   The Derby case is reminiscent of the case of the Hampstead
Asylum in an earlier chapter.[1] Both cases illustrate the doctrine
that statutory powers will be construed so as not to authorize
invasion of private rights unless the invasion is an inevitable
result of the exercise of the power conferred. In both cases, also,
the injunction was the remedy which effectively stopped the
local authority from using its powers so as to cause unauthorized
damage.

   Cases of nuisance are only one example of the efficacy of the
injunction. It is no less a general remedy, in its own sphere,
than is the action for damages; it may be the means of preventing the commission or continuance of any tort or breach of
contract. Just as, in the *Wandsworth* case, damages were awarded
for trespass because the local authority pulled down the building without giving the owner a hearing,[2] so in a case at Rotherham an injunction was granted to restrain the Corporation from
carrying out a demolition order without a proper hearing of
the owner's appeal for exercise of the statutory power of

[1] Above, p. 60.   [2] Below, p. 188.

postponement.[1] In both cases the action, being procedurally irregular, amounted to a tort, and the only difference was that in the *Rotherham* case the owner was able to act before the blow had fallen, and to prevent it from falling. The citizen is in a far stronger position if he can challenge the local authority before it has committed itself to action, and the value in this respect of the remedy by injunction need hardly be stressed.

Although primarily a remedy against tort and other actionable wrongs, the injunction may develop into a general remedy against unauthorized governmental action, as it has done in the United States. The Court of Appeal has granted an injunction to prevent a local education authority from ceasing to maintain schools without following the proper statutory procedure, although this default would not apparently have been an actionable wrong in itself.[2] Used in this way, the injunction may overlap the declaration and the prerogative remedies as a general remedy against *ultra vires* action.[3] Several of the cases mentioned in the following paragraphs on the Crown and Parliament were attempts at using injunctions in this way. But in none of the cases has the court discussed this question.

The Crown and its servants

An injunction will not be granted against the Crown. This is both on general grounds, because the court will not make an order which it has no means of enforcing, and also because of the provisions of the Crown Proceedings Act 1947. But the Act allows the court to make a declaratory order of similar scope,[4] and since any such order will certainly be respected, there is no lack of a suitable remedy against the Crown. It has, however, been held that the Act authorizes only a definitive order (corresponding to a final injunction) and not a provisional order (corresponding to an interim injunction).[5] This is an unjustifiable lacuna, for interim relief may be just as necessary against the Crown as against any other defendant.

An important question is how far the special rules relating

---

[1] *Broadbent v. Rotherham Corporation* [1917] 2 Ch. 31.
[2] *Bradbury v. Enfield L.B.C.* [1967] 1 W.L.R. 1311 (above, p. 56).
[3] Below, pp. 120, 138.
[4] See below, p. 292, for declaratory orders against the Crown.
[5] *International General Electric Co. v. Commissioners of Customs and Excise* [1962] Ch. 784.

to the Crown also extend to the Crown's servants. The Act provides that an injunction shall not issue against an officer of the Crown if the effect would be to give a remedy against the Crown which could not have been obtained in proceedings against the Crown.[1] The object of this is to prevent the Crown's immunity being stultified by substituting an individual official as the defendant, since the whole point of the immunity is that the machinery of central government shall not be brought to a halt by an injunction. Otherwise, applying the principle that wrongs done by servants of the Crown render the servant liable personally, an injunction might be sought against the servant and thus, in effect, a specific remedy would be obtained against the Crown instead of the declaratory order which is the more seemly form of relief. There have been cases in the past (though the examples are rare and perhaps open to doubt) where injunctions have been granted to restrain ministers of the Crown acting in their official capacity.[2] But the Act appears to have taken away this possibility with one hand while giving the new declaratory order with the other. An attempt was made in 1955 to obtain a mandatory injunction against the Minister of Agriculture in order to make him withdraw a draft scheme for potato marketing which had been laid before Parliament and which was alleged to be *ultra vires*. But it was plain that the Minister was acting in his official capacity, i.e. as a minister of the Crown; and although the Agricultural Marketing Acts provided that it was the Minister who was to make such schemes, so that the power resided in him rather than in the Crown itself, the court held that any remedy by injunction was barred by the Crown Proceedings Act.[3] Possibly a declaratory order could have been made if that had been asked for in proceedings under the Act against the Ministry (not the Minister), and possibly also the court could have made an ordinary declaration. At the present stage of the law the choice of remedy in such a case is not easy.

Parliament

Another limit to the injunction, imposed by the court itself,

[1] S. 21 (2).   [2] E.g. *Ellis v. Earl Grey* (1833) 6 Sim. 214.
[3] *Merricks v. Heathcoat-Amory* [1955] Ch. 567. But mandamus may be available: see below, p. 166.

is that it must not interfere with the processes of Parliament. As regards its proceedings within its own walls, Parliament is, of course, privileged from any judicial intervention. But there are extra-mural matters where a line has to be drawn. The court follows the principle that it will not intervene to prevent some matter being brought before Parliament as a question of public policy, even though it may be a breach of contract to bring it forward. Thus in one case the Wolverhampton Corporation had contracted with the Bilston Corporation that it would not oppose any application to Parliament by the Bilston Corporation for a local Act of Parliament for obtaining a water-supply from any area outside the Wolverhampton Corporation's area. The Wolverhampton Corporation did oppose such an application and were held to be in breach of their contract. The court, however, refused to restrain them by injunction, because that would have prevented Parliament from hearing all sides of the question in determining whether, as a matter of public policy, the Wolverhampton Corporation ought to be released from their obligation by statute.[1] This was a strong case, since the contract itself had been confirmed and made binding by an earlier local Act. It is not, therefore, that such contracts are void as contrary to public policy. The judges have repeatedly held that they have jurisdiction to grant an injunction in such cases, but they have invariably refused to grant it. But where the court makes it a rule to refuse the only effective remedy, it would be more straightforward to admit that no remedy exists.

A dramatic case arose in 1954 which for a time seemed as if it might cause a clash between the courts and Parliament. The Boundary Commission, which had statutory powers to make schemes for the rearrangement of parliamentary constituencies, proposed some changes in the Manchester area which were opposed by local voters who would thereby be transferred. The Home Secretary had laid the Commission's report before Parliament and both Houses had approved draft Orders in Council for giving effect to it under the statutory procedure. It only remained, therefore, for the orders to be approved by the Queen in Council. The objectors, who claimed that the Commission had not complied with their statutory duties, asked for

[1] *Bilston Corporation v. Wolverhampton Corporation* [1942] Ch. 391.

an interim injunction to restrain the Home Secretary from sub-
mitting the orders to the Queen in Council before a date which
would give time for their legality to be determined. They were,
in fact, granted this injunction at first instance, but were deprived of it on appeal.[1] The Court of Appeal held that it could
not be right for the court to intervene where the statutory procedure was subject to express parliamentary approval, and this
approval had been given. For grave constitutional questions
would arise if the courts ordered ministers not to do what the
two Houses of Parliament, acting with full statutory power,
had said that they should do. Any irregularity in the Commission's procedure (and no irregularity was in fact found) was a
matter for Parliament and for Parliament only. A further point,
which we have met above, was that relief by way of injunction
was probably barred by the Crown Proceedings Act.

Injunction in aid of statute

Mention should be made of one other use of the injunction,
very different from those already described, where it is not a
defence against abuse of authority but a weapon in the hands of
authority to prevent the abuse of statute. The Crown, represented by the Attorney-General, who will act on the application
of the governmental authority concerned, can ask the court
for an injunction to prevent repeated contravention of statute,
or abuse of statutory rights, by any offending person. Here,
therefore, the injunction comes to the aid of the government.

In one case the defendant had often broken the provisions
of the Town and Country Planning Act by using his land as a
a site for caravans without permission. He refused to pay fines,
and was eventually sentenced to imprisonment for non-pay-
ment. But the local planning authority also moved the Attorney-
General to apply for an injunction to prohibit illegal use of the
land, and the injunction was granted.[2] It was held that there
was jurisdiction to grant this additional remedy to prevent
violation of the public policy enforced by the Act, and that the
fact that the Act contained its own provisions for enforcement
did not fetter the Attorney-General's discretion, as an administrative matter, to ask for an injunction either as an alternative

---

[1] *Harper v. Home Secretary* [1955] Ch. 238. Contrast below, p. 133.
[2] *Attorney-General v. Bastow* [1957] 1 Q.B. 514.

to or in addition to the statutory penalties. In a later case the court went even further, and granted an injunction to prevent the use of land in a manner expressly permitted by the Act.[1] This was another caravan case where the offender moved the caravans from one site to another in the same neighbourhood, making a fresh application for permission in each case and appealing to the Minister on each refusal, thus taking advantage of the manifold opportunities for delay which the planning machinery provided in the days before the Caravan Sites and Control of Development Act 1960. The Attorney-General, on behalf of the local authority, was granted an injunction prohibiting this person from using any land in the neighbourhood as a caravan site without first obtaining permission. The injunction was thus used as a means of supplementing the imperfect remedies provided by Parliament in the Act. Whether it is right to increase statutory penalties this way is a debatable question. The court has declined to use its powers over wards of court to help a local authority to enforce school attendance orders which were persistently disobeyed by a parent, on the ground that it ought not to impose more severe sanctions than those which Parliament thought suitable.[2]

DECLARATIONS

Development of this remedy

The right to ask the court to declare the law on some doubtful point is a very useful remedy, for it enables disputes to be settled before they reach the stage where a right is infringed. It is also useful—and especially in administrative law—in cases where it is difficult to choose the right remedy or where the ordinary remedy is for some reason unsatisfactory. Here again, the remedy is one which plays a large part in ordinary private law. It is in constant use, for example, as a means of finding the meaning of some provision in a will, or whether a statute applies to some particular case, or whether a contract has been properly performed. The surprising thing is that such a necessary remedy should be a relatively modern invention. The

---

[1] *Attorney-General v. Smith* [1958] 2 Q.B. 173. See also *Attorney-General* v. *Harris* [1961] 1 Q.B. 74.
[2] Re B. (Infants) [1962] Ch. 201.

courts long held that they had no jurisdiction to grant declarations without giving other relief at the same time; they did
their best to refuse such jurisdiction when Parliament attempted
to give it to them; and even the Judicature Acts 1873–5 did
not implant it in the remodelled judicial system. But in 1883 it
was provided in the new rules of court that:

> No action or proceeding shall be open to objection, on the ground
> that a merely declaratory judgment or order is sought thereby, and
> the Court may make binding declarations of right whether any
> consequential relief is or could be claimed, or not.[1]

This is still the rule today, and the courts have grown accustomed to using it very freely. A declaratory judgment by itself
leads to no remedy, but it enables a party to discover what his
rights are, so that they can then be enforced in the normal way.
But clearly it ought not to be used merely in order to evade the
conditions to which those remedies are subject in so far as the conditions are themselves desirable. Furthermore, something must
be done to discourage speculators and busybodies: the court
will not entertain hypothetical questions, or actions instituted
by parties with an insufficient interest. The courts have therefore decided that the declaration is a discretionary remedy.

In administrative law the great merit of the declaration is
that it is an efficient remedy against *ultra vires* action by governmental authorities of all kinds, including the Crown. If the
court will declare that some action, either taken or proposed,
is unauthorized by law, that concludes the point as between the
plaintiff and the authority. If then his property is taken, he has
his ordinary legal remedies; if an order is made against him, he
can ignore it with impunity; if he has been dismissed from an
office, he can insist that he still holds it.[2] All these results flow
from the mere fact that the rights of the parties have been
declared. This is a particularly suitable way to settle disputes
with governmental authorities, since it involves no immediate
threat of compulsion, yet is none the less effective.

A case of 1910 may be regarded as a landmark. It was one
of the many repercussions of Lloyd George's celebrated budget
proposals for a tax on land values, which the House of Lords

---

[1] R.S.C., Order 25, rule 5, now replaced by R.S.C. 1965 Order 15, rule 16.
[2] As in *Ridge v. Baldwin* [1964] A.C. 40 (see below, p. 201).

rejected in 1909 with results so disastrous to themselves. Under the Act as finally passed in 1910 landowners were required, under threat of penalty, to complete a return to the Inland Revenue showing the annual value of their land on a certain basis. An owner objected that this demand was not authorized by the Act; and he succeeded in persuading the Court of Appeal to make a declaration against the Crown in proceedings instituted against the Attorney-General.[1] By suing the authorities and seeking a declaration the owner was able to take the initiative, and the court rejected the Crown's argument that his right course was to take no action and then dispute the form when he was sued for the penalty. On the other hand, declarations cannot be granted merely because a party prefers to attack rather than to defend. If that is his only motive, the court may say to him 'Wait until you are attacked and then raise your defence', and dismiss his action. Everything therefore depends upon the merits of his motives for making this move. Lord Justice Fletcher Moulton said:

So far from thinking that this action is open to objection on that score, I think that an action thus framed is the most convenient method of enabling the subject to test the justifiability of proceedings on the part of permanent officials purporting to act under statutory provisions. Such questions are growing more and more important, and I can think of no more suitable or adequate procedure for challenging the legality of such proceedings. It would be intolerable that millions of the public should have to choose between giving information to the Commissioners which they have no right to demand and incurring a severe penalty.

This decision gave a fair wind to the action for a declaration, particularly in administrative cases. As the quotation shows, the court considered that a question as to the legality of administrative action was in itself a good reason for asking for the intervention of the court at the earliest possible moment. The decision is all the stronger for the fact that the Inland Revenue were not threatening any tort. They were merely making a demand which they had no power to make, and therefore no power to enforce.

---

[1] *Dyson v. Attorney-General* [1911] 1 K.B. 410.

The Crown and its servants

It will also be observed that the declaration in the land tax case was granted against the Crown. This is a particularly valuable point, since there is no possibility of obtaining an injunction against the Crown or a servant of the Crown acting as such.[1] Here is a characteristic example of the more modern remedy showing its worth, for it is no hardship for the subject to be deprived of an injunction if he can, instead, have a declaration—provided only that the declaration will be respected, and there is no ground for fear on that score. The Crown Proceedings Act 1947 does not seem to have restricted the jurisdiction in any way, but it has altered the procedure. Any relief which could have been obtained by an action against the Attorney-General is now subject to the standard procedure, i.e. the action must be brought against the appropriate government department, and against the Attorney-General only if no appropriate department is listed.[2]

It is equally possible to obtain a declaration against a servant of the Crown if he is threatening to commit some wrongful act in his official capacity. But if his action is merely *ultra vires*, without amounting to a tort or other positive wrong, it is doubtful whether he (as opposed to the Crown) is the right defendant, for it is not he who legally possesses the power or who (therefore) oversteps it. But where, as so often happens, the power is given directly by statute to a minister, it seems probable that actions challenging its exercise should be instituted in accordance with the Crown Proceedings Act, and not against the minister personally.[3]

Another occasion for seeking a declaration against the Crown is for determining nationality. Thus where a prince of Hanover wished to establish his claim to British nationality under the somewhat dubious authority of an Act of Queen Anne's reign, he sought (and obtained) a declaration that he was a British subject by bringing an action against the Attorney-General.[4]

Other authorities

Declarations are also freely granted against other authorities,

[1] Above, p. 114.   [2] S. 23 (2). See below, p. 291.
[3] As was done, before the Act, in *Dyson v. Attorney-General*, above, p. 120; compare *Merricks v. Heathcoat-Amory*, above, p. 115.
[4] *Attorney-General v. Prince Ernest Augustus of Hanover* [1957] A.C. 436.

including statutory tribunals.[1] A ratepayer may obtain a declaration that a city council is misapplying moneys, as in the case
from Birmingham which appears in an earlier chapter.[2] A dock
worker may obtain a declaration that he has been irregularly
dismissed by a dock labour board so as to preserve his right
to employment under the dock labour scheme.[3]

In cases of the latter kind difficult questions may have to be
settled. Where the relationship is merely that of master and
servant, a declaration that there has been no effective dismissal
will not be granted; for the master always has power to dismiss
the servant, even though in breach of contract, and the servant's
remedy is to sue for damages. Employment by a statutory authority may also be ordinary contractual employment. Thus where
a doctor was dismissed by a hospital board he failed to obtain
the required declaration, despite the 'strong statutory flavour'
which the National Health Service gave to his contract of
employment.[4] But a chief constable holds a statutory office and
has a right to it which the court will declare.[5] Likewise a dock
worker has not only a contract but also a statutory status under
the dock labour scheme, and the court will protect him against
being deprived of this illegally.[6] On the same principle a declaration was granted against the dismissal by the Sunderland
Corporation of school-teachers who had refused to collect
money for pupils' meals, since the Education Act provided (as
the court held) that teachers could not be required to act as
collectors.[7] The question in each case is whether the public
authority is acting as an ordinary employer, who has power to
dismiss his employees subject to payment of damages for any
breach of contract, or whether it has only a statutory power of
dismissal which is restricted by the statute. In the former case
the court can, indeed, declare that the dismissal was a breach of

---

[1] See for example, *Cooper v. Wilson*, below, p. 179; *Taylor v. National Assistance
Board* [1957] P. 101 at 111, affirmed [1958] A.C. 532; *Ridge v. Baldwin* [1964]
A.C. 40 (see below, p. 201).

[2] Above, p. 75.   [3] See next paragraph.

[4] *Barber v. Manchester Hospital Board* [1958] 1 W.L.R. 181. Cf. *Vidyodaya University
Council v. Silva* [1965] 1 W.L.R. 77.

[5] *Ridge v. Baldwin* [1964] A.C. 40; see below, p. 201.

[6] *Vine v. National Dock Labour Board* [1957] A.C. 488; see above, p. 63, and
below, p. 141.

[7] *Price v. Sunderland Corporation* [1956] 1 W.L.R. 1253. Cf. *Sadler v. Sheffield Cpn.*
[1924] 1 Ch. 483.

contract.[1] But in the latter case it can give a specific remedy by declaring the dismissal to be *ultra vires* and so inoperative.

Limits of the declaration

The declaration is a most useful and popular remedy, but there are limits to its efficacy. Since certain of these limits do not apply to the remedy of certiorari, they have an important effect on the choice of remedies. Their advantages and disadvantages will be compared later on.[2]

First, the object of a declaratory judgment is to declare the legal position of the plaintiff. In a case where he has no legal rights or no legal standing this remedy is therefore useless to him. Suppose, for instance, that a planning authority grants permission for the building of a school, but does not follow the statutory procedure, so that the permission is legally invalid. A neighbour who objects to the school cannot obtain a declaration invalidating the permission.[3] Planning permission concerns only the applicant and the planning authority, and is not legally the business of a mere neighbour; he has no right or standing to sue unless some wrong such as nuisance or trespass is committed against him. Whether the same objection applies to a ratepayer challenging unlawful expenditure is uncertain, as mentioned below.[4] At least it does not apply merely because the plaintiff is one of many people whose legal position may be affected; thus the declaration is an effective remedy against an invalid by-law or general order.[5]

Secondly, a declaration merely declares. As already explained, this is no disadvantage where the action in question is *ultra vires*, for the action is then effectively stripped of its legal authority as against the plaintiff. But there is one situation where action may be *intra vires* and yet subject to control by the courts: where there is error on the face of the record.[6] Merely to declare that such an error appears can avail nothing, for the

---

[1] *McClelland v. Northern Ireland General Health Services Board* [1957] 1 W.L.R. 594 appears to be such a case.

[2] Below, p. 142.   [3] *Gregory v. Camden London Borough Council* [1966] 1 W.L.R. 899.

[4] See p. 126. In the United States even a federal taxpayer may be allowed standing to obtain a declaration and injunction: *Flast v. Cohen* 392 U.S. 83 (1968).

[5] *Nicholls v. Tavistock U.D.C.* [1923] 2 Ch. 18 (invalid by-law prohibiting use of market); *Brownsea Haven Properties Ltd. v. Poole Corporation* [1958] Ch. 574 (invalid order for one-way street). See Zamir, The Declaratory Judgment, 278.

[6] See above, p. 97.

action is *intra vires* and remains lawful. It is not void but only voidable. Certiorari is then the only effective remedy; for certiorari 'quashes', i.e. positively invalidates the action, not only as against the applicant but as against all the world. This defect of the declaration was established after a sharp conflict of opinion in the Court of Appeal, in a case where unemployment benefit was refused to some shipyard workers thrown out of work by a strike. It was alleged that the Commissioner's decision was erroneous on its face, and it was admitted that the applicants could have challenged it by certiorari if they had applied for that remedy in time. But the court in the end held that there was no jurisdiction to grant a declaration, since the Commissioner's decision would remain legally effective and would bar any award of unemployment benefit absolutely.[1] Since challenge for error on the face is so common, this is a serious deficiency in the declaration. It derives from the theoretical anomaly of the court controlling *intra vires* action. But it is no more satisfactory on that account.

Thirdly, a declaration may not be used as a substitute for an exclusive statutory remedy available from some specified court or tribunal—as for instance where a tax allowance can be claimed only by appeal to the Commissioners of Inland Revenue.[2] This is a general doctrine affecting other remedies, and is explained later.[3]

Finally, the declaration is a discretionary remedy. What this means is also explained later.[4]

RELATOR ACTIONS

A relator action is an action brought by the Attorney-General at the relation (i.e. at the instance) of some other person. By using this device it is possible for a private person to set in motion for his own purposes a form of action which really exists for the benefit of the Crown—as happens also with the prerogative remedies. A relator action is not so much a distinct remedy as a distinct form of procedure which will lead to one of the

---

[1] *Punton v. Ministry of Pensions and National Insurance (No. 2)* [1964] 1 W.L.R. 226; remarks in *Healey v. Minister of Health* [1955] 1 Q.B. 221 are partly consistent and partly inconsistent with this position.

[2] *Argosam Finance Co. Ltd. v. Oxby* [1965] Ch. 390.

[3] Below, p. 147.   [4] Below p. 144.

other remedies, usually an injunction or a declaration. It derives from the Crown's special power—or perhaps duty—to protect public rights and to see that the law is obeyed. Just as the Attorney-General may proceed against charities or public trusts which abuse their funds, so he may proceed against any public authority which is abusing its power. For the Crown, as *parens patriae*, has a special interest in enforcing the law for the general public benefit. The Attorney-General may act either of his own motion or on the relation of any other person; but the majority of his actions are at the instance of a relator, i.e. a litigant who has some motive for raising the question at issue, and at the relator's expense. In either case the Attorney-General has a free discretion whether to proceed or not.

The advantage of invoking the aid of the Attorney-General is that it overcomes problems of *locus standi*. A private plaintiff can sue for a declaration or injunction only if he is in some way specially concerned, e.g. if obstruction of the highway (a public nuisance) also obstructs access to his own premises, or if some wrongful administrative act threatens to render him liable to some penalty. To remedy public nuisances and to require public authorities to keep within their powers is not otherwise the business of the ordinary citizen. But it is the business of the Crown, and the Crown will lend its special status to any subject who reasonably wants to borrow it. This is not a logical arrangement, since it means in effect that the plaintiff's *locus standi*, which is a question of law, is decided by a minister of the Crown rather than by the court. But it is a beneficial arrangement, since it enables a private citizen to assert his concern as a member of the public that public authorities should not abuse their powers. It also provides a definite way of access to the court in cases where otherwise there might be an infinite number of plaintiffs. Both by this procedure and by certiorari (as we shall see) the citizen can come to the aid of the machinery of government. It is important that a system of public law should afford opportunities for this.

Since the Attorney-General is liberal in his decisions, the relator action works well. A typical case was where the London County Council, being empowered by statute to purchase and operate tramways, purchased a tramway company and also carried on a bus service which the company had run. The proprietors of a rival bus service, who were also ratepayers, caused the Attorney-General to sue for an injunction against the operation of buses by the Council, which was duly granted.[1] But a local authority may itself use a relator action to prevent persistent disregard of the law.[2]

This form of proceeding has been much used by ratepayers to challenge the legality of local authorities' expenditure. Since a ratepayer will seldom suffer special personal damage, but has a clear interest in restraining his Council's spending, the procedure fills an obvious need. But it has now been discovered that the court may grant a declaration to a ratepayer without any objection on the ground of *locus standi*. The case was again that of the Birmingham bus service where it was declared that the Corporation had no power to allow free travel to old-age pensioners on the grounds explained in an earlier chapter.[3] This opens an alternative avenue which may prove popular in future. No local authority is likely to disregard a declaration by the court, and in any case the district auditor, whose function it is to disallow any irregular expenditure by local councils,[4] will certainly disallow any items condemned by the court. It therefore seems possible that one of the many results of the court's present willingness to grant declarations will be that the relator action will be less used. But since the Court of Appeal, in the *Birmingham* case, said nothing about the plaintiff ratepayer's *locus standi*, it is not yet safe to conclude that the Attorney-General can be by-passed in this way. The law, in fact, is now far from clear.

Several statutes have given power to local authorities to bring legal proceedings 'for the promotion or protection of the interests of the inhabitants of their area' or to 'assert and protect the rights of the public' over highways. But the courts construe these so narrowly that a local authority may not sue without the Attorney-General's name in respect of a public nuisance[5]

---

[1] *London County Council v. Attorney-General* [1902] A.C. 165; above, p. 55. Cf. *Attorney-General v. Crayford U.D.C.* [1962] Ch. 575 (relator action at instance of mere commercial rival).

[2] See above, p. 117.

[3] Above p. 75.

[4] Above, p. 27.

[5] *Prestatyn U.D.C. v. Prestatyn Raceway, Ltd.* [1970] 1 W.L.R. 33.

or an obstruction of the highway.[1] There seems to be no good reason why the local government should not be as competent in its own area as the central government in the country at large, or why 'these Acts should not be construed beneficially.

Relator actions fall outside the Crown Proceedings Act 1947,[2] so that their scope and procedure remain unchanged.

THE PREROGATIVE REMEDIES

Prerogative remedies

We now enter the realm of the prerogative remedies. They were always called the prerogative writs until they were (with the exception of habeas corpus, which was too sacred to be tampered with) changed to 'orders' by an Act of 1938.[3] In administrative law habeas corpus plays a small (though important) part, but most of our attention here is required by certiorari and prohibition. These are primary remedies for the control of governmental powers. Mandamus, which is the prerogative remedy concerned with duties, is treated separately.

In the case of these 'prerogative' remedies the Crown is always the nominal plaintiff; but in their modern use it is usually a subject who is benefited. The Crown will lend its legal prerogatives to the subject so that they may collaborate to ensure good and lawful government. Habeas corpus will test the legality of a prisoner's detention in both the Crown's and the prisoner's interest. Certiorari and prohibition are both part of the machinery for controlling the administration of justice, which is primarily the Crown's concern, and are designed to keep inferior courts within their proper jurisdiction. All these remedies issue from the High Court, and must be sought by their own special procedure.

Certiorari and prohibition are both discretionary remedies, as is further explained below.[4]

Habeas corpus

The writ of habeas corpus provides an efficacious means of

---

[1] *Hampshire C.C. v. Shonleigh Nominees, Ltd.* [1970] 1 W.L.R. 865.
[2] See s. 23 (3).
[3] Administration of Justice (Miscellaneous Provisions) Act, 1938, s. 7.
[4] P. 144.

testing the validity of a person's imprisonment or detention. Nominally sought by the Crown, the remedy is in reality freely available to any prisoner and to any one acting on his behalf, without regard to nationality.

Where the validity of the imprisonment turns on the legality of some administrative act, habeas corpus becomes a remedy for enforcing the principle of *ultra vires*. Thus an alien detained pending deportation can apply for habeas corpus to question the validity of the deportation order, for example by alleging that what is asserted to be lawful deportation is in fact unlawful extradition at the request of a foreign government.[1] A mental defective detained unlawfully can be released by habeas corpus if it is shown that the detention order is *ultra vires*,[2] or vitiated by error on the face of the record[3] or supported by no evidence.[4] Since personal liberty is of paramount importance, the courts seem more disposed to review for 'no evidence' in these cases than in others. For the same reason they require the detaining authority to prove every fact which is legally necessary to justify the detention.[5]

Certiorari

Certiorari is used to bring up into the High Court the decision of some inferior tribunal or authority in order that it may be investigated. If the decision does not pass the test, it is quashed— that is to say, it is declared completely invalid, so that no one need respect it.[6] This is therefore a remedy of public rather than of private law.

The underlying policy is that all inferior courts and authorities have only limited jurisdiction or powers and must be kept within their legal bounds. This is the concern of the Crown, for the sake of orderly administration of justice, but it is usually a private complaint which sets the Crown in motion. The applicant must apply *ex parte* to the Divisional Court of the Queen's Bench Division for leave to apply for the order, and if this is granted (and if the case is contested) the Divisional Court will

[1] As (unsuccessfully) in *R. v. Home Secretary ex parte Soblen* [1963] 2 Q.B. 243.
[2] *R. v. Board of Control* [1956] 2 Q.B. 109.
[3] See the *Armah* case, above, p. 100, note 1.
[4] *R. v. Board of Control* (above), *per* Lord Goddard C.J.
[5] *R. v. Governor of Brixton Prison* [1969] 2 Q.B. 222.
[6] See above, p. 124.

later hear argument and decide whether to grant the order. The Crown is the nominal plaintiff but is expressed to act on behalf of the applicant, so that an application by Smith to quash an order of (for instance) a rent tribunal would be entitled *R. v. The —— Rent Tribunal, ex parte Smith*. The tribunal must then persuade the court that its order was within its powers. From the Divisional Court there is an appeal to the Court of Appeal, and thence with leave to the House of Lords.

Certiorari, therefore, is one of the various means by which an *ultra vires* act may be challenged. The form of the old writ was that of a royal demand for information, and it was used for that as well as for a number of other purposes only loosely related to the control of jurisdiction. Its great period of development as a means of controlling administrative authorities and tribunals began in the later half of the seventeenth century. Something was needed to fill the vacuum left by the Star Chamber, which had exerted a considerable degree of central control over justices of the peace, both in their judicial and their administrative functions, but was abolished in 1640. There was also the problem of controlling special statutory bodies, which had begun to make their appearance. The Court of King's Bench addressed itself to these tasks, and became almost the only co-ordinating authority until the modern system of local government was devised in the nineteenth century. And the most useful instruments which the Court found ready to hand were the prerogative writs. But not unnaturally the control exercised was strictly legal, and no longer political. Certiorari would issue to call up the records of justices and commissioners for examination in the Court of King's Bench and for quashing if error appeared on their face or if there was an excess of jurisdiction.

Certiorari had the special advantage, unique before the rise of the declaration, that it would effectively quash an illegal decision or order which by itself inflicted no actionable wrong on the applicant, and against which the remedies of private law were therefore useless.

Prohibition

Prohibition was a remedy of very similar scope; but it looked to the future rather than to the past. It was used

primarily to prohibit an inferior tribunal from continuing to
exceed its jurisdiction. But like certiorari it was extended to
administrative authorities generally, for example so as to
prevent an electricity authority from proceeding with a scheme
which was outside its powers,[1] or a housing authority from
requiring the demolition of a house which was improperly
condemned.[2]

Prohibition stands in much the same relation to certiorari
as the injunction stands in relation to the declaration. Certiorari
and prohibition rest on common principles and frequently go
hand in hand, as where an order is quashed by certiorari and
at the same time a prohibition is awarded to prevent any
further irregularity being committed. But either remedy may
be sought by itself, and it is possible on an application for prohibition to raise the same points of jurisdiction as can be raised
on certiorari.

The scope of these remedies. 'Judicial' functions

Certiorari and prohibition are primarily suited for the control of inferior courts: justices of the peace, recorders, coroners,
and all the special statutory tribunals (except where Parliament
provides otherwise) are liable to have their decisions quashed
for excess of jurisdiction or (as we have seen) for error on the
face of the record.[3] Prohibition, in particular, was an important
weapon of the Court of King's Bench in earlier times, when
that court waged war on competing jurisdictions such as those
of the ecclesiastical courts and the Admiralty Court. In one
respect prohibition is more potent than certiorari: it will issue
to prevent unauthorized proceedings in an ecclesiastical court,
but certiorari will not lie to review an ecclesiastical court's
decision[4]; for ecclesiastical law is a different system from the
common law on which the ordinary courts cannot sit in judgment. This is an illogical distinction in any case where the
question is not whether the ecclesiastical court is right, but
whether it is trespassing outside its jurisdiction. In a later case,
however, the House of Lords showed no favour to a contention

---

[1] See below, p. 132.
[2] *Estate and Trust Agencies Ltd. v. Singapore Improvement Trust* [1937] A.C. 898.
[3] Above, p. 94.
[4] *The King v. Chancellor of St. Edmundsbury and Ipswich Diocese* [1948] 1 K.B. 195.

that certiorari could not issue to a tribunal where the issue turned on scientific technicalities.[1]

But the concept of what is a 'court' has been greatly stretched, as has also the concept of what is a 'judicial' function; so that certiorari and prohibition have grown to be comprehensive remedies for the control of all kinds of administrative as well as judicial acts. This is because the judges very naturally saw no reason to abdicate the control which they achieved at the zenith of their power in the eighteenth century. In that age the chief organs of local government were the justices of the peace, who in addition to their regular judicial business had many administrative functions such as the upkeep of roads and bridges, the licensing of ale-houses, and the administration of the poor law. These administrative duties were discharged in the most judicial style possible: not only were the justices themselves primarily judicial officers, whose proceedings naturally tended to follow legal patterns—they were also almost completely free from central political control. Maitland, the great legal historian, epitomized the position of 'the amphibious old justice who did administrative work under judicial forms':

Whatever the justice has had to do has soon become the exercise of a jurisdiction; whether he was refusing a licence or sentencing a thief, this was the exercise of jurisdiction, an application of the law to a particular case. Even if a discretionary power was allowed him, it was none the less to be exercised with 'a judicial discretion'; it was not expected of him that he should have any 'policy'; rather it was expected of him that he should not have any 'policy'.[2]

Local administration thus had a strong judicial tradition. When, in the nineteenth century, most of the administrative functions of the justices were transferred to elected local councils or to new statutory authorities, they carried this tradition with them. Political control was imposed, but a judicial technique was inherited. The courts had fallen into the habit of calling many administrative acts 'judicial', meaning simply that the person wielding the power was required by law to keep within his jurisdiction and to observe the elements of fair procedure, such as giving a hearing to any one who would be affected. For a long

---

[1] *Baldwin & Francis Ltd. v. Patents Appeal Tribunal* [1959] A.C. 663.
[2] Maitland, *Collected Papers*, i. 478.

time this abuse of language was masked by the mixture of
functions which were performed by justices of the peace. When
these functions were later sorted out, the label 'judicial' still
stuck to administrative acts. Certiorari and prohibition were
still described as remedies for the control of judicial functions,
and for preventing excess of jurisdiction. But 'jurisdiction' had
become synonymous with 'power', and in fact certiorari and
prohibition were used to control all kinds of irregular administrative acts, from those of justices to those of ministers. Their
scope expanded automatically with the development of the
doctrine of *ultra vires*. Certiorari also had its special function of
controlling error on the face of the record, which is still one of
its most important applications.[1]

Rights and remedies

It is impossible to keep rights and remedies in separate compartments. Remedies ought to be mere adjuncts of the positive
principles of law, i.e. of the rules for the judicial control of
powers. But in practice the rules of law have a stubborn habit
of concealing themselves behind the remedies which happen to
be available. To discuss the scope of certiorari and prohibition
is merely to renew, though in a narrower context, the discussion
in an earlier chapter of what acts the court will control. Nevertheless, it is essential to review the subject from this angle.

The classic statement which serves as the starting-point for
the modern law comes from a case of 1923. This concerned an
electricity scheme for the London area, where the Electricity
Commissioners had statutory power to make schemes for
grouping electricity authorities into districts for the general
improvement of the supply. Any scheme was subject to confirmation by the Minister of Transport, and to approval by
both Houses of Parliament; it was also subject to the usual
public inquiry procedure in case of objection. There was a
difference of opinion between the London County Council,
which wanted one district for the whole area, and the electric
supply companies, who wanted two districts. The Commissioners attempted to compromise by making a scheme under
which there was only one district, but the district authority was
to be required to delegate its powers to two committees, so

---

[1] See above, p. 94.

that there would be a division of the kind that the companies wanted. The companies, however, challenged the legality of the scheme, and the Court of Appeal held it *ultra vires* on the ground that the Act did not permit the Commissioners to set up two authorities in the form of one.[1] A writ of prohibition was granted against the Commissioners at the instance of the companies, who had applied for it only a few days after the public inquiry had opened. It was objected that the function was not judicial but executive; that the application was premature as nothing decisive had yet happened; and that in any case the court should not intervene where the scheme had to be approved by Parliament. All these objections were swept aside, and the court made it plain that any statutory authority acting *ultra vires* could be called to order by the prerogative writs—by prohibition, to prevent them proceeding further with an unauthorized scheme, and by certiorari, to declare that any decision already taken was ineffective. The judgments explained how this wide power had been exercised for centuries. It had been said in a case of 1700:

For this court will examine the proceedings of all jurisdictions erected by Act of Parliament. And if they, under pretence of such Act, proceed to incroach jurisdiction to themselves greater than the Act warrants, this Court will send a certiorari to them, to have their proceedings returned here.[2]

This was restated in modern terms by Lord Justice Atkin in what has become the definitive statement, approved in many later cases:

Wherever any body of persons having legal authority to determine questions affecting the rights of subjects, and having the duty to act judicially, act in excess of their legal authority, they are subject to the controlling jurisdiction of the King's Bench Division exercised in these writs.[3]

Acting 'judicially'

It will be observed that the two statements just quoted, though separated by so long an interval of time, are generally similar in meaning. But the former speaks of 'jurisdiction', the latter of persons 'having the duty to act judicially'. The former

---

[1] *The King v. Electricity Commissioners* [1924] 1 K.B. 171.
[2] Cited in [1924] 1 K.B. at 183.   [3] [1924] 1 K.B. at 205.

is the more accurate, since 'jurisdiction' can easily include all kinds of administrative power, whereas 'the duty to act judicially' suggests a judicial as opposed to an administrative function. In reality nothing could be plainer than that the acts controlled, both in the cases themselves and in many other cases decided both before and since, were administrative acts. The case of 1700 concerned a rate levied by justices for the repair of Cardiff Bridge.[1] The *Electricity* case concerned a scheme which was plainly administrative in nature. Provided only that there was some determination of a question affecting or capable of affecting legal rights (as opposed for example to a mere report or recommendation[2]), certiorari would issue to quash it if it exceeded the statutory power. As it was put in a leading case,

> The true view of the limitation could seem to be that the term "judicial act" is used in contrast with purely ministerial acts. To the latter the process of certiorari does not apply, as for instance to the issue of a warrant to enforce a rate, even though the rate is one which could itself be questioned by certiorari. In short, there must be the exercise of some right or duty to decide in order to provide scope for a writ of certiorari at common law.[3]

In the *Electricity* case the Court of Appeal cited a long series of precedents where certiorari or prohibition, or both, had issued to administrative authorities such as the Board of Education, the Poor Law Commissioners, the Tithe Commissioners, licensing justices, &c. Plenty of other authorities could be added to this list, including ministers of the Crown. Lord Justice Atkin's rule was not confined to a 'body of persons' as opposed to an individual. Nor was it confined to cases where formal 'determinations' were made: any decision or order which produced legal consequences,[4] or was a step in a process which might produce them,[5] was controllable. The truth was that certiorari and prohibition were general remedies for the judicial

---

[1] *The King v. Inhabitants of Glamorganshire* (1701) 1 Ld. Raym. 580.

[2] *R. v. St. Lawrence's Hospital Statutory Visitors* [1953] 1 W.L.R. 1158. Cf. *R. v. Church Assembly Legislative Committee* [1928] 1 K.B. 411. But see Appendix, B.

[3] *R. v. Woodhouse* [1906] 2 K.B. 501 at 535 (Fletcher Moulton L.J.).

[4] *R. v. Paddington Valuation Officer* [1966] 1 Q.B. 380. But see Appendix, B.

[5] See *R. v. Criminal Injuries Compensation Board* [1967] 2 Q.B. 864 at 884, citing cases where medical certificates were quashed.

control of administrative[1] decisions, and could be invoked just as freely where a minister made an invalid clearance order[2] or a local authority wrongfully granted a licence,[3] as where justices of the peace convicted without jurisdiction. But the courts failed to give candid expression to this truth. They clung to their habit of calling administrative decisions 'judicial' in order that they might seem to have a pretext for controlling them. It was as if they had never quite convinced themselves of their title to interfere with administration pure and simple, although in fact they had been doing that for centuries.

So long as the courts instinctively understood that 'judicial' had for this purpose acquired an artificial meaning which included 'administrative', no trouble arose. But from time to time the penalty for misuse of language had to be paid. In the late nineteenth century the courts began to mislead themselves by holding that the decisions of licensing authorities were not 'judicial' and that certiorari could not therefore control the liquor-licensing functions of magistrates. Although they soon cleared up this fallacy decisively,[4] its traces still linger on an illogical way.[5] Confusion again began to reign about 1950 in other licensing cases in which the established law was apparently overlooked, and in which it was held that because an act was administrative it was not 'judicial'. These decisions involved the principles of natural justice, which similarly apply to 'judicial' acts, and they are discussed in the next chapter.[6] But they also shook the whole basis of the prerogative remedies. For it was no longer possible to be sure what the courts meant by 'judicial', or when they might turn round and say that, because an act was administrative, it could not be controlled.

[1] But not legislative: see the *Church Assembly* case, above.
[2] As in *R. v. Minister of Health ex parte Davies* [1929] 1 K.B. 619 (prohibition); *R. v. Minister of Health ex parte Yaffe* [1930] 2 K.B. 98 (certiorari), reversed on other grounds, [1931] A.C. 494.
[3] As in *R. v. London County Council* [1931] 2 K.B. 215 (expressly rejecting the argument that since the function was administrative it was therefore not judicial).
[4] The turning-point was *R. v. Woodhouse* [1906] 2 K.B. 501 (see especially p. 535). In *Frome United Breweries Co. v. Bath Justices* [1926] A.C. 586 (below, p. 137), Lord Sumner explains how licensing functions, though administrative in nature, are subject to certiorari. Counsel contesting this in 1953 was told that he was about sixty years too late: *R. v. Brighton Borough Justices* [1954] 1 W.L.R. 203.
[5] Below, p. 163.
[6] Below, pp. 198, 199.

This atmosphere of uncertainty pervaded a decision of the Court of Appeal in 1952, in which certiorari was granted to quash the decision of a Legal Aid Committee.[1] The Committee had held that legal aid could be awarded to a bankrupt's trustee in bankruptcy on the basis of the bankrupt's means and not the trustee's. This was *ultra vires*, and it was just the type of act that certiorari had for centuries been used to control: an excess of power by a statutory body. But the court made heavy going over the question whether the Committee's act was 'judicial'; and it was said that there was no duty to act judicially where the authority had before it no form of *lis* and had throughout to consider the matter from the point of view of policy and expediency. But if anything is plain about the use of these remedies in the past, it is that they have been freely employed to control illegal acts of policy where a statutory power was exceeded. The *Electricity Commissioners* case itself arose out of a question of pure policy and expediency: how best to organize the electricity companies in London. Policy and expediency play a large part in licensing cases but there is abundant authority for the control of licensing authorities by certiorari.[2]

In similar vein distinguished judges referred to 'an important but, as I think, a most unfortunate limitation ... the scope of certiorari is confined to acts of a judicial nature and does not embrace the purely administrative decision'[3]; and to 'one of the defects of certiorari', that it is confined to judicial acts and so may not be available when a minister is acting administratively, for example when granting planning permission.[4] Thus the false antithesis 'administrative or judicial?' began to undermine the long-settled law.

'Judicially' reinterpreted

A determined and (it may be hoped) successful attempt to extirpate the confusion has now been made by the House of Lords, in a case which is likely to prove as important and as

---

[1] *The Queen v. Manchester Legal Aid Committee* [1952] 2 Q.B. 413.
[2] Above, pp. 131, 135.
[3] Lord MacDermott, *Protection from Power under English Law*, 88 (1957).
[4] Lord Denning in *Pyx Granite Co. v. Ministry of Housing and Local Government* [1958] 1 Q.B. 554, [1960] A.C. 260.

beneficial as any decided in this branch of the law.[1] This again was a case involving natural justice: the House of Lords held, contrary to the decisions mentioned above, that the Chief Constable of Brighton could not validly be dismissed by the Watch Committee under their statutory powers without being given a fair hearing. It was not a case of certiorari but of a declaratory judgment; and as a case on natural justice it belongs to the following chapter. But it is of outstanding importance here because it has reinterpreted Lord Justice Atkin's words about 'the duty to act judicially' so as to remove the stumbling-block which had been made out of them. Lord Reid has explained that it was a mistake in earlier cases to take these words as expressing a superadded condition: they merely express what follows automatically from the power to affect the rights of subjects. Wherever there is 'legal authority to determine questions affecting the rights of subjects', which really means wherever there is power to make a decision or order, there is also a 'duty to act judicially'. The power and the duty go hand in hand. Lord Justice Atkin might therefore have said ' . . . and *accordingly* having the duty to act judicially, . . . '. Lord Reid explained how any other interpretation was impossible to reconcile with a long line of unquestionable authorities,[2] including the *Electricity Commissioners* case itself; and Lord Hodson criticised the fallacy of saying that 'the giver of the decision is acting in an executive or administrative capacity as if that was the antithesis of a judicial capacity.'

As the result of all this effort, certiorari and prohibition are presumably now restored to their historic and indispensable function as general remedies for the control of administrative decisions. They simply give effect to the principle that powers cannot be exercised illegally. The case-law has accordingly returned to a state of consistency.[3] The absurdity of describing administrative decisions as 'judicial' remains. But it is now seen

[1] *Ridge v. Baldwin* [1964] A.C. 40.
[2] Lord Reid's interpretation is also strongly supported by the decision of the House of Lords in *Frome United Breweries Co. v. Bath Justices* [1926] A.C. 586 (above, p. 135; below, p. 177). A further proof (if needed) of the absurdity of the 'judicial' fallacy was the courts' willingness to evade it by the use of mandamus: see below, p. 163.
[3] See, e.g. *R. v. Paddington Valuation Officer* [1966] 1 Q.B. 380; *Maradana Mosque Trustees v. Mahmud* [1967] 1 A.C. 13; *R. v. Chief Immigration Officer, Lympne Airport* [1969] 2 Q.B. 333; *R. v. Gaming Board for G.B.* [1970] 2 W.L.R. 1009.

for what it is: a vestigial survival from history. Unfortunately we have not, even now, heard the last of it. For it also seriously unsettled the principles of natural justice, as must be explained in Chapter 5.

Who may obtain the remedies?

'Orders of certiorari and prohibition are concerned principally with public order, it being part of the duty of the High Court to see that inferior courts confine themselves to their own limited sphere.'[1] As the form of the proceedings shows, the Crown is here concerned to see that the machinery of public administration works properly, as well as to see that justice is done to individuals. These remedies thus have a special 'public' aspect, which is one of their valuable features.

It follows that an applicant for certiorari or prohibition does not have to show that some legal right of his is at stake. If the action is an excess or abuse of power, the court will quash it at the instance of a mere stranger, though it retains discretion to refuse to do so if it thinks that no good would be done to the public.[2] In other words, these remedies are not restricted by the notion of *locus standi*. Every citizen has standing to invite the court to prevent some abuse of power, and in doing so he may claim to be regarded not as a meddlesome busybody but as a public benefactor. Lord Parker has said of certiorari:

Anybody can apply for it—a member of the public who has been inconvenienced, or a particular party or person who has a particular grievance of his own. If the application is made by what for convenience one may call a stranger, the remedy is purely discretionary. Where, however, it is made by a person who has a particular grievance of his own, whether as a party or otherwise, then the remedy lies *ex debito justitiae* . . .[3]

In practice the applicant normally has a grievance of his own, for this concept is not restrictively interpreted—it extends, for example, to a ratepayer and to a trade rival.[4] An instance of the award of certiorari to a (technical) stranger is where it is granted to a trade union acting on behalf of one of its members.[5]

---

[1] Devlin J. in *R. v. Fulham &c. Rent Tribunal* [1951] 2 K.B. 1.
[2] *R. v. Surrey J.J.* (1870) L.R. 5 Q.B. 466.
[3] *R. v. Thames Magistrates' Court* (1957) 55 L.G.R. 129.
[4] *Ibid; R. v. Paddington Valuation Officer* [1966] 1 Q.B. 380.
[5] E.g. *Minister of Social Security v. Amalgamated Engineering Union* [1967] 1 A.C. 725.

The wide scope of these remedies may be of crucial importance where the applicant is in fact genuinely aggrieved but has no grievance in the eye of the law. He may, for example, object strongly to a building for which his neighbour has been granted planning permission, although legally this is no concern of his. If he can show that the permission is void, for example because the principles of natural justice have been violated, he may have it quashed by certiorari[1] even though he could not have obtained a declaratory judgment because of his lack of personal legal right.[2] This emphasis on public interest rather than private right is not confined to the prerogative remedies (we have noticed it already in the relator action[3]), but it is one reason why they play so vital a part in our public law. In private law they are quite out of place, so that they cannot be used, for instance, for enforcing a contract of employment.[4]

Procedure

If we turn to procedure, we find that the 'public' character of certiorari and prohibition has much less fortunate consequences. For the prerogative remedies as a body have hereditary defects due to the fact that they escaped the great procedural reforms of the nineteenth century and have survived as special forms of action with their own special procedure.

In order to obtain certiorari or prohibition, a motion must first be made to the court for leave to apply. The rules of court prescribe a time-limit of six months (relatively to most other proceedings, a very short time) for certiorari, though the court has discretion to extend it.[5] There is no proper interlocutory process, as there is in ordinary actions, so that it is impossible to obtain an order (for example) for discovery of documents by the other side, which may be of the utmost importance. At the hearing itself, evidence is given on affidavit, i.e. in writing rather than orally; and it is exceptional for the court to allow cross-examination on the affidavits. The court's only means of

---

[1] As in R. v. Hendon R.D.C. [1933] 2 K.B. 696 (see below, p. 179).
[2] As in Gregory v. Camden L.B.C. [1966] 1 W.L.R. 899 (see above, p. 123).
[3] Above, p. 125.
[4] Vidyodaya University Council v. Silva [1965] 1 W.L.R. 77; below, p. 205. This limitation appears to have been overlooked in R. v. Aston University Senate [1969] 2 Q.B. 538: see below, p. 350.
[5] R.S.C. 1965 Order 53 rule 2; Order 3 rule 5.

deciding issues of fact in the normal manner is to direct a special issue to be tried; but that is a roundabout procedure, and the court may dismiss the application rather than resort to it. If the case turns upon a conflict of evidence,[1] certiorari and prohibition may therefore be useless.[2]

In addition to all these handicaps is the fact that prerogative remedies cannot be sought alternatively to other remedies. The remedies of private law, such as damages, injunction and declaration are all available in the ordinary form of action and a plaintiff may seek any or all of them simultaneously. But the prerogative remedies can be sought only by their own special procedure, in which the court is asked to extend a royal privilege to a subject. Certiorari and a declaratory judgment cannot therefore be sought alternatively in one action. But in recent cases[3] the courts have allowed litigants to apply for certiorari in the course of appeal proceedings, and it may be that they will be able to mitigate this procedural incompatibility.

Should the declaration supplant certiorari?

The topical question to-day is whether the work of certiorari (and prohibition) would be better done by the declaration, aided where necessary by the injunction. In the course of legal history progress has often been made by a shift from inferior to superior remedies. In the United States declarations and injunctions have taken the place of certiorari to quash in federal administrative law for over fifty years. In 1913 the Supreme Court made a profound muddle of the question what was a 'judicial' function—just the same question which plagued the English courts until half a century later[4]—and so destroyed the utility of certiorari.[5] There have been signs that a similar change

---

[1] As it may well do in a case of jurisdictional fact: see above, p. 90.
[2] See *R. v. Fulham &c. Rent Tribunal* [1951] 2 K.B. 1 at 11–13.
[3] *Chapman v. Earl* [1968] 1 W.L.R. 1315; *Metropolitan Properties Ltd. v. Lannon* [1969] 1 Q.B. 577. See 85 L.Q.R. at p. 20.
[4] Above, p. 135.
[5] *Degge v. Hitchcock*, 229 U.S. 162 (1913). Professor Jaffe of Harvard has commented: 'One can only wonder whether so grossly flagrant a misreading of history was deliberate.' And he calls the case 'reminiscent of recent English decisions': [1956] Public Law, 230. The confusion spread to many State courts, some of which circumvented it by allowing mandamus to be used in place of certiorari—a remedy which became known as 'certiorarified mandamus'. Cf. below, p. 163.

might take place in England, where likewise the evolution of remedies is governed by the survival of the fittest.

The advantages of the declaration were brought into prominence by the case of some London dock workers who were suspended from employment for refusing to operate a new system for the unloading of raw sugar. Notices of suspension were sent out by the port manager, and the men appealed unsuccessfully to the statutory appeal tribunal. They were then dismissed. Some time later—after there had been a prolonged dock strike —the men began actions for declarations that their dismissal had been illegal. In due course they obtained discovery of documents from the Dock Labour Board, and it was then revealed for the first time that they had been suspended by the port manager personally and not by the local board. This gave an entirely new aspect to the case, since it disclosed that their suspension (and therefore their dismissal) had been irregular under the statutory scheme. They duly obtained declarations to this effect, and so were successful.[1] Had they instead applied for certiorari, they would most probably have failed. For one thing, the six months' time-limit had expired. For another, they would not have obtained discovery of documents, and would never have lighted on their best point. Lord Justice Denning (as he then was) put the matter on the broadest plane:

It is axiomatic that when a statutory tribunal sits to administer justice, it must act in accordance with the law. Parliament clearly so intended. If the tribunal does not observe the law, what is to be done? The remedy of certiorari is hedged round by limitations and may not be available. Why then should not the court intervene by declaration and injunction? If it cannot so intervene, it would mean that the tribunal could disregard the law, which is a thing no one can do in this country.

The court is thus encouraging the litigant to circumvent the limitations of certiorari and implying that they are an obstacle to justice. This policy has twice been adopted by the House of Lords in later cases. One was a somewhat similar case of a dock worker who had been invalidly dismissed, to whom the House granted a declaration which had been refused by the Court of Appeal.[2] In the other case the question was whether planning

---

[1] *Barnard v. National Dock Labour Board* [1953] 2 Q.B. 18.
[2] *Vine v. National Dock Labour Board* [1957] A.C. 488, above, p. 122.

permission was needed for quarrying operations in the Malvern Hills, and, if so, whether conditions imposed by the Minister were valid.[1] The time limit for certiorari had expired and the quarrying company asked instead for declarations as to its rights. These were granted by the House of Lords, and the Minister's argument that the right remedy, if any, was certiorari was rejected on the ground that the two remedies are in no way mutually exclusive. In the Court of Appeal Lord Denning praised the declaration as a means of avoiding the confusion caused by the nominal restriction of certiorari to 'judicial' functions, thus showing once more how absurd and injurious that confusion was.

The present dilemma

The remedies discussed in this chapter are in general comprehensive and efficacious. But it is unfortunate that certiorari and the declaration each have advantages which the other lacks, and that they cannot be asked for in the alternative in one proceeding. The litigant is forced to make a choice at his peril. This is so obviously unreasonable that there is an urgent need for reform.

The disadvantages of certiorari are first its procedural peculiarities and secondly the trap that has been made out of the word 'judicial'. The latter disadvantage ought now to disappear, thanks to the recent judgment of the House of Lords. But the inconvenient procedure remains. It was condemned as 'archaic, cumbrous and too inelastic' by the Committee on Ministers' Powers in 1932,[2] but only minor improvements were made by statute in 1933 and 1938. Curiously enough, the Committee on Administrative Tribunals and Enquiries in 1957 merely recommended that certiorari should be given wider operation (as has since been done) and that there was nothing wrong with the procedure.[3]

At the time when the confusion over 'judicial' was rife, the courts attempted (following in American footsteps) to escape from their own entanglement by encouraging the use of the declaratory judgment. But the declaration has its own deficien-

---

[1] *Pyx Granite Co. Ltd. v. Ministry of Housing and Local Government* [1960] A.C. 260.
[2] Cmd. 4060 (1932) pp. 62, 99, 117.
[3] Cmnd. 218 (1957) para. 117. For the wider operation see below, p. 154.

cies.[1] It lacks the 'public' character of certiorari, so that the court may decline to interfere with some wrongful administrative act because the plaintiff has not the necessary personal standing.[2] It also has the serious defect of being unable to control error on the face of the record.

What then needs to be done? The right course, probably, will be to reform the procedure of certiorari rather than to abandon that historic remedy in favour of the declaration. The latter course would shift the basis of judicial control from public interest to private right, and this would be retrogressive. It may however be reasonable that the 'public' remedy should have a relatively short time limit. A complaint against the administration has to be lodged within two months in France and within one month in West Germany. This makes the time limit of six months for certiorari look generous—and the Committee of 1957 recommended that it be reduced.[3] Yet the time limit for declaratory relief is in most cases indefinite, at the discretion of the court. A scheme of reform will have to remove such arbitrary differences. It may be that the solution should be set to a fairly short time limit for 'public' proceedings aiming at specific relief, i.e. asking for some act or order to be quashed, and to allow 'private' proceedings started later to entitle the plaintiff to financial compensation only, where that is appropriate.

In the past few years the vicissitudes of the case-law have been such that different policies have seemed desirable at different times. In 1949 Lord Denning said:

Just as the pick and shovel is no longer suitable for the winning of coal, so the procedure of mandamus, certiorari and actions on the case are not suitable for the winning of freedom in the new age. They must be replaced by new and up-to-date machinery, by declarations, injunctions and actions for negligence ... The courts must do this. Of all the great tasks that lie ahead, this is the greatest.[4]

But in 1959 he said:

There is nothing more important, to my mind, than that the vast

---

[1] See above, p. 123, and also below, p. 154.

[2] It is probably due to the disuse of certiorari to quash in the United States that questions of standing cause more trouble there than here.

[3] Cmnd. 218 (1957) para. 114.

[4] Freedom Under The Law, 126.

number of tribunals now in being should be subject to the supervision of the Queen's courts. This can only be done if the remedy
by certiorori is maintained in the full scope which the great judges
of the past gave to it. . . . this historic remedy has still a valuable
part to play: or at any rate, it should have, if we wish any longer
to ensure that the rights of the people are determined according
to law.[1]

What is needed to reconcile these two ideals is that reform
should be undertaken not by the courts but by legislation. The
best of both worlds might then be attainable. Perhaps action
may be taken before long, since the Lord Chancellor has
referred the subject of remedies to the Law Commission.

RESTRICTION OF REMEDIES

Discretion and its consequences

The most important remedies discussed in this chapter—
declaration, injunction, certiorari, prohibition—are discretionary and the court may therefore withhold them if it thinks fit.
The conduct of the applicant may have been unmeritorious,[2]
or the case may be trivial.[3] The applicant may also have raised
his objection too late.[4] If for example a party appearing before
a tribunal knows that it is improperly constituted because one
of the members has an interest in the case, but raises no objection at the time, he may be refused certiorari.[5] He is treated,
in effect, as having waived the objection by accepting the tribunal's jurisdiction.

This discretion is exercised with great care, so that in any
normal case the remedy accompanies the right. But the very
fact that there is discretion involves the possibility that an applicant might be refused relief against unlawful action, perhaps
because of his own unreasonable conduct. What then is the
position? If the action is *ultra vires*, it has no legal effect. But
if the court withholds the remedy, must the applicant submit?
The courts have not often explored these problems, but the
decisions suggest that the answer depends upon the nature of

[1] *Baldwin & Francis Ltd. v. Patents Appeal Tribunal* [1959] A.C. 663 at 697.
[2] As in *White v. Kuzych* [1951] A.C. 585 (breach of contract).
[3] As in *Ex parte Fry* [1954] 1 W.L.R. 730; below, p. 200.
[4] As in *R. v. Stafford J.J.* [1940] 2 K.B. 33; *R. v. Aston University Senate* [1969]
2 Q.B. 538 (below, p. 350).
[5] *R. v. Williams* [1914] 1 K.B. 608.

the remedy. Certiorari and prohibition are remedies designed to preserve order in the legal system by controlling clear cases of abuse of power; they are not suited to the final determination of private rights. If certiorari is refused in discretion, the applicant is not prevented from disputing the legality of the action in other proceedings, e.g. by suing his tenant for the original rent after a rent tribunal has ordered a reduction and an application for certiorari has failed.[1] In other words, he cannot be met with a plea of *res judicata*, and the tribunal's jurisdiction is always open to question.[2]

But if a declaration is refused, or damages or an injunction, that is *res judicata* and conclusive as to the questions in issue, so that where the validity of the action is in issue the applicant cannot later contest it. The paradox of the enforcement of *ultra vires* action, if indeed this should ever arise, would be explicable by the estoppel resulting from the judgment of the High Court, which like every other estoppel would bar proof of the true facts.

Exhaustion of administrative remedies

The court does not require what is sometimes called 'the exhaustion of administrative remedies'. In other words, illegal administrative action can be challenged as soon as it appears, and there is no need first to pursue any administrative procedure or appeal that may be available in order to see whether the action will in the end be taken or not. Thus in the *Electricity Commissioners* case, even though the Minister might in the end not have confirmed the scheme, the proceedings were halted by prohibition as soon as it was shown that the scheme would be invalid.[3] And where a police officer, invalidly dismissed by a Watch Committee, did not appeal to the Home Secretary, this was held no bar to his obtaining a declaration from the court.[4] It is never too early to invoke the aid of the law to resist govern-

---

[1] *Per* Devlin J. in *R. v. Fulham &c. Rent Tribunal* [1951] 2 K.B. 1; *R. v. Judge Pugh* [1951] 2 K.B. 623; and see *London Cpn. v. Cox* (1867) L.R. 2 H.L. 239 at 262–3.

[2] *R. v. Judge Pugh* (above). The reason why there is no *res judicata* is explained by Lord Goddard in *A Note on Habeas Corpus*, 65 L.Q.R. 30 at 35.

[3] Above, p. 133. But contrast mandamus: below, p. 164.

[4] *Cooper v. Wilson* [1937] 2 K.B. 309; below, p. 179.

mental action which is contrary to law,[1] and even future action can be challenged if it is sufficiently imminent. But where there is a statutory right of appeal to a court of law, and the complaint is merely of error on the face of the record, it may be that the court will refuse certiorari on the ground that appeal is the more convenient remedy.

An opposite argument is sometimes put forward, to the effect that the exercise of an administrative appeal implies a waiver of judicial remedies. Thus the Court of Appeal held that a chief constable who did appeal to the Home Secretary had thereby waived his right to obtain a declaration from the court that his dismissal was invalid.[2] Fortunately this decision was reversed by the House of Lords. For it rests on an obvious confusion between appeal on the merits of the case and judicial review of the legality of the whole proceeding. These are quite different things, and it would be an illogical trap if they were mutually exclusive. Administrative remedies are highly desirable and people should be encouraged to use them. But to allow unlawful action to stand, merely because it has been appealed against on its merits, is indefensible.

Implied exclusion of remedies

A statutory scheme will often contain its own system of enforcement. In such cases the ordinary remedies may be excluded impliedly or expressly, or there may be a choice between a special statutory remedy and an ordinary remedy.

As a general rule, the courts are reluctant to hold that ordinary remedies are impliedly excluded, particularly where the statutory remedy is in the hands of an administrative body. Thus the court will grant a declaration that quarrying operations do not need planning permission, even though statute provides that the local planning authority may be asked to decide such questions.[3] For the plaintiff is here merely seeking

---

[1] See *R. v. Stepney Cpn.* [1902] 1 K.B. 317; *R. v. North* [1927] 1 K.B. 491 and cases there cited; *Lawler v. Union of Post Office Workers* [1965] Ch. 712; *Munnich v. Godstone R.D.C.* [1966] 1 W.L.R. 427; *R. v. Paddington Valuation Officer* [1966] 1 Q.B. 380. In the United States, where the principle of *ultra vires* is less clear-cut, exhaustion of administrative remedies is sometimes required and this is a source of uncertainty.

[2] *Ridge v. Baldwin* [1963] 1 Q.B. 539, [1964] A.C. 40. In *Annamunthodo v. Oilfield Workers' Trade Union* [1961] A.C. 945 Lord Denning rejected this line of argument, but in *James v. Minister of Housing and Local Government* [1966] 1 W.L.R. 135 (reversed on other grounds, [1967] 1 W.L.R. 171) he accepted it.

[3] *Pyx Granite Co. Ltd. v. M.H.L.G.* [1960] A.C. 260 (above, p. 142).

to establish that the planning legislation does not affect his ordinary legal liberties, which the courts protect by their ordinary remedies.

On the other hand there are situations where the statutory remedy is the only remedy. For example, where a taxing statute gives a right of appeal to the Commissioners of Inland Revenue on a disputed assessment, the court will not grant a declaration that the taxpayer is entitled to certain allowances.[1] Similarly where a river authority is given a statutory right to recover certain expenses in a magistrates' court, it cannot obtain a declaration from the High Court that its claim is good.[2] These are cases where the right given by the statute does not exist at common law, and can be enforced only in the way provided by the statute.

Difficult cases arise out of ministerial 'default powers', i.e. special powers under which ministers may take steps to compel local authorities to perform their statutory duties, for example to provide schools. These powers are described on a later page, where it is suggested that the courts interpret them too strictly.[3] For the courts are very ready to infer from the mere existence of the default power that the duty is to be enforced only by the minister, and they will then refuse any remedy to a private person.[4] But they will protect a private person's statutory right, such as his right to send his children to school free of charge[5]; and they may grant a remedy against the doing of something positively forbidden by the statute, since (as already mentioned) they may look upon this as equivalent to an actionable wrong for which ordinary remedies will lie.[6]

---

[1] *Argosam Finance Co. Ltd. v. Oxby* [1965] Ch. 390. Cf. *Harrison v. Croydon L.B.C.* [1968] Ch. 479. Contrast *Re Vandervell's Trusts* [1970] Ch. 44.

[2] *Barraclough v. Brown* [1897] A.C. 615.

[3] Below, p. 158.

[4] *Pasmore v. Oswaldtwistle U.D.C.*, below, p. 164; *Watt v. Kesteven C.C.* [1955] 1 Q.B. 408, refusing a declaration that education must be provided at a school chosen by the parents; *Wood v. Ealing L.B.C.* [1967] Ch. 364, refusing an injunction against a scheme for comprehensive schools.

[5] *Gateshead Union v. Durham C.C.* [1918] 1 Ch. 147 (declaration).

[6] *Bradbury v. Enfield L.B.C.* [1967] 1 W.L.R. 1311 (above, pp. 56, 114), granting an injunction against closing schools in a manner prohibited by the Act, but refusing an injunction against mere default since the default power belonged exclusively to the minister.

Comprehensive statutory remedies

It is common for statutes to make comprehensive provision for remedies by providing either for application to be made to the court in certain circumstances, or for the ordinary remedies to be restricted, or for both. For example, Part XI of the Town and Country Planning Act 1962 contains a complicated scheme of remedies for challenging the validity of plans, orders, decisions, &c., made under the Act. Its purport is to abolish all the usual remedies, but to give the court power to quash action not legally authorised by the Act [1] if any person aggrieved makes application within six weeks. It also provides certain rights of appeal to the court from the Minister on points of law. The legislation which governs compulsory purchase orders contains a generally similar provision, which is mentioned below. But, although there are certain common forms, statutory provisions about remedies are extensive in their variety. Sometimes certiorari and other specified remedies are taken away; sometimes all ordinary remedies are taken away; sometimes it is provided that some question is to be decided by a minister or tribunal and that the decision shall be final or unchallengeable. The precise effect of any such provision must always be a question of construction of the particular legislation. But it is important to illustrate the courts' attitude to such provisions, and this can be done by looking at certain common types.

The key to the attitude of the courts is their determination to preserve, even in the face of express statutory prohibition, their control over action which is *ultra vires*. If they allow this to be taken from them, they allow power to be made uncontrollable and the rule of law to collapse. This suffices to explain some of the remarkable feats of judicial construction which will be mentioned. Restrictive interpretation has done much to keep legislative deprivation of remedies within due bounds, thus redressing Parliament's tendency to take away fundamental legal safeguards without full appreciation of the consequences.

'Persons aggrieved'

One common device, already instanced, is to give an exclusive statutory remedy to 'any person aggrieved'. Contrary to their

---

[1] This paraphrase is subject to the doubts created by the *East Elloe* case (see Appendix, A).

usual policy, the courts have sometimes given a narrow meaning to this simple-looking phrase. Instead of holding it to mean 'any person who feels aggrieved' (a form in which it appears in some statutes[1]), they hold it to mean 'any person legally entitled to be aggrieved' or 'any person with a legal grievance'. An example comes (once again) from the position of a person who objects to some proposed activity on his neighbour's land for which the neighbour is given planning permission. Even if the objector has opposed the proposal at a public inquiry, he is unable to take advantage of a statutory remedy allowing any person aggrieved to challenge the legality of the permission.[2] The reason is that no legal right of his is infringed by the grant of permission.[3] But if the statute had provided no remedy, he might well have been able to obtain certiorari, and for that purpose would have counted as a person aggrieved.[4] This anomaly may be due more to the weak position of objectors under planning law than to any general rule of interpretation. In other contexts eminent judicial opinion now favours greater liberality.[5] It would be unfortunate if statutes which apparently give wide remedies were held to cut down the citizen's opportunities for disputing unlawful action, and to shift the basis of the remedy from public order to private interest.

Finality clauses

In order to preserve their control the courts have made it a firm rule to put a narrow construction on the finality clauses which are commonly found in statutes. If it is provided that some decision 'shall be final' or 'shall be final and conclusive', this is interpreted to mean that there is no further appeal, but that the decision is still subject to judicial control if it is *ultra vires*, or even if it merely shows error on the face of the record.[6] 'Parliament only gives the impress of finality to the decisions

---

[1] E.g. National Insurance Act 1911, s. 66(1). In the Act of 1965, s. 65, this has become 'any person aggrieved'. Cf. London Building Act 1930 s. 52(2) ('who may deem himself aggrieved').

[2] *Buxton v. Minister of Housing and Local Government* [1961] 1 Q.B. 278.

[3] See above, p. 123; below, p. 237.   [4] See above, p. 139.

[5] *Attorney-General of the Gambia v. N'Jie* [1961] A.C. 617; *Maurice v. L.C.C.* [1964] 2 Q.B. 362 (Lord Denning).

[6] *R. v. Medical Appeal Tribunal* [1957] 1 Q.B. 574.

of the tribunal on condition that they are reached in accordance with the law.'[1] The same principle applies equally to certiorari and to the grant of a declaration.[2] This robust attitude virtually deprives finality clauses of meaning for this purpose, since there is no right of appeal anyway unless expressly given by statute. But these clauses may be important for other purposes, for example when the question is whether the finding of one tribunal may be reopened before another.[3]

'*No certiorari*' clauses

One of the most striking feats of judicial construction is the rule that an act or decision which is *ultra vires* can be quashed by certiorari even in the face of a statute saying expressly that no certiorari shall issue.[4] 'Those statutes were passed chiefly between 1680 and 1848, in the days when the courts used certiorari too freely and quashed decisions for technical defects of form. In stopping this abuse the statutes proved very beneficial, but the court never allowed those statutes to be used as a cover for wrongdoing by tribunals. If tribunals were to be at liberty to exceed their jurisdiction without any check by the courts, the rule of law would be at an end.'[5] Here therefore we again meet the fundamental necessity for unified jurisdictional control which is essential for a coherent legal system.[6] The courts refuse to believe that Parliament can intend to violate this principle. As was said in one case, 'the consequence of holding otherwise would be that a Metropolitan magistrate could make any order he pleased without question'.[7]

'*Shall not be questioned*' clauses

A still more drastic restriction of remedies is commonly found in modern statutes, of which the Acquisition of Land (Authorisation Procedure) Act 1946 is typical. This Act governs

---

[1] *Ibid.*, (Denning L.J.).

[2] *Pyx Granite Co. Ltd. v. M.H.L.G.* [1960] A.C. 260.

[3] See *R. v. Deputy Industrial Injuries Commissioner* [1967] 1 A.C. 725; *R. v. National Insurance Commissioner* [1970] 1 Q.B. 477.

[4] Examples are *Ex parte Bradlaugh* (1878) 3 Q.B.D. 509; *R. v. Hurst* [1960] 2 Q.B. 133. Cf. the licensing cases noted below, p. 178.

[5] *R. v. Medical Appeal Tribunal* (above) (Denning L.J.).

[6] Cf. above, p. 92.

[7] *Ex parte Bradlaugh* (above).

the procedure for the compulsory acquisition of land. Any person aggrieved by a compulsory purchase order who 'desires to question the validity thereof' is given six weeks in which to apply to the High Court on the ground that the order is not empowered by the Act. Subject to this, the order 'shall not . . . be questioned in any legal proceedings whatsoever'.[1] The object of this type of clause is to give the acquiring authority a cast-iron title. Public authorities would be in an impossible position if they acquired land and built a housing estate or a hospital on it, yet were liable to have their title to the land invalidated in legal proceedings which might take place some years later. But so freely are these clauses now used that they are becoming an insidious habit. They apply indiscriminately throughout the planning legislation mentioned already and in various other cases where no necessity is evident.[2]

When these ouster clauses (as they have been called) first came before the courts, they were taken at face value.[3] In the *East Elloe* case the House of Lords held that after six weeks a compulsory purchase order could not be challenged on grounds of fraudulent motive.[4] The decision also created confusion as to the availability of various grounds of challenge even within the prescribed six weeks, but that problem is discussed separately in the Appendix.

In 1968 the House of Lords dramatically reversed its attitude in the *Anisminic* case.[5] Quoting with approval the remarks of Lord Justice Farwell cited elsewhere,[6] and endorsing the long-settled policy of the courts towards 'no certiorari' clauses, the House declared a decision of the Foreign Compensation Commission to be *ultra vires* despite a statute saying that a determination of the Commission 'shall not be called in question in any court of law'.[7] The House held unanimously that this provision

---

[1] 1st Sched., para. 16.

[2] Above, p. 148; and see 85 L.Q.R. at 208.

[3] But see *Webb v. M.H.L.G.* [1965] 1 W.L.R. 755, where a way of escape was found by the Court of Appeal in special circumstances.

[4] *Smith v. East Elloe R.D.C.* [1956] A.C. 736 (no fraud was in fact proved).

[5] *Anisminic Ltd. v. Foreign Compensation Commission* [1969] 2 A.C. 147, upholding a notable judgment of Browne J., for which see [1969] C.L.J. 230 and [1969] 2 A.C. at 223. For comment see 85 L.Q.R. 198.

[6] Above, p. 92.

[7] Foreign Compensation Act 1950. s. 4 (4).

would bar any challenge for mere error within jurisdiction, but would not protect any decision which was *ultra vires*. Moreover, the House by a majority held that the Foreign Compensation Commission had acted *ultra vires* in rejecting a mining company's claim to a share of the compensation fund paid over by the Egyptian Government to the British Government as compensation for British-owned properties expropriated by Egypt after the Suez operations in 1956. By misconstruing certain regulations the Commission had required the claimants to show that their successors in title were of British nationality, whereas on a true construction this requirement was irrelevant. This error, the House of Lords held, amounted to imposing a condition which the Commission had no power to impose. Thus a mistake which might well have been considered a mere error within jurisdiction[1] was held to involve excess of jurisdiction, and by stretching the doctrine of *ultra vires* to an extreme point the House of Lords was able to circumvent the ouster clause.

One result of this striking case was to focus attention on the dangers of ouster clauses and to persuade Parliament to provide limited rights of appeal from the Commission to the courts.[2] There can be no doubt that Parliament had previously intended to prohibit judicial control of the Commission entirely.[3]

Another important question is how the decision will affect the much commoner cases where the prohibition is not absolute but takes effect only after some period such as six weeks. The House of Lords emphasised the similarity of both kinds of ouster clause, rejecting the *East Elloe* case as contrary to precedent and principle. It seems therefore that the expiry of the six-weeks period will no longer prevent an order being challenged on the ground that it is made in bad faith or on wrong grounds, or is unreasonable, contrary to natural justice or in any other way *ultra vires*. But then there will be in-

---

[1] The Court of Appeal so held.

[2] Foreign Compensation Act 1969, s. 3, providing for appeal on questions of construction and jurisdiction to the Court of Appeal only, but not restricting proceedings based on natural justice. Since breach of natural justice goes to jurisdiction (below, pp. 185, 204), there may now be alternative remedies in natural justice cases.

[3] It was expressly exempted from s. 11 of the Tribunals and Inquiries Act 1958 (p. 154, below).

soluble problems for public authorities, who will not know (for example) whether they can rely on a compulsory purchase order and safely build a hospital or a motorway. The solution to this dilemma, it is suggested, should be to apply the *Anisminic* principle only to absolute ouster clauses. Where recourse to the courts is restricted only after a prescribed time, the eventual barring of legal remedies may be as necessary as under a normal statute of limitation, except possibly where an order is *ultra vires* on its face.[1] Thus a way might be found between the House of Lords' two extremes which would make both their decisions reconcilable.

What really matters in these cases is that the time allowed for recourse to the courts should be reasonable. The Committee on Ministers' Powers said that the six week period was too short, and Lord Radcliffe has called it pitifully inadequate.[2] It requires reconsideration along with the other reforms needed in the system of remedies.

'As if enacted' clauses

Another form of protective clause is to the effect that a statutory order shall 'have effect as if enacted in this Act' and that confirmation by the minister shall be 'conclusive evidence that the requirements of this Act have been complied with, and that the order has been duly made and is within the powers of this Act'. Hard though it might seem to find a loophole in this formula, the House of Lords has suggested that it applies only to orders which themselves conform to the Act, since it is only such orders that the Act contemplates.[3] Thus the court could still control procedural or other legal errors, and the exclusion clause would be virtually meaningless. The clause is now less common than it was (it came into use in the nineteenth century), and Parliament has instead resorted to the 'shall not be questioned' type of clause, which in most respects at least is more effectively 'judge-proof'.

More about exclusion clauses of this type will be found in the chapter on delegated legislation.[4]

---

[1] The order may need to be one which 'bears no brand of invalidity upon its forehead' (Lord Radcliffe in the *East Elloe* case).
[2] *Ibid.*
[3] *Minister of Health v. The King* [1931] A.C. 494.   [4] Below, p. 329.

Statutory reform

Manifestly the sole object of these clauses is to legalise illegalities and exempt them from judicial control. Lawyers are naturally hostile to this policy, for it opens the door to dictatorial power. The Committee on Ministers' Powers recommended in 1932 that it 'should be abandoned in all but the most exceptional cases',[1] and in 1957 the Franks Committee recommended that no statute should contain words purporting to oust the prerogative remedies.[2] The Tribunals and Inquiries Act 1958 has done something towards fulfilling the latter recommendation. Section 11 provides that

any provision in any Act passed before the commencement of this Act that any order or determination shall not be called into question in any court, or any provision in such an Act which by similar words excludes any of the powers of the High Court, shall not have effect so as to prevent the removal of the proceedings into the High Court by order of certiorari or to prejudice the powers of the High Court to make orders of mandamus.

But there are various exceptions, including any case 'where an Act makes special provision for application to the High Court . . . within a time limited by the Act'.

The Act therefore steers between two extremes in the manner already advocated. It makes no change in the law (whatever it may now be) where access to the courts is cut off only after a period of time. But in other cases it restores the court's powers of control—and not only over *ultra vires* acts but also, it seems, over error on the face of the record. But for no apparent reason it assumes that certiorari and mandamus[3] are the only relevant remedies in England, ignoring the declaratory judgment which may often be more useful and appropriate.[4] Yet another anomaly has thus been added to the contrast between certiorari and the declaration. There is no such discrimination in Scotland, where the Act safeguards the whole jurisdiction of the Court of Session over the validity of any decision, without reference to particular remedies.[5]

[1] Cmd. 4060 (1932) p. 65.
[2] Cmnd. 218 (1957) para. 117.
[3] For mandamus see below, p. 158.
[4] As in the *Anisminic* case (above).
[5] S. 11 (2).

ENFORCEMENT OF PUBLIC DUTIES

The remedies so far investigated deal with the control of *powers*, i.e. with the control of illegal acts. But there can also be illegal inaction, by neglect of some positive *duty*. This is particularly true of public authorities, who have many legal duties, imposing an obligation to act, as opposed to their legal powers, which give them a discretion whether to act or not.

Criminal prosecution

The natural way for a statute to enforce a public duty in the case of a private person is to invoke the criminal law, for example by making it an offence to fail to make an income-tax return. The common law took the same approach to the problem of making public authorities carry out their duties. Neglect of a public duty was held to be an indictable misdemeanour, punishable by fine or imprisonment. It was impossible, of course, to indict the Crown. But the inhabitants of counties, townships, and parishes were often indicted for failure to repair highways and bridges. The legal basis of this procedure was that a public nuisance (a crime) had been perpetrated. But there is also a wider doctrine that any neglect of a public duty is an indictable offence. A private prosecutor may indict members of the defaulting authority. In highway cases, however, the procedure by indictment has now been abolished in favour of statutory proceedings which any one may institute against the highway authority, with the ultimate sanction that the complainant may carry out the work himself and recover the cost from the defaulting authority.[1] An example of the wider proposition that any neglect of public duty is an offence may be seen in the case of a magistrate who was indicted (but acquitted) in 1832 for failing to take proper steps to suppress a riot.[2] Indictment is obviously an unsatisfactory remedy, and has rarely been used in modern times—though perhaps it is well that public authorities should be aware that it lingers on in the background.

---

[1] Highways Act 1959 s. 59. For the former procedure see Halsbury's *Laws of England*, 3rd ed., vol. 19, p. 139.

[2] *R. v. Pinney* (1832) 3 B. & Ad. 947.

Actions for damages and declarations

Ordinary civil actions may sometimes be of use, though it is not often that the law is clear enough to be satisfactory. Actions for damages are sometimes allowed for non-performance of statutory duty but the statute usually says nothing of any such remedy, and the question is whether the court will construe it as impliedly intended. The Act which forbids (under penalty) use of a motor-car without third-party insurance, for example, has been held to give an action for damages by an injured person against the owner of the car who allowed an uninsured person to drive it.[1] But a statutory order making it an offence to use a motor-car on the road in a dangerous condition has been held to give no civil action.[2] Similarly, when a water company failed to maintain the statutory pressure in its mains, and the plaintiff's house was burned down because the hoses would not work, it was held that the Act did not thereby intend to make the company liable in damages for the results of their default.[3] In one famous case of 1703 (which, however, no longer represents the law[4]) actions for damages were allowed to voters whose votes had been wrongfully refused at the poll.[5] The court is usually sympathetic to an action for damages if the statute has no scheme of its own for penalties or enforcement. 'For, if it were not so, the statute would be but a pious aspiration.'[6] Thus an action for damages may lie against a local authority which refuses a licence out of malice or spite, thereby violating its duty to act fairly.[7]

But where the statute itself provides penalties, there is *prima facie* no civil remedy,[8] for otherwise crimes would too freely be turned into torts. Actions have, indeed, sometimes been allowed in such cases, for example for breaches of the Factory Acts,[9] and in the case about motor insurance already mentioned. But in what is perhaps a more typical case, a bookmaker failed in

---

[1] *Monk v. Warbey* [1935] 1 K.B. 75.
[2] *Phillips v. Britannia Hygienic Laundry Co. Ltd.* [1923] 2 K.B. 832.
[3] *Atkinson v. Newcastle Corporation Waterworks Co.* (1877) 2 Ex. D. 441.
[4] Representation of the People Act 1949, s. 50.
[5] *Ashby v. White* (1703) 2 Ld. Raym. 938.
[6] Lord Simonds in *Cutler v. Wandsworth Stadium, Ltd.* (below). An example is *Ching v. Surrey C.C.* [1910] 1 K.B. 736 (failure to keep a school in repair).
[7] *David v. Abdul Cader* [1963] 1 W.L.R. 834; above, p. 85.
[8] *Phillips v. Britannia Laundry* (above) at 841.
[9] *Groves v. Lord Wimborne* [1898] 2 Q.B. 404.

an action against the proprietors of a dog-racing track for failure to provide him with facilities as required by the Betting and Lotteries Act 1934 which made this an offence punishable with fine and imprisonment.[1]

We are not here concerned with incidental wrongdoing, i.e. acts of negligence or other wrongs committed in the course of carrying out duties: for injuries of that kind ordinary actions will lie, as already explained.[2]

Actions for declarations play relatively little part in the enforcement of duties. Plaintiffs seeking damages often ask also for declarations, but the two remedies tend to stand or fall together. For the court will take the view either that Parliament intended the duty to be enforceable by a civil action or that it did not: in the first case, an action for damages will lie; in the second, no action will lie for any remedy. In this field, therefore, the declaration has no special advantages of the kind which has made it a competitor with certiorari.

There is a further factor which makes the courts slow to encourage private actions for non-performance of statutory duties. A *power* enables an authority to do what would otherwise be illegal. It is subject to legal limits, and it is safe to assume that Parliament did not intend it to be exercised beyond those limits. A *duty*, on the other hand, may or may not be legally enforceable. Parliament has recently become fond of imposing duties of a kind which, since no compulsive machinery is provided, are probably not *legal* duties at all, in the sense that they can be enforced by legal process. This is particularly common in statutes concerned with social services and nationalization. Thus the opening words of the National Health Service Act 1946 are

It shall be the duty of the Minister of Health . . . to promote the establishment in England and Wales of a comprehensive health service, . . .

and the Coal Industry Nationalization Act 1946 charges the Coal Board with the duties of 'working and getting coal in Great Britain', 'making supplies of coal available', and so on. These duties are imposed by statute, but it seems plain that it

---

[1] *Cutler v. Wandsworth Stadium Ltd.* [1949] A.C. 398.
[2] Above, p. 57.

must be by political rather than legal means that they are to
be enforced.

Default powers

Ministers are frequently given special powers to compel local
authorities to carry out their duties or to step in and remedy any
default themselves. For example, the Education Act 1944
provides that if the minister is satisfied, on complaint by any
interested person or otherwise, that a local authority has
failed to discharge any duty under the Act, the minister may
by order judge them to be in default and give them such
directions as he thinks expedient for performing the duty; and
that any such directions may be enforced by mandamus on
the minister's application.[1] Other examples of default powers
are to be found in the Public Health Act 1936,[2] the Housing
Act 1957[3] and the Town and Country Planning Act 1962.[4]
They are a standardized mechanism for enabling the central
government to deal with an inefficient or recalcitrant local
authority.

These powers are very rarely used, though their actual
existence puts a powerful lever in the minister's hands. In law
their principal effect is that, as has already been seen, they are
sometimes held to represent the only legal machinery for
enforcing the statutory duties, so that other remedies are not
available.[5] The courts are perhaps unduly strict in their
decisions, since the fact that the minister is equipped with
default powers for administrative purposes is not necessarily
an argument for depriving the citizen of his normal right, where
his interests are affected, to require public authorities to obey
the law.

Mandamus

The prerogative remedy of mandamus has for long been the
normal weapon for compelling performance of public duties, at
least where the plaintiff does not wish to run the hazard of an
action for damages. Mandamus came into general use for this

---

[1] S. 99.   [2] S. 322.   [3] S. 171.   [4] S. 207.
[5] Above, p. 147; below, p. 164.

purpose in the eighteenth century, having formerly been used mainly for restitution of offices to persons who had been wrongfully deprived of them. It proved to be one of the few effective instruments of public policy in the era between the abolition of the Star Chamber in 1640 and the creation of new administrative authorities in the nineteenth century. During that interregnum the business of administration was carried on mainly under judicial forms, and mandamus was virtually the only judicial order which could be used for forcing public authorities to perform their duties.

The essence of mandamus is that it is a royal command, issued in the name of the Crown from the Court of King's Bench (now the Queen's Bench Division of the High Court), ordering the performance of a public legal duty. It is a discretionary remedy, and the Court assumes a free discretion to grant it in suitable cases and withhold it in others. It has never lost the wide scope which the courts gave it in the eighteenth and early nineteenth centuries, when it was so vital a part of the machinery of government. But in the highly organized administrative system of the modern state it has no longer this prominent role to play. Governmental bodies today respond more naturally to the political stimulus, and the ultimate legal sanction has to be invoked only in a handful of stubborn cases.

Disobedience to a mandamus is a contempt of court, for which the normal penalty is imprisonment. A mandamus is therefore very like a mandatory injunction: both are commands from the court that some legal duty be performed. But the two remedies have different spheres. The injunction is an equitable remedy, and it is very rare to find mandatory injunctions outside private law. Mandamus is a common law remedy, based on royal authority, which is used only in public law.

Who may obtain mandamus?

As with the other prerogative remedies, it is usually a private person who sets proceedings for mandamus into motion. But the non-performance of a public duty seems to be regarded as less of an offence against public order than is the unlawful exercise of power. An applicant for mandamus must therefore show that he has a substantial interest in the performance of the

duty. But on the whole the courts are more generous in awarding mandamus than some of their statements might suggest.
The court may say that it proceeds 'on a very strict basis'.[1] But
it seems willing to allow a ratepayer to enforce the local
authority's statutory duties;[2] and it has not refused to consider
a claim by a Member of Parliament that the police should be
ordered to prosecute gaming clubs more actively.[3]

The 'interest' which has to be shown is not a technical legal
interest. It merely marks the distinction between persons who
are particularly concerned with the performance of a public
duty, and other people generally. An application for mandamus
may fail because the applicant is not specially concerned as well
as on the ground (which is not always clearly distinguished)
that the court decides in its discretion to refuse the remedy. It
is easy for the argument to proceed in a circle, for the question
whether a duty is owed to the applicant is really determined by
the question whether he has a remedy for enforcing it.

Commercial rivalry will not necessarily amount to a sufficient
interest. Thus where the government were required by statute
to collect the annual tax on betting shops in two instalments,
but as a concession collected in it twelve monthly instalments,
mandamus was refused to bookmakers whose concern was to
put their rivals out of business.[4] But there is usually *locus standi*
where the applicant has been a party to some kind of legal
process. The Manchester Corporation once obtained a special
Act of Parliament for the construction of tramways, against the
opposition of an insurance company which insured against
road accidents. The company procured a clause in the Act
requiring the Corporation to make by-laws for a prescribed
minimum distance between successive trams, but the Corporation made a by-law which instead of prescribing a distance left
the matter to the police. The company were granted a mandamus to compel the Corporation to make a by-law as required
by the Act, and it was held that their initiative in procuring the
clause gave them a superior interest to that of the general

---

[1] *R. v. Commissioners of Customs & Excise* [1970] 1 W.L.R. 450.

[2] *R. v. Paddington Valuation Officer* [1966] 1 Q.B. 380; *R. v. Hereford Cpn.* [1970]
1 W.L.R. 1424.

[3] *R. v. Metropolitan Police Commissioner* [1968] 2 Q.B. 118 (point left open).

[4] *R. v. Commissioners of Customs & Excise* (above).

public.[1] In another case a clergyman opposed an application
to justices for the transfer of a liquor licence from one house to
another. The justices allowed the transfer, but in so doing they
exceeded their statutory powers. The clergyman then obtained
a mandamus to direct them to hear and determine the case
correctly.[2] His special interest in the legality of the justices'
decision lay in the fact that he had appeared as an objector
when the application for the transfer was made to them. These
examples show a healthy disinclination to make technical rules
about *locus standi*. The court always has a discretion to refuse the
remedy to an undeserving applicant. But in general the court is
concerned to see that the law is observed.

Scope of mandamus

Mandamus may be used by one public authority against
another. The Borough Council of Poplar in London on one
occasion refused to pay their statutory contributions to the
London County Council for rates. The County Council obtained a mandamus ordering the proper payments to be made
—and, moreover, when the payments were not forthcoming
they obtained writs of attachment for imprisonment of the
members of the Poplar Council who had disobeyed the mandamus.[3] Thus the remedy may fortify the internal machinery
of government where specific legal duties exist. Statutes also
sometimes provide expressly that a duty owed by one authority
to another authority may be enforced by mandamus, as well as
providing special enforcement procedures of their own.

Unlike its less fortunate relative certiorari, mandamus was
never subject to the misguided notion that it could apply only
to 'judicial' functions. It applies to all sorts of functions indiscriminately. Thus it will issue to compel such bodies as railway
and dock companies to carry out duties imposed on them by
statute, to compel the levying of a rate by a local authority, to
compel the payment of statutory compensation, to compel the
production of public documents, to compel a returning officer
or a local authority to hold an election correctly, to compel the
allowance of an item in an assessment for income tax, and to

[1] *The King v. Manchester Corporation* [1911] 1 K.B. 560.
[2] *The Queen v. Cotham* [1898] 1 Q.B. 802.
[3] *The King v. Poplar Borough Council* [1922] 1 K.B. 72, 95.

compel the repayment of a sum due to the taxpayer.[1] In connexion with compulsory purchase of land, the court will compel
the purchasing authority to proceed with the purchase once it
has given notice of its decision to act, so that the owner will
not be left with unmarketable land on his hands for longer than
necessary.[2]

Another important sphere in which mandamus operates
freely is that of inferior courts and tribunals. If they refuse to
entertain a case where they have jurisdiction, they can be
ordered to hear and determine it according to law. Thus
magistrates, licensing justices, county courts, statutory tribunals[3] and other jurisdictions subject to the High Court can
be prevented from refusing jurisdiction wrongfully. A county
court judge, for instance, who mistakenly declined to hear an
action for possession by mortgagees on the ground that the
county court had no jurisdiction, was ordered to hear and determine the case on a mandamus from the Queen's Bench Division.[4] But there must be some *public duty* to exercise jurisdiction.
Mandamus will not issue to a private arbitrator or to a tribunal
voluntarily acting as arbitrator under a government contract.[5]

Mandamus and certiorari

Where some act or order is challenged as *ultra vires*, mandamus is often used as an adjunct to certiorari. Where the act is
done with no jurisdiction at all, certiorari will issue to quash it
and prohibition to prevent further proceedings. Where there is
jurisdiction, but it has been abused, certiorari will quash, and
a proper re-hearing can be ordered by mandamus. A typical
example is provided by the case of the schools at Swansea,
soon to be explained: the Board of Education's decision was
quashed by certiorari, since they had addressed their minds to
the wrong questions; and they were then ordered by mandamus
to consider the right questions, and determine them according
to law.[6] In such cases the prerogative remedies supplement one

---

[1] Halsbury's *Laws of England*, 3rd ed., vol. 11, pp. 91–94. A classic instance is
Bagg's Case (1615) 11 Co. Rep. 236 (reinstatement of wrongfully disfranchised
burgess of Plymouth).

[2] *Ibid.*, 91.

[3] *The King v. Housing Tribunal* [1920] 3 K.B. 334.

[4] *The Queen v. Judge Dutton Briant* [1957] 2 Q.B. 497.

[5] *R. v. Industrial Court* [1965] 1 Q.B. 377.

[6] *Board of Education v. Rice* [1911] A.C. 179; below, p. 192.

another, and their availability is governed by the same principles.

But even where certiorari seems to be required, mandamus can also be used by itself. If the lower tribunal is ordered to rehear the case, the mandamus amounts also to an implied declaration that the previous decision was a nullity, thus doing the work of certiorari automatically. Mandamus alone was awarded, for instance, in the case where a county council's theatrical licensing committee had refused to allow a theatre to continue to sell alcoholic refreshments, and were ordered to reconsider.[1] This use of mandamus as a substitute for certiorari has become a habit in liquor licensing cases. This is because it was liquor licensing cases that were first bedevilled by doubts as to whether the function was sufficiently 'judicial' to allow certiorari[2]; and though the doubts no longer exist, the habit does.

It has been suggested in one case that mandamus might be granted in advance of certiorari, so that the initial act could be kept in force until replaced by a valid act in obedience to the mandamus.[3] The object of this is to avoid administrative inconvenience. But it is founded on the heresy that unauthorised action is voidable rather than void, which is criticised elsewhere. A mandamus 'to hear and determine' necessarily assumes that the tribunal's earlier determination is inoperative in law.[4] 'The previous order must either be quashed on certiorari or ignored; and it is better for it to be quashed.'[5]

The limits of mandamus

What, then, are the limitations of mandamus? It will not of course lie where the authority has a discretion on the point[6]

---

[1] *The Queen v. Flintshire Licensing Committee* [1957] 1 Q.B. 350; above, p. 101.

[2] See above, p. 135. *The Queen v. Cotham* (above, p. 161) is an example of a case decided when the fallacy was uncorrected. Certiorari was refused but mandamus was granted. This was the equivalent of the American 'certiorarified mandamus' (above, p. 140, note 5).

[3] *R. v. Paddington Valuation Officer* [1966] 1 Q.B. 380 (Lord Denning M.R.). For this case see above, p. 104.   [4] *Ibid., per* Salmon L.J.

[5] *Baldwin v. Francis Ltd. v. Patents Appeal Tribunal* [1959] A.C. 663 at 694 (Lord Denning, here expressing the opposite opinion).

[6] As in *Re Fletcher* [1970] 2 All E.R. 527 (no mandamus to Parliamentary Commissioner for Administration).

since then it is a matter of power rather than duty. Of its more technical limitations mention must be made of two. It will not lie against the Crown. And it will not lie if Parliament has provided some other remedy which is construed as being exclusive. It will be convenient to treat the latter restriction first.

The doctrine that mandamus is excluded if Parliament has provided an exclusive remedy is illustrated by a decision of the House of Lords in a case where the owner of a paper mill was trying to force the local authority to build sewers adequate to the discharge of effluent from his mill. Under the Public Health Act 1875 the local authority had the duty to provide such sewers as might be necessary for effectually draining their district. The Act also provided that if complaint was made to the Local Government Board about failure to provide sewers, the Board after duly inquiring into the case might order performance of the duty within a fixed time, and might enforce their order by mandamus, or else appoint some person to perform the duty. This scheme of enforcement was held to bar the right of a private person to seek mandamus on his own account, since the Act implied that his right course was to complain to the Board.[1] The decision is an application of the general doctrine (already criticised with reference to default powers) that a statutory remedy may be exclusive if it relates to some special right or duty created by the statute.[2]

The court may similarly refuse mandamus if there is a right of appeal which has not been exercised.[3] This is a situation where it may be reasonable to require the prior exhaustion of other remedies.[4] But there is always discretion to award mandamus, as was done in one case where licensing justices had rejected an application without reasons given, so that it was difficult for the applicant to appeal effectively.[5]

Mandamus could, of course, be eliminated by express statutory provisions, but in fact these do not occur. In so far as it might be affected by wide clauses excluding judicial control, of the type we have met in connexion with certiorari, it now enjoys

---

[1] *Pasmore v. Oswaldtwistle U.D.C.* [1898] A.C. 387.
[2] Above, p. 147.
[3] *The King v. Assessment Committee of City of London Union* [1907] 2 K.B. 764.
[4] Contrast p. 145, above.
[5] *The Queen v. Thomas* [1892] 1 Q.B. 426.

the protection of the Tribunals and Inquiries Act 1958, already cited in the same context.[1]

Mandamus must be sought by the special 'prerogative' procedure which is incompatible with that for seeking ordinary remedies.[2] But since ordinary remedies are little used in this field, this procedural peculiarity is not so important as it is in the field of certiorari and prohibition.

The Crown and its servants

Finally we come to the Crown. It will be obvious from what has been said about the prerogative remedies that, since they emanate from the Crown, they cannot lie against the Crown.

That there can be no mandamus to the Sovereign, there can be no doubt, both because there would be an incongruity in the Queen commanding herself to do an act, and also because disobedience to the writ of mandamus is to be enforced by attachment.[3]

This does not matter with certiorari and prohibition, since they lie to control inferior jurisdictions, and extend to ministers of the Crown and other public authorities wielding statutory powers. But it is serious in the case of mandamus, since the Crown itself has public duties. How is their performance to be enforced?

There is a clear legal distinction as to the duties of Crown servants. Where the Crown servant is merely the instrument selected by the Crown for the discharge of the Crown's duty, any complaint of default must be made against the Crown and not against the servant. No mandamus can then lie. For example, an army officer disputed the terms of his retiring pay and compensation, which had to be determined under the terms of a royal warrant (a prerogative instrument making regulations as to terms of service in the army), and sought a mandamus against the Secretary of State for War in order to enforce what he thought were his rights under the royal warrant. In fact the royal warrant imposed no legal obligation on the Crown. But even if it did, the action could not succeed, since the Secretary of State was merely one of the Crown's servants

---

[1] Above, p. 154.
[2] See above, p. 140.
[3] *The Queen v. Powell* (1841) 1 Q.B. 352 at 361.

who owed no legal duty as such to any individual affected by
the warrant.[1] Similarly no mandamus will issue to the Treasury
to pay moneys appropriated by Parliament for a given purpose,
since the money is granted to the Crown and even though it is
in the hands of the Treasury, they are merely the instrument of
the Crown for handling the money.[2]

On the other hand, where Parliament has imposed a duty on
particular persons acting in some particular capacity, mandamus will issue notwithstanding that those persons are servants
of the Crown and acting on the Crown's behalf. This is because
the legal duty is cast upon them personally, and no orders given
to them by the Crown will be any defence. If therefore the Act
requires 'the Minister' to do something, mandamus will lie to
compel the Minister to act.[3] Similarly mandamus was granted
against the Special Commissioners of Income Tax, acting as
servants of the Crown, commanding them to authorise repayment to a taxpayer where the Act said that 'the ... Commissioners shall issue an order for the repayment, &c.'[4]. This
rule is all the more valuable because the Crown Proceedings
Act 1947 prevents the use of a mandatory injunction.[5]

Nevertheless, it should make no difference in principle
whether the duty is cast upon the Crown as such, or upon some
government department or other agency of the Crown. It is a
pity that this untidy situation was left unaltered by the Crown
Proceedings Act 1947. The Act did, indeed, provide that no
right to mandamus should be lost merely because the Act
had now created additional remedies.[6] But it did nothing to empower the courts to declare the Crown liable to perform some
duty.

It is possible that the court itself will fill this lacuna by exercising its ordinary jurisdiction to grant declaratory relief. For
it is established that this jurisdiction is effective against the
Crown.[7] But there seems to be no case in which it has been
used to declare the Crown to be subject to a duty.

---

[1] *The Queen v. Secretary of State for War* [1891] 2 Q.B. 326.
[2] *The Queen v. Lords Commissioners of the Treasury* (1872) L.R. 7 Q.B. 387.
[3] *Padfield v. Minister of Agriculture* [1968] A.C. 997.
[4] *The Queen v. Special Commissioners of Income Tax* (1888) 21 Q.B.D. 313.
[5] See above, p. 115.
[6] S. 40 (5).
[7] See above, p. 121.

Mandamus may be used *by* the Crown or a government department, for example for compelling a local authority to levy a rate to finance a payment due to the Treasury.[1]

COMPENSATION FOR PROPERTY TAKEN OR AFFECTED

Although the right to compensation is not itself a remedy of the kind discussed in this chapter, something may be said here of the position of owners of property which is taken under or adversely affected by legislation.

The presumption of a right to compensation

There is an established presumption that 'an intention to take away the property of a subject without giving him a legal right to compensation for the loss of it is not to be imputed to the Legislature unless that intention is expressed in unequivocal terms'.[2] On this ground the House of Lords invalidated a government scheme for assessing compensation on an *ex gratia* basis for property taken under war-time regulations, holding that there was a legal right to have compensation assessed in the ordinary way under the Lands Clauses Act 1845.[3] For the same reason the Privy Council held that an Australian statute vesting Melbourne Harbour in commissioners did not override private rights which had been acquired over part of the land.[4] But there is no restriction, as there is in the constitutions of some countries,[5] on the power of Parliament to provide for expropriation without compensation. The Leasehold Reform Act 1967 provided no compensation for the expropriated owners of freehold interests in houses let on long leases. The War Damage Act 1965 was enacted for the express purpose of

---

[1] *The Queen v. Maidenhead Corporation* (1882) 9 Q.B.D. 494.
[2] *Central Control Board v. Cannon Brewery Co. Ltd.* [1919] A.C. 744 (Lord Atkinson).
[3] *Ibid.*
[4] *Colonial Sugar Refining Co. Ltd. v. Melbourne Harbour Trust Commissioners* [1927] A.C. 343. See also *Hartnell v. Minister of Housing and Local Government* [1965] A.C. 1134.
[5] E.g. United States (fifth amendment, also fourteenth amendment as interpreted); Federal Republic of Germany (art. 14). Both constitutions confine the power to public purposes. The Leasehold Reform Act 1967 expropriated one class of owner for the benefit of another.

depriving a successful litigant of compensation awarded by the House of Lords for the destruction of property in wartime.[1] The planning legislation is in effect an extensive system of expropriation without compensation, since no compensation is normally payable where permission to develop land is refused, even though the land is thereby greatly reduced in value.

Compulsory purchase

When land is taken under a compulsory purchase order, compensation is payable in accordance with the Land Compensation Act 1961. The order must first be confirmed by a minister, and before that it must be advertised and served on every owner, lessee and occupier. Any such person who objects has a statutory right to a hearing, which often takes the form of a public inquiry.[2] If the order is confirmed, the acquiring authority must within three years serve a 'notice to treat', which sets in motion the machinery for assessing compensation. Any dispute over compensation is decided by the Lands Tribunal, from which appeal lies direct to the Court of Appeal. The basis of compensation is open market value, except in certain special cases.[3] This used to be assessed as at the date of the notice to treat, but the unfairness of this rule when there has been delay and a fall in the value of money has led the House of Lords to hold that the correct time is when the compensation is assessed or when possession is taken.[4]

In many cases it is impossible to assess the open market value without knowing what development might be permitted by the planning authorities. The Act of 1961 therefore lays down rules as to the assumptions to be made, and in certain cases allows either party to apply to the local planning authority (with a right of appeal to the minister) for a certificate of 'appropriate alternative development' specifying what planning permission might reasonably have been expected to be

---

[1] In *Burmah Oil Co. Ltd. v. Lord Advocate* [1965] A.C. 75.
[2] Acquisition of Land (Authorisation Procedure) Act 1946, 1st Sched.
[3] Land Compensation Act 1961, s. 5.
[4] *West Midland Baptist Association v. Birmingham Corpn.* [1970] A.C. 874.

granted. But this does not prevent it being assumed that additional permission would be granted where this could reasonably be expected in the particular case.[1]

The owner is also entitled to compensation for 'injurious affection' of his remaining land, if its value is impaired by severance or by the use made of the land taken from him.[2] If part of his land is taken for a motorway, for example, he may claim compensation for any fall in the value of his adjacent land caused by the noise and disturbance of traffic, but only in so far as it proceeds from the land actually taken from him.[3]

Uncompensated injury

No statutory compensation is in general payable to an owner from whom no land is taken, however injuriously affected his property may be. In some cases he may have a remedy for nuisance at common law; but, as explained elsewhere, this is of no avail against lawful exercise of statutory power.[4] In particular it is of no avail in the case of roads, owing to the unrealistic rule that ordinary user of the highway is not a nuisance,[5] and it is of no avail in the case of aircraft, because they are exempted by legislation.[6] There is therefore an artificial contrast between those from whom some land is taken, who receive compensation, and those from who nothing is taken but who are equally injured and who may suffer heavy uncompensated loss. This situation is a strong inducement to many people to resist projects for roads, airports and other public works by every possible means, and it leads to many lengthy public inquiries into objections. Parliament has enacted elaborate legislation to ensure that increased land values created by the community should be taxed for the benefit of the community.[7] But it does not seem to be concerned with the converse case, in which injury inflicted for the benefit of the

---

[1] Ss. 14–20.
[2] Compulsory Purchase Act 1965, ss. 7, 10.
[3] See *Edwards v. Minister of Transport* [1964] 2 Q.B. 134.
[4] Above, p. 60.
[5] *Hammersmith Rly. Co. v. Brand* (1869), I.R. 4 H.L. 171 at 196.
[6] Civil Aviation Act 1949, ss. 40, 41.
[7] Land Commission Act 1967, Pt III (cf. Town and Country Planning Act 1947, Pt VII, repealed in 1953).

community has to be borne by those upon whom it happens to fall. French administrative law has at least made some progress in awarding compensation to individuals who suffer exceptional injury for the general benefit.[1]

---

[1] E.g. C.E. 14 janv. 1938, *Société Anonyme 'La Fleurette'*; C.E. 25 janv. 1963, *Ministre de l'Intérieur c. Bovero*; C.E. 22 févr. 1963, *Commune de Gavarnie*.

5

NATURAL JUSTICE

Procedural standards

THIS and the two following chapters are concerned with administrative procedure. Should the procedure followed by an administrative authority affect the legality of its actions? It is reasonably obvious that the law should intervene against unlawful action. It is less obvious that it should attempt to impose a particular technique of administration on government departments, local authorities and so on. Yet the law undertakes to do this in certain respects, and in doing so it makes one of its most notable contributions to the art of government. For however wide the powers of the state, and however wide the discretion they confer, it is always possible to require them to be exercised in a fair manner; and if exercised fairly, they will be exercised more efficiently. Justice and efficiency go hand in hand.

Procedure is not a matter of secondary importance. It is only by procedural fairness that drastic governmental powers are rendered tolerable. A judge of the United States Supreme Court has said: 'Procedural fairness and regularity are of the indispensable essence of liberty. Severe substantive laws can be endured if they are fairly and impartially applied.'[1] He went on to say that it might be preferable to live under Russian law applied by common-law procedures than under the common law enforced by Russian procedures. One of his colleagues said: 'The history of liberty has largely been the history of the observance of procedural safeguards.'[2] How English judges have devised procedural safeguards will be seen in this chapter. They are one of the most essential elements in the rule of law.

---

[1] *Shaughnessy v. United States*, 345 U.S. 206 (1953) (Jackson J.).
[2] *McNabb v. United States*, 318 U.S. 332 (1943) (Frankfurter J.).

Administrative justice and natural justice

'Natural justice' is the name given to certain fundamental rules which are necessary to the proper exercise of every kind of power. In English law it covers two rules: first, that a man may not be judge in his own cause; and secondly, that a man may not be condemned unheard. These rules can be taken for granted in the administration of justice in courts of law. They should equally apply to the decisions of statutory tribunals. Finally, they should apply to all administrative acts in so far as the nature of the case admits. For all power ought to be exercised fairly, both in appearance and reality. It is the universality of this ideal of justice which leads to its being called 'natural'.

There are both broad and narrow aspects to consider. The narrow aspect is that the rules of natural justice are merely a branch of the principle of *ultra vires*, and should really find their home in Chapter 3. Violation of natural justice is then to be classified as one of the varieties of wrong procedure, or abuse of power, which violate the implied conditions which Parliament is taken to have intended to impose. Just as a power to act 'as it thinks fit' does not allow a public authority to act unreasonably or in bad faith, so it does not allow disregard of the elementary doctrines of fair procedure. As Lord Selborne once said[1]:

> There would be no decision within the meaning of the statute if there were anything of that sort done contrary to the essence of justice.

Thus violation of natural justice makes the decision void, as in any other case of *ultra vires*.[2]

But in its wider aspect the subject contains the very kernel of the problem of administrative justice: how far ought both judicial and administrative power to rest on common principles? How far is it right for the courts of law to try to impart their own standards of justice to the administration? When

---

[1] *Spackman v. Plumstead District Board of Works* (1885) 10 App. Cas. 229. In *General Medical Council v. Spackman* [1943] A.C. 627 at 640 the distinction between *ultra vires* and natural justice is based on a narrower sense of *ultra vires*.

[2] *Ridge v. Baldwin* [1964] A.C. 40; *Hoggard v. Worsbrough U.D.C.* [1962] 2 Q.B. 93. On this point see pp. 185, 204, below.

special powers to take action or to decide disputes are vested in administrative bodies with the very object of avoiding the forms of legal process, is there yet a residuum of legal procedure which ought never to be shaken off? The judges have long been conscious of this problem, and it has prompted them to some of their most notable achievements in judicial control. Rules of common law, which became in effect presumptions to be used in the interpretation of statutes, developed and refined the rules of natural justice over a period of centuries.[1] From time to time difficult questions arose about the precise content of the rules, but their general applicability to governmental action was never doubted. After the Second World War there was a setback, and the whole subject threatened to become unsettled, in a manner which is all too characteristic of our case-law. This was closely connected with the parallel confusion over the remedy of certiorari.

For the future of administrative justice it is of great importance that these rules should be settled clearly. They form, so to speak, the bridgehead which the legal ideals of justice and fair play have secured in the territory of administration. What is needed is to secure this position by firm rules of law, and to use it as a base for further exploration. The right of a person to be given a fair hearing, before he suffers in some way under the official rod, is a vital principle which, if only the judges themselves apply it consistently, will both protect the citizen's interests and improve the quality of administration. Just as the broad constitutional guarantee of 'due process of law' has proved of such importance in the United States for the imposition of a general standard of justice, so in England the concept of natural justice should provide the legal foundation on which administrative procedure should rest.

Natural justice in the common law

The rules as they now exist can be traced back to medieval precedents, and, indeed, they were not unknown in the ancient world. In their medieval guise they were regarded as part of the immutable order of things, so that in theory even the power of the legislature could not alter them. This theory lingered into

---

[1] The only mention of natural justice in a statute appears to be Foreign Compensation Act 1969, s. 3 (10) (see above, p. 152).

the seventeenth and faintly even into the eighteenth century, though by then it was incompatible with the modern theory of parliamentary sovereignty which was supplanting the old ideas. It reached its high-water mark in *Dr. Bonham's* case (1610), where Chief Justice Coke went so far as to say that the court could declare an Act of Parliament void if it made a man judge in his own cause, or was otherwise 'against common right and reason'.[1] This was one of his grounds for disallowing the claim of the College of Physicians to fine and imprison Dr. Bonham, a doctor of physic of Cambridge University, for practising in the City of London without the licence of the College of Physicians. The statute under which the College acted provided that fines should go half to the king and half to the College, so that the College had a financial interest in its own judgment and was judge in its own cause.

No modern judge could repeat this exploit, for to hold an Act of Parliament void is to blaspheme against the doctrine of parliamentary sovereignty. As we shall see, there are plenty of cases under modern statutes where authorities are in a sense (sometimes even a financial sense)[2] judges in their own affairs. Coke's opinion was by no means clear law even to his contemporaries, although it was approved by another great judge, Chief Justice Holt, in 1701. Holt said that it was 'far from any extravagancy, for it is a very reasonable and true saying, that if an Act of Parliament should ordain that the same person should be party and Judge . . . it would be a void Act of Parliament.'[3] He also said that an Act of Parliament could not make adultery lawful, though it could legalize divorce and remarriage. Natural justice, natural law, the law of God and 'common right and reason' were all aspects of the old concept of fundamental and eternal law. They no longer represent any kind of limit to the power of statute. Natural justice has had to look for a new foothold, and has found it as a mode not of destroying enacted law but of fulfilling it. Its basis now is in the rules of interpretation. The courts may presume that Parliament, when it grants powers, intends them to be exercised in a right and proper way. Since Parliament is very unlikely to make provision to

[1] 8 Co. Rep. 113*b* at 118*a*.
[2] See *Wilkinson v. Barking Corporation*, below, p. 180.
[3] *City of London v. Wood* (1701) 12 Mod. 669.

the contrary, this allows considerable scope for the courts to devise a set of canons of fair administrative procedure, suitable to the needs of the time.

The courts also apply similar doctrines in the private sphere, in the interpretation of contracts. Members of trade unions or of clubs, for example, cannot normally be expelled without being given a hearing, for their contracts will be construed as including a duty to act fairly.[1] The same may apply to members of universities, including students.[2] Natural justice is by no means confined to powers of public authorities, though the latter are what matter in administrative law.

Where an administrative act or decision is vitiated by a breach of natural justice, the court may award any appropriate remedies. Frequently the remedy will be certiorari to quash. But actions for declarations are sometimes successful,[3] and so occasionally are actions for damages.[4]

The two main rules which the courts have laid down will be discussed in their traditional order: first, the rule against bias; and secondly, the rule which gives the right to a hearing. It is, however, the second of these rules which has the greater scope in the sphere of administrative action, and which is the subject of the more difficult case-law.

THE RULE AGAINST BIAS

'No man a judge in his own cause'

A judge is disqualified from hearing any case in which he has a pecuniary interest, or any other interest likely to be a real cause of bias. The classic example from the regular courts of law is that of Lord Chancellor Cottenham in 1852, who in a Chancery suit had made a number of decrees in favour of a canal company in which he was a shareholder to the extent of several thousand pounds. His decrees were set aside by the House of Lords on account of his pecuniary interest.[5] It was not shown that his

---

[1] See *Russell v. Duke of Norfolk* [1949] 1 All E.R. 109; *Abbott v. Sullivan*, [1952] 1 Q.B. 189 (below, p. 201); *Lee v. Showmen's Guild of Great Britain* [1952] 2 Q.B. 329; *Lawlor v. Union of Post Office Workers* [1965] Ch. 712.

[2] See Appendix, C.

[3] See below, pp. 179, 201.

[4] See below, p. 188.

[5] *Dimes v. Grand Junction Canal* (1852) 3 H.L.C. 759.

judgment was in any way affected by his shares; in fact it was clearly not affected at all, for Lord Campbell said:

No one can suppose that Lord Cottenham could be, in the remotest degree, influenced by the interest that he had in this concern; but, my Lords, it is of the last importance that the maxim, that no man is to be a judge in his own cause, should be held sacred. . . . And it will have a most salutary influence on [inferior] tribunals when it is known that this high Court of last resort, in a case in which the Lord Chancellor of England had an interest, considered that his decree was on that account a decree not according to law, and was set aside. This will be a lesson to all inferior tribunals to take care not only that in their decrees they are not influenced by their personal interest, but to avoid the appearance of labouring under such an influence.

As an example of bias of a non-pecuniary kind we may take the case of the solicitor whose firm were acting for a client in a claim against him for damages caused in a road accident. The solicitor was also acting clerk to the local justices before whom the client was convicted of dangerous driving, and he retired with them when they were considering their decision. The fact that the convicted man was his firm's client was held to invalidate the conviction, even though it was proved that the justices did not in fact consult their clerk, and that he made no reference to the other case.[1] For this is a matter where appearance is almost as important as reality. 'Justice should not only be done, but should manifestly and undoubtedly be seen to be done.' Nevertheless, a line has to be drawn between genuine and fanciful cases. Where, for instance, a county council had prosecuted a trader under the Food and Drugs Act, it was held no objection that the justices' clerk was a member of the council, upon proof that he was not a member of the council's Health Committee, which had in fact directed the prosecution.[2] The Court of Appeal protested against the tendency to impeach judicial decisions 'upon the flimsiest pretexts of bias', and against 'the erroneous impression that it is more important that justice should appear to be done than that it should in fact be done'.

These are examples of the rule against bias as applied to the

---

[1] R. v. Sussex Justices [1924] 1 K.B. 256.
[2] R. v. Camborne Justices [1955] 1 Q.B. 41.

ordinary courts of law. But the question before us is how far
the same rule can be applied to administrative decisions. The
answer depends on whether the statutory power is entrusted
to persons in the singular or in the plural, and whether the bias
is personal or collective.

Collective authorities

Where powers are vested in collective bodies such as committees or councils, and there is some latitude in their membership, it is easy to apply the rule in much the same way as in
courts of law. Justices of the peace, for instance, have important
administrative functions in liquor licensing which can be made
subject to the rule against bias just as easily as can their judicial functions, for it is not necessary for any particular justice to
sit at any one time. Thus in one case the licensing justices of
Bath referred an application for renewal of a liquor licence to
another body of justices called the Compensation Authority,
and took steps to oppose the renewal at the hearing before the
Compensation Authority. But three of the licensing justices
were also members of the Compensation Authority and took
part in the decision to refuse the renewal. The House of Lords
held that this invalidated the decision, for the fundamental rule
that persons who had taken part in a dispute were disqualified
from judging it applied, in the Lord Chancellor's words, 'not
only in the case of Courts of justice and other judicial tribunals,
but in the case of authorities which, though in no sense to be
called Courts, have to act as judges of the rights of others'.[1]
Here again there is, of course, a limit to the doctrine, and it is
confined to cases where the bias is likely to be a real one. The
court refused, accordingly, to interfere with a justices' order
allowing the Bradford Corporation to appropriate certain
streams for its waterworks merely because two of the justices
were trustees of funds which had invested money in the Corporation's bonds, which might conceivably be better secured by any
improvement of the Corporation's assets.[2]

Disqualifying interests

The rule at common law is that any direct pecuniary interest,

---

[1] *Frome United Breweries Co. v. Bath Justices* [1926] A.C. 586. See above, pp. 135, 137.
[2] *R. v. Rand* (1866) L.R. 1 Q.B. 230.

however small, disqualifies the adjudicator, while personal
interest of any other kind must be such as to raise a real likelihood of bias. A justice of the peace is not disqualified, merely
because he subscribes to a society for preventing cruelty to
animals, from hearing a prosecution instituted by the society.[1]
Nor is a member of a disciplinary body disqualified merely by
membership of a professional 'defence union' which institutes
disciplinary proceedings.[2] In liquor licensing there are special
statutory provisions against justices acting in cases where they
have an interest in the profits of the premises; but it is also
provided that their acts shall not be invalid merely because of
that disqualification.[3] By a subtle construction the courts confine this last provision to what they call 'the technical disqualification created by the Act', and will nevertheless set aside
any order where a real likelihood of bias is shown.[4] Their attitude, if a little difficult to explain by pure reason, shows a
laudable reluctance to interpret a statute as making a serious
inroad on the rules of natural justice. For if the protecting
clause were allowed its full meaning, people's rights would be
legally settled by judges who by fundamental doctrine are incompetent to act. In a modern case where a spirits licence was
granted to a co-operative society, the fact that six out of the
seven justices were members of the society and derived small
dividends from it was held to be a mere technical disqualification under the Act, and thus within the protecting clause, since
there was no evidence of real bias.[5]

There are many kinds of administrative proceedings where a
decision can be attacked because disqualified people took part
in it. There is no way of defining them comprehensively except
to say that they include all cases where a decision affecting
some one's legal rights is taken by persons who (a) can be dispensed with, and (b) are not (or may appear not to be) impartial. Two well-known examples may be added to those already
given. In one, a police sergeant had been dismissed by the
Chief Constable of Liverpool, and his appeal against dismissal

---

[1] R. v. Justices of Deal (1881) 45 L.T. 439.
[2] Leeson v. General Medical Council (1889) 43 Ch. D. 366; Allinson v. G.M.C.,
[1894] 1 Q.B. 750.
[3] Licensing Act 1953 s. 48, replacing earlier legislation.
[4] R. v. Tempest (1902) 86 L.T. 585.
[5] R. v. Barnsley Licensing Justices [1960] 2 Q.B. 167.

was rejected by the Watch Committee. But the Chief Constable himself was present with the Watch Committee when they decided the appeal. In fact, as it was held, the police sergeant had succeeded in resigning before the purported dismissal, so that it had no legal effect, and did not prejudice his right to recover his pension contributions. But the court also granted a declaration that the presence of the Chief Constable, whose mind was made up in advance and who was in effect the respondent to the appeal, was fatal to the validity of the Watch Committee's decision.[1] Lord Justice Scott said:

The risk that a respondent may influence the court is so abhorrent to English notions of justice that the possibility of it or even the appearance of such a possibility is sufficient to deprive the decision of all judicial force, and to render it a nullity.

In the other case the court invalidated the decision of a Rural District Council to allow some property in Hendon to be converted into a garage and restaurant. Under the planning legislation the Council had power to permit this development and as matters then stood the owners of the property would have a right to compensation if their intentions were later frustrated by a planning scheme. One of the councillors, however, was the estate agent who was acting for the owners, and he was present at the meeting which approved the application. A neighbouring owner was granted certiorari to quash the permission on this ground, for it was held that the agent's interest in the business disqualified him from taking part in the Council's consideration of it, even though the evidence was that he took no active part.[2] Similarly the court quashed the decision of a rent assessment committee where it was shown that the chairman had been active in assisting proceedings by other tenants against the same landlord, even though it was not alleged that he was in fact influenced.

These cases show that the court is more concerned with appearance than with reality. The test is not whether there is a real likelihood of bias, but whether a reasonable man would suspect it.[3] 'Justice must be rooted in confidence.'[4]

[1] *Cooper v. Wilson* [1937] 2 K.B. 309.
[2] *R. v. Hendon Rural District Council* [1933] 2 K.B. 606 (see above, p. 139).
[3] *Metropolitan Properties Ltd. v. Lannon* [1969] 1 Q.B. 577. But the 'real likelihood' test is important in liquor licensing cases, as explained above.
[4] *Ibid.* (Lord Denning M.R.).

All these were cases concerning justices, councils, or committees. On all those bodies there are enough members to allow any
disqualified member to be dispensed with, and the presence
of a single disqualified member is fatal.

Indivisible authorities

Where statute empowers a minister or an official to act, he
will often be the one and only person who can do so. There is
no way of escaping responsibility if he is personally interested.
Transfer of responsibility is, indeed, a recognized type of *ultra
vires*.[1] Accordingly, it is generally supposed that the minister
(say) must act as best he can even in a case where, for example,
he himself owns property which will be benefited if he approves
a development plan. It is not possible to give an example from
a modern decided case of private and personal interest on the
minister's part which would be comparable to the case of Lord
Cottenham in the judicial sphere.[2] But a case involving public
funds can be cited, where a local authority and the minister
were given power to decide the pension rights of employees.
The Local Government Superannuation Act gave employees
of local authorities statutory rights to pensions under certain
conditions, but provided that any question concerning these
rights should be decided first by the local authority, and then in
case of dispute by the minister, whose decision on questions of
fact was to be final. The Court of Appeal held that there was
no escape from these clear provisions.[3] Lord Justice Scott, whose
concern for administrative justice used sometimes to enliven
the law reports with strong language, said of the Act:

. . . its first provision is to subject the duty to pay to the jurisdiction, not of a court, not of a lay tribunal, not even of an impartial
third party, but of the debtor himself! That . . . almost converts
its right into a mere discretionary privilege. At any rate the local
authority is made, purely and simply, a 'judge in its own cause'. It is
true that a so-called appeal is allowed to the aggrieved employee

---

[1] Above, p. 62.
[2] Above, p. 175.
[3] *Wilkinson v. Barking Corporation* [1948] 1 K.B. 721.

from the decision of that far from impartial judge, but to what court? To the Minister!

And he added, speaking of questions of fact such as loss of pension on the ground of fraud or misconduct:

> Such an issue involves a question of character on which a wrong decision may ruin a man for life. . . . This state of affairs is not consonant with British justice or the rule of law on which British democracy depends for its very existence.

But no change was made when a new Local Government Superannuation Act was enacted in 1953.[1] There could hardly be a better example to show how remote from the modern world are the ideas expressed in *Dr. Bonham's* case.[2]

The same point also made an appearance in the famous case concerning Lord Cottenham, already recounted.[3] Before the appeal from the Vice-Chancellor to the Lord Chancellor could be taken, the Lord Chancellor had to sign an order for enrolment. But it was held that his shareholding in the company, which disqualified him from hearing the appeal, did not disqualify him from ordering the enrolment, since he was the only person with power to do so. 'For this is a case of necessity, and where that occurs the objection of interest cannot prevail.' Similarly the Privy Council held that there could be no legal objection on the score of bias to an order of the New Zealand Dairy Board which allocated areas of supply among various companies, even though the Board had made large loans to one of the companies and so had an interest in its prosperity.[4] For both these functions had been given to the Board by statute.

Another case where bias cannot be helped is where an authority makes a void decision, perhaps by failing to give a fair hearing, and then has to reconsider the case in order to decide it validly. This is explained below.[5]

Departmental bias

Administrative cases raise, in particular, the problem of what

---

[1] See s. 21. Another example is a minister's power to make an order for costs in his own favour: below, p. 243.
[2] Above, p. 174.   [3] Above, p. 175.
[4] *Jeffs v. New Zealand Dairy Board* [1967] 1 A.C. 551.
[5] P. 214.

may be called 'departmental bias'. Ministers and their departments are committed to their own policies, which inevitably
they tend to favour. This makes them unsatisfactory judges in
judicial cases, where policy ought to be eliminated. It does not,
of course, disqualify them for administrative decisions which
are intended to be based on policy. As regards judicial cases,
we have already noticed the comments of the Court of Appeal
in the case where a local authority and the minister were made
judges of the pension rights of the local authority's employees.
The Ministers' Powers Committee considered the subject generally in their report of 1932, and recommended that judicial
decisions should be entrusted to independent tribunals. They
painted a pathetic picture of a minister's dilemma in situations
where his impartiality would be in inverse ratio to his efficiency:

> An easy-going and cynical Minister, rather bored with his office
> and sceptical of the value of his Department, would find it far easier
> to apply a judicial mind to purely judicial problems connected with
> the Department's administration than a Minister whose head and
> heart were in his work. . . . Parliament should be chary of impos-
> ing on Ministers the ungrateful task of giving judicial decisions in
> matters in which their very zeal for the public service can scarcely
> fail to bias them unconsciously.[1]

As a general rule it may be said that Parliament does observe
this principle. It is, indeed, the observance of it that has led to
the great growth of administrative tribunals in this century.
They have in turn brought their own problems, as we shall see,[2]
and one of the regular complaints about some of them is that
they appear to the public to bear a taint of 'departmental bias',
perhaps because the clerk is an official of the ministry, or because they sit in ministry premises, or because their proceedings
are not wholly free from the tinge of policy. It was to this second
generation of grievances that the Franks Committee addressed
themselves in their Report of 1957, of which more will be said
in due course.

The Stevenage case

A case of great interest and some difficulty was that of the
new town at Stevenage, where the contest revolved round alle-

---

[1] Cmd. 4060 (1932) p. 78.
[2] See below, Chapter 7.

gations of ministerial bias.[1] The Minister of Town and Country Planning had determined that Stevenage should be the first of the new towns under the New Towns Act 1946. Local people at Stevenage objected, and they were fully heard at a public local inquiry conducted by an inspector of the Ministry. The inspector duly sent in his report to the Minister, and the Minister, after considering the report (as the Act required him to do), confirmed the order designating the new town. But before this procedure was set in train the Minister had visited Stevenage and made a speech at a public meeting. There was heckling and jeering, and there were cries of 'dictator' and 'gestapo'. But the Minister firmly stated his policy, and according to the report he said 'It is no good your jeering: it is going to be done— (applause and boos).' The objectors maintained that by this positive statement of policy the Minister had in effect declared that his mind was made up in advance. He had precluded himself, they said, from 'considering' the subsequent report of the inspector fairly and without bias. This is precisely the problem of 'departmental bias'. Three courts succeeded in reaching three different conclusions, showing all possible variations both on the law and on the facts. The High Court held that the law required impartial consideration, and that in fact it had not been given. The Court of Appeal held that the law required impartial consideration, but that it had been given. It was left for the House of Lords to hold that the law did not require impartial consideration at all: the Minister could be as biased as he liked, provided that he observed the procedure laid down by the Act.

On the facts of the case, there seems much to be said for the middle road followed by the Court of Appeal. It is a virtue in a minister to have a policy and to advocate it. He also has to face opposition and to make public speeches. If, when he does so, he lets fall a defiant remark, that is by no means inconsistent with an ability to consider, or reconsider, the whole project when later the inspector's report arrives. The law must allow for the departmental bias which he is expected and indeed required to have. Even if the objectors had succeeded in invalidating the order, the Minister could have made a fresh one to the same effect.

[1] *Franklin v. Minister of Town and Country Planning* [1948] A.C. 87.

The decision of the House of Lords would also be easy to understand if it were merely that the Minister had, in fact, observed both the letter and the spirit of the Act. But Lord Thankerton, who delivered the only reasoned speech, used language which threw doubt on the applicability of the rule against bias to any kind of administrative case. He said:

> In my opinion, no judicial, or quasi-judicial, duty was imposed on the respondent [the Minister], and any reference to judicial duty, or bias, is irrelevant in the present case. The respondent's duties under s. 1 of the Act and Schedule I thereto are, in my opinion, purely administrative. . . . I am of opinion that no judicial duty is laid on the respondent in discharge of these statutory duties, and that the only question is whether he has complied with the statutory directions to appoint a person to hold the public inquiry, and to consider that person's report.

Lord Thankerton here treats 'judicial duty' and statutory functions as two mutually exclusive things. But there were many cases then in the law reports in which it had been held that a minister considering the report of a public inquiry had a quasi-judicial duty, meaning that although his decision was a purely administrative act, he was bound by the rules of natural justice so far as they could reasonably apply to the case.[1] But no reference was made to these cases. Lord Thankerton went on to say:

> My Lords, I could wish that the use of the word 'bias' should be confined to its proper sphere. Its proper significance, in my opinion, is to denote a departure from the standard of even-handed justice which the law requires from those who occupy judicial office, or those who are commonly regarded as holding a quasi-judicial office, such as an arbitrator.

But a quasi-judicial act is nothing if not an act based on policy, the act of an administrator. An arbitrator, on the other hand, is a kind of private judge appointed by agreement or under statute. No questions of policy enter into his decisions. The typical case of an office 'commonly regarded' as quasi-judicial, and supported by many authorities including previous decisions of the House of Lords, is that of a minister proposing to make or confirm an order subject to the hearing of objections.[2]

---

[1] See below, p. 194.   [2] See below, p. 190.

This case, therefore, endangered the 'basic English' of administrative law. It did, indeed, mark the beginning of the period when the meaning of 'judicial' functions was misunderstood, as already explained in connexion with remedies, and as explained further below.[1] This was more than a mere matter of words: the danger was that the rules of natural justice and the remedies of certiorari and prohibition would cease to apply to administrative acts, and that wide fields of judicial control would be surrendered.

Void or voidable?

In the case of Lord Cottenham's judgment, with which this discussion started, the judges advised the House of Lords that Lord Cottenham's disqualifying interest made his judgment not void but voidable. This has sometimes been repeated as if it was true of all cases involving bias.[2] But in that case the remedy was by way of appeal from one of the superior courts of law, and the court's decision would naturally be valid unless and until reversed on appeal. That is to say, it would be voidable as opposed to being void from the beginning.[3]

But where the case is one of review as opposed to appeal, the basis of the court's jurisdiction to intervene is that the administrative decision is unauthorised by law, i.e. of no legal effect whatever and so void.[4] There is no valid analogy with an appeal from a court of law. Judgments dealing with administrative decisions therefore proceed on the footing that the presence of bias means that the tribunal is improperly constituted, so that it is without jurisdiction and its decision is void.[5] This fits correctly into the framework of the *ultra vires* principle, whereas the notion of a voidable decision does not.

---

[1] Above, p. 135; below, p. 199.

[2] See de Smith, Judicial Review of Administrative Action, 2nd ed., 260; Rubinstein, Jurisdiction and Illegality, 203.

[3] *McPherson v. McPherson* [1936] A.C. 177.

[4] *Ridge v. Baldwin* [1964] A.C. 40. For fuller discussion see 84 L.Q.R. at p. 104.

[5] *R. v. Cheltenham Commissioners* (1841) 1 Q.B. 467 (decision 'invalid'); *Allison v. General Medical Council* [1894] 1 Q.B. 750 ('wholly void'); *R. v. Nat Bell Liquors Ltd.* [1922] 2 A.C. 128 at 160 ('without jurisdiction'); *R. v. Paddington and St. Marylebone Rent Tribunal* [1947] 1 All E.R. 448 and also [1956] 1 Q.B. 229 ('no jurisdiction'); *Cooper v. Wilson,* quoted above, p. 179 ('a nullity'). The Privy Council has held bias to render a trial *coram non judice* and the judgment a nullity: *Vassiliades v. Vassiliades* [1945] All I.R. 38. And see *Oscroft v. Benabo* [1967] 1 W.L.R. 1087 at 1100; *Anisminic Ltd. v. F.C.C.* [1969] 2 A.C. 147 at 171.

There are three further persuasive arguments. First, the courts have in several 'bias' cases awarded remedies which are inexplicable except on the assumption that the decision is void: in one case a declaration,[1] and in another a mandamus unaccompanied by certiorari.[2] Secondly, it is established that failure to give a fair hearing makes an administrative decision void, not voidable, and the two rules of natural justice should operate similarly.[3] Thirdly, it has never been allowable to call evidence in addition to the record except to prove lack of jurisdiction[4]—and such evidence must obviously be called to prove the bias alleged.[5]

A suggestion that unlawful administrative action may be valid until condemned by the court has appeared in some recent decisions, but seems to be based on no authority, and is criticised elsewhere.[6]

THE RIGHT TO A HEARING

'Hear the other side'

The other fundamental rule of natural justice is that a man has a right to be heard: *audi alteram partem*. This rule embraces the whole notion of fair procedure, or due process, and is capable of great elaboration in detail. Granted that a party must always be heard, ought he to have an oral hearing? Has he the right to bring witnesses and to cross-examine the other side? Ought he to have notice of the other side's case? Furthermore, unlike the rule against bias, the rule requiring a hearing is of almost universal validity. It can be transplanted without incompatibility from its native judicial soil into any part of the territory of administration. Its only limits are those which the courts themselves, and occasionally Parliament, decide to set. Here, therefore, is a fruitful source for principles of administrative justice.

An ancient rule

According to one picturesque decision, the rule first made its

---

[1] *Cooper v. Wilson* (above). See above, p. 123, for explanation.
[2] *R. v. L.C.C.* [1892] 1 Q.B. 190. For the implications of this see above, p. 163.
[3] See below, p. 204.
[4] Rubinstein, Jurisdiction and Illegality, 78; above, p. 94.
[5] See [1922] 2 A.C. at 160 (cited above, p. 185, note 5).
[6] Above, p. 104.

appearance in the Garden of Eden. When the University of
Cambridge deprived the recalcitrant Bentley of his degrees, he
was able to have the act declared a nullity because he had not
first been heard in his own defence; one of the judges observed
that even Adam had been called upon by God to meet the
charge of having eaten of the forbidden tree, before suffering
expulsion.[1] This is a nice example of the old manner of looking
on such rules as eternal truths, whereas today they are looked
on as presumptions, based on the principle of fairness, for the
construction of Acts of Parliament.[2]

As Bentley's case shows, the courts took their stand several
centuries ago on the broad principle that bodies entrusted with
legal power could not validly exercise it without first hearing
the person who was going to suffer. This principle was applied
very widely to administrative as well as to judicial acts, and to
the acts of individual ministers and officials as well as to the acts
of collective bodies such as justices and committees. The hypothesis on which the courts built up their jurisdiction was that
the duty to give every victim a fair hearing was just as much a
canon of good administration as of good legal procedure. If the
court cannot control administrative discretion within its proper
sphere, it can at least see that the discretion is not exercised
without consideration of both sides of the case. Nothing is more
likely to conduce to just and right decisions than the habit of
first giving a hearing to any affected party.

This duty to 'hear the other side' would seem to be so self-
evident that no trained professional, whether judge or administrator, could overlook it. But the perpetual stream of cases that
come before the courts throughout the British Commonwealth
shows that overlooking it is one of the most common legal
errors to which human nature is prone. Courts of law themselves overlook it from time to time, and there is no need to go
to old books for examples.[3] Still more so do administrators.

Some classic examples

Until quite recently English judges seized every opportunity

---

[1] *R. v. University of Cambridge* (1723) 1 Str. 557.
[2] As in *Ridge v. Baldwin* [1964] A.C. 40; *Wiseman v. Borneman* [1969] 3 W.L.R.
706.
[3] See *Abraham v. Jutsun* [1963] 1 W.L.R. 658; *Sheldon v. Bromfield Justices* [1964]
2 Q.B. 573.

to apply their doctrine uniformly. In particular, they applied it to all kinds of administrative acts. A leading example comes from a case of 1863. Under an Act of 1855 it was provided that no one might put up a building in London without giving seven days' notice to the local Board of Works. If any one did so, it was provided that the Board of Works might have the building demolished. A builder, nevertheless, began to build a house in Wandsworth without having given the requisite notice, and when his building had reached the second storey the Board of Works sent men late in the evening who demolished it. The Board did exactly what the Act said they might do in exactly the circumstances in which the Act said they might do it. And their action was, of course, purely administrative. Nevertheless, the builder brought a successful action for damages for the injury to his building, and won it merely on the ground that the Board had no power to act without first asking him what he had to say for himself.[1] Erle C.J. said:

I think the board ought to have given notice to the plaintiff and to have allowed him to be heard. The default in sending notice to the board of the intention to build, is a default which may be explained. There may be a great many excuses for the apparent default. The party may have intended to conform to the law. He may have actually conformed . . . though by accident his notice may have miscarried. . . . I cannot conceive any harm that could happen to the district board from hearing the party before they subjected him to a loss so serious as the demolition of his house; but I can conceive a great many advantages which might arise in the way of public order, in the way of doing substantial justice, and in the way of fulfilling the purposes of the statute, by the restriction which we put upon them, that they should hear the party before they inflict upon him such a heavy loss. I fully agree that the legislature intended to give the district board very large powers indeed: but the qualification I speak of is one which has been recognised to the full extent. It has been said that the principle . . . is limited to a judicial proceeding, and that a district board ordering a house to be pulled down cannot be said to be doing a judicial act. . . . I do not quite agree with that; . . . I think the appeal clause would evidently indicate that many exercises of the power of a district board would be in the nature of judicial proceedings.

---

[1] *Cooper v. Wandsworth Board of Works* (1863) 14 C.B. (N.S.) 180.

Two of the other judgments in this case are important. Willes J. said:

I am of the same opinion. I apprehend that a tribunal which is by law invested with power to affect the property of one of Her Majesty's subjects, is bound to give such subject an opportunity of being heard before it proceeds: and that the rule is of universal application, and founded on the plainest principles of justice. Now, is the board in the present case such a tribunal? I apprehend it clearly is. . . .

And Byles J. also said:

It seems to me that the board are wrong whether they acted judicially or ministerially. I conceive they acted judicially, because they had to determine the offence, and they had to apportion the punishment as well as the remedy. That being so, a long course of decisions, beginning with Dr. Bentley's case, and ending with some very recent cases, establish that, although there are no positive words in a statute, requiring that the party shall be heard, yet the justice of the common law will supply the omission of the legislature.

These judgments of a unanimous Court of Common Pleas reveal very plainly what the judges conceived their task to be. They were engaged in laying the foundation of a far-reaching system of administrative law by imposing the elements of fair procedure on administrative authorities generally. This was at the beginning of the era described by Dicey as 'The Period of Collectivism',[1] when Parliament had already begun to pour out the stream of regulatory legislation which has become more swollen with every subsequent year. But in his more legal writings Dicey paid little attention to the work of the judges in their efforts to keep control of this great tide.[2] If authors and critics had paid more heed to what the judges were achieving, later generations of lawyers might have been spared much trouble.

'Judicial' and 'quasi-judicial' acts

It will have been noticed that in the *Wandsworth* case the ominous word 'judicial' played, once more, a confusing part. The court justified its intervention on the ground that the act of the Board of Works was judicial, although really it was plainly administrative. In the *Smethwick* case of 1890, which was

[1] Dicey, *Law and Opinion in England*, chs. vii and viii.
[2] Above, p. 7.

almost exactly parallel with the *Wandsworth* case, and which followed it to the same result, Mr. Justice Wills said:

> In condemning a man to have his house pulled down, a judicial act is as much implied as in fining him £5; and as the local board is the only tribunal that can make such an order its act must be a judicial act, and the party to be affected should have a notice given him. . . . in the present case there is nothing in the Act of Parliament to limit the natural inference as to the nature of the act. [1]

In both cases the injured party's action was for damages for trespass, the board having entered and damaged the property unlawfully. All that he was doing was resisting an unlawful administrative invasion.

But the administrative function had to be miscalled 'judicial' for the supposed reason that it was only to judicial functions that the principles of natural justice applied. This is exactly the same fallacy that beset the remedies of certiorari and prohibition, and to which so much unprofitable discussion has already been devoted. [2] In the sphere of natural justice it was an equally meaningless and dangerous shibboleth. The argument goes round in a circle: natural justice must be observed where the function is judicial; and the function is called judicial where natural justice is required to be observed.

Subsequently the term 'quasi-judicial' came into vogue, and this at least was not quite so evident a misnomer as 'judicial'. It had the advantage of obscurity of meaning, so that by merely describing administrative functions as quasi-judicial the courts could continue their good work of applying the principles of natural justice widely. The term was much used in the housing cases, related below. It may also be illustrated from a case which arose in Oxford, where the city council demolished two walls which a housing company had built across roads on their land. The action was held illegal on the ground (amongst others) that the company had not been given an opportunity of endeavouring to dissuade the council from this drastic step. [3] The Master of the Rolls referred to 'that most salutary principle' which laid down

---

[1] *Hopkins v. Smethwick Local Board of Health* (1890) 24 Q.B.D. 713. See similarly *Smith v. The Queen* (1878) 3 App. Cas. 624.

[2] Above, p. 135.

[3] *Urban Housing Co. Ltd. v. Oxford City Council* [1940] Ch. 70.

that a local authority exercising such a power of demolition as this, in coming to its decision to demolish, is acting in a quasi-judicial capacity and must give the person concerned either a notice that they intend to take this matter into their consideration with a view to coming to a decision, or, if they have come to a decision, that they propose to act upon it, and give him an opportunity of showing cause why such steps should not be taken.

Although the term 'quasi-judicial' is in this context as meaningless as 'judicial', it is still in constant use, even since the House of Lords has explained away 'judicial'.[1]

The three-cornered cases

So far we have examined only cases where administrative power is exercised by a single public authority. But frequently there are several authorities involved, and the procedure is more formal. The typical situation is where the local authority has power to take the initiative in making some order (for instance for a planning scheme, or for the compulsory purchase of property for slum clearance) but the order does not take effect unless confirmed by the minister. The normal statutory procedure is that if any person concerned objects to the proposed order, a public inquiry is held before the minister's inspector who eventually makes a report which the minister must consider before making his decision.[2] Here the business begins to assume the appearance of a *lis inter partes*, since the matter comes before the minister, in a contested case, as an issue between the local authority and the objectors. This is a misleading analogy, but it runs right through the decisions. They are sometimes referred to as the Housing Act cases, since many of them arose from closing orders or slum clearance orders.

The first case, however, concerns education. In 1911 the House of Lords had to decide whether the Board of Education had properly determined a dispute between a body of school managers and the Local Education Authority of Swansea. The local authority had refused to pay teachers in church schools at the same rate as teachers in the authority's own schools. Teachers gave notice to leave, and the managers complained

[1] Above, p. 137; below, p. 203. See for example *Maradana Mosque Trustees v. Mahmud* [1967] 1 A.C. 13.
[2] For inquiries see Chapter 6.

that the local authority were failing to keep the schools efficient, as the Education Act required. A public inquiry was held before a barrister who made a report in favour of the managers, but the Board of Education decided in favour of the local authority. The House of Lords upheld the award of certiorari and mandamus to quash this decision and to order a proper determination of the dispute; for the Board had not dealt with the question which arose under the Act, which was whether they could legitimately discriminate between the two classes of schools.[1] But the Lord Chancellor, Lord Loreburn, spoke about the Board's duties in general terms:

> Comparatively recent statutes have extended, if they have not originated, the practice of imposing upon departments or officers of State the duty of deciding or determining questions of various kinds. In the present instance, as in many others, what comes for determination is a matter to be settled by discretion, involving no law. It will, I suppose, usually be of an administrative kind; but sometimes it will involve matter of law as well as matter of fact, or even depend upon matter of law alone. In such cases the Board of Education will have to ascertain the law and also to ascertain the facts. I need not add that in doing either they must act in good faith and listen fairly to both sides, for that is a duty lying upon every one who decides anything. But I do not think they are bound to treat such a question as though it were a trial. They have no power to administer an oath, and need not examine witnesses. They can obtain information in any way they think best, always giving a fair opportunity to those who are parties in the controversy for correcting or contradicting anything prejudicial to their view.

Although the case itself involved no breach of natural justice, Lord Loreburn's epitome was so apt that it became the most frequently quoted statement on the subject. It combined a complete acceptance of the rule requiring a fair hearing as 'a duty lying upon every one who decides anything' with an acknowledgment of its practical limitations when applied to administration.

The Hampstead case

This leading case was decided by the House of Lords in

---

[1] *Board of Education v. Rice* [1911] A.C. 179.

1914. The Hampstead Borough Council made a closing order against a house as being unfit for human habitation. The owner appealed, as the Act allowed, to the Local Government Board, and the usual public local inquiry was held—though the owner did not attend it. The appeal failed, and the owner then took his case to the courts. He complained that the Board had not given him a fair hearing on his appeal because he was not allowed to appear before the officer who actually decided the matter and because he was not allowed to see the report of the inspector who held the inquiry, which, of course, was the principal document in the proceedings. These complaints succeeded in the Court of Appeal but failed in the House of Lords.[1] The judges all agreed that the general importance of the case 'can scarcely be overestimated'. Where they differed was in their willingness to compromise between the procedure of courts of law and the needs of practical administration. The argument that prevailed was that by entrusting the power to a government department, Parliament must have intended that the department should act in its normal manner, and should therefore be able to take its decision without making public its papers and without having to conduct itself like a court of law. Lord Haldane, then Lord Chancellor but previously a minister with wide experience, said:

My Lords, when the duty of deciding an appeal is imposed, those whose duty it is to decide it must act judicially. They must deal with the question referred to them without bias, and they must give to each of the parties the opportunity of adequately presenting the case made. The decision must be come to in the spirit with the sense of responsibility of a tribunal whose duty it is to mete out justice. But it does not follow that the procedure of every such tribunal must be the same. . . . The Minister at the head of the Board is directly responsible to Parliament like other Ministers. The volume of work entrusted to him is very great. . . . Unlike a judge in a court, he is not only at liberty but is compelled to rely on the assistance of his staff. When, therefore, the Board is directed to dispose of an appeal, that does not mean that any particular official of the Board is to dispose of it. . . . It is said that the report of the inspector should have been disclosed. It might or might not have been useful to disclose this report, but I do not think the board was bound to do so,

---

[1] *Local Government Board v. Arlidge* [1915] A.C. 120.

any more than it would have been bound to disclose all the minutes made on the papers in the office before a decision was come to.

This case was a turning-point, representing a reaction against the judicialisation of administrative procedure. In so far as it reconciled the procedure of a government department with the legal standard of natural justice, the result was useful. But it was unfortunate that the House of Lords set their faces against the disclosure of the inspector's report. In ordinary cases, where the objector makes full use of his hearing before the inspector, it is unreasonable to deny him a sight of the report, and the argument that it is on a par with other departmental papers is misconceived. It was not until the government accepted the recommendations of the Franks Committee in 1957 that the battle for the disclosure of reports was won—and it was not won in the courts, but by the pressure of public opinion. Reports are now made available under statutory rules of procedure or as a matter of departmental practice.[1] But the law still stands where the House of Lords left it in the *Hampstead* case.[2] This was a missed opportunity. In the United States disclosure of similar reports has normally been regarded by the courts as essential in the interests of justice.

Subsequent housing cases

Other Housing Act cases dealt with the Minister's relations with the local authority promoting the order. In the normal course of business the central and local authorities work in close touch, and when a statutory scheme is in preparation they may be in almost daily communication over all kinds of details. But as soon as a draft order is published and objection is lodged, this is what the courts call a *lis*. From that point onwards the Minister must bear in mind that there are two opposing parties, and that he must not deal with one of them without due consideration of the other. Before that stage is reached he has no judicial duty. Objectors have tried to have orders set aside on the grounds that the Ministry advised the local authority before it published its proposed order,[3] and because the Ministry encouraged the local authority to suppose that

---

[1] See below, p. 235.
[2] *Denby (William) and Sons, Ltd. v. Minister of Health* [1936] 1 K.B. 337.
[3] *Frost v. Minister of Health* [1935] 1 K.B. 286.

if it made an order, it would be of a kind likely to be confirmed[1]; but these complaints have rightly been rejected by the courts on the ground that they are really objections to the ordinary departmental procedure. Parliament must have intended to allow efficient administration.

These seemingly extravagant claims were perhaps prompted by another decision in which the Court of Appeal went so far as to upset an order on the ground of dealings between the Ministry and the local authority. But there was the vital difference that the dealings took place during the stage of the *lis*, when both order and objections were, so to speak, *sub judice* with the Ministry. This was the case of the clearance order at Jarrow. Objections were made and the public inquiry was held, but after receiving the report the Ministry made efforts to persuade the Jarrow Corporation to accept a less expensive scheme. The Corporation resisted and asked the Minister to receive a deputation. The Minister replied that in view of his quasi-judicial function he did not think he ought to receive a deputation representing one side only. But it was arranged that an official of the Ministry and also the inspector who had held the inquiry should visit Jarrow and confer with the local authority on the site. After this meeting the Corporation submitted further evidence and argument to the Ministry. In the end the Minister confirmed the order. But the objectors impugned it, and with success, on the ground that these dealings between the Corporation and the Ministry after the public inquiry had been closed were a breach of natural justice.[2] For at that stage issue had been joined, and evidence had been heard, yet the Ministry were giving a further hearing to one party behind the back of the other. It was an example of an administrative authority failing to observe the duty enshrined in Lord Loreburn's words: 'They can obtain information in any way they think best, always giving a fair opportunity to those who are parties in the controversy for correcting or contradicting anything prejudicial to their view.'

Effects of the Jarrow *case*

This decision was received without enthusiasm in Whitehall;

---

[1] *Offer v. Minister of Health* [1936] 1 K.B. 40.
[2] *Errington v. Minister of Health* [1935] 1 K.B. 249.

and one must admit that the mixture of administrative and judicial responsibilities makes it difficult for the Ministry to fulfil their functions. As soon as an objection is lodged, they must either give up their normal dealings with the local authority, or else they must allow the objectors to intrude into the daily work of the department. When the inquiry has been held, the Ministry cannot refer back to the local authority without reopening the whole subject of the inquiry. What makes the position seem artificial is the idea that the local authority is a party to the dispute, and that the Minister is an independent judge. In fact, the two authorities are working— or should be working—hand in glove, one at the local and one at the national level. Both are wielding administrative power, and there is no real difference in the nature of their activities.[1] The notion of the *lis* is therefore fallacious.[2] If the scheme had been promoted by a local office of the Ministry, instead of by the local corporation, any amount of subsequent consultation might have taken place and have been passed over as ordinary departmental work.[3]

The government made a counter-move in the Planning Act of 1947 by obtaining from Parliament an express provision that the Minister might, in the case of development plans, consult the local authority or any one else at any stage without any obligation to allow further objections, or to hold any further hearing.[4] This applied only to development plans, and in all other cases the ruling in the *Jarrow* case is still respected.

An enterprising but unsuccessful attempt was made to apply the doctrine of the *Jarrow* case to a case concerning the Manchester airport. A compulsory purchase order was proposed, and during the local inquiry the inspector was flown over the site in an aircraft piloted by one of the witnesses supporting the scheme. The objectors said that they too should have been represented on the flight, but the court disagreed.[5] On the other hand, in a case where a compulsory purchase order was made for land forming part of a farm, the owner succeeded in chal-

---

[1] See below, p. 229.
[2] It was criticised by Lord Greene M.R. in the *Johnson* case (below).
[3] As to consultation with another government department, see below, p. 237.
[4] Town and Country Planning Acts 1947 s. 10 (3), 1962 s. 10 (3).
[5] *Re Manchester (Ringway Airport) Compulsory Purchase Order* (1935), 153 L.T. 219.

lenging the order because the Ministry sent his reasoned notice of objection to the local authority but never let him see the detailed reply which the local authority then made.[1] This was under the temporary war-time procedure by which the Minister might dispense with a public local inquiry, but that did not affect the substance of Lord Loreburn's principle, which the court once again applied.

What the Minister cannot be required to disclose is evidence which came into his department's possession before issue was joined by the notice of objection. For this would be to require the production of reports, files, and minutes which lie behind the departmental screen. In rejecting one claim of this kind Lord Greene M.R. truly said: 'It is manifest that, in the operation of hybrid functions of that kind, no perfectly logical result is to be expected.'[2]

Cases originated by the deciding ministry

The dilemma became still more plain in a case concerning the Kingston by-pass. This was a trunk road, and therefore the responsibility of the Minister of Transport rather than of a local authority. A scheme for improving the road required a compulsory purchase order, which led to objections and a public inquiry. At the inquiry a ministry official read a statement of the proposals and produced documents and plans; but he called no witnesses, made no attempt to controvert the objections put forward, and declined to answer the objectors' questions about the necessity for the scheme and the merits of alternative schemes. The court held that this was nevertheless a valid inquiry.[3] The Minister was 'in a somewhat peculiar position', being both the author of the scheme and the person behind the inquiry; and as a matter of public interest it was most important that he should give full information to the public and to objectors. But at the inquiry the only object was to hear the objections, not to call for evidence from the Ministry. This conclusion made the public inquiry seem farcical. In 1950 a Scottish court

---

[1] *Stafford v. Minister of Health* [1946] K.B. 621. A similar case is *R. v. Housing Appeal Tribunal* [1920] 3 K.B. 334.
[2] *B. Johnson & Co. (Builders), Ltd. v. Minister of Health* [1947] 2 All E.R. 395 at 399.
[3] *Re Trunk Roads Act 1936* [1939] 2 K.B. 515.

refused to follow the Kingston decision in a case concerning the amalgamation of police forces.[1] But there the inquiry had to be held by an independent inspector, and his report had to be laid before Parliament. The need for both sides of the case to be considered was thus self-evident in the public interest, rather than in the objector's interest. As we shall see, the Government eventually accepted the recommendation of the Franks Committee (1957) that it is essential to expound 'the official case' at public inquiries.[2]

All these decisions show how a main principle of natural justice can be fitted into modern administrative procedure. Instead of taking the view that statutory inquiry procedures are intended to supplant the rules of the common law, the courts have held rather that they are a framework within which the traditional concept of natural justice should continue to operate. The statutory procedure and the common law supplement each other harmoniously.

Judicial retreat: The Ceylon textile *case*

Suddenly a counter-current began to disturb the broad stream of these decisions, although it had been flowing so steadily and for so long. For some unknown reason the courts seemed disposed to turn their back on the long line of precedent which required statutes conferring administrative powers to be interpreted according to the rules of natural justice.

The first clear breach of the principle *audi alteram partem* occurred in a case from Ceylon in which the Privy Council held that a textile trader could be deprived of his trading licence without any kind of hearing.[3] The charge against him was that his firm had falsified paying-in slips when banking coupons under the scheme of control. The Controller in fact wrote to the trader and offered him the opportunity of explaining himself and of inspecting the documents in the case; he also allowed the trader's lawyer to appear before him; and finally he arranged an inquiry before an assistant controller at which the trader and his witnesses were heard. The Supreme Court of Ceylon,

---

[1] *Ayr (Provost, &c.) v. Lord Advocate*, 1950 S.C. 102.
[2] Below, p. 233.
[3] *Nakkuda Ali v. Jayaratne* [1951] A.C. 66. For the other (and better) aspect of his case see above, p. 88.

following familiar English authorities, held that the circumstances demanded a fair hearing, but that it had in fact been given. Certiorari was therefore refused. The Privy Council agreed that a fair hearing had been given—but, going out of their way to raise the question, they held that it had never been necessary.

The judgment, delivered by Lord Radcliffe, stated that there was no ground for holding that the Controller was acting judicially or quasi-judicially; that he was not determining a question but withdrawing a privilege; and that nothing in the regulations or in the conditions of his jurisdiction suggested that he need proceed by analogy to judicial rules. It said that the power 'stands by itself on the bare words of the regulation'. It assumed that there was nothing to consider beyond the bare words, and that the right to a hearing could be determined as if the question had never before arisen in an English court. No attention was paid to the long established presumption that 'the justice of the common law will supply the omission of the legislature'.[1] Nor was it remembered that licensing had long been held to be a judicial function.[2] Primary principles of law were abandoned in favour of the fallacious doctrine, resting on no authority, that a licence was a mere privilege and that therefore the holder could be deprived of his livelihood without ceremony.

The taxi-driver's case

Not long afterwards the Queen's Bench Division held that a London taxi-driver could be deprived of his licence without a hearing.[3] The power to grant and revoke licences rested with the Metropolitan Police Commissioner. Here again, the licensing authority did not in fact act without granting a hearing: the driver was allowed to appear before the Licensing Committee, but the Committee would not allow him to call a witness to controvert the evidence of the police. His licence was revoked and he applied for certiorari on the ground that the hearing given to him had not been full and fair. The Divisional Court replied that he was not entitled to a hearing at all. The relevant

[1] Above, p. 189.
[2] Above, p. 135; below, p. 209.
[3] *The Queen v. Metropolitan Police Commissioner* [1953] 1 W.L.R. 1150. Contrast the American case of *Hecht v. Monaghan*, 307 N.Y. 461 (1954), and the French case of *Trompier-Gravier*, Sirey, 1945, 3. 14.

part of the London Cab Order provided for revocation by the Commissioner 'if he is satisfied . . . that the licensee is not a fit person to hold such a licence'. In language very similar to the Privy Council's, Lord Goddard C.J. said that the Commissioner if he wished could summarily withdraw a licence without any sort of hearing or inquiry; that the Order did not intend that he should act as a judge or quasi-judge; and that there was no order to bring up before the court, since the Commissioner had simply decided that the applicant was not a fit person to hold a licence. He added:

> He was exercising what I may call a disclplinary authority, and where a person, whether he is a military officer, a police officer, or any other person whose duty it is to act in matters of discipline, is exercising disciplinary powers, it is most undesirable, in my opinion, that he should be fettered by threats of orders of certiorari and so forth, because that interferes with the free and proper exercise of the disciplinary powers which he has.

Disciplinary powers

Not the least disturbing feature of this last case was the novel argument that disciplinary powers should be beyond judicial control. A disciplinary power is a power to inflict punishment for an offence, and if there is one case more than another which demands fair procedure and the right of self-defence, that is it.[1] But in a subsequent case, where a fireman had disobeyed an order to clean a superior officer's uniform and was given a caution by the Chief Fire Officer, the Court of Appeal declined to hold that disciplinary powers were immune from judicial control.[2] They refused the discretionary remedy of certiorari,[3] which the determined fireman had sought, on the ground that in so small a matter he should have obeyed the order and complained afterwards. The danger of Lord Goddard's doctrine, which he had repeated in this case, was that the court would deny jurisdiction altogether, so that the good and the bad cases would be rejected indiscriminately.

The law at the crossroads

It was impossible to see what defensible reasoning prompted

---

[1] As to university disciplinary powers see Appendix, C.
[2] See above, p. 144.   [3] *Ex parte Fry* [1954] 1 W.L.R. 730.

the judicial retreat from the principle that a victim of drastic administrative action has a right to be heard. It had long been established as 'a principle of universal application', 'a duty lying upon every one who decides anything', and in the analogous sphere of contractual powers the courts consistently recognized that the protection of a man's livelihood was as important as the protection of his property.[1] Lord Denning said of a trade union committee, whose powers derived from the union's contractual relationship with its members:

These bodies, however, which exercise a monopoly in an important sphere of human activity, with the power of depriving a man of his livelihood, must act in accordance with the elementary rules of justice. They must not condemn a man without giving him an opportunity to be heard in his own defence: and any agreement or practice to the contrary would be invalid.[2]

Yet our law appeared suddenly to be open to the reproach that though a man must be heard before being expelled from his trade union or his club, he need not be heard before being deprived of his livelihood by a licensing authority.

The Brighton police case

In 1963, however, the tide turned once again, when the House of Lords went back to the classic authorities in a case which is an important landmark.

The Chief Constable of Brighton had been tried and acquitted on a criminal charge of conspiracy to obstruct the course of justice. Two other police officers were convicted, and the judge twice took opportunities to comment adversely on the chief constable's leadership of the force. Thereupon the Brighton Watch Committee, without giving any notice or offering any hearing to the chief constable, unanimously dismissed him from office. His solicitor then applied for a hearing and was allowed to appear before a later meeting. The Committee confirmed their previous decision, but by a vote of nine against three. The chief constable exercised his right of appeal to the Home Secretary, but his appeal was dismissed. Finally he turned to the courts of law, claiming a declaration that his dismissal was void

---

[1] Above, p. 175.

[2] *Abbott v. Sullivan* [1952] 1 K.B. 189 at 198; see also *Russell v. Duke of Norfolk* [1949] 1 All E.R. 109 at 119; *Lee v. Showmen's Guild* [1952] 2 Q.B. 329.

since he had been given no notice of any charge against him and no opportunity of making his defence. This was refused by the High Court and by a unanimous Court of Appeal. But it was awarded by the House of Lords by a majority of four to one.[1]

The initial dismissal was not only a breach of the principles of natural justice: it was contrary to the express provisions of the statutory regulations governing police discipline, which in cases of misconduct require notice of the charge and an opportunity for self-defence. They apply 'where a report or allegation is received', and much intellectual effort was therefore spent on the question whether this piece of loose draftsmanship meant that the safeguards in the regulations (which justice plainly demands in any case) applied only where there was a formal 'receiving' of the complaint. A more absurd point on which to decide an important case it would be hard to find. But great benefit flowed from it, since although the dismissal was held void on this ground by the majority of four, three of them felt impelled to consider what the situation might be if the regulations did not apply. Thus they came to the question of principle, and this became the dominant theme in their opinions.

A watch committee is empowered to dismiss any constable 'whom they think negligent in the discharge of his duty, or otherwise unfit for the same'.[2] Therefore in the committee's eyes the constable must be convicted of negligence or unfitness before they have power to dismiss him. This makes the case considerably stronger than many of the classic natural justice cases, and it is certain that the judges who decided those cases would have held that there could be no legal exercise of the power without notice of the charge and a fair hearing. For how can the committee fairly find negligence or unfitness without hearing the defence? It was on this simple ground that the majority upheld the chief constable's rights. The hearing given to his solicitor was held to be irrelevant, since even then no notice of any specific charge was given, and natural justice was again violated.

The leading speech of Lord Reid is of the greatest significance because of its extensive review of the authorities, which inevi-

---

[1] *Ridge v. Baldwin* [1964] A.C. 40.
[2] Municipal Corporations Act 1882 s. 191.

tably exposed the fallacies underlying some of the previous decisions. He attacked the problem at its root by demonstrating how the term 'judicial' had been misinterpreted, and this fundamental point has already been explained in connexion with certiorari.[1] This led to the conclusion that the Ceylon textile case, holding that a licensing authority did not act judicially in cancelling a licence, was based on 'a serious misapprehension of the older authorities and therefore cannot be regarded as authoritative'. Strangely enough, the taxi-driver's case was not cited, but it has since necessarily been disapproved.[2]

In setting out to review the law Lord Reid said:

> The authorities on the applicability of the principles of natural justice are in some confusion. . . . The principle audi alteram partem goes back many centuries in our law and appears in a multitude of judgments of judges of the highest authority. In modern times opinions have sometimes been expressed to the effect that natural justice is so vague as to be practically meaningless. But I would regard these as tainted by the perennial fallacy that because something cannot be cut and dried or nicely weighed or measured, therefore it does not exist.

He observed that if the case had arisen thirty or forty years ago the courts would have had no difficulty in allowing the appeal, and that none of the authorities which were then so respected had ever been disapproved or doubted. He also said:

> We do not have a developed system of administrative law— perhaps because until fairly recently we did not need it. . . . But I see nothing in that to justify our thinking that our old methods are any less applicable today than ever they were to the older types of case. And if there are any dicta in modern authorities which point in that direction then, in my judgment, they should not be followed.

Among the numerous cases reviewed were the *Wandsworth* and *Smethwick* cases, and the *Liverpool* case which had already held that the principles of natural justice applied to dismissal of a police officer.[3] Lord Reid emphasised that whether the cases

---

[1] Above, p. 137. In *Re H. K. (an infant)* [1967] 2 Q.B. 617 the court has very sensibly held that an immigration officer has a duty to act fairly without having to act judicially. See also *R. v. Gaming Board for Great Britain* (below, p. 210); *R. v. Birmingham City Justice* [1970] 1 W.L.R. 1428.

[2] See *R. v. Gaming Board for Great Britain* [1970] 2 W.L.R. 1009; *Banks v. Transport Regulation Board* [1968] A.L.R. 445, *per* Barwick C.J.

[3] Above, p. 179.

concerned property or tenure of an office or membership of an institution, they were all governed by one principle, and he aptly celebrated the centenary of the *Wandsworth* case by approving the excellent general statements which have been quoted earlier.[1] Shortly afterwards the Police Act 1964, which gave power for senior police officers to be retired compulsorily in the interests of efficiency, gave an express right for any officer affected to make representations.[2]

Void or voidable?

The *Brighton* case settled the point—though many earlier cases had also decided it[3]—that failure to give a fair hearing renders the decision void, not voidable.[4] The courts have always adopted the natural attitude that this omission, like the disregard of any other mandatory procedural requirement, deprives the action of its statutory authority and makes it *ultra vires*. Nevertheless on this point the House of Lords were divided three to two. There is a contrast between the majority opinions, solidly based on numerous precedents and on principle, and the minority opinions which advocate new and ominous doctrine.

The motive behind the minority opinions is the desire to enlarge judicial discretion. It is said, though it by no means follows, that if the action is voidable the court need quash it only if justice so requires. This would introduce dangerous uncertainty—one might say, palm-tree injustice. Natural justice has for centuries been enforced as a matter of law and not of discretion. But the uncertainties of the period before the *Brighton* case have unfortunately undermined the clear principle that used to prevail. Of the nine judges concerned in that case, five denied that there was a right to a fair hearing. In this situation it is not discretion that is needed but consistency. The right to natural justice should be as firm as the right to personal liberty.

The uncertainty is aggravated by an exceptionally difficult

---

[1] Above, p. 188. See also *Wiseman v. Borneman* [1969] 3 W.L.R. 706.
[2] Ss. 5 (5), 6 (5), 39 (2).
[3] E.g. *Kanda v. Government of Malaya* [1962] A.C. 322; below, p. 212.
[4] For this question see also pp. 103 and 185, above, and 84 L.Q.R. at p. 101.

decision of the Privy Council.[1] Its principle is impeccable:
failure to give a fair hearing will not (for example) entitle a
stranger to treat the dismissal of a chief constable as void unless
he himself elects to do so. But for this self-evident truth it
invokes the dissenting opinions in the *Brighton* case, which
argued that the dismissal was voidable only at the court's discretion. Yet the Privy Council very properly denies that there
is any such discretion as against the chief constable himself. The
confusion here seems inextricable.

Another serious objection to holding action voidable is that
the litigant is then deprived of what is often his best and sometimes his only remedy, a declaratory judgment.[2]

Offices and employments

We have already met the problem that a statutory office or
status is sometimes difficult to distinguish from ordinary contractual employment.[3] The distinction is important also for
purposes of natural justice, since natural justice does not apply
to the ordinary contractual relationship of master and servant.
For this reason the Privy Council refused certiorari to a university lecturer who had been dismissed without a hearing
from his post in Ceylon—though the case itself looked more like
one of statutory status since the university's power to dismiss
was statutory and was restricted (just as in the *Brighton* case) to
cases of incapacity or misconduct.[4] But where the employee has
a right of appeal to an appeal committee, natural justice may
apply to the appeal proceedings.[5]

Another case where natural justice is excluded, according to Lord Reid's analysis in the *Brighton* case, is that of an
office held merely at pleasure, where the office-holder can be
dismissed for any reason or no reason. What made the difference
in that case was that under the statute the chief constable could
be dismissed only 'for cause', to wit for some inadequacy or
default on his part. Justice obviously demands, and the law

---

[1] *Durayappah v. Fernando* [1967] 2 A.C. 337, criticized in *Denton v. Auckland City*
[1969] N.Z.L.R. 256 at 268 and in 83 L.Q.R. at p. 502. See below, p. 217, above,
p. 106.

[2] See above, p. 123.   [3] Above, p. 122.

[4] *Vidyodaya University Council v. Silva* [1965] 1 W.L.R. 77, following *Barber v.
Manchester Hospital Board* (above, p. 122).

[5] *Pillai v. Singapore City Council* [1968] 1 W.L.R. 1278.

accordingly provides, that he should not be found to be at fault without an opportunity to defend himself.

Although it was not in issue in the *Brighton* case, the position of a man who holds a statutory office at pleasure only may need further consideration. The argument appears to be that since he need be given no reason for his dismissal, his side of the case need not be heard. But for this there is no earlier authority of any weight,[1] and the logic seems faulty. As will be seen from many of the cases already discussed, natural justice has been held to apply to a great many decisions and acts for which there was no obligation to give reasons. And if the office-holder is subject to some accusation, he ought to be allowed to defend himself in any case, whatever the terms of his tenure. In a perfect world, even a mere contractual employee would doubtless have a right to be heard if subject to some charge of misconduct. Why then does the law stop short of this case? And where ought it to stop short?

The key to this puzzle is perhaps to be sought in the notion of specific enforcement. Contracts of employment are not specifically enforceable: therefore dismissal, however wrongful, is legally effective; and the employee, though he may be entitled to damages, is as we have seen not entitled to a declaration of 'no dismissal'. A person with a statutory office or status, on the other hand, is given specific protection.[2] He can be dismissed only in the manner provided by the statute, and if that is not observed a declaration of 'no dismissal' (with or without an injunction) is available to him. Wrongful dismissal is then *ultra vires* and void. It is surely right that the rules of natural justice should extend to all such cases where specific protection is given. If a schoolteacher cannot be dismissed for reasons which conflict with the statute,[3] why should he be liable to dismissal in breach of natural justice? These are both forms of *ultra vires*, and the latter should apply just as much as the former. Even in contractual cases the courts enforce natural justice where there is some status that they are prepared to protect

---

[1] *R. v. Darlington School Governors* (1844) 6 Q.B. 682 is a doubtful authority, more evaded than followed: see [1964] A.C. at p. 66. A subsequent unreported case is *Tucker v. British Museum*, The Times, 8 December 1967 (C.A.).

[2] Above p. 122.

[3] As in *Price v. Sunderland Corporation* [1956] 1 W.L.R. 1253; above, p. 122.

specifically, for instance membership of a trade union[1] or of a club.[2] If the case is one where the law is prepared to protect the office, whether held at pleasure or otherwise, it should protect the holder against wrongful deprivation of every kind.

The problem of 'policy'

We have been preoccupied with cases where the question was whether some person was guilty of some default, and it is in these that a sense of justice most obviously demands a fair hearing. But what if the question is rather one of government policy? If schoolteachers are dismissed because the education authority is closing schools, or if taxi-drivers' licences are cancelled because there are thought to be too many taxis, will this alter the case?

Since the courts have not been faced with these questions, it is not very profitable to speculate. But throughout the decisions there runs a certain element of 'policy', and it is important to consider its effect.

Although it is easy to see when policy plays a dominating part, it is probably wrong to regard it as an isolated element in some kinds of administrative decision. Even in the plainest case of individual merit, where for example a licensee is accused of misbehaviour, it is a question of policy what penalty should be inflicted, if any, and what standards should be required. In truth, every discretionary administrative decision involves policy, to some extent. What is variable is the effect that the circumstances of affected individuals may have on policy. But even in the most extreme case, such as where schools have to be closed and teachers dismissed, the right to be heard may not be inappropriate. For there is another side to natural justice quite apart from fairness to the individual: it helps the administrator to take a better decision if he hears the objections to his policy from those who have the strongest interest in contesting it. It may be that the courts will decide that this is not the concern of the law. But there would seem to be no real reason why they should so decide, for legal rights in such situations are not out of place. For example, the number of separate police forces in

---

[1] As in *Lee v. Showmen's Guild* [1952] 2 Q.B. 239 (declaration and injunction); above, p. 201.

[2] As in *Fisher v. Keane* (1878) 11 Ch. D. 353 (declaration and injunction).

the country is at present being drastically reduced by a scheme of compulsory amalgamations, as a matter of policy, but the legislation allows every police authority affected by the scheme to have its objections heard at an inquiry.[1] The principles of natural justice might well extend thus far themselves.

Although the *Brighton* case in no way raised such questions, Lord Reid at one point made some problematical remarks about policy. He said that where a minister was not dealing with a single isolated case, but with something like, say, a scheme for an important new road, his primary concern would be not with the damage to landowners' rights but with the fulfilment of his policy; and that it would be quite wrong to require the minister to act in the same sort of way as a board of works deciding whether a house should be pulled down. The passage is only a short digression and is plainly not intended to change established law. But it seems to suggest that in such a case the minister would be entitled to acquire land compulsorily without giving the owner a hearing—a suggestion which conflicts not only with a decision on natural justice[2] but with the enacted law of compulsory purchase.[3] The slum clearance schemes in issue in the Housing Act cases involved just such acts of policy, but the courts did not hesitate to apply the rules of natural justice by quashing the minister's decision when he consulted the local authority behind the backs of the objectors.[4]

It is in just these 'policy' cases that Parliament reinforces the common law by providing for statutory inquiries, which is the best possible proof of the importance and appropriateness of the right to be heard. The dominance of policy in no way affects the minister's duty to hear a landowner's case. What it affects is the weight that he may give to that case after he has heard it. But that in any event is the minister's affair and outside the sphere of the law.

It is true that the great majority of the decisions deal with cases where some deficiency or default on the part of the person affected has to be found. But they contain no hint (apart from Lord Reid's) that the principle *audi alteram partem* is restricted

---

[1] Police Act 1964, 3rd sched.
[2] *Stafford v. Minister of Health* [1946] K.B. 621; above, p. 197.
[3] Above, p. 168.
[4] *Errington v. Minister of Health* [1935] 1 K.B. 249; above, p. 195.

to such cases, and Lord Loreburn's celebrated formulation is
really a direct denial of any such restriction. The principle is
that drastic powers cannot lawfully be exercised against
particular people without giving them the opportunity to state
their case. It should make no difference whether the occasion
for the exercise of the power is personal default or an act of
policy. Good administration demands fair consultation in
either case, and this the law can and should enforce.

Licensing

Licensing cases, in particular, contain a large element of
policy, since in many cases a licensing authority will be free
to grant or withhold licences as it thinks best in the public
interest. Very extensive licensing powers are possessed by the
central government, local authorities, the police, magistrates,
tribunals and other authorities, and in many cases they give
what might be called power of commercial life or death over
a person's trade or livelihood. Yet there is a surprising absence
of clear law about the procedure required when licences are
refused or revoked, except where there is a formal tribunal
such as the traffic commissioners. Occasionally the statute will
provide that the appellant or licensee must first be given notice
and offered a hearing.[1] Sometimes it will give a right of appeal.[2]
More commonly it will say nothing. Nor have the courts been
able to fill this lacuna successfully in the past. Relatively
few cases have been reported, and it is in this area, as we
have seen, that there have been confused and unfortunate
decisions.[3]

Since the *Brighton* case it seems that the principles of natural
justice will in general apply to licensing in the same way as to
other administrative powers. The bad decisions have been
disapproved and the courts are alive to the injustice of depriving anyone of liberty, property or livelihood without fair
procedure. In a recent case the Court of Appeal had to consider the statutory licensing system governing gaming clubs,
under which the Gaming Board must give a certificate of
consent before a gaming club can apply to the magistrates for a

[1] E.g. Prevention of Fraud (Investments) Act 1958, s. 6.
[2] E.g. Licensing Act 1964, s. 21.
[3] Above, pp. 135, 198.

licence. The court decided that in refusing a certificate for reasons concerning the character and suitability of the applicants the Board must act fairly and obey the principles of natural justice.[1] In fact it was held that they had done so, since they had given the applicants full opportunity to know and contest the case against them, even though they had not revealed the sources of their information or given their reasons.

Government departments have important powers of commercial and industrial regulation under which many decisions are made from day to day and which have no statutory procedural safeguards. Examples are import and export licensing; foreign exchange control; the licensing of buildings costing more than £100,000; the grant of office development permits and industrial development certificates; and the drastic powers over insurance companies possessed by the Board of Trade. Natural justice ought to play its normal part in these areas, subject to administrative necessities impliedly recognized by the legislation. But the authorities have succeeded in wielding these far-reaching powers without provoking challenge in the courts.[2]

An important form of licensing is planning control, but even here it is an open question whether a local planning authority ought to give an applicant an opportunity to make representations before planning permission is refused.[3] There is a right of appeal to the minister, but in principle that is no reason for not requiring the procedure to be fair at the initial stage. The Act itself is silent.

Similar obscurity surrounds the multitudinous licensing powers of local authorities over such things as cinemas, nursing homes, road vehicles, animal boarding establishments, knackers' yards, fireworks factories, pawnbrokers and slaughter-houses. Police licensing powers cover, *inter alia*, firearms, pedlars, taxicabs and taxi-drivers. Many of these arrangements might be thought to cry out for administrative rationalization and procedural regularity. But only rarely do they come before the courts. Liquor-licensing, on the other hand, has been in the

---

[1] *R. v. Gaming Board for Great Britain* [1970] 2 W.L.R. 1009.
[2] See now *Re Pergamon Press Ltd.* (below, p. 218).
[3] Some planning authorities do so. Cf. *Denton v. Auckland City* [1969] N.Z.L.R. 256.

hands of magistrates since the sixteenth century and has made a full contribution to the case-law of natural justice.

What is a fair hearing?

'Convenience and justice are often not on speaking terms.'[1] But an administrative authority cannot be expected to act as if it were a court of law,[2] and justice must therefore be reconciled with practical needs. What matters is substance, not form. Normally a hearing means an oral hearing at which a party may be legally represented and may call and cross-examine witnesses. But in a suitable case the 'hearing' may be held on paper, and the objector may merely be given the opportunity to submit objections and arguments in writing.[3] Few such cases, however, have appeared in the courts.

Ministers and government departments are very commonly given statutory power to hold hearings, as the next chapter explains. If the minister duly appoints some one to hold the hearing, there is no right of personal appearance before the minister himself.[4] Where delegation is not expressly authorised it does not follow that it will be unlawful, if it is a normal and reasonable administrative arrangement of the kind that the statute may be taken to have contemplated. Thus an authority might appoint a committee to hear evidence and argument and report them, either in full or in an accurate summary, to the authority so that it could itself decide.[5] But where, as happened in a case from New Zealand, a Dairy Board appointed a committee for these purposes which in its report did not say what the evidence was, it was held that the hearing was defective.[6] For the Board had taken its decision in ignorance of the evidence; and therefore its order, which allotted the milk supply from certain areas to certain factories, was quashed by certiorari.

Where the hearing is given by a body of persons, it is neces-

[1] Lord Atkin in [1943] A.C. at 638.
[2] See above, p. 192, and Re H.K. (an infant) [1967] 2 Q.B. 617 (immigration officer must nevertheless act fairly).
[3] R. v. Housing Appeal Tribunal [1920] 3 K.B. 334; Stuart v. Haughley Parish Church Council [1935] Ch. 452; Jeffs v. New Zealand Dairy Board [1967] 1 A.C. 551.
[4] Local Government Board v. Arlidge [1915] A.C. 120; above, p. 193.
[5] Osgood v. Nelson (1872) L.R. 5 H.L. 636; Jeffs v. New Zealand Dairy Board (above).
[6] Ibid.

sary that all its members should hear the whole of the evidence, unless the parties otherwise agree; and this rule applies equally to an assessor, where there is power to appoint one.[1]

Whatever sort of hearing is given, it must always include 'a fair opportunity to those who are parties in the controversy for correcting or contradicting anything prejudicial to their view.'[2] A hearing where the party does not know the case he has to meet is no hearing at all.[3] Accordingly where a police officer was dismissed in Malaya, after a hearing before an adjudicating officer, the Privy Council declared the dismissal void because the adjudicating officer was in possession of a report of a board of inquiry which made charges of misconduct but which was not available to the police officer.[4] A similar case in England led to the quashing by certiorari of a decision of an Industrial Injuries Commissioner.[5] After hearing the case the Commissioner obtained, as he was empowered to do, a report from an independent medical expert; but the parties were not notified and were therefore unable to comment on the report. The Commissioner had, in effect, taken further evidence, unknown to the parties, between the hearing and the decision. The same principle applies where a party is allowed to know only part of the real charge against him.[6] It also applies where a rent tribunal, having inspected the property before the hearing, fails to inform the landlord of unfavourable conclusions formed at the inspection.[7] But it does not, of course, require a minister to disclose all the information about a proposed housing scheme which his department collected before any objection to the scheme was lodged.[8]

The right to know the case to be met does not necessarily involve any right to know the sources of adverse information or to confront informants, for in some cases it will be quite

[1] *R. v. Deputy Industrial Injuries Commissioner* [1962] 2 Q.B. 677.
[2] Above, p. 192.
[3] *Ridge v. Baldwin* (above, p. 202); *Stafford v. Minister of Health* (above, p. 197).
[4] *Kanda v. Government of Malaya* [1962] A.C. 322. A corresponding case from Ceylon is *Shareef v. Commissioner for Registration of Indian and Pakistani Residents* [1966] A.C. 47.
[5] *R. v. Deputy Industrial Injuries Commissioner* [1962] 2 Q.B. 677.
[6] *Maradana Mosque Trustees v. Mahmud* [1967] 1 A.C. 13.
[7] *R. v. Paddington &c. Rent Tribunal* [1949] 1 K.B. 666.
[8] Above, p. 197.

proper for the authority to employ confidential sources.[1] What natural justice requires is that the information itself should be disclosed so that there is a fair opportunity of contesting it.

Evidence and procedure

Where an oral hearing is given, a tribunal must, it has been laid down, (*a*) consider all relevant evidence which a party wishes to submit; (*b*) inform every party of all the evidence to be taken into account, whether derived from another party or independently; (*c*) allow witnesses to be questioned; (*d*) allow comment on the evidence and argument on the whole case.[2] The right to call and to cross-examine witnesses is therefore, as a general rule, part of the procedure required by natural justice.[3] But there is no need for the strict legal rules of evidence to be observed. In an industrial injuries case the Commissioner was therefore held entitled to take into account evidence given at the hearing of medical reports made in previous cases, although in a court of law these might have been inadmissible under the rule against hearsay.[4]

In the same case it was stated by the Court of Appeal that natural justice demands that the decision should be based on some evidence of probative value. This is a novel suggestion, and it conflicts with the well established proposition that to find facts supported by no evidence is not *ultra vires*.[5] But, as we have seen elsewhere, the courts are now showing a disposition to develop 'no evidence' as a head of judicial control,[6] and if they do so it may be that natural justice will supply the peg on which to hang it.

The right to legal representation may prove to be a part of natural justice in suitable cases, but this is not as yet clearly established.[7]

---

[1] *Ceylon University v. Fernando* [1960] 1 W.L.R. 223 (accusation against student taking examination); *R. v. Gaming Board for Great Britain* [1970] 2 W.L.R. 1009 (above, p. 210); *Re Pergamon Press Ltd.*, below, p. 218.

[2] *R. v. Deputy Industrial Injuries Commissioner* [1965] 1 Q.B. 456.

[3] See *Osgood v. Nelson* (1872) L.R. 5 H.L. 636.

[4] *R. v. Deputy Industrial Injuries Commissioner* [1965] 1 Q.B. 456.

[5] Above, p. 98.

[6] Above, p. 99.

[7] See *Pett v. Greyhound Racing Association Ltd.* [1969] 1 Q.B. 125; [1970] 1 Q.B. 46 and 67; *Enderby Football Club v. Football Association* [1970] 3 W.L.R. 1021.

Reasons and reports

Natural justice does not require that reasons should be given for decisions.[1] But now that the duty to give reasons has been introduced as a general principle for statutory tribunals,[2] including licensing bodies such as traffic commissioners and the Air Transport Licensing Board, it might well be thought to be required generally by natural justice. An additional argument is that unless the court insists upon reasons being stated, it is handicapped in asserting its control over error on the face of the record.[3] Furthermore, the law has already gone some distance towards requiring reasons to be given for discretionary decisions.[4]

Much the same might be said about the disclosure of the report of the officer who held the hearing, where the hearing can lawfully be held by a subordinate such as a departmental inspector. As explained earlier, the courts have held that natural justice does not require the disclosure of the report.[5] But it is now recognized that ordinary fairness does require it, and in the majority of cases disclosure is now made under the statutory inquiry procedures described in the next chapter. The courts having missed their opportunity, other means have been found.

Hearing held after decision

What is an administrative authority to do if it has failed to give a fair hearing, so that its decision is quashed or declared void? It still has the duty to give a proper hearing and decide the case, but it has prejudiced itself by its defective decision, which it may well have defended in legal proceedings. It cannot be fair procedure to take a decision first and hear the evidence afterwards, even though the first decision is legally a nullity.

But in most cases the only possible course is for the same authority to rehear the case. For that authority will be the only authority with statutory power to proceed, and there is therefore 'a case of necessity' of the kind we have already met.[6]

---

[1] *R. v. Gaming Board for Great Britain* [1970] 2 W.L.R. 1009. Cf. *Minister of National Revenue v. Wrights' Canadian Ropes Ltd.* [1947] A.C. 109.
[2] Below, pp. 236, 270.   [3] Above, p. 96.   [4] Above, p. 79.
[5] Above, p. 193.   [6] Above, p. 181.

This was acknowledged in the *Brighton* case: ' . . . if an officer or body realizes that it has acted hastily and reconsiders the whole matter afresh, after affording to the person affected a proper opportunity to present his case, then its later decision will be valid.'[1] In the *Brighton* case the hearing, when given, was deficient, so that the second decision was as void as the first. But a Canadian case, arising out of disciplinary proceedings by the Toronto Stock Exchange, affords an example of a second hearing and second decision being valid, since everything possible was done to review the case fully and fairly.[2]

A different but comparable situation is where the hearing is given after action has been decided upon, but in time to prevent the decision being void. This happened in Trinidad where the Governor had power to transfer the indentures of immigrant workers from one estate to another. The Governor made an order for such a transfer without consulting the estate owner, but as soon as he heard that the owner objected he gave him a fair hearing. He then declined to cancel the order. Since the hearing was given while there was still power to cancel the order, the procedure was held valid.[3] A late hearing is better than no hearing at all, but the law ought to be cautious in admitting such dubious procedure.

Limits and exceptions

Like all other rules, *audi alteram partem* has its limits. It does not apply to contracts of service.[4] There must be numerous discretionary powers to which it is inherently inapplicable, such as power to take urgent action to prevent crime or the spread of disease. It has been held inapplicable to the minister's power to permit development of a major airport.[5] Other powers are probably not subject to the rule because the law makes provision for them to be challenged subsequently, for example the issue of a subpoena to a witness, and preliminary rulings under the statutory procedure in tax avoidance trans-

[1] [1964] A.C. at p. 79 (Lord Reid).
[2] *Posluns v. Toronto Stock Exchange* (1968) 67 D.L.R. (2d) 165. Cf. *King v. University of Saskatchewan* (1969) 6 D.L.R. (3d) 120.
[3] *De Verteuil v. Knaggs* [1918] A.C. 557.
[4] Above, p. 205.
[5] *Essex C.C. v. M.H.L.G.* (1967) 66 L.G.R. 23. The true reason may be that planning permission does not legally concern third parties (above, p. 123).

actions.¹ But in principle there is no difference between final decisions and those which are not final. The House of Lords has emphasized that Parliament will be presumed to intend statutory procedure to be fair at all stages, but that sometimes the subsequent procedure may determine the fairness of the preliminary procedure.² But these are conjectures, and as a general rule the existence of a right of appeal is no argument against the right to be heard before the initial decision: fair procedure is equally necessary at all stages.³

The rule applies primarily to an exercise of legal *power*, and it may or may not apply to the making of a report or recommendation which has no effect on legal rights.⁴ It may also be presumed that there is no right to a hearing before the exercise of *legislative* power, so that there is no room for the rule in relation to the making of statutory regulations—although in a few special cases Parliament makes provision for inquiries.⁵

But in truth the lesson of the host of cases that have been brought before the courts is that exceptions are conspicuous by their absence wherever genuine administrative power has been exercised under statute with any serious effect on a man's property, liberty or livelihood. Where the courts have denied a right to be heard it is more probably a bad decision than a true exception. The rule must come close to deserving the judicial tributes quoted earlier: 'a principle of universal application', 'a duty lying upon every one who decides anything'.

Aliens have been held to have no right to be heard in their own defence when subjected to deportation orders.⁶ But this also may well be a bad decision. Lord Denning has suggested that a hearing should at any rate be given before the order is executed.⁷ The hollowness of the objections is shown by two developments. First, the Home Secretary was obliged by a European convention to arrange for a judicial hearing in a wide

---

¹ *Wiseman v. Borneman* [1969] 3 W.L.R. 706.
² *Ibid.*
³ *Leary v. National Union of Vehicle Builders* [1970] 3 W.L.R. 434.
⁴ Contrast *R. v. St. Lawrence's Hospital Statutory Visitors* [1953] 1 W.L.R. 1158 with *Re Pergamon Press Ltd.*, below, p. 218.
⁵ See below, p. 338.
⁶ *Ex parte Venicoff* [1920] 3 K.B. 72; cf. *Musson v. Rodriguez* [1953] A.C. 530.
⁷ *R. v. Governor of Brixton Prison ex parte Soblen* [1963] 2 Q.B. 243.

class of deportation cases.[1] Secondly, Parliament has enacted a new system of tribunals and appeals, which has been extended to aliens, giving procedural rights in cases of exclusion, deportation, non-renewal of residence permits, and so forth.[2] Parliament has therefore moved ahead of the courts in recognizing that a civilized system of law must treat aliens fairly as well as citizens.

This position is confirmed in the latest decisions, which hold that no hearing need be given either in the case of refusal of admission or in the case of non-renewal of a limited entry permit, on the ground that in such cases there is 'no legitimate expectation' that permission will be given.[3] Whether this new test of 'legitimate expectation' will prove satisfying remains to be seen. It is necessarily very difficult to find good reasons for making exceptions to 'a principle of universal application'.

Who may complain?

It is obvious that a denial of a fair hearing is a wrong which is personal to the party aggrieved. If he himself does not wish to complain, it is not the business of other people to do so, for as against them there is nothing legally wrong with the decision.[4] An example has already been given, based on a judgment of the Privy Council.[5] In that case the Minister of Local Government in Ceylon exercised his power to dissolve a municipal council and appoint commissioners to discharge its duties, since it appeared to him that the council was not competent to perform them.[6] But the council were given no opportunity to meet this charge, in breach of natural justice. The council itself did not challenge the Minister's action: it was only their mayor who did so. But he, it was held, was not entitled to complain individually, since although he had lost his office this was merely a consequence of a wrong done to the council. His applications for

---

[1] See 557 H.C. Deb. Written Answers 174 (1956).

[2] Immigration Appeals Act 1969, extended to aliens by S.I. 1970 No. 151.

[3] *Schmidt v. Home Secretary* [1969] 2 Ch. 149 (refusal to vary landing conditions restricting stay of students of 'scientology'). The Act of 1969 as extended gives an alien a right of appeal against refusal of leave to land and refusal to revoke or vary any landing condition.

[4] For explanation see 84 L.Q.R. at 109.

[5] Above, pp. 106, 205.

[6] *Durayappah v. Fernando* [1967] 2 A.C. 337.

certiorari and a declaration therefore failed. The confusing language used in this decision has been criticized already.[1]

It does not follow that no third party can ever complain of a breach of natural justice. If a biased licensing authority grants an application, it is the public interest which is wronged rather than any individual. Thus a third party may be granted a remedy, as happened in the *Hendon* case.[2]

Statutory powers of inquiry

In its latest decision, reported too late for incorporation above (p. 211), the Court of Appeal has held that the rules of natural justice apply to an inquiry into the affairs of a company held under statutory powers by inspectors appointed by the Board of Trade.[3] The inspectors have no judicial or quasi-judicial function, and they make no legal decision: they merely inquire and report. But since their findings may be very damaging they have a duty to act fairly and in accordance with natural justice. This means that before making an adverse finding they must tell the party affected the substance of the charge and give him a fair opportunity to deal with it. But they need not show him the evidence itself or allow him to cross-examine any witness. 'In the application of the concept of fair play, there must be real flexibility.' This is a good illustration of the universality of the principles so widely but so accurately stated by Lord Loreburn in 1911.[4]

The extension of natural justice to merely investigatory powers is important. But its application is bound to depend on circumstances.[5] In the present case the inspectors were acting correctly and could therefore compel officers of the company to answer questions in accordance with the Act. Had they acted incorrectly, the court could presumably have intervened to prevent action being taken on what was not a proper report.

---

[1] Pp. 106, 205.   [2] Above, pp. 139, 179.
[3] *Re Pergamon Press Ltd.* [1970] 3 W.L.R. 792.   [4] Above, p. 192.
[5] Contrast *Essex C.C. v. M.H.L.G.* (1967) 66 L.G.R. 23 (proposed development order for Stansted Airport).

6

STATUTORY INQUIRIES

THE PROBLEMS OF INQUIRIES

An administrative technique

THE statutory inquiry is the device most frequently used by Parliament for giving a fair hearing to objectors before the final decision is made on some important scheme. It is a prominent feature of our administrative law in comparison with that of other countries. In France and Italy, for example, where there are special administrative courts, there is sometimes more ample jurisdiction to deal with complaints, but the complaint must in most cases follow the event. In the English system, where there are no special courts for administrative cases, and control is of a strictly legalistic (or jurisdictional) character, there are better opportunities to make objections and obtain a hearing before the decision is taken. This is consistent with the English conception of the proper spheres of administrative and judicial power. It underlies, as we have already seen, the legal rules of natural justice: although an official act cannot be challenged if it is within the powers conferred, rules can still be laid down for ensuring that the elements of fair procedure are followed *before* the moment of decision. Not only is there the common-law rule, *audi alteram partem*; there are many statutes which contain their own scheme of natural justice and which lay down the procedure for dealing with objections. Every Act contains its own code, usually in a schedule at the end of the Act; but the provisions have become stereotyped and may be discussed without much differentiation.

Although the whole object of these inquiries is to assuage the feelings of the citizen, and to give his objections the fairest possible consideration, they have given rise to many complaints. They are a hybrid legal-and-administrative process, and for the very reason that they have been made to look as much as possible like a judicial proceeding, people grumble at the way in which they fall short of it. They have in fact formed one of the principal battlegrounds between legal and official opinion in the past fifty years. They were reviewed both by the Ministers' Powers Committee of 1932 and by the Committee on Tribunals and Enquiries (the Franks Committee) of 1957. The first report had little practical effect; but the government's acceptance of the Franks Committee's recommendations marked a turning-point at which repeated criticisms at last achieved something.

Statutory inquiries are now so common that it is unusual to find a statute concerned with planning control or with the acquisition of land, or indeed with any important social service or scheme of control, which does not provide this machinery for one or more purposes. Acts concerned with housing, town and country planning, new towns, roads, agriculture, health, transport, aviation, rivers, police, local government—these are merely a few examples to show the range of subjects covered by what has now become a standard technique. Many inquiries have to be held in cases of compulsory acquisition, as, for example, where land is taken for roads, schools, hospitals, airfields, housing estates, town development, open spaces and playing fields, swimming baths, cemeteries, children's homes, markets, slaughterhouses or smallholdings. There are also very many planning inquiries. The Ministry of Housing and Local Government, which arranges inquiries concerning local authorities and some central departments, as well as all its own cases of housing and planning, has a corps of over 200 inspectors responsible for about 6,000 inquiries a year.

In all these cases the decision that the minister must take is a decision of policy. Should a county council's development plan be approved? Should land be compulsorily acquired for a motorway? Should a slum clearance scheme be authorised? Should an appeal against refusal of planning permission be allowed? This is the characteristic situation. But, as noted in the next chapter, the inquiry procedure is also used where a minister has to give a decision of a more judicial character, for example on an appeal against a district auditor's surcharge.[1]

Inquiries held under the Housing Acts may be taken as typical. We have already met several cases[2] which arose out of

---

[1] Below, p. 257.   [2] Above, p. 193.

the earlier Housing Acts; the present Housing Act of 1957 contains four separate sets of detailed rules for inquiries among its schedules. It may be helpful to summarize the procedure for clearance orders, as set out in the fifth schedule. A clearance order is an order for the wholesale demolition and clearance of an area of bad housing (slum clearance) which may or may not then be redeveloped under the Act. The initiative here rests with the local authority.

Specimen procedure (clearance orders)

The first step is for the local authority to pass a resolution to denote some definite area as a clearance area. This they may do (and indeed must do, if they are satisfied as to certain facts) 'upon consideration of an official representation or other information in their possession', so that it is clear from the Act that there is no right for an objector to be heard at that stage. The resolution is only a preliminary step to prepare the way for either a clearance order or a compulsory purchase order, and two separate schedules provide similar procedures for each case. These orders require the consent of the Minister of Housing and Local Government before they can become effective, and the time for making objections is between the making of the order and the Minister's decision upon it. Before the local authority may submit a clearance order to the Minister they must make it available for inspection and advertise it in the local press. They must also notify owners, occupiers, and mortgagees of the land, and inform them of their opportunities for making objections. If no objection is made, the Minister may confirm the order with or without modification. But the important provision is:

If any objection duly made is not withdrawn, the Minister shall, before confirming the order, either cause a public local inquiry to be held or afford to any person by whom an objection has been duly made as aforesaid and not withdrawn an opportunity of appearing before and being heard by a person appointed for the purpose, and, after considering any objection not withdrawn and the report of the person who held the inquiry or of the person appointed as aforesaid, may, subject to the provisions of this Schedule, confirm the order with or without modification.[1]

[1] The power of modification allows the minister to modify an invalid order so as to make it a valid one: *Minister of Health v. The King* [1934] A.C. 494.

16—A.L.

If the order is confirmed, the local authority must again advertise it and inform objectors. A period of six weeks is then allowed within which any one who wishes to challenge the order on legal grounds (e.g. *ultra vires*) must apply to the High Court. Subject to any legal dispute, the order becomes operative at the end of the six weeks, and 'shall not be questioned in any legal proceedings, whatsoever'. The significance of this drastic clause is explained elsewhere.[1] Standardized provisions of the same kind are found in the law governing the compulsory purchase of land, both under the Housing Act and under the general statute, the Acquisition of Land (Authorisation Procedure) Act 1946. The Town and Country Planning Act 1962 also follows this standard pattern.[2]

When there is opposition to the local authority's order the usual sequence of events is that objection is lodged and a public local inquiry is held. The 'person appointed for the purpose' is in the great majority of cases one of the Ministry's inspectors. The 'case' is thus 'heard' before an official of the ministry concerned. Both the local authority and the objectors may be legally represented, and an important inquiry will have some of the atmosphere of a trial. The inspector may conduct the inquiry as he wishes, subject in some cases to procedural regulations. The objectors will call witnesses and examine them, and the local authority's representatives may cross-examine them. The authority will also frequently call witnesses of its own. The inspector, like a judge, will often take very little part in the argument; his task is to hear the objections and the argument and then give advice to the Minister. In due course the inquiry is closed, and the inspector makes his report. Until 1957 the normal practice was to refuse disclosure of this report to the objectors: it was treated as an official document like any other paper on the Ministry's files, and like any other report from a civil servant to his department, it was treated as confidential.[3] Eventually the Minister's decision would be given; but often, under the old practice, it would be unaccompanied by reasons. Occasionally the statute would require reasons to be given; for instance, the schedule dealing with clearance orders under the Housing Act 1957, quoted above, provides that the Minister shall give reasons, if requested, for treating a building as unfit

[1] Above, p. 151.   [2] Above, p. 148.   [3] See above, p. 193.

for human habitation if this has been disputed by the owner at the inquiry.

Dissatisfaction with inquiries

In the normal case of inquiries held before departmental inspectors, the general line of complaint was that what began with much of the openness and regularity of a court of law degenerated into a decision taken by an unseen power, behind closed doors, and on grounds unspecified. How strongly people could feel about this is shown by Lord Hewart's attack on it in *The New Despotism*, published in 1929, when he was Lord Chief Justice. He wrote:

> The departmental policy of secrecy, which is inveterate, is in itself sufficient to condemn the system under which the public departments act as tribunals to decide disputes of a judicial nature. This secrecy naturally leads to the conclusion that the departments are afraid of their proceedings being made public, and tends to destroy confidence in the fairness of their decisions. How is it to be expected that a party against whom a decision has been given in a hole-and-corner fashion, and without any grounds being specified, should believe that he has had justice? Even the party in whose favour a dispute is decided must, in such circumstances, be tempted to look upon the result as a mere piece of luck.[1]

Turning then to inquiries specifically, he continued:

> It is sometimes enacted that, before the Minister comes to a decision, he shall hold a public inquiry, at which interested parties are entitled to adduce evidence and be heard. But that provision is no real safeguard, because the person who has the power of deciding is in no way bound by the report or the recommendations of the person who holds the inquiry, and may entirely ignore the evidence which the inquiry brought to light. He can, and in practice sometimes does, give a decision wholly inconsistent with the report, the recommendations, and the evidence, which are not published or disclosed to interested individuals. In any case, as the official who decides has not seen or heard the witnesses, he is as a rule quite incapable of estimating the value of their evidence. . . . the requirement of a public inquiry is in practice nugatory. . . . It seems absurd that one official should hold a public inquiry into the merits of a proposal,

[1] P. 48.

and that another official should be entitled, disregarding the report of the first, to give a decision on the merits.[1]

The essential compromise

The fact that has to be faced is that there is no reason why the final decision should be based on evidence given at the inquiry at all—and often it will not be. Suppose, to take the example of the *Stevenage* case,[2] that the local residents oppose a scheme for imposing a new town on them on the grounds that it will be difficult to provide for a satisfactory water-supply or for sewage disposal. These objections are certainly relevant to the scheme, but they have to be weighed by the Minister and his advisers against the demands of national policy. It may be that these objections apply to all the other eligible sites for the new town. It may be, also, that the need to develop new towns is so great that the expense of overcoming serious physical obstacles will justify itself. It may be, again, that the other advantages of the site outweigh the objections. These are eminently the sort of matters upon which the final decision will turn. But it is impossible to bring them to a head at a public inquiry in the same way in which a legal issue can be brought to a head in a court of law. For the question before a court of law is self-contained: the evidence on matters of fact and the argument on matters of law provide the judge with all the material for his decision. If fed with the right data he should deliver the right answer. Since a judge is not a machine, he will have his own opinions which will influence his judgment. But this does not alter the fact that his duty is to decide the issues raised before him on the materials laid before him.

A minister's decision on a planning scheme or a clearance scheme or a new town order is a different kind of mental exercise. The public inquiry cannot provide him with all that he has to consider, for there is the whole exterior world of political motive. Even if the Minister sends, as he sometimes does, representatives to argue questions of policy before the inspector, this does not solve the problem. For the inspector cannot bear the responsibility for the decision in the same way in which a judge is responsible for deciding a case at law. It is fundamental

[1] P. 51.   [2] Above, p. 183.

to the constitution that the judge should be independent and bear his own responsibility. But it is equally fundamental that political decisions should be taken by a minister responsible to Parliament, and that the political responsibility should rest entirely upon him and not upon his officials or advisers. Furthermore, the place where policy should be explained is Parliament, where the responsibility lies. Nothing, therefore, can prevent the real responsibility lying outside the forum of an inquiry, whereas it must lie inside the forum of a court of law.

This contrast may be indistinct in borderline cases. Courts of law may appear to take decisions of policy and ministers may decide particular cases into which policy does not seem to enter. But, all the same, legal decisions and political decisions are different things and require different procedures.

'Blowing off steam'

It is natural, then, that objectors should often be left with a sense of frustration, feeling that they are fighting a phantom opponent, and that they have no assurance of coming to grips with the real issues which are going to decide the case. In the *Stevenage* case the judge of first instance said:

> To take any other view [*sc.* than that the minister must have reasonable grounds for his decision] would reduce the provisions for objections, the holding of a local public inquiry, the report of the officer who holds it, and the consideration of that report by the Minister to an absurdity, because when all has been said and done the Minister could disregard the whole proceedings and do just as he pleased. The Attorney-General argued that that was, indeed, the position, and that the sole use of the liberty to make objections was that the objectors (I am quoting his words) might 'blow off steam' and so rally public opinion to which alone the Minister might bow.[1]

But as we know, and as the appellate courts held,[2] the minister's decision cannot be dictated to him by the inspector's conclusions from the inquiry. Does this then mean that inquiries must be regarded merely as opportunities for objectors to blow off steam? If one takes the view that it is waste of time to call evidence and make representations before one person when the final decision will be taken by some different person, who is not bound by the report of the first, then the only good done by the

[1] [1947] 1 All E.R. at 398.   [2] Above, p. 183.

inquiry is to give the objectors such satisfaction as they may derive from making their objections publicly.

But this view is cynical and unrealistic. It assumes that a government department will take no notice of its inspector's report unless it is legally obliged to do so, and that is obviously wrong. The important thing is not that the decision should be dictated by the report but that the objectors' case should be fairly heard and should be fairly taken into account. The law can ensure that their case is heard. But it cannot ensure that any particular weight is given to it.[1] That, after all, is precisely the basis on which the judges have developed the rules of natural justice. In imposing the general rule that a man is entitled to be heard in his defence before his property or his livelihood can be taken from him, the law has never required that there must be any rational connexion between the defence put forward and the final order made. It is enough to assume that a responsible official will pay due regard to the other side of the case once his mind is directed to it. The real risk is not that he will perversely disregard the evidence, but that he will be tempted to act before he has discovered that there is another side to the case. The same applies to public inquiries, which are merely a statutory and formal method of giving effect to the same principle of justice which the judges developed by case-law.

The running fire of adverse comment from the legal profession has not therefore always been directed at the right target. The statutory inquiry has proved to be an essential piece of mechanism and the committees who have reported upon it have been unable to suggest anything better. It is incessantly in use, and it is now as familiar as any other governmental procedure. But it has required substantial improvement in its details, as we shall see.

PROCEDURAL IMPROVEMENTS

Statutory inquiries and natural justice

Before looking at the procedural reforms which have been made administratively and by statute we should consider the relationship between a statutory inquiry procedure and the

[1] Subject to the rules as to judicial control for unreasonableness, &c.: above, p. 70.

principles of natural justice. Clearly there is a close kinship, for the statutory inquiry is merely a Parliamentary and formalized version of the hearing which in any case would be required by the common law. There is a basic consistency, so that the inquiry provisions of a statute can be treated as a framework within which natural justice can operate and supply missing details. Natural justice is founded on the presumption that Parliament intends powers to be exercised fairly; and this presumption is all the stronger where Parliament itself has provided for a hearing.

We have already seen how the statutory and common law procedures interacted in the Housing Act cases. In the *Hampstead* case the House of Lords imposed restrictions that were thought to be necessary in the interests of departmental efficiency. But in the *Jarrow* case the Court of Appeal filled in a gap in the statutory procedure by invalidating the minister's order where he consulted one party behind the back of the other.[1] The minister's quasi-judicial duty was discussed on the footing that the statutory inquiry made no material difference. Lord Loreburn's famous formula was taken as the rubric, and the minister's function was held to be quasi-judicial—as the inspector's has been held to be also.[2] Natural justice was also applied in another case where the normal inquiry procedure was modified by war-time legislation; but even that discouraging background did not prevent the court from holding that a landowner must be given a fair opportunity to object to a compulsory purchase order.[3] The principle of these cases was that the law could not be content with seeing merely that the form of the inquiry procedure had been followed.

It is to be hoped that these cases are still sound law. But their principle is threatened by dicta in the *Stevenage* case, saying that the minister need do nothing but follow the statutory procedure, and in the *Brighton* case, saying that natural justice has no part to play where ministers have to attach importance to their policy. It would be lamentable if these dicta were to unsettle the law, but there is no need to repeat the criticism made already.[4]

[1] Above, p. 195.
[2] *Denby & Sons Ltd. v. Minister of Health* [1936] 1 K.B. 337.
[3] *Stafford v. Ministry of Health* [1946] K.B. 621; above, p. 197.
[4] Above, pp. 184, 208.

The Ministers' Powers Committee (1932)

The first full-scale report on the system of inquiries was made by the Committee on Ministers' Powers of 1932.[1] The whole tenor of its approach was that the statutory procedure was a vehicle for the principles of natural justice, and it was recommended that those principles should go further than they did. Natural justice ought, it was suggested, to include a right to have reasons for the decision, and perhaps also a right to see the report of the inspector. And the Committee concluded that in any case, regardless of natural justice, the right solution to the dilemma of inspectors' reports was to publish them. The right to a hearing should also include the right for the objector to know in good time the case which he had to meet.

None of these recommendations resulted in any change in the law or in departmental practice, and twenty-five years were to pass before the same questions were taken up with greater success by the Franks Committee. Meanwhile complaint continued unabated, especially on the non-disclosure of inspectors' reports. Discontent was aggravated by comparison with the enlightened practices of certain departments which already employed independent inspectors, published their reports, and gave reasons for their decisions.

The Franks Committee (1957)

The Committee on Tribunals and Enquiries (the Franks Committee) surveyed the whole ground again in its report of 1957.[2] This was a more extensive, factual and practical report than the report of 1932; and it caught a favouring tide of public opinion. Although it made many important recommendations, none of them were very radical. The inquiry system as such was accepted as the best method of hearing that could be devised. Although there was a recommendation (not accepted) that inspectors should be put under the control of the Lord Chancellor, no real attempt was made to follow the American lead in separating the functions of 'prosecutor' and 'judge'. The value of the Committee's work lay rather in its proposals for improving the existing system, which have achieved considerable success and have greatly reduced the volume of public complaint. Of

---

[1] Cmd. 4060.   [2] Cmnd. 218.

outstanding importance were the recommendations (accepted) that inspectors' reports should be published and that objectors should be able to know as early as possible what case they had to meet.

Looking at the nature of the inquiry process, the Committee contrasted 'two strongly opposed views': the 'administrative' and the 'judicial' views. The administrative view, which had been dominant previously, stressed that the minister was responsible to Parliament and to Parliament only for his decision, and that it could not in any way be governed by rules. The judicial view held that an inquiry was something like a trial before a judge and that the decision should be based wholly and directly on the evidence. Both these extremes were rejected —and this involved rejecting the established philosophy that justified non-disclosure of the government's case and non-disclosure of the inspector's report. The Committee said:

If the administrative view is dominant the public enquiry cannot play its full part in the total process, and there is a danger that the rights and interests of the individual citizens affected will not be sufficiently protected. In these cases it is idle to argue that Parliament can be relied upon to protect the citizen, save exceptionally. . . . If the judicial view is dominant there is a danger that people will regard the person before whom they state their case as a kind of judge provisionally deciding the matter, subject to an appeal to the Minister. This view overlooks the true nature of the proceeding, the form of which is necessitated by the fact that the Minister himself, who is responsible to Parliament for the ultimate decision, cannot conduct the enquiry in person.

The Committee rejected the notion that objectors could not expect the same standard of justice when the scheme was initiated by the same minister who had ultimately to decide its fate rather than by some other authority. This misconception had gained currency because of the difficulty of finding any other explanation for the curious language used by the House of Lords in the *Stevenage* case.[1] But one anomaly does not justify another. The Committee put fallacious distinctions firmly aside:

These and other possible distinctions are useful in considering

[1] Above, p. 184.

detailed aspects of the various procedures, but they are misleading when what has to be considered is their general nature. Not only is the impact of these various procedures the same so far as the individual citizen is concerned, for he is at issue with a public authority in all of them, but they also have basic common features of importance when regarded from a wider point of view. All involve the weighing of proposals or decisions, or˜ provisional proposals or decisions, made by a public authority on the one hand against the views and interests of individuals affected by them on the other. All culminate in a ministerial decision, in the making of which there is a wide discretion and which is final.

The plan of reform

Two of the Committee's primary recommendations relating to inquiries were that there should be a permanent and independent body, the Council on Tribunals, and that the Council should formulate rules of procedure for inquiries which would have statutory force. The Council on Tribunals was constituted by the Tribunals and Inquiries Act 1958, but is a purely advisory body. It has to consider and report on such matters as may be referred to it by the Lord Chancellor, or as it may itself determine to be of special importance, concerning 'administrative procedures involving, or which may involve, the holding by or on behalf of a Minister of a statutory inquiry.'[1] There is thus standing machinery for dealing with the problems of inquiries as and when they arise. The work of the Council will be mentioned below under a number of different headings. An example of a matter referred to it by the Lord Chancellor will be found under *Costs*. An example of a special report by the Council will be found under *Evidence from other sources*. In addition, as its work has developed, the Council has entertained complaints from members of the public, and the special report just mentioned arose out of such a complaint. Thus the Council has, in its limited sphere of operation, undertaken the work of an Ombudsman. Its constitution and other activities are explained in the next chapter.

Power to make procedural rules for inquiries was given by an Act of 1959, which added a new section to the Tribunals and Inquiries Act.[2] The power is conferred on the Lord Chan-

---

[1] S. 1 (1) (c).
[2] S. 7A, added by Town and Country Planning Act 1959, s. 33.

cellor, acting by statutory instrument and after consultation with the Council on Tribunals. Rules have been made for certain of the commoner types of inquiries, as mentioned below.

In Scottish affairs the Secretary of State for Scotland acts in place of the Lord Chancellor.

Of the Committee's detailed recommendations about inquiries the following are the most noteworthy.

(1) A public authority should be required to make available, in good time before the inquiry, a written statement giving full particulars of its case.

(2) The minister should, whenever possible, make available before the inquiry a statement of the policy relevant to the particular case; but he should be free to direct that the statement be wholly or partly excluded from discussion at the inquiry.

(3) If the policy changes after the inquiry, the letter conveying the minister's decision should explain the change and its relation to the decision.

(4) The main body of inspectors should be placed under the control of the Lord Chancellor.

(5) The initiating authority (including a minister) should explain its proposals fully at the inquiry and support them by oral evidence.

(6) Statutory codes of procedure should be formulated by the Council on Tribunals.

(7) Public inquiries are preferable to private hearings in cases of compulsory acquisition of land, development plans, planning appeals and clearance schemes.

(8) The inspector should have power to administer the oath and subpoena witnesses.

(9) Costs should be more generally awarded and the Council on Tribunals should keep the subject under review.

(10) The inspector's report should be divided into two parts: (i) summary of evidence, findings of fact, and inferences of fact; and (ii) reasoning from facts, including application of policy, and (normally) recommendations.

(11) The complete text of the report should accompany the minister's letter of decision and also be available on request centrally and locally.

(12) Further, if any of the parties wish for an opportunity to propose corrections of fact, the first part of the report should, as soon as possible after the inquiry, be sent both to the authority and to the objectors. They should have 14 days in which to propose corrections.

(13) The minister should be required to submit to the parties for their observations any new factual evidence, including expert evidence, obtained after the inquiry.

(14) The minister's letter of decision should set out in full his findings and inferences of fact and the reasons for the decision.

The great majority of these recommendations were accepted by the government and have since been put into effect. Only nos. (2) and (4) were rejected outright, though nos. (9) and (12) were reserved for further consideration. The remainder were declared to be 'wholly or partly acceptable'—a form of acceptance which left open a way of retreat, as appeared later in connection with no. (13).[1]

The necessary changes have been effected more by administrative directions than by alteration of the law. The Tribunals and Inquiries Act 1958, in addition to setting up the Council on Tribunals, made provision for reasons to be given for decisions. The statutory rules of procedure which have now been made for some inquiries also give legal force to some of the other improvements. But the chief instrument of reform has been the ministerial circular, a document which has no legal operation but which 'invites' local authorities and other bodies to make arrangements suggested by the minister. The circulars in question here are published documents which are therefore a most useful aid to public understanding of the administrative scheme. Comprehensive circulars were in fact issued some months before the Tribunals and Inquiries Act was passed, and this brought the new system into being in so far as the government did not itself do so by ordinary departmental instructions.[2]

The action taken on the various recommendations of the Franks Committee is set out in an appendix to the annual report of the Council on Tribunals for 1963.

[1] See below, p. 237.
[2] See for example Circular No. 9/58 of the Ministry of Housing and Local Government.

The right to know the opposing case

One important requirement of natural justice is that the objector should have the opportunity to know and meet the case against him.[1] 'The case against him', in the context of an inquiry, is usually some scheme backed by government policy. The Franks Committee stressed that the reasons behind, say, a compulsory purchase order for the acquisition of land are capable of explanation to an objector and should be explained in advance of the inquiry, so that he has time to prepare his case.

Ministerial instructions therefore ask local authorities to prepare written statements setting out the reasons for their proposals and to make these available to objectors in good time before the inquiry. This has now become standard practice. In the cases where rules of procedure now apply, they require the authority to serve on the objector a written statement of their reasons for seeking confirmation of their order or else a written statement of the submissions which they will make at the inquiry. If directions or opinions of other government departments are to be relied upon, they must be disclosed in advance. And facilities must be given for inspection and copying of relevant documents and plans. Where the minister is himself the originating authority, he will of course act similarly.

But there are some inquiries, not as yet covered by rules of procedure, which are of narrower scope. The ordinary statutory provision requires the minister to hold an inquiry and consider the inspector's report. But some statutes say that the inquiry shall be merely an inquiry into the objection. Thus the formula in the New Towns Act, which was in question in the *Stevenage* case, provides for an inquiry to be held 'with respect to the objection.'[2] To the same effect is the Local Government Act 1958 as regards objections by local authorities threatened by proposals for altering local government areas. Another instance is in the Police Act 1964, which deliberately confined inquiries into police amalgamation schemes to inquiries into objections in order to prevent the inquiry going into the merits

---

[1] Above, p. 212.
[2] New Towns Act 1965, 1st Schedule; above, p. 183.

of the scheme as opposed to the merits of the objection. The Scottish decision requiring both sides of the case to be expounded at such inquiries was accordingly nullified.[1] Nor does the law require the inspector to be at liberty to consider alternative schemes or, indeed, to make any recommendation at all.[2]

A restricted inquiry of this kind is fundamentally faulty, for as the Franks Committee observed, 'an objection cannot reasonably be considered as a thing in itself, in isolation from what is objected to.'[3] But inquiries which range widely and are expensive in time and money may be a serious obstacle to schemes which need speedy execution, and there is a genuine dilemma. Inquiries are concerned with the local or personal aspects of some proposed action, but these have to be weighed against general policy and it is impossible to detach one from the other. Inquiries 'into objections' ought therefore to be confined to special situations where it can reasonably be demanded that the proposal itself should be taken for granted. This was the position in the only such case which has come before the courts recently, where it was clear from the statutory scheme that the merits of the proposals (for local government reorganization) were to be canvassed elsewhere than at the inquiry.[4] There seems little risk of a general drift back to the old practice exemplified in the *Kingston By-pass* case, for the objector's right to know the case against him is now recognized in principle.

Although the government rejected the recommendation that the deciding minister, as opposed to the initiating authority, should provide a statement of policy before the inquiry, there has been an improvement in the issue of explanatory material (particularly from the Ministry of Housing and Local Government) which helps policy to be understood.

Publication of Inspectors' Reports

None of the reforms achieved by the Franks Committee was of greater importance than the successful termination of the

---

[1] See above, p. 198. This change was recommended by the Royal Commission on the Police, 1962, Cmnd. 1728, para. 289.

[2] *Wednesbury Corpn. v. Minister of Housing and Local Government* [1966] 2 Q.B. 275.

[3] Cmnd. 218, 1957, para. 271. This paragraph erroneously assumes that the standard form of inquiry is into objections only. For the standard form, see above, p. 221.

[4] *Wednesbury Corporation v. M.H.L.G.* (above).

long struggle to secure publication of inspectors' reports. Before the Committee there was strong official opposition to the proposal. The Ministry of Housing and Local Government testified that publication would embarrass the Minister, would be administratively impracticable, would require many more inspectors, would impair frankness, would put inspectors under an 'enormous strain' in polishing up their reports for publication, would do no good, would bewilder the objectors, and so forth. Another witness said that publication would entail delay since the inspector would have to be so careful about his grammar and spelling. Yet the official case was not so weak as one might think from some of the arguments used to defend it. It had been accepted by the House of Lords in the *Hampstead* case[1] and treated with respect by the Ministers' Powers Committee, though the Committee were in favour of publication. But no argument could alter the overriding fact that it was impossible to persuade people that they had received justice if they were not allowed to see the document which was based on their evidence. If inquiries were to be acceptable to public opinion, the 'administrative view' had to make concessions.

It is now the standard practice for a copy of the report to accompany the minister's letter of decision. Where statutory rules apply, they require this specifically. None of the evils that were feared seem to have resulted. The work of inspectors is more respected than before, since objectors can see how carefully it is done. It was not long before the Chief Inspector of the Ministry of Housing and Local Government stated publicly that the disclosure of reports had led to markedly better public relations. At the same time it is easier for objectors to tell whether legal remedies may be open to them or whether there is cause for complaint to the Council on Tribunals. Above all, the sense of grievance has been removed. Good administration and the principles of justice have once again proved to be friends, not enemies. The departments that were most tenacious of secrecy have found that it has done them good to abandon it.

The government however rejected the recommendation that the part of the report dealing with the evidence and findings of fact should be disclosed in time for the parties to suggest corrections before the decision. This practice is, in fact, followed

---

[1] Above, p. 193.

in Scotland,[1] and ideally England ought to follow suit. But in England the delays caused by over-centralized procedures, particularly for development plans and planning appeals, are so serious that the government felt unable to agree to a step which would increase the time taken by an inquiry. Administrative congestion has here affected procedural fairness. Fortunately inspectors' findings of fact are a very rare subject of complaint.

Reasons for decisions

As mentioned already, the Tribunals and Inquiries Act makes provision for the giving of reasons for decisions.[2] This is a matter of great importance. It enables the citizen to understand the connection between the inspector's report and the minister's decision. It also enables the court to quash the decision if the reasons are not adequately given, thus making a notable extension of judicial control over inquiry procedures.

The terms and effect of the Act are explained in the chapter on tribunals, where it is noted that the statutory duty to give reasons applies only where reasons are requested.[3] But in practice a reasoned decision letter is now sent out as a matter of course. Where procedural rules have been made (as explained below[4]), they impose an unqualified duty to give reasons, so that there is no need to make any request. It has been held that reasons given under the rules must be as full and as adequate as reasons given under the Act, and that where a bad decision letter leaves real and substantial doubt as to the reasons the minister's decision may be quashed.[5] The court's insistence on adequate decision letters shows how far the law has progressed from the time when the objector saw neither the inspector's report nor the reasons for the action taken upon it.

Evidence from other sources

Acute difficulty can arise where the minister bases his deci-

---

[1] See e.g. Town and Country Planning Appeals (Inquiry Procedure) (Scotland) Rules 1964, S.I. No. 181, rule 10 (1) and *J. & A. Kirkpatrick v. Lord Advocate* 1967 S.L.T. (Notes) 27 (decision of Secretary of State quashed for failure to observe this rule).

[2] S. 12.   [3] Below, p. 270.   [4] Below, p. 239.

[5] *Givaudan & Co. Ltd. v. Minister of Housing and Local Government* [1967] 1 W.L.R. 250 (decision quashed under Town and Country Planning Act 1962 s. 179). Cf. *Iveagh v. Minister of Housing and Local Government* [1964] 1 Q.B. 395.

sion on facts which he obtains otherwise than through the inquiry. For here the mixture of semi-legal procedure and political decision readily causes misunderstanding. If the objector finds that the minister has taken account of facts which there was no opportunity of contesting at the inquiry, he may feel that the inquiry is waste of time and money. But, as has been emphasized already, it is inherent in most inquiry procedures that in the end the minister takes a decision of policy, and that the inquiry provides him with only part of the material for his decision. *Ex hypothesi*, he may take account of other material. But of what sort of other material?

Controversy centred round this question in the case of the Essex chalkpit in 1961. [1] A company had been refused planning permission to dig and work chalk on their own land. They appealed to the minister and the usual local inquiry was held. Neighbouring landowners appeared at the inquiry and opposed the appeal, giving evidence that the dust from chalk working would be injurious to their land and their livestock. On these grounds the inspector recommended that the appeal be dismissed. But the minister rejected the inspector's recommendation and granted permission after consulting the Ministry of Agriculture whose experts advised that there was no likelihood of serious injury if a particular process ('kibbling') was used and if other conditions were imposed as to fencing of stockpiles and other matters. This evidence was not before the inquiry, and the objectors were aggrieved that they had not been able to dispute it. After an unsuccessful attempt to obtain a legal remedy (explained in an earlier chapter[2]), they complained to the Council on Tribunals. The Council took up the question with government departments and made a special report to the Lord Chancellor. There were also several debates in Parliament and much public comment. The government, it appeared, had not fully accepted the Franks Committee's recommendations about new factual evidence. [3]

The Council on Tribunals criticized the rejection by the minister of his inspector's recommendation in cases where (i)

---

[1] See Annual Reports of the Council on Tribunals, 1960, para. 111; 1961, para. 56.

[2] Above, p. 149 (the *Buxton* case).

[3] Cmnd. 218, 1957, paras. 347–350.

the rejection was based on ministerial policy which could and should have been made clear at the inquiry or (ii) the minister took advice after the inquiry from persons who neither heard the evidence nor saw the site, but yet controverted the inspector's findings as to the facts of the local situation. These final words contain the heart of the matter. The minister's policy may be formed on the basis of all kinds of facts, reports and advice which have nothing to do with the local situation which is the subject of the inquiry, and which therefore need not necessarily be known to the objectors or investigated at the inquiry. But the facts of the local situation are in a different category, and there is bound to be complaint if due respect is not paid to the inspector's findings. In the chalkpit case the government's explanations were not clear on this vital question: was the advice given by the Ministry of Agriculture general advice, to the effect that a certain mode of chalk-working was incapable of creating excessive dust; or was it really advice about the local situation, to the effect that chalk-working in that particular pit would be innocuous? It was the feeling that the advice was of the latter character that underlay all the complaint.

The Council on Tribunals recommended that there should be a rule for future cases providing that the minister, if differing from the inspector's recommendation on a finding of fact or on account of fresh evidence (including expert opinion) or a fresh issue (not being a matter of government policy), should first notify the parties and allow them to comment in writing; and that they should be entitled to have the inquiry reopened if fresh evidence or a fresh issue emerged. This was accepted by the government and is now followed in practice, and it is also embodied in the statutory rules of procedure which have been made for some inquiries including planning appeals.[1] But it may be difficult to tell what is a finding of fact and what is a matter of opinion. The rule was held not to apply recently where the minister rejected his inspector's finding that a house in a particular place would be unobjectionable, since the minister was held not to be differing from the inspector on the facts but

---

[1] See S.I. 1969 no. 1092, rule 12 (2), replacing earlier orders.

enforcing a general policy of not permitting building outside village boundaries.[1]

The same principle may be seen in a case of 1954, in which an objector unsuccessfully challenged a compulsory purchase order for the acquisition of land for a school.[2] At the inquiry the owner persuaded the inspector that another piece of land would be a better site. But that land was already in course of development as a municipal housing estate. The Minister of Education therefore asked the Minister of Housing and Local Government whether the land could be released, and was told that it could not be since the development was too far advanced. The court held that this was a matter of policy on which one minister was always at liberty to consult another between the inquiry and the decision. But, the court added, the situation would have been wholly different if the Minister of Housing had replied that the land was not wanted because it was water-logged or otherwise unsuitable for building. Information of that kind, concerning the relative merits of the two sites, should be disclosed to an objector so that its accuracy could be challenged. This decision suggests that the principles of natural justice might have achieved substantially the same result as the rule recommended by the Council on Tribunals.

Procedural rules

Although the Tribunals and Inquiries Act 1958, as amended in 1959,[3] gives general power to the Lord Chancellor to make statutory rules of procedure for inquiries, rules have so far been made only for inquiries arising from compulsory purchase of land in various cases, from planning appeals and from a few other matters.[4] These are large and important classes, but at the present rate of progress it will be a long time before

[1] *Luke (Lord) v. Minister of Housing and Local Government* [1968] 1 Q.B. 172. A technical defect of the rule is that it does not apply where the inspector makes no recommendation: see *Westminster Bank Ltd. v. M.H.L.G.* [1970] 2 W.L.R. 645.

[2] *Darlassis v. Minister of Education* (1954) 52 L.G.R. 304. This may be compared with the *Jarrow* case, above, p. 195.

[3] Town and Country Planning Act 1959, s. 33.

[4] S.I. 1962, no. 1424 (compulsory purchase by local authorities); 1967, no. 720 (compulsory purchase by ministers); 1968 no. 1952 and 1969 no. 1092, replacing earlier orders (planning); 1966 no. 1375 (gas storage); 1967 no. 450 (electricity wayleaves); 1967 no. 1769 (pipe-lines).

inquiries generally will be subject to statutory rules. In the meantime administrative practice follows the rules by analogy where they are not legally applicable. The making of rules has been welcomed by people professionally concerned.

The rules already made provide a timetable for various steps and formalities. Among their more important substantial provisions are those dealing with—

the written statement of its case by the initiating or opposing authority;[1]
the persons entitled to appear at the inquiry;
the right of representation;
evidence by government departments concerned with the proposal;
the right to call evidence and cross-examine witnesses;
procedure for site inspections;
evidence obtained after the inquiry;[2]
notification of the decision, with reasons;[3]
the right to obtain a copy of the inspector's report.[4]

The persons entitled to appear as of right under the rules are those who have some statutory standing in the matter—the appellant in a planning appeal, for example, but not a neighbour who wants to object.[5] But the rules also provide that any person may appear with the inspector's leave, and the usual practice (as also in cases not covered by the rules) is to throw open the inquiry to all who wish to appear. This is good administration, since neighbours and others may often be able to point out serious objections; and the object is to obtain the best decision in the public interest. But those who appear at discretion rather than as of right do not under the rules obtain the full rights of a party. They are not entitled to be sent the statement of the initiating or opposing authority's case; and they are not entitled to the benefit of the rule, discussed above, about disclosure of evidence from sources other than the inquiry. The Council on Tribunals was unsuccessful in asking for an assurance that the benefit of the latter rule should in practice be extended to them.[6] But usually they have similar interests

---

[1] Above, p. 233.   [2] Above, p. 237.   [3] Above, p. 236.
[4] Above, p. 235.   [5] See above, p. 123.
[6] Annual Report for 1962, para. 37.

to one of the statutory parties, who will be officially encouraged to keep them informed.[1]

An objector's right of representation is unrestricted, so that he may appear by a lawyer or by any other person, as well as by himself.

The rules contain no requirement that the proceedings should be held in public. Although public hearings are the rule, the inspector is able (as in a court of law) to exclude the public and even other parties where the evidence to be given is confidential, for example a secret commercial process. In such cases there is an irreconcilable conflict between the objectors' rights to know the case against them and to cross-examine witnesses and, on the other hand, the need for secrecy in genuine cases. A partial solution is that the objector's professional representatives may be allowed to be present, since they are bound by their professional standards of conduct and can be expected to respect confidences.[2]

Discretionary inquiries

The Tribunals and Inquiries Act 1958 defined a 'statutory inquiry' as an inquiry held under a statutory duty. The jurisdiction of the Council on Tribunals and the other provisions of the Act therefore applied where an Act provided that the minister *shall* hold an inquiry, but did not apply where the provision was merely that the minister *may* hold an inquiry. But there are many discretionary inquiries of the latter class, and it is just as important that they should conform to the best practice. It is also sometimes difficult, where the statute is ambiguous, to tell whether there is a duty or a discretion. Clear examples of discretionary inquiries are those held under the Local Government Act 1933, where departments have a general power to hold inquiries in connexion with their functions under the Act,[3] inquiries into objections to compulsory purchase orders for defence purposes,[4] and inquiries held under the National Health Service Act 1946.[5]

[1] *Ibid.*, para. 39.
[2] See Annual Report for 1969 of the Parliamentary Commissioner for Administration (H.C. 138, 1969–70), p. 55.
[3] S. 290.
[4] See Council on Tribunals' Annual Report for 1961, para. 79.
[5] S. 70.

The law was therefore amended by the Tribunals and Inquiries Act 1966, which gives power to apply the relevant parts of the Act of 1958 to discretionary inquiries designated by statutory instrument. An order has been made bringing large numbers of such inquiries within the scope of the Act.[1] Sixty-five varieties of inquiries are specified, including those held under the Local Government Act 1933 and the National Health Service Act 1946, and the statutory duty to give a reasoned decision on request is expressly made applicable.

Since discretionary inquiries are by definition not legally necessary, and since any inquiry into anything may always be held administratively, ministers sometimes prefer to avoid statutory procedure altogether and hold non-statutory inquiries. The first inquiry into the development of Stansted airport, which might well have been held under the planning legislation, was in fact held as a mere administrative inquiry after which the government proposed to authorize the development by special order. Similarly the Minister may ask regional hospital boards to hold non-statutory inquiries into complaints against hospitals instead of using his own powers under the National Health Service Act 1946. In such cases objectors have no procedural rights (apart from the principles of natural justice), their complaints cannot be taken up by the Council on Tribunals, and the safeguards intended by the Act of 1966 cannot operate. The Council on Tribunals has publicly criticized these procedures.[2]

Planning inquiry commissions

Big projects for such things as major airports and power stations often raise difficult questions about alternative sites and other problems of more than local character which cannot well be handled at an ordinary local inquiry.[3] A new procedure is provided by the Town and Country Planning Act 1968, under which the Minister may refer applications and appeals, and also the government's own proposals, to a 'planning inquiry commission' consisting of from three to five persons.[4]

[1] S.I. 1967, no. 451.
[2] Annual Report for 1967, para. 116; for 1968, para. 52.
[3] See above, p. 234.
[4] Ss. 61–63.

The commission must then proceed in two stages: first, it must conduct a general investigation; secondly, it must hear objectors at a local inquiry before one or more of its members. It is only the second stage which is subject to the Tribunals and Inquiries Acts and to the usual safeguards. The first stage is to be an unrestricted investigation comparable to an inquiry by a royal commission, and the only formal requirement is that notice of the reference to the commission shall be published and served on certain parties. The right to object to a specific proposal at the second stage is, as in other cases, confined to persons with a statutory status; but it will no doubt be the practice, as also in other cases, to allow anyone genuinely concerned to be heard.

Costs

Ministers have power under numerous statutes to make orders for the recovery of costs incurred (either by the department or by other parties) in connection with inquiries, including for example compulsory purchase and planning inquiries.[1] But until recently the power was very rarely exercised. In 1964 the Council on Tribunals made a report on the subject at the request of the Lord Chancellor.[2] The principal recommendations were that the power should be extended to cover all inquiries and hearings; that it should be exercised more freely, particularly against any party who behaves unreasonably and vexatiously (including a public authority); that a higher standard of behaviour should be expected from a public authority than from the citizen; that costs should normally be awarded to successful objectors in compulsory purchase and similar cases; and that inspectors should always make recommendations as to costs in their reports.

The government accepted the recommendation in favour of successful objectors, and this together with other recommended changes has been put into force administratively. The changes which require legislation still remain to be implemented.

Inspectors

All the evidence before the Franks Committee was to the

[1] The provisions commonly made applicable are those of the Local Government Act 1933, s. 290.
[2] Cmnd. 2471.

effect that the inspectors were competent, patient, and open to very little criticism as to the manner in which they controlled the proceedings. Their reputation has been strengthened still further by the practice of publishing their reports, which reveal a high standard of skill and care. But certain questions of principle remain. What should the inspector's status be? Is it right that he should be a permanent official of the ministry concerned with the scheme? Or should he be an independent person, with a position more like that of a judge? The 'administrative' and the 'judicial' views can both be supported by an appeal to precedent.

The Ministry of Housing and Local Government, which holds more inquiries than any other ministry, has a permanent staff of inspectors for housing and planning inquiries. These men are its own officials, and usually serve as inspectors for the rest of their careers once they have been assigned to that work. Certain other ministries, and all the Scottish departments, normally employ independent persons such as surveyors, lawyers or retired officials. Indeed, the Ministry of Housing and Local Government does this in certain cases, such as inquiries into new town orders (since the minister himself is the originator of the scheme) and inquiries into food and water supply schemes of exceptional difficulty. Sometimes an inquiry is held by two inspectors, one or both of whom may have technical qualifications. Thus a major proposal for an atomic power station or an overhead electricity line may be held before a planning inspector and an engineering inspector sitting together. Alternatively technical assessors may sit with an inspector to assist him. But the most common situation in England is that the inquiry is presided over by a single government official.

Two factors affect the question of departmental versus independent inspectors. The first is, once again, 'policy'. It is obviously easier to entrust the case to an independent arbiter if it is a decision which will turn more on local facts than on broad national policy, such as a decision to acquire one site rather than another for a school, or to acquire a piece of land for road widening. An important planning scheme, depending very much on the degree of control which can rightly be imposed on private interests, or a proposal to create a new town, obviously lies more in the sphere of policy; and when policy has to be weighed against private interest, the minister must take responsibility and employ trained officials.

The ideal would be for the Minister himself to hold the enquiry and thus hear the evidence at first hand, but since this is clearly out of the question the next best course is for one of his own officers, who can be kept in touch with developments in policy, to perform this function.[1]

The other factor is the volume of work. The Ministry of Housing and Local Government, with a corps of about 200 inspectors, may have to provide for more than 6,000 inquiries in a year. This pressure of business, combined with the strong element of policy in many of the cases, makes it almost inevitable that professional administrators should take charge of it. Continuity of work demands continuity of policy.

There are other arguments for the departmental inspector which are entitled to some respect. One is than an independent inspector may positively mislead the objectors into supposing that the process is judicial, and that the decision will be based entirely on the evidence heard at the inquiry. Then, when they find in the end that this is not so, they are all the more dissatisfied. At some stage or other the objector must face the fact that he is the object of an administrative, not a judicial, process, and that policy must play a large part. A more practical point is that the departmental inspector may often be more skilled in this particular work.

The Franks Committee's conclusion on this dilemma was that inspectors should be placed under the control of the Lord Chancellor, so that they would no longer be identified in the minds of the objectors with the department of the deciding minister.[2] But even this modest proposal was not accepted by the government. It was felt to be essential that the corps of professional inspectors, whose lives are spent in an endless succession of inquiries, should remain an integral part of their departmental organization. The pleas made in Parliament that the inspectors should become 'Lord Chancellor's men' achieved nothing. Independent inspectors continue to be used in some

[1] *The Franks Committee's Report*, para. 293.
[2] Para. 303.

cases as before. The use of departmental inspectors has ceased to be a subject of complaint. Indeed, the employment of an independent inspector in one case was the cause of a complaint to the Council on Tribunals.

Inspectors have now been given the responsibility of deciding certain categories of planning appeals themselves instead of merely making a recommendation to the Minister.[1] The object of this innovation is to reduce the delays in planning appeals. At the same time, it strengthens the case for a trained departmental inspectorate.

The Council on Tribunals

Various complaints reach the Council on Tribunals from people dissatisfied with inquiries. Details of some are to be found in the Council's annual reports. These complaints are taken up with government departments when they seem to be justified, and a number of improvements in practice have resulted.

In most of these cases no legal right has been infringed, but nevertheless the complainant feels that injustice has been done. In one case a London borough council had put forward a scheme for a large housing estate which involved demolishing an area of old houses. An inquiry was held at which local landowners objected to the scheme and argued that the best plan was that the old houses should be rehabilitated. The Minister dismissed the appeal, apparently on the ground that the objectors had made out their case. But the borough council prepared a modified scheme and after negotiations with the Minister, who had meanwhile become the authority to whom application for permission had to be made, they obtained permission for it. From these negotiations the objectors were excluded. They had no right to take part, nor indeed had they had any legal right to take part in the original inquiry. But after their successful opposition to the first scheme it seemed less than fair to exclude them from the consideration of the modified scheme, since the two were so closely connected. The Council on Tribunals issued a special report criticizing the handling of this case, and it was debated in Parliament.[2]

[1] Town and Country Planning Act 1968, s. 21; S.I. 1968 No. 1972. Procedural rules have been made by S.I. 1968 No. 1952.
[2] Annual Report for 1965, para. 77 (Packington Estate, Islington).

Another source of complaint to the Council has been the informal procedure by which appellants in planning appeals are invited by the Ministry to agree to have their appeals decided on written representations only, without an inquiry.[1] The attraction of this procedure is that it saves time and expense and is frequently quite satisfactory—so much so that about half of all planning appeals are dealt with in this way. Each side is allowed to see and comment upon the submissions made by the other, but the report of the officer who inspects the site and makes a factual report to the Minister is not disclosed. The delay in disposing of planning appeals is so serious that many appellants are willing to waive their legal right to a statutory inquiry for the sake of a quicker and less formal procedure. This useful device is characteristic of the fondness of government departments for informal and non-statutory methods. But a procedure which plays so important a part ought to be statutory. One defect of its not being so is that there is no power in the Minister to award costs. Another defect is that there is no provision for the views of third party objectors. In any case, the inspector's report should be disclosed, as the Council has advocated.

These are examples of the Council's 'ombudsman' function in receiving and investigating complaints, which is illustrated further in the next chapter.

Experiments in the United States

An attempt to 'judicialize' departmental procedure, much in the manner the House of Lords refused to approve in the *Hampstead* case, has led the courts of the United States through some interesting gyrations. In a famous case of 1936, which concerned the Secretary of Agriculture's power to fix prices for sales of livestock after a public hearing, the Supreme Court invalidated a price-fixing order merely on the ground that the Secretary himself had not personally heard or read any of the evidence or considered the arguments submitted, but had decided the matter merely on the advice of his officials in consultations at which the objectors were not present.[2] A heroic decision! The opinion given by Chief Justice Hughes rejected

[1] Annual Report for 1964, para. 76; 1966, para. 89.
[2] *Morgan v. United States*, 298 U.S. 468 (1936).

the very essence of administrative practice by refusing to allow that 'one official may examine evidence, and another official who has not considered the evidence may make the findings and order'. He said:

> That duty [*sc.* of decision] cannot be performed by one who has not considered evidence or argument. It is not an impersonal obligation. It is akin to that of a judge. The one who decides must hear.

It would be stimulating to hear the comments of senior civil servants, on both sides of the Atlantic, upon this doctrine. It has since been made subject to severe qualifications, including statutory modification, as indeed was inevitable if it was not to bring the work of administration to a standstill. The facts of life make it quite impossible for a minister personally to peruse all the evidence when the case comes finally to him for decision, nor can it be right to subpoena him in every case and demand to know his exact state of mind and how much of his homework he did before he signed the order.[1] Obviously the work of holding the inquiry and reporting on the evidence must be delegated to officials, and in many cases the evidence will be so voluminous that the minister will have to have it summarized. But what the Supreme Court does require is that the decision should be the personal decision of the minister in the sense that he sees the record and exercises his personal judgment upon it. The case may be predigested for him in his department, but he is the one who is required to decide. He must therefore 'hear' in the sense of applying his mind to both sides of the case. He may not simply accept a decision taken by his subordinates, as he may in England.[2]

The Federal Administrative Procedure Act

Congress adopted a new line of attack in the Administrative Procedure Act of 1946. This Act is an ambitious attempt to deal with many of the problems discussed in this book. It does, indeed, adopt the ideal 'the one who decides must hear' for the inquiries to which it applies, meaning obligatory statutory inquiries held by agencies of the federal government and decided 'on the record'. But instead of attempting to control the

---

[1] *United States v. Morgan*, 313 U.S. 409 (1941); see also *Morgan v. United States*, 304 U.S. 1 (1938).
[2] Above, p. 64.

final decision of the minister or agency, and postponing the substantial decision until the last possible moment, it allows a substantial decision to be taken by the official who holds the hearing. The object is to meet the complaint that hearing officers may be—or at any rate appear to be—too much the puppets of their agencies. The position of these officers is therefore strengthened under the American statute, which endeavours to give them a position of independence and responsibility almost like that of a judge of first instance. Hearing officers are formed into something like a special corps, and are removable only for good cause established before the Civil Service Commission; and their salaries and conditions of service are controlled by the Commission rather than by their own agencies. Having given them a status of greater independence, the Act then provides that, unless they submit the whole record to the agency, they shall decide the case, and not merely make a recommendation to the agency. The Act says:

> In cases in which the agency has not presided at the reception of the evidence, the officer who presided . . . shall initially decide the case or the agency shall require (in specific cases or by general rule) the entire record to be certified to it for initial decision. Whenever such officers make the initial decision and in the absence of either an appeal to the agency or review upon motion of the agency within time provided by rule, such decision shall without further proceedings then become the decision of the agency.[1]

Thus the ideal has become: 'The one who hears must decide.' If the case is heard on the lower level, the parties will obtain a decision from the hearing officer himself, subject to appeal to the agency. Reasons must be given for the decision, and also for any further decision by the agency, so that the agency's appellate function is much less free from constraint than it would be if it were taking an initial decision on an unpublished report from its hearing officer.

Would this 'judicialized' procedure improve the system of statutory inquiries in Britain? The Franks Committee in their report of 1957 did not think so: it was fallacious, they said, to regard the inspector as 'a kind of judge provisionally deciding the matter, subject to an appeal to the minister.'[2] This is

---

[1] S. 8.   [2] Above, p. 229.

undoubtedly correct in the cases for which statutory inquiries are primarily designed: the cases where the decision is likely to be dominated by ministerial policy. It is a mistake to suppose that the person in the best position to decide on the site of an atomic power station or of a new town is the inspector who held the inquiry. The inquiry can determine the local aspects, but it cannot determine the national aspects.

But in cases where policy is stereotyped or easy to ascertain, the position may be otherwise. These are the cases for which the American procedure is designed; and it reflects the American feeling that policy ought to be crystallized in rules and formulae rather than left at large.[1] This class of cases is not so extensive in Britain, where many powers of regulation are either purely political (like control of nationalized industries) or commercial (like those of the Independent Television Authority) or else are allotted to special tribunals (like the Restrictive Practices Court). But something like the American system is to be found in British road passenger transport and air transport licensing, where the initial decision is made by an independent tribunal but is subject to an appeal to the minister.[2] And something like it now applies to certain appeals from the refusal of planning permission by local planning authorities, where some kinds of appeals which turn mainly on their own local circumstances are in fact decided by the inspector, subject only to intervention by the minister in special cases.[3] But what appears to be the standard case in the United States is likely to remain the exceptional case in Britain.

Administrative procedure is now the concern of the Administrative Conference of the United States, which was appointed in 1968. This body is in some respects comparable to the Council on Tribunals, though it is much larger in size and contains many official members.

There are certain other kinds of inquiry which need brief explanation. Inquiries are not always concerned with land, though it is those inquiries which tend to monopolize attention.

---

[1] This is discussed in 81 L.Q.R. 357.
[2] See below, p. 256.
[3] Above, p. 246.

Accident inquiries

Railway accidents, shipwrecks, air crashes, factory accidents, and so forth, often have to be inquired into, and in general the familiar form of the public inquiry is followed. But under the various statutes providing for such inquiries the practice varies a good deal. It is obviously of great importance that it should be satisfactory, since the reputation and livelihood of drivers, pilots, and others—not to mention the safety of their passengers—will often depend on the findings. Curiously enough, although these inquiries appeared to fall within the terms of reference of the Franks Committee, and details were laid before them by the government departments responsible, the Committee did not investigate them, and confined itself to the more controversial inquiries affecting land.

If we take railway accident inquiries as an example, we find that there are no rules of procedure, there is no right to legal representation, no right of cross-examination, and no right of appeal. The minister has, indeed, power to direct a more formal inquiry, but since that has not been done since 1879, it is hardly material. Shipping casualty inquiries, on the other hand, where there is power to cancel a mariner's licence, are much more formal and judicial (with legal representation and cross-examination) and there is a right of appeal to the High Court. In the case of aircraft accidents, for which there is an up-to-date procedure,[1] an inspector first makes a private investigation, but must invite representations from anyone whom he proposes to criticize in his report. Any such person is entitled to have his case reviewed by a Review Board appointed by the Lord Chancellor, which normally sits in public and accords full procedural rights. In important cases the Board of Trade may alternatively order a formal public inquiry, which takes place before a commissioner (an experienced barrister) and at least two skilled assessors, all appointed by the Lord Chancellor. The case is then presented under the control of the Attorney-General. The reports of inspectors, review boards and commissioners are normally to be published. Investigations and reviews may be re-opened on the directions of the Board of Trade.

[1] Civil Aviation (Investigation of Accidents) Regulations 1969, S.I. No. 833; also S.I. 1969 No. 1437.

Although accident inquiries raise very difficult questions, their procedure plainly needs to be kept under review as much as that of other inquiries. For this at the moment there is no clear policy. On the one hand, accident inquiries were omitted from the order which brought numerous discretionary inquiries within the Tribunal and Inquiries Acts.[1] On the other hand, the Council on Tribunals were consulted about the new procedure for inquiries into aircraft accidents. They pointed out that the Review Board is an obligatory inquiry and therefore within the Tribunals and Inquiries Act 1958, so that the Council may consider complaints. But the other parts of the procedure are discretionary, and will not therefore be subject to the Act of 1958 unless an order is made under the Act of 1966, as is believed to be intended.

Tribunals of inquiry

There is one type of public inquiry which from time to time attracts much attention: the special inquiry which Parliament may at any time constitute under the Tribunals of Inquiry (Evidence) Act 1921. This procedure is reserved for special occasions where a full-dress inquiry into allegations is required in the public interest, and it has been put into operation seventeen times since the Act was passed. Such inquiries have been held into premature disclosures of budget details by ministers, the receipt of gifts by ministers, allegations that a change in bank rate was prematurely divulged, accusations of brutality against the police, exceptional accidents and other matters of urgent public concern.[2]

These inquiries are themselves fundamentally extra-legal, like those previously mentioned. The Act of 1921 merely clothes them with powers to summon witnesses, send for documents, administer oaths, and so forth, reinforced by the sanction of punishment for contempt of court. In order to bring the Act into play both Houses of Parliament must resolve that a tribunal shall investigate some matter described as being 'of urgent public importance'; the tribunal must then be appointed by the Crown or a Secretary of State in a document reciting that the Act is to apply.

[1] See above, p. 242, and in particular item 49 of the Schedule to the Order, S.I. 1967 No. 451.
[2] See Trial by Tribunal by Professor G. W. Keeton.

Experience of these inquiries has revealed their dangers as well as their advantages. They are inquisitorial in character, and usually take place in a blaze of publicity. Very damaging allegations may be made against persons who may have little opportunity of defending themselves and against whom no legal charge is preferred. The tribunal is usually presided over by a High Court judge, who can be relied upon to mitigate these dangers so far as possible. But an inquisitorial public inquiry is not always easily controllable, and its evils would be grave if its use were not infrequent.

A Royal Commission has reviewed this procedure and has recommended the observance of certain safeguards, with a view particularly to assisting any witness to know of any allegations against him in time to defend himself. The Commission emphasizes that this species of inquiry is justifiable only on the exceptional occasions when there is something like a nation-wide crisis of confidence. But it is also emphasized that some procedure of this kind must be available for use in such emergencies.[1] A supplementary report has recommended that the Act of 1921 should be amended so as to make it clear that the tribunal's power to take proceedings for contempt is not to be used so as to stifle free discussion of the subject matter of the inquiry in the press and elsewhere.[2]

[1] Cmnd. 3121 (1966).   [2] Cmnd. 4078 (1969).

7

SPECIAL TRIBUNALS

MERITS AND DEFECTS OF TRIBUNALS

The growth of tribunals

OUTSIDE the ordinary courts of law there is a host of special statutory tribunals with jurisdiction to decide legal disputes. They are one of the by-products of an age of intensive government, and in particular they multiply under the welfare state. The movement of progressive society nowadays might be said (inverting the famous remark of Maine) to be from contract to status. Less and less are people left to rely on personal transactions enforced by the ordinary law courts. More and more are they made subject to regulatory schemes—national insurance, the health service, state education, agricultural control, rent control, and many other such things are administered under elaborate Acts of Parliament. Here is a new source of social friction, for there are bound to be many disputes. What benefit may A claim under the insurance scheme? Ought Dr. B to be removed from the health service? Is C entitled to a reduction of rent? Should D be allowed to give notice to his farm tenant?

To add all this work to the tasks of the ordinary courts would not only cause a breakdown: it would also in many cases be wrong in principle. The process of the courts is elaborate, slow, and costly. Its defects are those of its merits, for the object is to give the highest standard of justice; generally speaking, the public wants the best possible article, and is prepared to pay for it. But in administering social services the aim is different. Disputes must be disposed of smoothly, quickly and cheaply. The object is not the best article at any price, but the best article that is consistent with efficient administration. Moreover, many of these disputes are best decided by bodies on which technical experts can sit. Special forms of tribunal have therefore been devised, and the contrast between them and the ordinary courts is striking. A new system for the dispensation of justice has grown up side by side with the old one. National insurance tribunals, rent tribunals, transport tribunals, health service tribunals, together with many others, have come to play a part in the life of the ordinary citizen which is (assuming the ordinary citizen to be law-abiding) likely to be of more direct concern to him than that of the courts of law. The total number of the tribunals falling within the scope of the Tribunals and Inquiries Act 1958 now amounts to about 2,000, when all their local subdivisions are aggregated.

The various classes of tribunals are constituted by express provision in numerous Acts of Parliament. It is only rarely that Parliament gives delegated power to set up a new kind of tribunal by ministerial order.[1] But naturally power is given to ministers to provide for the membership, organization and proceedings of the tribunals which the statutes constitute.

These bodies are often called 'administrative tribunals', but this does not mean that their decisions are necessarily administrative. In the great majority of cases they are judicial, in the sense that the tribunal has to decide facts and apply rules to them impartially, without considering executive policy. Such tribunals are in substance courts of law. They are 'administrative' because the reasons for preferring them to the ordinary courts of law are administrative reasons. An administrative tribunal is, in fact, one part of a scheme of administration of some statutory service or system of control for which, as a whole, a minister is responsible to Parliament. When, for example, unemployment benefit is awarded by a national insurance local tribunal, its decision is as objective as that of any court of law. Only two elements enter into it: the facts as they are proved, and the statutory rules which have to be applied. The rules will often give the tribunal a measure of discretion. But discretion is given to be used objectively, and no more alters the nature of the decision than does the 'judicial discretion' which is familiar in courts of law. These tribunals therefore have the character of courts but they are enmeshed in the administrative machinery of the state, and subject to the same control by the courts.

---

[1] A number of compensation appeal tribunals are constituted under delegated power, e.g. boards of referees under S.I. 1963 no. 999. See Tribunals and Inquiries Act 1958, 1st Sched., Part I, Annex. See also Town and Country Planning Act 1962 s. 44 (but the power has not been exercised).

The responsibilities of tribunals are just as great as those of the courts of law in many respects. Mental health review tribunals, for instance, determine whether a mental patient shall be compulsorily detained, whereas questions affecting his property are determined by the courts.

Tribunals and inquiries contrasted

There is a clear contrast between the standard statutory tribunal and the standard statutory inquiry. The tribunal finds facts and decides the case by applying legal rules. The inquiry finds facts and leads to a recommendation to a minister who then takes a decision in which there may be a large element of policy. The tribunal need look no further than the facts and the law, for the issue before it is self-contained. The inquiry, as pointed out previously, is concerned only with the local aspects of what may be a larger issue.[1] Tribunals are used where cases have to be decided but the minister in charge of the scheme does not want to be responsible for the decisions. Inquiries are used where the minister wants to be responsible for the decision, but to be properly informed before he makes it. In other words, tribunals make judicial decisions and inquiries are preliminary to administrative decisions.

But Parliament has experimented with many different bodies and procedures and has in some cases set up tribunals where one would expect to find inquiries and vice versa. Transport licensing, in particular, has been affected by the tradition of employing independent tribunals for deciding what are really questions of policy. The Railway Commission (1873), the Railway and Canal Commission (1888), the Railway Rates Tribunal (1921), and the Transport Tribunal (1947) were successively empowered to control railway rates and charges. This was essentially a commercial and political matter, yet an independent tribunal was employed. Rate control for railways generally has now been found unnecessary, but the Transport Tribunal still controls passenger fares in London. Similarly the licensing of commercial road services is entrusted to tribunals, the Traffic Commissioners; appeals lie from them to the Transport Tribunal in respect of goods services and to the Minister of Transport in respect of passenger services. The logic of these

[1] Above, p. 238.

arrangements is not evident, but they work well and have survived several investigations.[1] Air transport licensing, which
was introduced in 1960 to control the allocation of routes and
the scales of charges, is assigned to a tribunal, the Air Transport
Licensing Board, from which however appeal lies to the minister.
This curious system at least recognizes that ultimately the decision is one of policy.

Where the decision has to be taken by a minister, he must
necessarily appoint some one to hear the case and advise him
how to decide it. The procedure is therefore that of an inquiry,
and the Tribunals and Inquiries Acts will apply accordingly,
even though the subject-matter seems more suitable to a tribunal. This is the situation where ministers have to decide
questions of fact and law, for example under the national
insurance scheme where certain important questions in claims
for benefit are 'minister's questions', subject to a right of appeal
to the court on a point of law.[2] Similarly appeal from the decision of a district auditor lies to the minister in some cases, even
though the only question may be the legality of the local authority's expenditure, thus raising only issues of fact and law.[3]
Sometimes appeal lies to the minister from a fully formed tribunal, as in the case of air transport licensing mentioned above,
and as in the case of appeals to the Minister of Health by doctors
found guilty of default by the National Health Service Tribunal
or a local executive council. In some of these situations the minister's function may be explained as a kind of prerogative of
mercy or as an ultimate political appeal, but in others it defies
logical analysis. We are here in an area where tribunal and
inquiry procedures are strangely intermixed.

Composition and operation

The common feature of all statutory tribunals, as opposed to
inquiries, is that they make their own decisions independently
and are free from political influence. In the abnormal cases

[1] Franks Committee's Report, Cmnd. 218 (1957), para. 229.

[2] National Insurance Act 1965 ss. 64, 65; National Insurance (Industrial
Injuries) Act 1965, s. 35. Cf. *Healey v. Minister of Health* [1955] 1 Q.B. 221 (minister's
power to decide category of employment). The National Superannuation and
Social Insurance Bill 1970 proposed to transfer this jurisdiction to a special
tribunal.

[3] Above, p. 27.

where appeal lies to a minister, the minister's policy may indirectly influence them. But from direct political control they are as free as are the courts of law, and this independence is jealously preserved.

Tribunals are therefore as a rule staffed by independent persons, not by civil servants. Even if in a sense they are people's courts, they have at least their full share of judicial independence. The public by no means always gives them credit for their impartiality, often because of minor factors which arouse suspicion. For instance, a pensions appeal tribunal or a national assistance appeal tribunal will usually have a civil servant as its clerk, who will tell the appellant how to proceed and require him to fill up forms emanating from his department. The tribunal may sit in the department's premises, and the part played by the official representing the department before the tribunal, as well as the position of the clerk, may give an impression of influence. But the truth is to the contrary. A typical tribunal (especially if it is an appeal tribunal) will consist of three persons. The chairman will in many cases be a practising lawyer, perhaps a local solicitor, who gives his services part-time. The other two members will be chosen from a panel of people willing to serve, none of whom will be in the employment of the department. In many cases they will represent certain interests, such as landlords and tenants in the case of Agricultural Land Tribunals, and employers and employed in the case of National Insurance Local Tribunals. The tribunal will then consist of an independent chairman, and one person chosen from each of the panels of names put forward by the employers and the trade unions respectively (or as the case may be). The chairman is usually paid, but the members will often be unpaid, and will regard the work as public service. In other cases members may have expert qualifications, as, for example, members of Pensions Appeal Tribunals, some of whom must be medical practitioners, and in that case they are normally paid. One special case is the Patents Appeal Tribunal, which consists of a High Court judge. Some of the important adjudicators, such as the National Insurance Commissioner (who hears appeals from the local tribunals), are paid at least as much as county court judges, or equivalent rates for part-time. At the other end of the scale, the chairmen and members of Rent Tribunals receive little more than token payments. These differences reflect—though by no means always faithfully—the wide variation in the type of work, which may range from highly skilled full-time employment of a most responsible kind to relatively petty adjudication undertaken voluntarily (like the work of a justice of the peace) as a service to the community. Tribunals' clerks, also, are subject to a variety of arrangements. For the most part they are civil servants, and form the one substantial link between the departments and the tribunals. But rent tribunals appoint and employ their own clerks, who accordingly have no civil service status.

The Special Commissioners of Income Tax are exceptional among tribunals in that they consist wholly of officials. But they are acknowledged in practice to be independent and their decisions are subject to appeal to the High Court on points of law.

Appeals

There is great diversity also in the arrangements for appeals. Sometimes there is a two- or three-tier structure, as with claims to benefit under national insurance. These claims are first determined by the local insurance officer, who is not a tribunal but an official of the ministry. From his decision there is an appeal to the local tribunal, consisting of an independent legal chairman appointed by the minister and two other members (not officials) representing employers and employed respectively. From the local tribunal a final appeal lies to the National Insurance Commissioner, who must be a barrister of at least ten years' standing. These authorities also adjudicate claims arising from industrial injuries,[1] which previously went to industrial injuries tribunals. The National Health Service has an elaborate appeal structure for the benefit of doctors and others against whom complaints are made by patients.[2] If the complaint is upheld by the initial tribunal (the local executive council) the doctor may appeal to the National Health Service Tribunal and thence further to the minister if threatened with removal from the health service; and if threatened with lesser penalties he may appeal to the minister direct. Other instances of appeals to ministers have already been noted.

[1] National Insurance Act 1966, s. 8.
[2] See *R. v. Ministry of Health* [1968] 1 Q.B. 84.

The above are cases where the appeal consists of a full re-hearing of the case on its merits. From many tribunals there is no such general right of appeal, but there is then usually a right of appeal to the courts on any question of law. Decisions of the Lands Tribunal and of the Transport Tribunal, for ex-ample, are subject to a right of appeal on a point of law to the Court of Appeal. Similar appeals lie to the High Court from many other tribunals, either under specific statutes [1] or under the general provision of the Tribunals and Inquiries Act 1958. [2] The latter statute gives an appeal on a point of law from rent tribunals, independent schools tribunals, compensation appeal tribunals and many others, including new tribunals such as industrial tribunals and rent assessment committees to which its provisions are extended by ministerial order. [3]

In a few cases there is no appeal of any kind: examples are supplementary benefit appeal tribunals, betting levy appeal tribunals and compensation appeal tribunals. In others there is an appeal to a higher tribunal and therefore no appeal to the courts: thus there is no appeal to the courts from the National Insurance Commissioner, the highest judicial authority in the hierarchy of tribunals dealing with national insurance and industrial injuries. But here it is important to remember that the court can intervene in case of error on the face of the record, so that these tribunals have become subject to a wider measure of judicial control than was contemplated when they were created. [4]

What is 'law'?

Where the right of appeal is restricted to questions of law, it is important to know what 'law' means. This formula allows appeal on the ground that a finding of fact is supported by no evidence. [5] But provided there is evidence, there can be no appeal on the primary facts of the case which have to be proved, such as the age and size of a building and the purpose for which

---

[1] E.g. from the Special Commissioners of Income Tax and from Mental Health Review Tribunals.
[2] S. 9.
[3] S.I. 1965, nos. 1403, 2151.
[4] See above, p. 97.
[5] Above, p. 100.

it is used. If the primary facts are established, the question whether the building is a 'house' within the meaning of the Housing Act is a question of law;[1] for the question is one of interpreting the law and applying it to ascertained facts. In other words, legal inferences and interpretations are matters of law. In a leading case the House of Lords held that for the purposes of an appeal on a point of law it was a question of law whether a transaction, the facts of which were ascertained, amounted to 'trade' within the meaning of a taxing statute.[2]

A question such as 'what is the rent of the premises?' may therefore be one of fact or of law, or of both, according to the issues in dispute. If the dispute is about the figure agreed, this is a question of fact. But if the facts of the case are established, and the question is whether a payment intended as a premium is in law 'rent', that is a question of law. Where both matters are in dispute, the question is sometimes called a mixed question of law and fact or a question of mixed law and fact. The latter expression is the less accurate, since law and fact are different things which do not mix.

But the courts are not always consistent. In the tax case mentioned above all the lower courts had held that the matter was 'purely a question of fact'. There is also a tendency to designate questions of legal interpretation as 'questions of fact and degree', for example for the purpose of deciding whether on established facts there has been a 'material change in the use' of land within the meaning of the planning Acts.[3] This reasoning would narrow the right of appeal on a point of law. But it is most desirable that this right should be liberally accorded,[4] so that the courts can give authoritative guidance on the difficult questions of law which tribunals have to solve—as for example under the complex statutes governing selective employment tax and redundancy payments, which have to be interpreted by industrial tribunals. At the same time, a court of

---

[1] *Re Butler* [1939] 1 K.B. 570.

[2] *Edwards v. Bairstow* [1956] A.C. 14.

[3] E.g. *Birmingham Cpn. v. Habib Ullah* [1964] 1 Q.B. 178. For criticism see 85 L.Q.R. 18.

[4] As in *O'Brien v. Associated Fire Alarms Ltd.* [1968] 1 W.L.R. 1916 (implied term in contract); *Instrumatic Ltd. v. Supabrase Ltd.* [1969] 1 W.L.R. 519 (exercise of discretion).

law is rightly inclined to respect the decisions of such tribunals on questions of legal interpretation which are peculiarly within the subject-matter of their jurisdiction, such as the classification of industrial operations for the purpose of exemption from selective employment tax.[1]

Appeal in relation to review

The existence of a statutory right of appeal does not deprive the High Court of its ordinary powers of quashing a tribunal's decision which is ultra vires or erroneous on its face.[2] It is possible, however, that the court would decline to grant discretionary remedies for those purposes where an appeal was the more suitable remedy.

Appeal and review are in theory two distinct procedures, appeal being concerned with merits and review being concerned with legality.[3] But in practice an appellant will often wish to raise questions which strictly are questions of legality, such as violation of natural justice or some objection to the tribunal's jurisdiction. It is important that this should be freely allowed, since otherwise many cases could not be fully disposed of on appeal. But in several recent appeals under the Tribunals and Inquiries Act 1958 the court has acted as if jurisdictional questions could not be decided on appeal, and has converted the proceedings into review by certiorari.[4] This would severely restrict the right of appeal and would make unnecessary difficulties for appellants wishing to appeal both on the merits and on some question of jurisdiction. There is abundant authority to the effect that jurisdiction can be challenged by way of appeal[5]; and the implication of the Act is to the same effect, since it gives the right of appeal to any one 'dissatisfied in point of law' and contains ample provision for remitting any case to the tribunal and for giving any decision which the tribunal might have given.

---

[1] *C. Maurice & Co. Ltd. v. Ministry of Labour* [1969] 2 A.C. 346.
[2] Above, p. 145.
[3] Above, p. 53.
[4] *Metropolitan Properties Ltd. v. Lannon* [1968] 1 W.L.R. 815; *Chapman v. Earl* [1968] 1 W.L.R. 1315. For criticism see 85 L.Q.R. 20.
[5] E.g. *Essex C.C. v. Essex Incorporated Church Union* [1963] A.C. 808; *Shell v. Unity Finance Co. Ltd.* [1964] 2 Q.B. 203.

Procedural anomalies

Before the reforms which followed the Report of the Franks Committee there were some striking procedural anomalies. Some tribunals sat in public, others sat in private. Some allowed unrestricted legal representation, others allowed none. Some followed the legal rules of evidence, others disregarded them. Some allowed full examination and cross-examination of witnesses, others allowed witnesses to be questioned only through the chairman. Some took evidence on oath, others did not. Some gave reasoned decisions, others did not. The insurance tribunals well illustrated some of these diversities. National Insurance local tribunals sat in private and allowed no legal representation before them. Industrial injuries local tribunals sat in public, unless they decided otherwise, and would permit legal representation with the chairman's consent for special reasons.

Most of these discrepancies had good reasons behind them originally. Tribunals which inquire into the intimate personal circumstances of poor people, such as supplementary benefit (formerly national assistance) appeal tribunals, ought to sit in private. And where a patient under the national health service wishes to make a complaint against a doctor, the whole procedure may fail to work if the complainant knows that he will have to face a hostile lawyer. But in other tribunals a rule that allows representation by any one except a lawyer is as unreasonable as a rule allowing any one but a doctor to prescribe medicine. Rules designed to produce cheapness and informality of procedure, which were suitable for some tribunals, were being applied indiscriminately.

Problems of tribunals

The statutory tribunal proved to be a most useful, indeed indispensable device, especially in the mechanism of the welfare state. The success of the tribunals (originally Commissioners) established under the first National Insurance Act of 1911 prompted Parliament to create many more, as it is still doing with no sign of abatement. Statute after statute created new tribunals and new jurisdictions, but until 1957 the pattern of all these bodies was never reviewed as a whole. Just as in the nineteenth century the accumulation of different courts of law with inconvenient jurisdictions had to be swept away by the Judicature Acts 1873–75, so in the twentieth century the jungle of statutory tribunals had to be mapped out and tidied. The anomalies were a source of complaint and there was an inherent tendency towards diversity and disorder. This was perhaps aggravated by the inclination of government departments to leave their tribunals to solve their own problems, applying somewhat rigidly the excellent principle that the executive should not interfere with judicial functions.

As a sample of the kind of complaint made by people whose livelihoods were greatly affected by tribunals' decisions may be cited the following comments on rent tribunals which were made to the Franks Committee by the Justice for Landladies Association.

(1) There is no appeal against the tribunal's decision. Tremendous power, which can ruin a person's life, has been put into the hands of three men. Yet there is no higher court in which their decisions can be tested.

(2) The three on the bench of the tribunal need have no proper legal qualifications. A court of no appeal has been put into the hands of men who are generally neither qualified lawyers, magistrates or judges.

(3) There is no evidence on oath, and therefore there can be no proper cross-examination as in a court of law. Statements are made on both sides, but the time-honoured method of getting to the truth cannot be used.

(4) Procedure is as the tribunal shall determine. No rules have been laid down as to the procedure at a tribunal hearing. Witnesses may be heard or not heard at their pleasure.

THE COMMITTEE ON ADMINISTRATIVE TRIBUNALS AND ENQUIRIES

Constitution and work of the Committee

The Committee presided over by Sir Oliver Franks (as he then was) was commissioned by the Lord Chancellor in 1955 as an immediate (though illogical) result of the *Crichel Down* case of 1954. That case really had nothing to do with tribunals and inquiries, but was a manifestation of public concern over the way in which government departments had handled a landowner's request (based on no legal right) to have land which had been compulsorily acquired returned after the war. This was a purely departmental matter. It was what might be called, with due apology to the civil service, ordinary maladministration. The correct remedy for this was the ombudsman, but the ground for him had not yet been prepared. Meanwhile the public outcry was to some extent appeased by commissioning the review of tribunals and inquiries, for which for other reasons the time was ripe. Inquiries have been dealt with in the preceding chapter.

The Committee was not primarily a legal body, though it had strong legal membership. Its published evidence contains a great deal of information, including a survey of all the tribunals of which classified details were supplied by government departments. As in the case of inquiries, the evidence revealed two different attitudes, the legal and the administrative. The legal attitude was that tribunals must be regarded as part of the machinery of justice and organized accordingly. The administrative attitude was that tribunals were primarily part of the machinery of administration. The head of the Lord Chancellor's Department and the Treasury Solicitor, being both lawyers and administrators, were able to appreciate both viewpoints and to give particularly valuable evidence. Certain witnesses from the universities put forward suggestions for a permanent body of some kind to concern itself with tribunal procedure, to supervise the making of procedural rules, and to make sure that the elements of justice were observed throughout the whole system with such uniformity as facts might allow.

The Committee's Report [1]

In its Report (1957) the Committee first acknowledged the merits of special tribunals and the undoubted need for this supplementary system of judicature. No general transfer of functions from tribunals to courts of law was suggested. On the other hand, the Committee firmly adopted the legal view as to tribunals' status. They said:

[1] Cmnd. 218 (1957).

Much of the official evidence, including that of the Joint Permanent Secretary to the Treasury, appeared to reflect the view that tribunals should properly be regarded as part of the machinery of administration, for which the government must retain a close and continuing responsibility. Thus, for example, tribunals in the social service field would be regarded as adjuncts to the administration of the services themselves. We do not accept this view. We consider that tribunals should properly be regarded as machinery provided by Parliament for adjudication rather than as part of the machinery of administration. The essential point is that in all these cases Parliament has deliberately provided for a decision independent of the Department concerned . . . and the intention of Parliament to provide for the independence of tribunals is clear and unmistakable.

To make tribunals conform to the standard which Parliament thus had in mind, three fundamental objectives were proclaimed: openness, fairness and impartiality.

In the field of tribunals openness appears to us to require the publicity of proceedings and knowledge of the essential reasoning underlying the decisions; fairness to require the adoption of a clear procedure which enables parties to know their rights, to present their case fully and to know the case which they have to meet; and impartiality to require the freedom of tribunals from the influence, real or apparent, of Departments concerned with the subject-matter of their decisions.

The Council on Tribunals

The Committee's central proposal was that there should be a permanent Council on Tribunals in order to provide some standing machinery for the general supervision of tribunal organization and procedure. It was to consist of both legal and lay members, with lay members in the majority—thus manifesting the spirit which runs all through the Report, that tribunal reform was to be based on broad public opinion, and was not a kind of lawyers' counter-revolution against modern methods of government. Such a body, it was hoped, would provide the focal point which had previously been lacking. It was to be appointed by the Lord Chancellor and to report to him, so that the Lord Chancellor would undertake a general responsibility for the well-being of tribunals, in somewhat the same way as he already does for the courts of law. This reflects the Committee's conception of tribunals as one branch of the judicial system. It also reflects dissatisfaction with *ad hoc* inquiries such as the Ministers' Powers Committee of 1932 and the Franks Committee itself. A body is needed which can deal with complaints as they arise, instead of leaving them to build up into a volume of public discontent which, every twenty-five years or so, discharges itself in a special but temporary inquest by a committee which merely reports once and then dissolves.

Other recommendations

The following are a selection from the Committee's other recommendations on tribunals.

(1) Chairmen of tribunals should be appointed and removed by the Lord Chancellor; members should be appointed by the Council and removed by the Lord Chancellor.

(2) Chairmen should ordinarily have legal qualifications—and always in the case of appellate tribunals.

(3) Remuneration for service on tribunals should be reviewed by the Council on Tribunals.

(4) Procedure for each tribunal, based on common principles but suited to its needs, should be formulated by the Council.

(5) The citizen should be helped to know in good time the case he will have to meet.

(6) Hearings should be in public, except only in cases involving (i) public security, (ii) intimate personal or financial circumstances, or (iii) professional reputation, where there is a preliminary investigation.

(7) Legal representation should always be allowed, save only in most exceptional circumstances. In the case of National Insurance Tribunals the Committee were content to make legal representation subject to the chairman's consent.

(8) Tribunals should have power to take evidence on oath, to subpoena witnesses, and to award costs. Parties should be free to question witnesses directly.

(9) Decisions should be reasoned, as full as possible, and made available to the parties in writing. Final appellate tribunals should publish and circulate selected decisions.

(10) There should be a right of appeal on fact, law and merits to an appeal tribunal, except where the lower tribunal is exceptionally strong.

(11) There should also be an appeal on a point of law to the courts; and judicial control by the remedies of certiorari, prohibition and mandamus should never be barred by statute.

(12) The Council should advise, and report quickly, on the application of all these principles to the various tribunals, and should advise on any proposal to establish a new tribunal.

In addition there were numerous recommendations about particular tribunals.

THE ACT OF 1958 AND AFTER

The Tribunals and Inquiries Act 1958

The government's general acceptance of the Report was signified by the Tribunals and Inquiries Act 1958, a short statute passed without any opposition.

The Act provides first for the Council on Tribunals. The Council has a maximum membership of sixteen;[1] but there is special provision for a Scottish Committee of the Council, since legal affairs in Scotland are so different, consisting partly of persons not members of the Council itself. The Council has emerged as a purely advisory body, without the function of appointing tribunal members, but with general oversight over tribunals and inquiries. The tribunals under its superintendence are listed in a schedule, which includes the great bulk of those considered by the Committee. It is no doubt right that such a body, which is intended to be a watch-dog and independent of ministerial control, should have no executive functions: it is to bark but not to bite. It is not therefore a court of appeal, or a council of state on the French or Italian model. But it has to keep under review the 'constitution and working' of the listed tribunals, and report on any other tribunal question which the government may refer to it. In practice it receives complaints from individuals and invites testimony from witnesses. It is also frequently consulted in the ordinary course of

---

[1] Including the Parliamentary Commissioner: below, p. 276.

departmental work. Its annual report must be laid before Parliament. It is specifically empowered to make *general* recommendations as to the membership of the listed tribunals, and it must be consulted before any new procedural rules for them are made. Some particulars of the Council's work will be found below.

Other relevant provisions of the Act are as follows:

(1) Chairmen of rent tribunals and of tribunals dealing with national insurance, industrial injuries, national assistance, and national service are to be selected by their ministries from panels nominated by the Lord Chancellor.

(2) Membership of any of the listed tribunals, or of a panel connected with it, can be terminated only with the Lord Chancellor's consent.

(3) No procedural rules or regulations for the listed tribunals may be made without consultation with the Council on Tribunals.

(4) A right of appeal to the High Court on a point of law is given in the case of a number of specified tribunals, including rent tribunals, rent assessment committees, and tribunals dealing with children, employment, schools, nurses, and mines. In various other cases this right already exists, as explained earlier.[1]

(5) Other tribunals may be brought within the Act by ministerial order. Since Parliament has continued to create new tribunals as fast as ever, many additions have been made to the schedule, including mental health review tribunals, betting levy appeal tribunals, industrial tribunals and rent assessment committees.

(6) Judicial control by means of certain remedies (certiorari and mandamus) is safeguarded. This is discussed elsewhere.[2]

(7) There is a legal right to a reasoned decision from any of the listed tribunals, provided this is requested on or before the giving or notification of the decision. This is discussed below.

(8) The ministers responsible under the Act, and to whom the Council on Tribunals reports, are the Lord Chancellor and the Secretary of State for Scotland.

[1] Above, p. 260. [2] Above, p. 154.

The Act falls short of the Committee's recommendations in certain respects, for instance in its arrangements as to the appointment of chairmen and members of tribunals. Perhaps the most notable divergence is in the failure to provide for appeals on questions of fact and merits. The Committee recommended a right of appeal on 'fact, law and merits', but the Act has provided only a right of appeal on a question of law. Thus the Committee's proposal that there should be a right of appeal from rent tribunals to county courts remains unfulfilled, and no right of appeal has been given, except on a point of law, from the rent assessment committees set up by the Rent Act 1965. Nor has the Council on Tribunals recommended any change: it has investigated the question of appeals from rent tribunals and concluded that the balance of advantage is in preserving the finality of the tribunals' decisions.[1]

Other recommendations of the Committee have been carried out by administrative measures and do not therefore appear in the Act. The inconsistencies in national insurance and industrial injuries tribunals as regards sitting in public and the right of legal representation were removed by order. These tribunals (now amalgamated) sit in public unless the tribunal for special reasons otherwise directs, and all restriction on legal representation has been removed.[2]

Administrative steps have also been taken to ensure that most chairmen of tribunals have legal qualifications. Supplementary benefit appeal tribunals are the principal remaining exception. The extent to which other recommendations of the Committee have been implemented may be seen from a survey published by the Council on Tribunals in 1964.[3]

Reasons for decisions

The statutory right to reasoned decisions is notable, for no such binding rule is applicable to the ordinary courts of law. The Act requires the tribunal or minister 'to furnish a statement, either written or oral, of the reasons for the decision if requested, on or before the giving or notification of the decision,

---

[1] Annual Report for 1962, para. 50.
[2] S.I. 1958, nos. 701, 702.
[3] Annual Report for 1963, Appendix A.

to state the reasons'.[1] Any such reasons are deemed to be incorporated in the record, and the importance of this point has already been noted.[2] There are certain exclusions, such as hearings in connexion with legislative measures, e.g. factory regulations. There is also power to exclude cases where the Lord Chancellor is of opinion that the giving of reasons is 'unnecessary or impracticable,' subject to consultation with the Council on Tribunals. The only exemptions granted under this provision have been in favour of certain tax tribunals, not because they should not give reasons but because there are other statutory provisions under which they can be required to do so.[3] No significant use of the escape clause has therefore been made. On the other hand there are many cases where extensive reasons cannot be given, for example where the tribunal merely finds facts on evidence. No tribunal can be expected to give fuller reasons than the nature of the case admits.

The High Court has held that reasons given under the Act must be 'proper, adequate reasons,' and 'reasons which will not only be intelligible but which deal with the substantial points which have been raised'. Furthermore, the court has treated inadequacy of reasons as error on the face of the record, so that the decision can be quashed, even if the duty to give reasons is not mandatory.[4] This case concerned an agricultural arbitrator (one of the scheduled tribunals) who found that a notice to quit was justified because the tenant had not done sufficient work to make good dilapidations which the landlord had specified under numerous different heads. It was held that the reasons given were too vague and the award was set aside.[5]

It is unfortunate that the Act gives a right to a reasoned decision only where reasons are requested. In practice requests are seldom made, and tribunals commonly give their reasons as a matter of course. In many cases also procedural rules impose

[1] S. 12. The word 'on' may have an 'elastic meaning': *Scott v. Scott* [1921] P. 107.
[2] Above, p. 97.
[3] Council on Tribunals, Annual Reports: 1959, para. 64; 1960, para. 90.
[4] See the *Brayhead* case, above, p. 57.
[5] *Re Poyser & Mills' Arbitration* [1964] 2 Q.B. 467. The Council on Tribunals declined to recommend exemption for agricultural arbitrators: Annual Report, 1959, para. 68.

an unqualified duty to give reasons, and the courts interpret this duty in the same way as they interpret the Act itself.[1]

Procedural powers and rules

A statutory tribunal has inherent power to control its own procedure. Normally it is not required to observe the legal rules of evidence.[2] It should allow the calling and cross-examination of witnesses, etc., as required by the principles of natural justice.[3] But its decision need not be confined to the evidence given before it: it may rely on its own knowledge and experience, provided it gives the parties a fair opportunity to comment on anything outside their own knowledge.[4] It may inspect a site or a building, though it should preferably do so in the presence of the parties.[5] Parties may enforce the attendance of witnesses and the production of documents by obtaining subpoenas from the High Court, which for this purpose will lend its aid to inferior tribunals freely.[6]

Experience has shown that published rules of procedure are highly desirable. Although the Council on Tribunals does not itself draw up procedural rules as the Franks Committee recommended, it has to be consulted before such rules are made.[7] The usual practice is for each type of tribunal to be equipped with its own set of rules by ministerial order. The Council therefore considers all rules for new tribunals, and any revised or amending rules for other tribunals. In the course of ten years the Council considered about a hundred sets of rules. A general account of this work is given in one of its reports,[8] and its annual reports contain details.

In scrutinizing procedural rules the Council endeavours to promote intelligibility and consistency, particularly on matters such as publicity of hearings, the right of representation and the right of cross-examination. A great many amendments in draft rules have been secured with the cooperation of government

---

[1] See the *Givaudan* case, above, p. 236.
[2] Above, p. 213.   [3] *Ibid.*
[4] *R. v. City of Westminster Assessment Committee* [1941] 1 K.B. 53; *Crofton Investment Trust Ltd. v. Greater London Rent Assessment Committee* [1967] 2 Q.B. 955.
[5] See *Salsbury v. Woodland* [1970] 1 Q.B. 324.
[6] *Soul v. Inland Revenue Commissioners* [1963] 1 W.L.R. 112.
[7] Tribunals and Inquiries Act 1958, s. 8.
[8] Annual Report for 1964, Pt. II.

departments, providing for example for the disclosure to both sides of information obtained by the tribunal, for freedom from the legal rules of evidence and for unrestricted rights of representation. A number of draft rules have been criticized as being *ultra vires* and have been withdrawn.

Tribunals are so diverse in their nature that, although considerable progress has been made towards procedural uniformity, there is nothing as yet resembling a common code of procedure, and there are exceptions to almost every rule. Even the principle that reasons must be given for decisions is modified by the Mental Health Act 1959[1] in the case of mental health review tribunals, since it may be against the patient's own interests to tell him the reasons for his detention. The rule allowing representation by a lawyer or any other person, which the Council on Tribunals tries to preserve in its widest form, is modified in the case of service committees which hear (in the first instance) complaints by patients against doctors and other professional men in the National Health Service. Before a service committee no-one may be represented by a paid advocate, whether legally qualified or otherwise. The advantages of keeping this procedure informal, and of avoiding the discouragement to complainants which professional representation of doctors would bring about, were recognized by the Council on Tribunals as justifying an exception—and this was endorsed by the professional associations themselves.[2]

It is therefore all the more necessary for every set of procedural rules to be judged on its own merits, and this work constantly occupies the Council on Tribunals. Examples of amendments made in special situations are the provisions in the Plant Breeders Rights Regulations 1965 allowing licensees to contest the cancellation of breeders' rights in which they may have purchased important interests, and in the Betting Levy Appeal Tribunals Rules 1963 allowing a bookmaker to object to having his accounts automatically investigated by an auditor if he appeals to the tribunal.[3]

Reorganization of tribunals

The tribunal system has an inherent resistance to uniformity

---

[1] S. 124. [2] Annual Report for 1960, para. 42.
[3] Annual Report for 1964, para. 30.

of any kind. It would seem beneficial to constitute fewer and stronger tribunals by amalgamating or grouping the existing tribunals according to their function, as by unifying those concerned with insurance and social security benefits, those concerned with land, those concerned with the National Health Service, &c. Thus the multifarious jurisdictions which new legislation is constantly augmenting would be rationalized. The Franks Committee however saw little scope for this at the time of their report. But subsequently the tribunals dealing with family allowances and industrial injuries were merged in the National Insurance tribunals. Another unifying tendency has been the use of industrial tribunals for a number of different purposes.[1] But the simplification of the National Health Service system that the Franks Committee favoured has not been carried out: the proposal was that the National Health Service tribunal should be the final tribunal of appeal and that appeals to the minister should be abolished; but all the professional associations opposed the suggestion, and the Council on Tribunals therefore felt unable to press it.[2]

A strong case for amalgamation, which the Council did press, arose when rent assessment committees were set up by the Rent Act 1965.[3] Rent tribunals dating from 1946 were already in existence and would have been improved by revision of their arrangements. But instead of constituting one type of tribunal for dealing with all rents, or empowering the minister to do so later, the Act of 1965 created rent assessment committees alongside but distinct from the existing rent tribunals, with an awkward jurisdictional division between them depending on whether the premises are furnished or unfurnished. The desirability of amalgamation was admitted in Parliament and minor provision was made for overlap of membership. But the Act was passed in such haste that a valuable opportunity for reorganizing these tribunals was lost.

Under the National Superannuation and Social Insurance Bill 1970 it was proposed to set up a new system of tribunals to deal solely with 'minister's questions'.[4] This was opposed by

[1] See below, p. 275.
[2] Annual Report for 1964, para. 47.
[3] Annual Report for 1965, para. 20.
[4] See above, p. 257.

the Council on Tribunals on the ground that a claimant should be able to put his whole case before a single tribunal, namely the regular national insurance local tribunal, and that separate jurisdictions for different classes of questions were unnecessary and objectionable. But once again the Council made its objections in vain.

The structure of industrial tribunals may also require alteration. These tribunals have grown greatly in importance and may possibly develop into labour courts with wide jurisdiction and a heavy case-load. Since they were first constituted for the sole purpose of hearing industrial training levy appeals, they have also been called up to deal with redundancy payments, selective employment tax, certain compensation appeals, and disputes under the Contracts of Employment Act 1963 and the Docks and Harbours Act 1966. Moreover, it is proposed to give them extensive jurisdiction over industrial contracts of employment and over equal pay for women employees. Their constitution will clearly require review. They may need reorganizing on the lines of the national insurance system, with local tribunals and a centralized appeal tribunal comparable to the National Insurance Commissioner.

When legislation is in preparation the line of least resistance is usually to leave existing tribunals as they are and to create new tribunals to deal with new problems. This tendency, if unchecked, leads to a jungle of different jurisdictions which are as inconvenient to the citizen as they are bewildering. In the interests of the machinery of justice this tendency needs to be reversed.

Miscellaneous

Although the Council on Tribunals has no legal right to be consulted about bills in Parliament constituting or affecting tribunals, it is in practice consulted as the Franks Committee intended. The Council comments on bills in much the same way as it does on procedural rules, and in particular it attempts to help departments drafting provisions for new tribunals. In this way it has been able, for example, to secure a statutory right to be heard for a licence-holder threatened with cancellation of his licence.

The Council has investigated many miscellaneous matters.

It has made a study of rent tribunals.[1] It has reported adversely on suggestions that witnesses before tribunals should be given absolute privilege and that tribunals need additional power to subpoena witnesses.[2] It has also investigated numerous complaints made to it by dissatisfied parties, and in some cases has been able to improve tribunals' practices. It has secured improvements in accommodation by following up complaints and also as a result of its members' visits to tribunal hearings. It has thus been acting as a kind of ombudsman in the sphere of tribunals (as also of inquiries).

The Parliamentary Commissioner for Administration, as appointed under the Act of 1967, is an ex officio member of the Council.[3] It was apparently the intention of this arrangement that their respective functions should be determined by informal agreement, since the Commissioner has discretion to decide whether to take up any case. But in fact the Commissioner's policy is to investigate all eligible complaints, even though they may also fall within the sphere of the Council, so that there are now two alternative avenues in the narrow class of cases connected with inquiries where the two jurisdictions overlap.[4]

It may be that the Council's present constitution, which is that of an advisory committee, will need some degree of assimilation towards that of the Parliamentary Commissioner, who has legal powers of investigation and a large staff. It may also be thought that both institutions are in need of greater resources of legal expertise.

[1] Annual Report for 1962, Pt. IV.
[2] Annual Report for 1960, paras. 75, 82.
[3] Parliamentary Commissioner Act 1967, s. 1 (5); above, p. 15.
[4] See e.g. the Commissioner's Annual Report for 1969, p. 55 (evidence at planning inquiry heard *in camera*).

8

LEGAL PROCEEDINGS INVOLVING THE CROWN

THE BACKGROUND

'The king can do no wrong'

ENGLISH law has always clung to the theory that the king is subject to law and, accordingly, can break the law. There is no more famous statement of this ideal than Bracton's, made 700 years ago: 'rex non debet esse sub homine sed sub deo et sub lege, quia lex facit regem.'[1] But in practice rights depend upon remedies, and the theory broke down—as Bracton's words suggest that it would—because there was no human agency to enforce the law against the king. The courts were the king's courts, and like other feudal lords the king could not be sued in his own court. He could be plaintiff—and as plaintiff he had many prerogatives in the law of procedure—but he could not be defendant. No form of writ or execution would issue against him, for there was no way of compelling his submission to it. Even today, when most of the obstacles to justice have been removed, it has been found necessary to make important modifications of the law of procedure and execution in the Crown's favour.

The maxim that 'the king can do no wrong' does not in fact have much to do with this procedural immunity. Its true meaning is that the king has no legal power to do wrong. His legal position, the powers and prerogatives which distinguish him from an ordinary subject, is given to him by the law, and the law gives him no authority to transgress. This also is implicit in Bracton's statement, and it provides the justification, such as it is, for the rule that the Crown could not be sued in tort until 1948. But the king has a personal as well as a politic capacity, and in his personal capacity he is just as capable of

[1] 'The king must not be under man, but under God and under the law, because it is the law that makes the king.'

acting illegally as is any one else—and the temptations in his path, in former times at least, were much stronger. English law has never succeeded in distinguishing effectively between the king's two capacities. One of the best illustrations of this is that, despite mystical theories that the Crown is a corporation and that 'the king never dies', the death of the king caused great trouble even in relatively modern times: Parliament was dissolved; all litigation had to be begun again; and all offices of state (even all commissions in the army) had to be regranted. Until numerous Acts of Parliament had come to the rescue the powers of government appeared wholly personal, and it could truly be said that 'on a demise of the Crown we see all the wheels of the state stopping or even running backwards'.[1]

But justice had somehow to be done, and out of the streams of petitions which flowed in upon medieval monarchs came the procedure known as petition of right. This held the field until the new system began in 1948, and many of the vagaries of its early procedure were rationalized by an Act of 1860.[2] In essence it was a petition by a subject which the Crown referred voluntarily to the decision of a court of law. The Crown's consent was signified by endorsing the petition 'Let Right be Done' (*fiat justitia*), so that after obtaining this fiat the plaintiff could obtain the judgment of one of the regular courts. Employed originally for the recovery of land or other property, this remedy made an important stride (as was to be expected) after the Revolution of 1688, when it was agreed by the judges that it would lie to enforce a contract. This was in the *Bankers'* case (1690–1700), in which various bankers attempted to sue the Crown for payments due on loans to Charles II on which that king had defaulted. It was, in fact, by other means that the bankers finally obtained their judgment—though not their money, for the problem of enforcement was as intractable as ever. No further case of importance arose until 1874, when an inventor of a new kind of heavy artillery sued for a reward promised to him by the War Office.[3] This case finally settled the point that judgment could be given against the Crown on a petition of right for breach of contract made by the Crown's agents. Since in any normal case the Crown would grant the

---

[1] Maitland, *Collected Papers*, iii. 253. [2] Petitions of Right Act 1860.
[3] *Thomas v. The Queen* (1874) L.R. 10 Q.B. 31.

fiat and respect the judgment, there was now a reasonably effective remedy in contract.

No liability in tort

Meanwhile the judges had set their face against any remedy in tort. This was an unfortunate by-product of the law of master and servant as it was understood in the nineteenth century. For obvious reasons it had become necessary that employers should be liable for torts—most commonly negligence —committed by their employees in the course of their employment. But in seeking a legal basis for this, judges at first tended to say that it depended on the implied authority given by the master to the servant, or that the fault was the master's for not choosing his servants more carefully. Neither line of thought would bring liability home to the Crown, for as we have seen the theory has always been that the Crown's powers cannot be exercised wrongly. Thus 'the king can do no wrong' meant that the Crown was not liable in tort—even though a breach of contract is just as much a 'wrong' as a tort, and even though the social necessity for a remedy against the Crown as employer was just as great as, if not greater than, the need for a remedy in contract. The first important case was an unsuccessful petition of right by Viscount Canterbury in 1842.[1] He had been Speaker of the House of Commons in 1834 when some workmen in the employ of the Crown, being told to burn the piles of old tallies from the Exchequer, succeeded in burning down both Houses of Parliament and the Speaker's house in addition. But the Speaker's claim against the Crown for the value of his household goods foundered on the objection that the negligence of the workmen could not be imputed to the Crown either directly or indirectly. Similarly, where a British naval commander, suppressing the slave trade off the coast of Africa, seized and burnt an allegedly innocent ship from Liverpool, the owner's petition of right was rejected.[2] It was later recognized that employer's liability is quite independent of fault on the part of the master, and depends rather on the fact that it is for the master's benefit that the servant acts and that the master, having put the servant in a position where he can do

[1] *Viscount Canterbury v. Attorney-General* (1842) 1 Ph. 306.
[2] *Tobin v. The Queen* (1864) 16 C.B.N.S. 310.

damage, must accept the responsibility. But it was then too late to challenge the doctrine that the Crown could have no liability in tort, which was an unshakeable dogma until Parliament abolished it in 1947. But for any claim which did not 'sound in tort'—such as for breach of contract, recovery of property, or for statutory compensation—a petition of right would lie.

Personal liability

The Crown's immunity in tort never extended to its servants personally. It was, and is, a principle of the first importance that officials of all kinds, high or low, are personally liable for any injury for which they cannot produce legal authority. The orders of the Crown are not legal authority unless it is one of the rare acts which the prerogative justifies, such as the detention of an enemy alien in time of war. Thus although in past times the Crown was not liable in tort, the injured party could always sue the particular Crown servant who did the deed, including any superior who ordered him to do it or otherwise caused it directly. A superior officer cannot be liable merely as such, for it is not he but the Crown who is the employer[1]; but if he takes part in the wrongful act he is no less liable than any other participant. Superior orders can never be a defence, since neither the Crown nor its servants have power to authorize wrong. The ordinary law of master and servant makes the master and the servant jointly and severally liable for torts committed in course of the employment. Before 1948, therefore, some one negligently injured by a Post Office van could sue the driver of the van but not the Postmaster-General or the Crown. Had the van been owned by a private employer, the action would have lain both against the driver and against the employer, although, of course, the damages could have been recovered only once.

The personal liability of officials was not only one of the great bulwarks of the rule of law: it also provided a peg on which a very proper official practice was hung. The Crown did in fact assume the liability which could not lie upon it in law by making a habit of defending actions brought against its servants for torts committed by them in their official capacities.

[1] *Bainbridge v. Postmaster-General* [1906] 1 K.B. 178.

The legal process was issued solely against the individual servant, but his defence was in practice conducted by the Crown's legal advisers, and if damages were awarded they were paid out of public funds. Government departments did their best to be helpful in making this practice work smoothly, and if there was any doubt as to which servant to sue they would supply the name of a suggested defendant. This was known as suing a 'nominated defendant',[1] and it was an effective antidote to the shortcomings of the law until two fatal flaws appeared. One was in a case where it was clear that some Crown servant was liable but the evidence did not make it clear which. A representative defendant might then be nominated merely in order that the action might in substance proceed against the Crown, but this practice was condemned by the House of Lords in 1946.[2] The other difficulty was that there can be torts (such as failure to maintain a safe system of work in a factory) which render only the employer liable, so that there could be no one to nominate in, say a Ministry of Supply factory where the occupier was in law the Crown.[3] These two cases exposed the weaknesses of the makeshift practice of suing the Crown indirectly through a nominated defendant. The favourite argument that juries would award extravagant damages against government departments had also lost its force, since juries were no longer used in most civil cases. The Minister of Transport had been made liable for his department in tort (as also in contract) since 1919.[4] The government decided that the time had come—and it was, indeed, overdue—for abolishing the general immunity in tort which had been an anomaly of the Crown's legal position for more than a hundred years. This was the genesis of the Crown Proceedings Act 1947. To some extent the Act followed the proposals of a committee which had reported in 1927, but whose report was shelved until the extralegal machinery had begun to show clear signs of breakdown. The Committee on Ministers' Powers, in their report of 1932,[5] had also emphasized this 'lacuna in the rule of law'. But reform had to wait for the more favourable climate which followed the

---

[1] Cf. Road Traffic Act 1930, s. 121 (2).
[2] *Adams v. Naylor* [1946] A.C. 543.
[3] *Royster v. Cavey* [1947] K.B. 204.
[4] Ministry of Transport Act 1919, s. 26.
[5] Cmd. 4060 (1932), p. 112.

Second World War, when the two above-mentioned cases supplied the immediate stimulus.

THE CROWN PROCEEDINGS ACT 1947

The law as it now stands under the Act may be divided under three headings: 1 Tort; 2 Contract; 3. Procedure and other matters.

LIABILITY IN TORT

General rules

The Act subjects the Crown to the same general liability in tort which it would bear 'if it were a private person of full age and capacity'.[1] The general policy, therefore, is simply to put the Crown into the shoes of an ordinary defendant. Furthermore, the Act leaves untouched the personal liability of Crown servants, which was the mainstay of the old law, except in certain cases concerning the Post Office and the armed forces, to be mentioned presently. The principle of the new law is that where a servant of the Crown commits a tort in the course of his employment, the servant and the Crown are jointly and severally liable. This corresponds to the ordinary law of master and servant.

The Act specifically makes the Crown liable for:

(a) torts committed by its servants or agents;
(b) breach of duties which a person owes to his servants or agents at common law by reason of being their employer; and
(c) breach of duties attaching at common law to the ownership, occupation, possession, or control of property.

Head (a) is subject to the proviso that the Crown shall not be liable unless the servant or agent would himself have been liable. This proviso gives the Crown a dispensation which a private employer does not enjoy in occasional cases where the servant has some defence but the employer is still liable as such; for the doctrine is that personal defences belonging to the servant do not extend to the employer unless he also is entitled to them personally, and they may not prevent the servant's act

[1] S. 2.

from being a tort even though he personally is not liable. But in other respects it seems that the three heads are comprehensive. Head (c) subjects the Crown to the normal rule of strict liability for dangerous operations (*Rylands v. Fletcher*), so that the position is more satisfactory than in the case of other public authorities.[1]

The Crown is also given the benefit of any statutory restriction on the liability of any government department or officer.[2] A number of statutes contain such limitations of liability, for example the Mental Health Act 1959 which protects those who detain mental patients under the Act unless they act in bad faith or without reasonable care.

Statutory duties

Statutory duties can give rise to liability in tort,[3] and the Act subjects the Crown to the same liabilities as a private person in any case where the statute binds both the Crown and other persons.[4] The Act makes no change in the general rule that statutes do not bind the Crown unless an intention to do so is expressed or implied[5]; so the Crown will normally be liable only where the statute in question says so. This rule might well be the other way round, so that (so to speak) the Crown would have to contract out instead of having to contract in. But many important statutes do expressly bind the Crown, such as the Road Traffic Act 1960, the Factories Act 1961, and the Occupiers' Liability Act 1957. Under the last of these Acts, for instance, the Crown becomes liable in the same way as any other occupier of premises for not taking reasonable care for the safety of visitors invited or permitted to be there. A visitor to a government office or workshop who was injured by a negligently maintained roof or staircase would be able to sue the Crown for the tort. So far as concerns the occupation of land, the Crown shares both the common law and statutory liabilities of its subjects. Nor does the Crown shelter behind the fact that powers may be given (either by common law or statute) to a minister or other servant of the Crown directly, and not to the Crown itself. In such cases the Crown is made liable as if the minister were acting on the Crown's own instructions.[6]

[1] Above p. 58. [2] S. 2 (4). [3] Above, p. 156. [4] S. 2 (2).
[5] S. 40 (2) (f); below, p. 293. [6] S. 2 (3).

These primary rules for imposing liability in tort may be said, in general, to achieve their object well. The Crown occasionally claims that its governmental functions entitle it to exemption on grounds of public policy. But this claim is now, as in the past, rejected by the courts. Thus where boys escaped from an 'open Borstal' and damaged a yacht, the Home Office was held to have no defence if negligent custody could be established.[1]

Who is a Crown servant?

In broaching the question who is a servant of the Crown, it must be remembered that the Crown is liable to the same extent as a private person for torts committed by its servants *or agents*, and that 'agent' includes an independent contractor.[2] The general principle in tort is that the employer is liable for the misdeeds of his servant done in the course of the servant's employment (the course of employment being widely interpreted) but not for the misdeeds of independent contractors, who bear their own responsibility. Where the employer can control what the employee does and how he does it, the relationship is likely to be that of master and servant, so that they are liable jointly. But where this relationship is absent, the employer is not liable at all. For example, a person who takes his car for repair to an apparently competent garage is not liable if, because of careless work by the garage, a wheel comes off and injures some one.[3] Yet there are some special cases where there is liability even for independent contractors, for example where the work is particularly dangerous—thus a householder had to share the liability when she called in workmen to thaw out frozen pipes and by using blowlamps they set fire both to her house and her neighbour's.[4] If this had happened on Crown land, the Crown would have been equally liable under the Act because of its general liability for the torts of its agents.

But in the case of *servants* the Act sets up a special criterion based on appointment and pay. It says that the Crown shall

---

[1] *Dorset Yacht Co. v. Home Office* [1970] 2 W.L.R. 1140.

[2] S. 38 (2).

[3] Cf. *Phillips v. Britannia Hygienic Laundry* [1923] 2 K.B. 832, where the plaintiff failed to circumvent this principle by pleading breach of statutory duty (above, p. 156).

[4] *Balfour v. Barty-King* [1957] 1 Q.B. 496.

not be liable for the torts of any officer of the Crown 'unless that officer has been directly or indirectly appointed by the Crown' and was at the material time paid wholly out of moneys provided by Parliament or out of certain funds (which in case of doubt may be certified by the Treasury), or would normally be so paid.[1] The final words cover the case of voluntary office-holders, such as ministers acting without salary. But the principal importance of this provision is that it prevents the Crown becoming answerable for the police. It can be said, as we know,[2] that in some of their functions at least the police act as officers of the Crown. Yet since the police, both in London and in the provinces, are at least partly paid out of local rates, and in the provinces are appointed by local authorities, they are all excluded by the Act.[3] This left an unsatisfactory situation until the Police Act 1964 remedied it by placing representative liability on chief constables as explained previously.[4]

Nor do there seem to be any other plausible complaints against the restriction. It has been suggested that it frees the Crown from responsibility for the acts of 'borrowed' servants— as where the servant of A is told to work to B's orders, so that B may be liable for his negligence—but the answer to this may be that if the Crown borrows A's servant, A's servant is not for that reason an 'officer of the Crown', so that the exclusion clause does not operate. There is also some doubt as to the Crown's liability for the servants of certain public corporations. It is clear that the nationalized industries and the B.B.C. are independent bodies and not servants or agents of the Crown.[5] But the less industrial and more governmental corporations, such as the New Town Development Corporations and the Regional Hospital Boards, stand in much closer relationship with the Crown, and whether they and their servants can render the Crown liable must depend on careful examination of their constituent Acts in cases as yet undecided. But this is unlikely to afford the Crown any exemption to which it would not be entitled on ordinary legal principles. What matters in practice is that there should be an employer with a long enough purse to satisfy a judgment, and there is no doubt of the capacity of public corporations on that score.

[1] S. 2 (6). [2] Above, p. 33. [3] Above, p. 32.
[4] Above, p. 35. [5] Above, p. 43.

Judicial functions

The Crown has one other general immunity in tort which is both noteworthy and proper. The Act provides against Crown liability in tort for any person discharging judicial functions or executing judicial process.[1] This expresses the essential separation of powers between executive and judiciary. Judges and magistrates are appointed by the Crown or by ministers. They are paid (if at all) out of public funds, and so may be said to be servants of the Crown in a broad sense—a sense that was brought home to them when their salaries were reduced as 'persons in His Majesty's service' under the National Economy Act 1931. But the relationship between the Crown and the judges is entirely unlike the relationship of employer and employee on which liability in tort is based. The master can tell his servant not only what to do but how to do it. The Crown has had no such authority over the judges since the days of Coke's conflicts with James I. The master can terminate his servant's employment, but the superior judges are protected by legislation, dating from 1700, against dismissal except at the instance of both Houses of Parliament.[2] Their independence is sacrosanct, and if they are independent no one else can be vicariously answerable for any wrong that they may do.

It is virtually impossible for judges of the Supreme Court to commit torts in their official capacity, since they are clothed with absolute privilege. Lower judges, such as magistrates, can probably offend if they act outside their jurisdiction, and the Act accordingly protects the Crown in the case of any one 'discharging or purporting to discharge' judicial functions. In this context the word 'judicial' ought not to bear the artificially wide meaning discussed elsewhere. It ought naturally to cover members of independent statutory tribunals, e.g. rent tribunals, even where they are whole-time employees of the Crown as are the Special Commissioners of Income Tax.[3] A more doubtful case is that of independent licensing authorities such as traffic commissioners. The functions of inspectors

[1] S. 2 (5).
[2] Below, p. 304.
[3] Contrast *Ranaweera v. Ramachandran* [1970] 2 W.L.R. 500, decided in the different context of the constitution of Ceylon.

holding public inquiries would seem not to be 'judicial' in this sense, though they are in the artificial sense.[1]

The Post Office and the armed forces

Both the Post Office and its employees were given remarkably wide dispensations by the Act.[2] But since the Post Office is no longer a Crown service, these are discussed elsewhere.[3]

In the case of the armed forces there are provisions designed to prevent the taxpayer from paying twice over for accidents in the services, once by way of damages and once more by way of disability pension to the injured person or his dependants. The dispensation therefore applies only where the injury is attributable to service for pension purposes, and it cannot affect the rights of plaintiffs outside the armed forces. The main provision is that, provided that pensionability is certified, neither the Crown nor the tortfeasor is liable for death or personal injury caused by one member of the armed forces, while on duty as such, to another member of the armed forces who is either on duty as such or is on any land, premises, ship, aircraft, or vehicle for the time being used for service purposes.[4] Similarly, the Crown and its servants as owners or occupiers of any such land, &c., are exempted if a certificate of pensionability is given and the injured party is a member of the forces. Ministers are empowered to give conclusive certificates to settle the question whether any person was or was not on duty, or whether any land, &c., was in use by the forces at the relevant time.

Although these provisions are clearly aimed at producing equitable results, there may still be anomalies. In one case a territorial reservist was accidentally killed by the firing of a live shell, and the death was duly certified as attributable to service for pension purposes; but the award was nil, since his parents, who were his nearest surviving relatives, did not themselves qualify under the pension scheme.[5] Thus the sole result was to deprive the parents of their remedy in damages, as their son's personal representatives, for his death. Accidents to the Crown's

---

[1] Above, p. 193.
[2] S. 9, now replaced by Post Office Act 1969, ss. 29–30.
[3] Above, p. 42.
[4] S. 10.   [5] *Adams v. War Office* [1955] 1 W.L.R. 1116.

civilian employees are governed by the ordinary law, in which the right to damages is modified only to a limited extent on account of state insurance benefits[1]—for these benefits are in part met from contributions and not from taxation.

LIABILITY IN CONTRACT

General principles

The Crown's liability for breach of contract was, as we have seen, acknowledged in principle long before the Crown Proceedings Act 1947, but was subject to the ancient procedure of petition of right. There were also a few special cases where statute had provided other remedies. The Minister of Transport was expressly made liable in contract by the Ministry of Transport Act 1919,[2] and could be sued by ordinary procedure; other departments were incorporated by statute (such as the former Office of Works), and it was held that this rendered them liable on their contracts; and some ministers or departments were by statute made able 'to sue and be sued', which was held to render them liable in contract, though not in tort.[3]

The Crown Proceedings Act 1947 has now modernized and simplified the procedure, without altering the general principle of Crown liability. The petition of right is abolished, together with a number of old forms of procedure. Also abolished are the special provisions as to the Ministry of Transport and as to departments able to sue and be sued. Instead, all actions in contract are brought against the appropriate government department, or against the Attorney-General, under the standard procedure laid down in the Act. Proceedings both in contract and in tort are thus covered by the same set of rules, which are explained in the next section.

The principal provision of the Act is that any claim against the Crown which might have been enforced, subject to the fiat, by petition of right or under any of the statutory liabilities repealed by the Act, may now be enforced as of right and without the fiat in proceedings under the Act.[4] Thus the scope of the

---

[1] Law Reform (Personal Injuries) Act 1948, s. 2.   [2] Above, p. 281.
[3] *Minister of Supply v. British Thompson-Houston Co. Ltd.* [1943] 1 K.B. 478.
[4] S. 1.

Act depends upon the scope of the petition of right and the other old procedures, and the old law relating to them will still be of importance if the Crown ever resists a claim on the ground that it falls outside the area of Crown liability. But apart from tort and certain cases such as actions by servants of the Crown (discussed elsewhere),[1] and the special case of salvage (now covered by the Act),[2] the scope of the old actions was probably comprehensive. The petition of right, for instance, appears to have been available for recovery of money from the Crown where an ordinary subject would have been liable in quasi-contract, a head of liability which is not truly contractual; and, as already noted, the petition of right could be used to recover money due from the Crown under statute. The substance of these remedies is thus infused into the new statutory scheme, and there are no obvious gaps.

There is perhaps a gap, more of theoretical than practical importance, as regards actions against the sovereign personally. A petition of right used to lie, and the Act of 1860 provided for payments from the privy purse; but now the Crown Proceedings Act both abolishes the petition of right and provides that nothing in the Act shall apply to proceedings by or against the sovereign personally.[3] Is the Crown then no longer personally liable in contract? It seems possible, following the words of the Act, that the petition of right is not abolished to that extent, so that it still survives for claims against the Crown in person, which remain under the old law. This result would be far from ideal, but at least it would preserve the remedy in some form.

Agents in contract

The Crown servant or agent who actually makes the contract —for example, a War Office official who orders boots for the army—is not in law a party to the contract, and is not liable on it personally. He is merely the Crown's agent, and the ordinary law is that where a contract is made through an authorized agent, the principal is liable but the agent is not. The agent is merely a mechanism for bringing about a contract between his principal and the other contracting party. Thus if the boots are ordered from a manufacturing company, the parties to the contract are the Crown and the company, and the agents on

---

[1] Below, p. 298.   [2] S. 8.   [3] S. 40 (1).

either side are not legally liable on it. It has long been clear that Crown servants, acting in their official capacity, are as immune as any other agents, for in 1786 it was decided that the Governor of Quebec could not be sued on promises made by him to pay for supplies for the army in Canada.[1] This immunity of the agent must be contrasted with the position in tort, where master and servant are both fully liable personally for torts committed by the servant in the course of his employment, and where the personal liability of Crown servants is an important safeguard—though not quite so important as it was in the era before the Crown itself became liable in tort.

Where a contract is made through an agent duly authorized, the principal is liable but not the agent. Where the agent is unauthorized, the agent is liable but not the principal. This latter result is achieved by allowing the other party an action against the agent for breach of warranty of authority. This is a contractual remedy, for a contract is implied by law to the effect that the agent promises, in consideration of the party agreeing to deal with him, that he has the authority of his principal. Thus the law finds a means of making agents responsible for any loss which they may cause by exceeding their authority. But it is doubtful whether this remedy is available against agents of the Crown. The Court of Appeal has indeed upheld a judgment to the effect that a Crown servant acting in his official capacity is, on grounds of public policy, not liable to actions for breach of warranty of authority. 'No action lies against a public servant upon any contract which he makes in that capacity, and an action will only lie on an express personal contract.'[2] There seem to be two distinct strands of argument, one that public policy requires Crown agents to be able to contract free of personal liability, and the other that in such cases the implied contract of warranty is unjustified on the facts. Public policy should weigh less heavily now that the Crown Proceedings Act has gone so far towards assimilating the Crown's prerogatives with the ordinary law of the land. The other argument is also of dubious validity. Since the case was one arising out of a contract of employment, where (as explained elsewhere)[3] the principles underlying the case law

---

[1] *Macbeath v. Haldimand* (1786) T.R. 172.
[2] *Dunn v. Macdonald* [1897] 1 Q.B. 401, 555.   [3] Below, p. 303.

are confused, it is sometimes regarded as a less formidable obstacle than it appears at first sight. There were also other alternative grounds for the decision in the Court of Appeal. Nevertheless, while this authority stands, Crown agents appear to have a privileged position and to enjoy complete personal immunity in making contracts on behalf of the Crown. If they exceed their authority, therefore, neither the Crown nor its agent is liable, and the law fails to provide the remedy which justice demands.

PROCEDURE AND OTHER MATTERS

The statutory procedure

The Crown Proceedings Act 1947 has much to say about procedure. The general policy is that the ordinary procedure in civil actions shall apply so far as possible to actions by and against the Crown, both in the High Court and in the County Court. But inevitably there must be modifications in detail. The Crown is not nominally a party to proceedings under the Act: where the Crown is suing, the plaintiff is a government department or the Attorney-General;[1] where the Crown is being sued, it is represented similarly. The Treasury issues a list of the departments which can sue and be sued under the Act, and if there is no suitable department in any particular case the Attorney-General will fill the gap. It is a departure from ordinary legal notions that departments which are not juristic persons (for some departments are not incorporated) should be able to be parties to actions, but all things are possible by Act of Parliament.

The Act also exempts the Crown from the compulsory machinery of law enforcement. This is not in order to enable the Crown to flout the law, but because it would be unseemly if, for example, a sheriff's execution could be issued against a government department or a minister could be committed for contempt of a court order. The Crown must be treated as an honest man, and the ordinary laws must have their teeth drawn. Therefore the Act provides that no execution or attachment or process shall issue for enforcing payment by the Crown.[2] Nor can the Crown be made the object of any injunction or order for specific performance or order for the delivery up of

[1] S. 17.   [2] S. 25 (4).

property.[1] Nor can such remedies be obtained indirectly by the issue of an injunction against an officer of the Crown. Instead of these remedies the court merely makes a declaratory order, so that the plaintiff's rights are recognized but not enforced. The restrictions on relief corresponding to an injunction have been explained in detail already.[2]

The remedy most often desired is the payment of money. Here the court's order states the amount payable, whether by way of damages, or costs, or otherwise, and the Act provides that the appropriate government department shall pay that amount to the person entitled.[3] It is also provided that payments made under the Act shall be defrayed out of moneys provided by Parliament.[4] A successful plaintiff against the Crown must thus be content with a declaration of his rights or with a mandatory, but unenforceable, order for payment. He may, however, be sure that it will be respected by the government.

In his or her private capacity the sovereign stands wholly outside the Act and under the older law.[5] Nor is there any Crown liability under the Act for matters arising outside the government of the United Kingdom.[6]

The ordinary legal rules as to indemnity and contribution now apply in Crown Proceedings.[7] The rule most likely to come into play is that which allows an employer, who has to pay damages for his servant's wrongful act, to recover the amount from the servant. This illustrates the general principle that where there are joint tortfeasors—and master and servant are in law joint tortfeasors—the tortfeasor who is innocent may claim contribution from the tortfeasor who is to blame. Thus if a postman driving a van knocks down and injures some one negligently, and the injured man sues the Crown and obtains damages, the Crown has a legal right as employer to make the postman indemnify it.[8] Since the salaries of Crown servants are in any case, legally speaking, at the Crown's mercy,[9] the Crown is in a particularly strong position to enforce this right if it should wish to do so.

[1] S. 21. For injunctions against other authorities see above, p. 111.
[2] Above, p. 114.   [3] S. 25 (3).   [4] S. 37.
[5] S. 40 (1). See above, p. 289.   [6] S. 40 (2).   [7] S. 4.
[8] See *Lister v. Romford Ice and Cold Storage Co. Ltd.* [1957] A.C. 555.
[9] Below, p. 302.

Since the Act now provides one uniform procedure for all actions against the Crown, it has abolished the petition of right and various other antiquated forms of procedure[1]—except possibly in the case of actions against the sovereign personally.[2]

Other Crown privileges

The Crown has various advantages under the general law, which fall outside the scope of this book. Under the law of limitation of actions the Crown's title to land is not barred until the land has been in adverse possession for thirty years,[3] whereas the normal period in ordinary cases is twelve years. Formerly the Crown and its servants shared with other public authorities the privilege of a very short limitation period for wrongful acts,[4] until the legislation was repealed in 1954.[5]

There is also the important rule that statutes do not bind the Crown in the absence of express provision or necessary implication.[6] This, though essentially only a rule of construction, makes it possible for the Crown and all its numerous servants to claim exemption on some occasions from the law of the land. In fact statutes usually make provision for their application to the Crown, and the rule gives rise to little complaint. There was once an unsuccessful prosecution of a War Office employee for exceeding a speed limit (he was driving a locomotive on the road at three miles an hour when the speed limit was two)[7]; but the speed limits now in force under the Road Traffic Act 1960 are expressly made applicable to the Crown by the Act itself.[8] The Crown is not bound by the Town and Country Planning legislation since it contains no such provision. Thus the Crown does not need planning permission if it wishes to develop Crown land.[9]

Crown privilege in the law of evidence is a special subject, treated later in this chapter.

LIMITATIONS OF STATE LIABILITY

Political action: tort

A line has to be drawn between governmental acts which can

---

[1] S. 23 and First Schedule.   [2] See above, p. 289.
[3] Limitation Act 1939, s.4.
[4] *Ibid.* s. 21 (one year); Public Authorities Protection Act 1893 (six months).
[5] Law Reform (Limitation of Actions, &c.) Act 1954.   [6] Above, p. 283.
[7] *Cooper v. Hawkins* [1904] 2 K.B. 164.   [8] S. 250 (1).
[9] *Ministry of Agriculture v. Jenkins* [1963] 2 Q.B. 317.

give rise to legal liability because they are analogous to the acts of ordinary persons, and acts which give rise to no such liability because the analogy breaks down. There is a certain sphere of activity where the state is outside the law, and where actions against the Crown and its servants will not lie. The rule of law demands that this sphere should be as narrow as possible. In English law the only available examples relate in one way or another to foreign territory.

In tort, the Crown and its servants can sometimes plead the defence of act of state. But this plea is only available for acts performed abroad. It would subvert the rights of the subject entirely if it would justify acts done within the jurisdiction, for it would be the same as the defence of state necessity, which has always been rejected. But acts of force committed by the Crown in foreign countries are no concern of the English courts. In the time of the naval campaign against the slave trade, for example, a Spanish slave trader failed in an action for damages against a British naval commander who destroyed one of his establishments in West Africa.[1] It is by this fundamental rule that acts of violence in foreign affairs, including acts of war, cannot be questioned in English courts. It also casts a complete immunity over all acts of the Crown done in the course of annexing or administering foreign territory.

A British Protectorate is in principle considered to be a foreign territory, so that a person arrested by the government's orders has no remedy.[2] But where, as used to happen in practice, a protectorate is in fact completely 'under the subjection of the Crown' and is ruled as if it were a colony, the courts will assert their jurisdiction and the Crown must act according to law.[3] The boundaries of the area within which the rule of law is upheld may thus sometimes be difficult to draw. But it is clear that within that area the Crown cannot extend its limited legal power by plea of act of state. Another naval case will illustrate this. The British and French governments had made an agreement for the control of lobster fishing in Newfoundland, by which no new lobster factory was to be established there without joint consent. A factory was in fact established by the plaintiff, contrary to the terms of the inter-governmental agreement, and

[1] *Buron v. Denman* (1848) 2 Ex. 167.
[2] *The King v. The Earl of Crewe ex parte Sekgome* [1910] 2 K.B. 576.
[3] *Ex parte Mwenya* [1960] 1 Q.B. 241 (Northern Rhodesia).

the defendant, a naval captain acting under Admiralty orders, seized it. The plaintiff was a British subject and his factory was within British territory. The Crown's attempt to justify the seizure as an act of state therefore failed, and the plaintiff was awarded damages against the responsible Crown officer. [1] To-day, under the Crown Proceedings Act, the Crown would also be liable directly. The enforcement of treaties, so far as it affects the rights of persons within the jurisdiction, must be authorized by Act of Parliament. The Crown has no paramount powers.

It is often said that act of state cannot be pleaded against a British subject. No such rule was laid down in the lobster-fishing case; but the case was treated as an illustration of some such rule in a number of *obiter dicta* in a later case in the House of Lords. [2] This is weighty authority, but even so there are grounds for thinking that the proposition may be too wide. All the cases in question were cases where the acts took place within the jurisdiction—and within the jurisdiction the rights of an alien (not being an enemy alien) are similar to those of a subject. If in British territory an alien has his property taken, or is detained, in any way not justified by law, he has full legal protection [3]—not because of his nationality, but because he is within the area where the government must show legal warrant for its acts. Conversely, if a British subject chooses to live outside the jurisdiction, it is hard to believe that he can thereby fetter the Crown's freedom of action in foreign affairs. If the house of a British subject living in Egypt had been damaged by British troops when seizing the Suez Canal, would its owner really have been able to recover damages in an English court?

An affirmative answer indeed appears to be given by Lord Reid in a recent case where a British subject claimed damages from the Crown for injury done to his hotel in Cyprus (a foreign country) by a 'truce force' of British troops. [4] But the other Lords of Appeal left this question open, holding that there was in fact no act of state. A negative answer is suggested by another case in which British subjects lost valuable

[1] *Walker v. Baird* [1892] A.C. 491.
[2] *Johnstone v. Pedlar* [1921] 2 A.C. 262.
[3] *Johnstone v. Pedlar* (above); *Kuchenmeister v. Home Office* [1958] 1 Q.B. 496.
[4] *Nissan v. A.-G.* [1970] A.C. 179.

concessions in Pondoland after its annexation by the Crown, and in which act of state was pleaded successfully.[1]

The latter case perhaps gives the right lead. Generalities about the immunity of British subjects ought probably to be confined to (*a*) acts done within the realm, and (*b*) acts against British subjects abroad which are not acts of international policy, such as the above-mentioned injury to the hotel in Cyprus. A logical basis for 'act of state' then emerges. It is not so much a matter of nationality as of geography—that is to say, the Crown enjoys no dispensation for acts done within the jurisdiction, whether the plaintiff be British or foreign; but foreign parts are beyond the pale (in Kipling's words, 'without the law'), and there the Crown has a free hand, whether the plaintiff be foreign or British.

Political action: contract

In contract there are also cases where ordinary business must be distinguished from political acts. It has been laid down that 'it is not competent for the Government to fetter its future executive action, which must necessarily be determined by the needs of the community when the question arises'.[2] But this was an isolated decision, and its scope is by no means clear. It concerned a Swedish ship which was detained in England in 1918 after its owners had been given an assurance through the British Legation in Stockholm, on behalf of the British government, that the ship would be given clearance if she brought (as she did) an approved cargo. The owners sued the Crown by petition of right for damages for breach of contract. The court held that this was not a contract at all—so far from being a commercial transaction, it was merely a statement by the government that it intended to act in a particular way in a certain event. Up to this point there is no difficulty, for plainly a boundary must be drawn between legal contracts and mere administrative promises not intended to be legally binding. That is a question of fact. But the judge went on to say that the Crown not merely *had* not made such a contract but *could* not make such a contract, because it could not hamper its freedom of action in matters which concerned the welfare of the state;

---

[1] *Cook v. Sprigg* [1899] A.C. 572.
[2] *Rederiaktiebolaget 'Amphitrite' v. The King* [1921] 3 K.B. 500.

and he argued *a fortiori* from the doctrine that Crown servants are always dismissible at will, which is discussed elsewhere.[1]

The rule thus laid down is very dubious; it rests on no authority, and it has been criticized judicially.[2] Its obvious weakness lies in the fact that the meaning of 'future executive action' is so uncertain. If the Admiralty makes a contract for the sale of a surplus warship, that fetters the Crown's future executive action in that the ship will have to be surrendered. Yet there ought surely to be a remedy against the Crown for breach of contract in that case as much as in any other. The only sound distinction is that already familiar in private law between contracts intended to be legally binding and other extra-legal promises which may be broken with impunity. Undertakings about future executive action, as in the case of the Swedish ship, may obviously sometimes fall into the latter class.

Another case which falls outside the ordinary law of contract is that of treaties. No English court will enforce a treaty, that is to say an agreement made between states rather than between individuals. 'The transactions of independent states between each other are governed by other laws than those which municipal courts administer.'[3] In the days when much of India was governed by the East India Company this principle was often invoked by English courts in order to disclaim jurisdiction over transactions between the Company, acting in effect as a sovereign power, and the native rulers of India. For the same reason the Company was given the benefit of the doctrine of act of state, so that it could commit acts of force with no legal responsibility.[4] Its commercial and its governmental activities had to be separated, so that while liable for the one it was not liable for the other. Similarly, where money is paid to the Crown under a treaty as compensation for injury inflicted on British subjects, those subjects cannot sue the Crown to recover the money, for the transaction is on the plane of international affairs out of which no justiciable rights arise.[5] The ordinary principles of trust or agency are no more suitable to the case

---

[1] Below, p. 300.   [2] In the *Robertson* and *Howell* cases, cited above, p. 68.

[3] *Secretary of State for India v. Kamachee Boye Sahaba* (1859) 13 Moo. P.C. 22.

[4] *Salaman v. Secretary of State for India* [1906] 1 K.B. 613.

[5] *Rustomjee v. The Queen* (1876) 2 Q.B.D. 69; *Civilian War Claimants Association v. The King* [1932] A.C. 14. The principle is not changed by the Foreign Compensation Act 1950.

than the law of contract is suitable for the enforcement of treaties.

THE LAW OF CROWN SERVICE

Nature of Crown service

Crown service is one of the most curious departments of English administrative law. In most other democratic countries the position and rights of state employees form an important branch of public law, and the tenure of posts in the civil service gives rise to many questions for the courts, whether they be ordinary courts of law or special administrative courts. In England the position is just the opposite. The civil service, despite its great size and importance, is largely staffed and regulated under arrangements which are not legally enforceable. This accords, perhaps, with the way in which the civil service works, withdrawn as much as possible from the public gaze, and screened from scrutiny by the doctrine of ministerial responsibility.[1] But legally it is anomalous. Civil servants of the Crown, and military servants also, have no legal right to their salaries, it seems, and no legal protection against wrongful dismissal. So far as the law goes, apart from a few statutes such as the Superannuation Act 1965, the civil service might still consist of a handful of secretaries working behind the scenes in the royal palace. Although it has lost its 'domestic' character in every other respect, it is still in a primitive state of legal evolution. It is also curious that the legal situation did not reveal itself clearly until late in the nineteenth century.

Another paradox is that in practice the situation is just the opposite of what these legal rules would suggest. The courts have to a large extent abrogated jurisdiction over contracts of service under the Crown. But Crown service, though legally the most precarious of all employments, is in reality the most secure. This is merely convention, but in the civil service the convention is so deeply ingrained that there are probably better grounds for complaining that civil servants are excessively protected than for criticizing their defencelessness in law. The Crichel Down affair of 1954 provides a good example. This was one of the rare cases where serious complaints were

---

[1] See above, p. 18.

made good against the conduct of officials. The charge was that they had not given proper attention to a landowner's claims for the restoration of land taken under compulsory powers before the war. There was no infringement of legal rights, but clearly there had been bad administration. A public inquiry was ordered by the Minister of Agriculture and all the correspondence was published [1]—a most unusual opportunity for the public to see the contents of official files. But despite the strong criticism which the report contained, there were no dismissals, and in the civil service the result of all the upheaval was no more than some rearrangement of duties. The Minister of Agriculture, however, resigned—although he personally was entirely free from blame, and had shown magnanimity in ordering the inquiry. There could hardly be a better illustration of the rock-like solidity of the civil service and, in contrast, of the irrational vicissitudes of politics. The doctrine of ministerial responsibility does not, indeed, require a minister to resign if his officials have done something which is not in accordance with his orders or his policy, and of which he does not approve. But, when the choice had to be made, it was in fact the Minister who elected to pay the penalty.

There is a close connexion between the responsibility of the Minister and the security of tenure of the civil servant. There is no real need for this connexion to produce such results as it did in the *Crichel Down* case; but since the public is accustomed to frequent changes of ministers and to complete stability in the administrative machine, there is a natural tendency for the sacrosanctity of tenure of official posts to be exaggerated. It is this which gives an atmosphere of unreality to the subject of Crown service. In law, the civil servant holds his office at pleasure and can be dismissed instantaneously by the government for misconduct or for any other reason. In practice, a civil servant's misconduct seems more likely to cause the downfall of his minister than of himself.

Tenure and remuneration

Crown servants of all ranks are in law the servants of the Crown and not of one another.[2] A civil servant therefore has no

---

[1] Cmd. 9176 (1954).
[2] *Bainbridge v. Postmaster-General* [1906] 1 K.B. 178.

contractual relationship with his department, with his minister, or with any superior officer. Whoever engages him acts merely as the Crown's agent, and the contract (such as it is) is between the servant and the Crown. Any remedy for breach of the agreed terms must therefore be sought against the Crown alone, subject to the procedure prescribed by the Crown Proceedings Act.

The best-known case on the legal insecurity of civil service tenure concerned the dismissal of a consular agent in Africa.[1] A Mr. Dunn had been engaged as consular agent in Nigeria for a term (as he said) of three years certain, but was prematurely dismissed. He sued the Crown by petition of right, but a strong Court of Appeal refused him any relief. The court substantially accepted the Crown's argument reported in the following words:

> . . . servants of the Crown hold office only during the pleasure of the Crown, except in cases where it is otherwise provided by statute. . . . The action of a civil servant of the Crown might, if he could not be dismissed, in some cases bring about a war. A contract to employ a servant of the Crown for a fixed period would be against the public interest and unconstitutional. It is not competent for the Crown to tie its hands by such a contract.

The basis of the rule that Crown servants are dismissible at pleasure, therefore, is the principle that the public interest requires that the government should be able to disembarrass itself of any employee at any moment.

This case had a sequel, for having failed against the Crown the consular agent sued the officer who had engaged him.[2] It was plain that this officer had no authority to promise a certain period of tenure, for the law as laid down by the court was that any such term was unenforceable. He was therefore sued personally for breach of warranty of authority, on the principle already explained. But here again he failed: first, because it was held that public policy excludes any remedy for breach of warranty of authority against a public servant who is acting purely in his public capacity[3]; and secondly, because in fact the agent *had* been duly authorized in this instance, and the complaint was really that the law gave no remedy against the

---

[1] *Dunn v. The Queen* [1896] 1 Q.B. 116.
[2] *Dunn v. Macdonald* [1897] 1 Q.B. 401, 555.
[3] Above, p. 290.

Crown's breach of the agreed terms of service rather than that any misrepresentation had been made by the agent. The first of these grounds is questionable in principle, for there is no obvious reason why civil servants should not be as responsible for misrepresenting their authority as anyone else. A more acceptable way of escape is to say that the misunderstanding was one of law, as to which one person cannot in theory mislead another, for all are supposed to know it. Artificial as this is,[1] it avoids the greater evil of inventing new official immunities.

The rule as laid down in *Dunn's* case, that the Crown can always dismiss a public servant at pleasure despite any engagement to the contrary, has been followed in a number of later decisions,[2] and the general policy of the judges has clearly been to treat Crown service as no concern of the ordinary law. Yet the reasons put forward for this policy will not really bear examination. It is said that the public interest demands that public servants should be subject to summary dismissal because of the damage that it may be in their capacity to do. But any employer can always dismiss a servant: the only question is whether, if he does so, he should pay damages for breach of contract.[3] No master can be compelled to employ a servant, any more than a servant can be compelled to serve a master. The argument that the Crown could not otherwise relieve the public of an undesirable servant therefore falls to the ground. The question is merely one of monetary compensation. It may be said that the Crown should not be put in the dilemma of ignoring the public interest or else committing a breach of contract—for a breach of contract, despite Mr. Justice Holmes's famous theory to the contrary,[4] is a wrongful act. But to that it can be answered that it is of even greater importance that engagements expressly entered into at least be honoured in the breach, even if not in the observance. The Crown should be an honest man, and if driven to break its contract ought to pay damages. As a learned judge has said:[5]

---

[1] It was also expressly rejected at first instance: see at p. 406.

[2] E.g. *Rodwell v. Thomas* [1944] K.B. 596; *Riordan v. War Office* [1959] 1 W.L.R. 1046, aff'd [1961] 1 W.L.R. 210.

[3] See above, p. 122.

[4] Holmes's theory was that a contract was a promise to perform or to pay damages, at the promisor's option.

[5] Bailhache J. in *Denning v. Secretary of State for India* (1920) 37 T.L.R. 138.

The Crown is under no obligation to accept the services of an officer . . . ; where the engagement is for a fixed term and the Crown wishes to dispense with the services of the officer before the agreed date, there is nothing to prevent it from suspending the officer and . . . paying him his agreed remuneration for the remainder of the contract period. The efficiency of the public administration would not be thereby impaired and the Crown would be acting in accordance with one of the most famous maxims of law, pacta sunt servanda. As it is, the Crown saves the public purse a relatively infinitesimal amount at the price of conduct which would be condemned in an individual.

In reality, the courts are equally reluctant to give a mere money judgment against the Crown on a contract of service, for they have held that a civil servant has not even a contractual right to arrears of pay.[1] An Indian civil servant had made default in payments of alimony to his wife under a separation order, and the wife attempted to attach, by a garnishee order, arrears of pay due to her husband. But debts can be attached only if legally due, and the Crown took the point that since the pay could not be sued for by the husband, it was not legally due to him and so not attachable by his creditors. This contention was upheld, following a very similar Scots case in which the Court of Session had decided that contracts of service under the Crown were subject to an implied condition that the right to salary should not be legally enforceable.[2] As is mentioned below, both these decisions have been rejected by the Privy Council.

In the armed forces the lack of any legal remedy for wrongful dismissal, or for recovery of pay, has been made clear in a parallel line of decisions which are, if anything, more categorical than those dealing with civil servants. It was in fact the decisions about military service which provided persuasive precedents for the decisions about civil service. Although it has occasionally been suggested that there is no necessary reason why the rules should be the same in both cases, there are no very convincing reasons for differentiation. On the whole, however, the military cases tend more to the conclusion that this type of Crown service is not contractual at all.

---

[1] *Lucas v. Lucas* [1943], P. 68.
[2] *Mulvenna v. The Admiralty* 1926 S.C. 842.

The law is as clear as it can be [said Lord Esher M.R. in 1890] . . . that all engagements between those in the military service of the Crown and the Crown are voluntary only on the part of the Crown and give no occasion for an action in respect of any alleged contract. . . . The courts of law have nothing whatever to do with such a matter. [1]

Lack of legal principles

What, then, are a civil servant's rights if he is unable to enforce his contract either for wrongful dismissal or for recovery of pay? The courts have reduced the contract almost to vanishing point, at least on the employee's side, and the whole tendency of the decisions has been towards the conclusion that Crown service is not contractual at all. In some provocative *obiter dicta* Lord Goddard C.J. took this logical step, saying that 'an established civil servant is appointed to an office and is a public officer, remunerated by moneys provided by Parliament, so that his employment depends not on a contract with the Crown but on appointment by the Crown . . .'.[2] This suggested legal divorce between the Crown and its servants is a new idea, which seems to run counter to the long-accepted principle that there is a true relationship of master and servant between them. Lord Goddard C.J. nevertheless also suggested that a civil servant should have a legal right to arrears of pay by claiming on a *quantum meruit*, i.e. for the value of the services rendered. But against whom this claim would lie, if not against the Crown, he did not say, nor did he consider the authorities which have expressly decided that arrears of pay are not legally recoverable.

The case-law in fact still gives ample scope for contrary arguments. On two occasions the Privy Council has more than hinted that there might be some contractual remedy for wrongful dismissal.[3] And recently, in holding that the law of Ceylon allowed a civil servant to sue the Crown for increments of salary, the Privy Council has rejected the English and Scots decisions

---

[1] *Mitchell v. The Queen* (1890) [1896] 1 Q.B. 121, note. The law has been altered in Australia: see 66 *L.Q.R.* at 480.

[2] *Inland Revenue Commissioners v. Hambrook* [1956] 2 Q.B. 641 at 654.

[3] *Shenton v. Smith* [1895] A.C. 229; *Reilly v. The King* [1934] A.C. 176. See also *Robertson v. Minister of Pensions* [1949] 1 K.B. 227 at 231; *Terrell v. Secretary of State for the Colonies* [1953] 2 Q.B. 482 at 499 (below, p. 305).

to the contrary.[1] Moreover, the only decision of the House of Lords is to the effect that a Crown servant can sue for his pay—but this is one of those mysteries where the House has displayed an Olympian detachment from familiar problems. A Post Office telegraphist had enlisted in the armed forces in 1915 on the strength of a Post Office circular which promised 'full civil pay in addition to military pay'. The question was whether he was entitled to increments of civil pay granted in the Post Office during the period when he was in the armed forces. He sued for this additional salary by petition of right and succeeded.[2] Even though the objection to his remedy was never raised, the case may well represent the future law. For it seems unlikely that the courts will continue to deny the remedy which justice obviously demands. The state of the decisions illustrates case-law at its worst, and Crown counsel have had to implore judges not to add to the confusion by propounding more doctrine.[3]

Nothing in the Crown Proceedings Act 1947 alters the judge-made law as to Crown service. The non-legal character of the public service is in some ways in keeping with its whole constitutional position, and it cannot be said to be a source of serious complaint. The Act has provided machinery corresponding to a garnishee order under which moneys due from the Crown may be attached like other debts, but there is an express exception in respect of wages or salary payable to an officer of the Crown.[4] Thus the Act adopts the same policy as the courts.[5]

The judiciary

Judges are regarded as servants of the Crown in the sense that they hold appointments granted by the Crown. It is, of course, a cardinal principle that they should have security of tenure. In the case of the judges of the High Court and of the Court of Appeal their tenure is protected by the Judicature Act of 1925, replacing the Act of Settlement of 1700, making them removable on an address of both Houses of Parliament (a pro-

---

[1] *Kodeeswaran v. A.-G. of Ceylon* [1970] 2 W.L.R. 456.
[2] *Sutton v. Attorney-General* (1923) 39 T.L.R. 294.
[3] *Riordan v. War Office* [1959] 1 W.L.R. 1046 at 1052.
[4] S. 27.   [5] Above, p. 302.

cedure which has only once been carried into effect).[1] But
the lower judiciary appear to have no better legal protection
against dismissal than have other office-holders. The question
arose in the case of a judge of the Supreme Court of Malaya
who had been appointed in 1930 on the understanding that the
retiring age should be 62. When Malaya was overrun by the
Japanese in 1942 he was retired on pension, some time before
he had reached 62, on the footing that his office had been
abolished. He claimed that he was protected by the Act of
Settlement or alternatively by a contract that the Crown should
employ him until the retiring age. Both claims were rejected,
the first on the construction of the Act, and the second because
the Crown had the power to dismiss him at pleasure which
could not (just as in the case of civil servants) be fettered by
contract.[2] Legal security of tenure for judges is in fact the
exception rather than the rule. In England county court judges
and magistrates are subject to removal by the Lord Chancellor
for inability or misbehaviour. But any undue interference with
judges of any kind would raise a political storm. Their tenure,
like that of civil servants, is as firmly protected by convention
as it could be by positive law. But in a number of other countries
of the Commonwealth legal protection is given by the constitution, which provides that judges can be removed only on the
recommendation of a judicial commission.

Loss of services

The Crown has from time to time brought actions to recover
damages for the loss of services of an employee. At common law
a master had an action against some one who injured his servant
and so deprived him of his services. Where a public servant is
injured by some one's negligence, so that the public loses the
benefit of his services, the government may feel that damages
should be recovered for the public purse. But, although a claim
of this kind was once allowed, the door has now been closed by
a decision of the Court of Appeal in a case where an Inland
Revenue official was injured in a road accident by a motor-
car.[3] The action for loss of services (known as the action *per*

---

[1] In 1830 (an Irish judge). Lords of Appeal in Ordinary in the House of Lords
are protected by the Appellate Jurisdiction Act 1876.

[2] *Terrell v. Secretary of State for the Colonies* [1953] 2 Q.B. 482.

[3] *Inland Revenue Commissioners v. Hambrook* [1956] 2 Q.B. 641.

quod servitium amisit) is now held to be confined to cases of 'menial' servants, meaning servants working *intra moenia* in a domestic establishment. It is therefore out of place where the injured servant is the holder of a public post, and in the case just mentioned the Crown's claim failed.

CROWN PRIVILEGE IN THE LAW OF EVIDENCE

The rule and the dilemma

The Crown has the special privilege of being able to prevent evidence from being given in court if its disclosure would be contrary to the public interest. This power has long existed at common law, and the judge-made rules are expressly preserved under the Crown Proceedings Act 1947. The ordinary procedure for obtaining discovery of documents and answers to interrogatories is made applicable to Crown proceedings. The Crown may therefore be required to authorize the disclosure of official information, which would otherwise be an offence under the Official Secrets Act 1911. But the Crown Proceedings Act contains a proviso that its provisions shall not prejudice the law about withholding documents or refusing to answer questions on grounds of public interest.[1] The standard procedure therefore continues to operate. If it is desired to prevent the disclosure of evidence, the minister submits a sworn affidavit stating that on grounds of public interest he objects to the disclosure of specified documents. Privilege may also be claimed in respect of oral evidence by certifying that evidence on some particular fact or matter is to be excluded.

The Crown need in no way be a party to the litigation. It may intervene to prevent the disclosure of evidence in any proceedings whatever, as it did in the *Thetis* case (below) where the action was between private parties. Nor will the court hear the evidence *in camera*, for disclosure to the parties may be as objectionable as disclosure to the public generally. Thus the Crown is enabled to suppress the evidence altogether.

This is a highly dangerous power, since it enables the executive to deprive a litigant of his legal rights. If he is prevented from putting forward the evidence on which he relies, he may lose an action which he ought to have won. In effect, he is

[1] S. 28.

expropriated without compensation. On the other hand, some protection must certainly be given to secrets of state. The difficult question is whether the courts can hold the scales of justice where private right and public interest thus come into conflict, or whether the last word must rest with the executive. In 1942 the House of Lords, departing from the current of earlier authority, declared in sweeping terms that a ministerial claim of privilege must be accepted at face value by the court. But this rule revealed the truth of the United States Supreme Court's statement that 'a complete abandonment of judicial control would lead to intolerable abuses'.[1] In 1956 the government announced administrative reforms. In 1964 a judicial rebellion began in the Court of Appeal. In 1968 the House of Lords finally re-established the law on a sound footing.

The Thetis case

The *Thetis* case[2] was for long a source of trouble because the House of Lords laid down the law in terms far wider than were required by the question before them. In 1939 the submarine *Thetis* sank during her trials with the loss of ninety-nine men. Many of their dependants brought actions for negligence against the contractors who had built the submarine, and this was a test case. The plaintiffs called on the contractors to produce certain important papers, including the contract with the Admiralty for the hull and machinery and salvage reports made after the accident. But the First Lord of the Admiralty swore an affidavit that disclosure would be against the public interest. The House of Lords held that this affidavit could not be questioned, so that the plaintiffs inevitably lost their case. After the war it was divulged that the *Thetis* class of submarines had a new type of torpedo tube which in 1942 was still secret. The case is a good example of the most genuine type, where it seems plain that the interests of litigants must be sacrificed in order to preserve secrets of state. Diplomatic secrets and methods for the detection of crime might demand similar protection.

Unfortunately the House of Lord's unanimous decision took

---

[1] *U.S. v. Reynolds* 345 U.S. 1 (1953).
[2] *Duncan v. Cammell, Laird & Co. Ltd.* [1942] A.C. 624.

the form of a sweeping rule that the court could not question a claim of Crown privilege made in proper form, regardless of the nature of the document. Thus the Crown was given legal power to override the rights of litigants not only in cases of genuine necessity but in any case where a government department thought fit. This had not been the law previously. In several English cases judges had called for and inspected documents for which privilege was claimed in order to satisfy themselves that the claim was justified. In 1931 the Privy Council held that the court could examine such a claim, and remitted a case to Australia with directions to examine the documents and strong hints that the claim of privilege should be disallowed.[1] In that case the plaintiff was suing a State government for faulty storage of his wheat, and the Privy Council did not see how the public interest could require non-disclosure of the documents showing how it has been allowed to go bad or how mice had got into it. An English court had actually disallowed a claim of privilege in one case, and the document (quite innocuous) may be seen in the report.[2]

'Class' claims

The principal danger of the *Thetis* doctrine was that it enabled privilege to be claimed merely on the ground that documents belonged to a class which the public interest required to be withheld from production, i.e. not because the particular documents were themselves secret but merely because it was thought that all documents of that kind should be confidential. A favourite argument—and one to which courts of law have given approval[3]—was that official reports of many kinds would not be made fearlessly and candidly if there was any possibility that they might later be made public. Once this unsound argument gained currency, free rein was given to the tendency to secrecy which is inherent in the public service. Privilege was claimed for all kinds of official documents on purely general grounds, despite the injustice to litigants. It is not surprising that the Crown, having been given a blank cheque, yielded to the temptation to overdraw.[4]

---

[1] *Robinson v. South Australia* (No. 2) [1931] A.C. 704.
[2] *Spiegelman v. Hocker* (1933) 50 T.L.R. 87 (statement to police after accident).
[3] *Smith v. East India Co.* (1841) 1 Ph. 50; *Hennessy v. Wright* (1888) 21 Q.B.D. 509.
[4] Quoted by Lord Pearce in [1968] A.C. at 985.

One case is said to be typical of many others not reported. A man awaiting trial and detained in the hospital wing of Winchester prison was violently assaulted by a convict who was under observation as a suspected mental defective. The Home Office claimed privilege for the police and medical reports which would have shown whether the prison authorities knew that the man was dangerous, and the injured man was therefore unable to make out his case, which alleged negligent custody of the convict.[1] Privilege was claimed on the 'class' basis, and the claim incurred strong judicial criticism. The judges considered that the evidence could have been made available without any injury to the public interest, and as we shall see this has since been officially admitted.

In another case the Secretary of State for War intervened in a soldier's divorce case so as to prevent disclosure of reports of a representative of the Soldiers', Sailors' and Airmen's Families Association who had attempted to reconcile the soldier and his wife.[2] The ordinary law gives privilege to marriage conciliators, but this privilege can be waived by the parties and Crown privilege was invoked to prevent this possibility. The court felt obliged to allow the claim, but it was able to reject a further Crown claim that the conciliator should not be called as a witness. It was held that the Crown could not render a witness totally incompetent, but could only object to evidence being given on specific matters. In fact the witness gave evidence without in any way jeopardizing the public interest.

Official concessions

Discontent with the position in England, where Crown privilege was being invoked to prevent the use in evidence of all kinds of commonplace official communications, caused the government to make important concessions administratively. The Lord Chancellor announced in 1956 that privilege would no longer be claimed for reports of witnesses of accidents on the road, or on government premises, or involving government employees; for ordinary medical reports on the health of civilian employees; for medical reports (including those of prison doctors) where the Crown or the doctor is sued for negligence;

[1] *Ellis v. Home Office* [1953] 2 Q.B. 135.
[2] *Broome v. Broome* [1955], P. 190.

for papers needed for defence against a criminal charge; for witnesses' ordinary statements to the police; and for reports on matters of fact (as distinct from comment or advice) relating to liability in contract.[1] These heads, which are defined in more detail in the statement, are said to comprise the majority of cases which come before the courts. It will be noted that they include medical reports on prisoners of the kind that the Crown refused to produce in the *Winchester* case. Privilege will still be claimed in cases of inspectors' reports into accidents not involving the Crown (such as factory inspectors' reports), though the inspector will not be prevented from giving evidence; for medical reports and records in the fighting services and in prisons in cases not involving negligence; and for departmental minutes and memoranda. These are said to be the cases where freedom and candour of communication with and within the public service would be imperilled if there were to be the slightest risk of disclosure at a later date. Two supplementary announcements have since been made.[2]

The concessions were a welcome indication that privilege would no longer be allowed to run riot. But, for the very reason that they were made, it became all the harder to accept the argument about 'freedom and candour of communication with and within the public service'. Why, for example, should this objection be waived in criminal cases but not in civil cases?[3] In private life candid reports have to be made by many professional men, yet they do not shrink from giving honest opinions because there is a distant chance that their report may one day have to be disclosed in court. Lord Radcliffe said in the House of Lords: 'I should myself have supposed Crown servants to be made of sterner stuff,' and he criticized the insidious tendency to suppress 'everything however commonplace that has passed between one civil servant and another behind the departmental screen.'[4]

---

[1] 197 *H.L. Deb.* (1956) col. 741.

[2] 237 *H.L. Deb.* col. 1191 (referring to this book) (1962); 261 *H.L. Deb.* col. 423 (1964).

[3] For a surprising answer to this question see [1968] A.C. at 942 (Lord Reid) and 84 L.Q.R. at 172. It seems that the object was to protect authors of reports from civil liability.

[4] In the *Glasgow* case, below.

The judicial rebellion

Meanwhile legal opinion was mobilizing for the overthrow of the extreme doctrine of the *Thetis* case and the unrestricted use of 'class' privilege. In 1956 the House of Lords held that in Scotland the court had power to disallow a claim by the Crown, and that in laying down the contrary in the *Thetis* case the House had failed to consider a long line of authority.[1] In 1964 the Court of Appeal declared that the same was true of England, holding that the Crown's claims were unquestionable only in cases of defence or other specific state secrets.[2] Otherwise the law of England would have fallen behind the law of Scotland, Canada, Australia, New Zealand and the United States.[3] The claim in question was purely a 'class' claim, and the Attorney-General admitted that there was nothing in the papers themselves that would make their disclosure injurious to the public interest. He claimed that in the interests of 'freedom and candour of communication' all communications with or within a government department should be withheld. The court rejected this argument and asserted its own power to inspect the documents in a 'class' case and if necessary order their production. But no such order was made, since it was held that the documents would not in fact help the appellants. Meanwhile privilege continued to be claimed on a wide basis by the Crown. 'It is not unnatural that its servants fight trench by trench to preserve the citadel of immunity which the years have built up for them.'[4] Moreover, having several times further asserted its controlling power without in fact exercising it,[5] the Court of Appeal changed its mind in 1967 and relapsed into the unqualified *Thetis* doctrine.[6]

Finally the House of Lords was given the opportunity to lay down more acceptable law. The House has now unanimously reversed what it unanimously stated in 1942, it has shattered

---

[1] *Glasgow Cpn. v. Central Land Board* 1956 S.C. 1. For a case of disallowance see *Whitehall v. Whitehall* 1957 S.C. 30.

[2] *Re Grosvenor Hotel* (No. 2) [1965] Ch. 1210 (Lord Denning M.R., Harman and Salmon L.JJ.).

[3] See particularly *R. v. Snider* (1953) 2 D.L.R. (2d) 9; *Corbett v. Social Security Commission* [1962] N.Z.L.R. 878; *Bruce v. Waldron* [1963] V.L.R. 3.

[4] Per Harman L.J. in the *Wednesbury* case (below).

[5] *Merricks v. Nott-Bower* [1965] 1.Q.B. 57; *Wednesbury Corporation v. Ministry of Housing and Local Government* [1965] 1 W.L.R. 261.

[6] In *Conway v. Rimmer* (below), Lord Denning M.R. strongly dissenting.

the basis of the unrestricted 'class' privilege, and it has successfully ordered the production of documents against the objections of the Crown.[1] These documents were reports by his superiors on a probationer police constable who was prosecuted by the police for theft of an electric torch and decisively acquitted. He sued the prosecutor for damages for malicious prosecution, and applied for discovery of five reports about himself which were in the police records and which were important as evidence on the question of malice. Both parties wished this evidence to be produced, but the Home Secretary interposed with a wide claim of 'class' privilege, asserting that confidential police reports were a class of documents the production of which would be injurious to the public interest.

The House of Lords heaped withering criticism on the overworked argument that whole classes of official documents should be withheld, at whatever cost to the interests of litigants, for the sake of 'freedom and candour of communication with and within the public service'. They also concluded that the earlier authorities had been misinterpreted in the *Thetis* case as regards England as well as Scotland. On the other hand they made it clear that the court would seldom dispute a claim of privilege based upon the specific contents of a document concerning, for example, Cabinet decisions, criminal investigations, national defence or foreign affairs. But in every case the court had the power and the duty to weigh the public interest of justice to litigants against the public interest asserted by the government. In many cases this could be done only by inspecting the documents, which could properly be shown to the court, but not to the parties, before the court decided whether to order production.

At a later date the House itself inspected the five documents in question, held that their disclosure would not prejudice the public interest, and ordered them to be produced to the plaintiff.[2]

Primarily therefore the House of Lords has now destroyed the foundation of excessively wide 'class' claims. But by insist-

---

[1] *Conway v. Rimmer* [1968] A.C. 910. Little mention was made of the precedents in the Court of Appeal and in other Commonwealth countries which had prepared the way for this reform.

[2] [1968] A.C. at 996.

ing upon the court's duty to weigh the two conflicting public interests it has put the whole subject on a far healthier basis. The essential dilemma remains. But a dangerous executive power has been brought back into legal custody.

9

DELEGATED LEGISLATION

Administrative legislation

ONE of the principal administrative activities is legislation. If we measure merely by volume, more legislation is produced by the executive government than by the legislature. All the orders, rules, and regulations made by ministers, departments, and other bodies owe their legal force to Acts of Parliament, except in the few cases where the Crown retains original prerogative power, for instance in declaring war and in governing the armed forces to some extent. But Parliament is obliged to delegate very extensive law-making power over matters of detail and to content itself with providing a framework of more or less permanent statutes. Law-making power is also vested in local authorities, in statutory corporations such as the nationalized industries, in professional bodies such as the Law Society, and in various other bodies authorized by statute.

This administrative legislation is traditionally looked upon as a necessary evil, an unfortunate but inevitable infringement of the separation of powers. But this is an old-fashioned view, for in reality it is no more difficult to justify it in theory than it is possible to do without it in practice. There is only a hazy border-line between legislation and administration, and the assumption that they are two fundamentally different forms of power is misleading. There are some obvious general differences. But the idea that a clean division can be made (as it can, more probably, in the case of the judicial power) is a legacy from an older era of political theory. It is easy to see that legislative power is the power to lay down the law for people in general, whereas administrative power is the power to lay down the law for them individually, or in some particular case. In the case of the scheme for centralizing the electricity supply undertakings in London, which has been instanced already as a matter of administrative power,[1] it might be said that the power was just as much legislative. In fact it is largely a question of taste where the line is drawn. Nor does it much matter in the present context. For legal purposes—judicial control, statutory interpretation, and the doctrine of *ultra vires*—there is common ground throughout both subjects. What does matter is that both involve the grant of wide discretionary powers to the government. Much that has already been said about the legal control of powers can be taken for granted in this chapter, which is concerned only with the special features of the administrative power to legislate.

If we look at the practical side, it is at once plain that administration must involve a great deal of general law-making, and that no theory which demands segregation of these functions can be sound. Parliament can lay down that cars must carry suitable lights, or that the price of eggs shall be fixed, or that the employment of dock workers shall be controlled, or that there shall be relief from double taxation. But where, as happens so frequently, such legislation can be properly administered only by constantly adjusting it to the needs of the situation, discretion has to be allowed. This is the work of administration, in the clearest sense of the term, and the fact that it may also be said to be legislation is of no relevance. As Parliament thrusts ever greater responsibilities onto the executive, and social and other regulatory services are constantly multiplying, delegated legislation is increasing simply as a function of the growth of discretionary power. The true constitutional problem presented by delegated legislation is not that it exists, but that its enormous growth has made it difficult for Parliament to watch over it.

The growth of a problem

Uneasiness at the extent of delegated legislation began to be evident towards the end of the nineteenth century. It was not a new device, but the scale on which it began to be used in what Dicey called 'The Period of Collectivism' was a symptom of a new era. Perhaps the most striking piece of delegation ever effected by Parliament was the Statute of Proclamations 1539 (repealed in 1547), by which Henry VIII was given wide

[1] Above, p. 132.

power to legislate by proclamation. In 1531 the Statute of Sewers delegated legislative powers to the Commissioners of Sewers, who were empowered to make drainage schemes and levy rates on landowners. These were early examples of a technique which Parliament has always felt able to use. But the flow of these powers was no more than a trickle until the age of reform arrived in the nineteenth century. Then very sweeping powers began to be conferred. The Poor Law Act of 1834 gave to the Poor Law Commissioners, who had no responsibility to Parliament, power to make rules and orders for 'the management of the poor'. This power, which lasted for over a century (though responsibility to Parliament was established in 1847), remained a leading example of delegation which put not merely the detailed execution but also the formulation of policy into executive hands.

But this was part of a particular experiment in bureaucratic government. As a thing in itself, delegated legislation did not begin to provoke criticism until later in the century. The publication of all delegated legislation in a uniform series under the title of Statutory Rules and Orders (since 1947, Statutory Instruments) began in 1890, and in 1893 the Rules Publication Act made provision (as will be explained) for systematic printing, publication and numbering, and for advance publicity. These measures brought the proportions of the problem to public notice. In 1891, for instance, the Statutory Rules and Orders were more than twice as extensive as the statutes enacted by Parliament. The First World War inevitably brought a great increase, as the government assumed almost unbounded emergency powers under the Defence of the Realm Act 1914. In 1920, when the war-time surfeit had not yet worn off, rules and orders were five times as bulky as the statutes. Delegated legislation therefore became a target when the outcry against the growth of administrative powers developed in the 1920's. It formed the first of the matters referred to the Committee on Ministers' Powers, whose Report was published in 1932.[1] Since that time, although delegated legislation has continued to grow in bulk and importance, it has not been such a subject of controversy. The Second World War brought another flood of regulations, which hardly abated at

[1] Cmd. 4060 (1932).

first when the war was succeeded by the welfare state. But, apart from the question of publication,[1] it was no longer felt that rules and regulations represented a problem about which anything could be done. Some people wanted more of them, and others less, but that they must continue in their accustomed form was assumed with resignation. A committee of the House of Commons which made a general review in 1953 was unable to recommend any important changes.[2]

Wide general powers

A standard argument for delegated legislation is that it is necessary for cases where Parliament cannot attend to small matters of detail. But, quite apart from emergency powers (considered below), Parliament sometimes delegates law-making power that is quite general. The provision of the Poor Law Acts 1834–1930 empowering regulations for 'the management of the poor' was exceptional for peace-time legislation of its period. But it was far surpassed by the powers conferred in the hey-day of state controls after the Second World War. Under the Supplies and Services (Extended Purposes) Act 1947 controls authorized by many regulations already in force were extended for the following additional purposes:

(a) for promoting the productivity of industry, commerce, and agriculture;
(b) for fostering and directing exports and reducing imports, or imports of any classes, from all or any countries and for redressing the balance of trade; and
(c) generally for ensuring that the whole resources of the community are available for use, and are used, in a manner best calculated to serve the interests of the community.

This was much more than 'emergency' legislation, in any fair sense of that overworked word. Subject to one single reservation for the sake of freedom of the press, the whole economic life of the community was subjected to executive power. The time seemed to have come to which a former minister had looked forward in the Report of 1932, when protesting against the view that delegated legislation was a necessary evil:

I feel that in the conditions of the modern state, which not only

---

[1] See below, p. 331.   [2] See below, p. 341.

has to undertake immense new social services, but which before long may be responsible for the greater part of the industrial and commercial activities of the country, the practice of parliament delegating legislation and the power to make regulations, instead of being grudgingly conceded, ought to be widely extended, and new ways devised to facilitate the process.[1]

These sweeping economic controls have now been removed, but statutory social services have inevitably extended the permanent field of delegated legislation. Some of the regulatory powers are wide, for instance the power in the National Health Service Act 1946 for the Minister to control the medical services to be provided, to secure that adequate personal care and attendance is given, and so on. In such cases the Act can do little more than provide an outline, and the only effective control left to Parliament is through the subsequent political responsibility of the Minister.

Taxation

Even the tender subject of taxation, so jealously guarded by the House of Commons, has been invaded to some extent. Under the Import Duties Act 1958 the Treasury is authorized to specify the classes of goods chargeable and the rates of duty, subject to affirmative approval by the House of Commons where duty is imposed or increased. The schedules of goods liable to purchase tax are similarly variable by Treasury order under the Purchase Tax Act 1963, but again subject to an affirmative vote of the House of Commons if the tax is increased or extended. Many Acts give power to prescribe charges for services rendered, for example by the Post Office or under the National Health Service.

Power to vary Acts of Parliament

It is quite possible for Parliament to delegate a power to amend statutes. This used to be regarded as incongruous, and the clause by which it was done was nicknamed 'the Henry VIII clause'—because, said the Committee of 1932, 'that King is regarded popularly as the impersonation of executive autocracy'. The usual object was to assist in bringing a new Act

---

[1] Miss Ellen Wilkinson in Cmd. 4060 (1932), p. 137.

into effect, particularly where previous legislation had been complicated, or where there might be local Acts of Parliament which some centralized scheme had to be made to fit. A well-known example—well known because it was said that the Act could not otherwise have been carried through at the time when Parliament was favourable to it—is the National Insurance Act of 1911, which provided that if any difficulty arose in bringing one part of the Act into operation, the Insurance Commissioners with the consent of the Treasury might do anything that they thought necessary or expedient for that purpose, and might modify the provisions of the Act, provided that they acted before the end of 1913. Such clauses were not uncommon, and sometimes they gave power to amend other Acts as well; but the Committee of 1932 criticized them as constituting a temptation to slipshod work in the preparation of bills, and said that they should be used only where they were justified before Parliament on compelling grounds.[1]

But in fact, as the intricacy of legislation grows steadily more formidable, some power to adjust or reconcile statutory provisions has to be tolerated. Although such clauses may no longer be cast in such striking terms, substantially similar devices have been even more in vogue since the Report than before it. One need look no further than the Statutory Instruments Act 1946 itself to find an example: the King in Council may direct that certain provisions about laying statutory instruments before Parliament shall not apply to instruments made under pre-existing Acts if those provisions are deemed inexpedient. Under the Factories Act 1961 there is wide power to modify or extend the provisions of the Act dealing with health or safety. Under the Protection of Birds Act 1954 there is again wide power to vary the Act by order. Many more examples could be given.[2] If there is to be delegated legislation at all, it is inevitable that it should affect statute law as well as common law.

Emergency powers

The common law contains a doctrine of last resort under which, if war or insurrection should prevent the ordinary courts

[1] Cmd. 4060 (1932), p. 61.
[2] For a case of modification of an Act by regulations see *Britt v. Buckinghamshire C.C.* [1964] 1 Q.B. 77.

from operating, the actions of the military authority in restoring order are legally unchallengeable. When the courts are thus reduced to silence, martial law (truly said to be 'no law at all') prevails. This principle has had to be called into play in Ireland as late as 1921, but it lies outside our subject. All other emergency powers derive from Parliament by delegation.

The one standing provision for peace-time emergencies is the Emergency Powers Act 1920, which is designed to protect the public from the effects of serious strikes. It was invoked in 1921, 1924, 1926 (the general strike), 1948 and 1949 (dock strikes), 1955 (rail strike) and 1966 (seamen's strike). The Crown may by proclamation declare an emergency on account of any threat to the supply and distribution of food, water, fuel, or light, or to the means of locomotion, if it appears that the community, or any substantial part of it, will be deprived of 'the essentials of life'. While the proclamation is in force the Crown may by Order in Council make regulations 'for securing the essentials of life to the community', and may confer on ministers or others any powers and duties deemed necessary for a wide variety of purposes connected with public safety and the life of the community. But there are some limits. No form of compulsory military service or industrial conscription may be imposed. Nor can it be made an offence to take part in a strike. Nor, thirdly, can there be any alteration of criminal procedure, or any right to inflict fine or imprisonment without trial. Trial by courts of summary jurisdiction may be authorized, subject to maximum penalties of three months' imprisonment and a fine of £100. A proclamation of emergency must at once be communicated to Parliament, which must be summoned if necessary; the regulations must be laid before Parliament as soon as possible, and will expire in seven days from the time when they are so laid, unless both Houses approve them by resolution. The proclamation itself expires in a month, but without prejudice to a further proclamation.

The powers granted in war-time are naturally much wider, and are too wide to describe in detail. In 1914 the Defence of the Realm Act, in a single short section, gave power to the King in Council to make regulations 'for securing the public safety and the defence of the realm', including trial by court martial in wide classes of cases. As we shall see, the courts found this formula to be subject to a number of implied restrictions, for instance as regards taxation, expropriation, and access to the courts. By the end of the war many things of questionable legality had been done, and it was thought necessary to pass the Indemnity Act 1920 and the War Charges Validity Act 1925. Profiting by this lesson, Parliament granted more elaborate and specific powers in the Emergency Powers (Defence) Act 1939. The King in Council was empowered to make defence regulations, being such regulations 'as appear to him to be necessary or expedient for securing the public safety, the defence of the realm, the maintenance of public order and the efficient prosecution of any war in which His Majesty may be engaged, and for maintaining supplies and services essential to the life of the community'. A series of specific powers was then added, providing for such things as detention of persons and requisitioning of property, for amending, modifying, or suspending any statute, and for delegating any of the powers to other authorities. The Treasury was given power to make orders imposing charges in connexion with any scheme of control under the regulations, subject to affirmative resolution by the House of Commons within twenty-eight days. In 1940 a further Act provided that defence regulations might require persons 'to place themselves, their services, and their property at the disposal of His Majesty' if it appeared to him to be necessary or expedient for public safety, the defence of the realm, &c. Under these virtually unlimited powers the government undertook the close control of industrial employment as well as of very many other matters. So extensive were the powers that no Indemnity Act was found necessary. Powers which for some purposes were even wider were continued in the post-war decade by a succession of Acts of Parliament which adapted the war-time governmental machine to peace-time control of economic activity, and under which rationing schemes continued to be administered.[1] Although the number of operative controls was much reduced from 1951 onwards, it took a long time to dispose of the framework of 'emergency' laws.[2]

---

[1] See above, p. 317.
[2] A few powers linger on under the Emergency Laws (Re-enactments and Repeals) Act 1964.

LEGAL CONTROL OF DELEGATED LEGISLATION

Control by the courts

Judicial control of delegated legislation rests on exactly the same foundations as judicial control of administrative powers, the subject of Chapter 3. Any order or regulation which is not authorized by statute (or in a few special cases by the royal prerogative) can have no legal effect, and is therefore *ultra vires* and void.[1] Delegated legislation in no way partakes of the immunity which Acts of Parliament enjoy from challenge in the courts, for there is a fundamental difference between a sovereign and a subordinate law-making power. Acts of Parliament have sovereign force, but legislation made under delegated power can be valid only if it conforms exactly to the power granted. Thus a County Council's by-law will be void if it conflicts with statute law, as was the case where the by-law forbade betting in public places altogether whereas the applicable Acts of Parliament allowed it under certain conditions.[2] Similarly the House of Lords invalidated an order of the Minister of Labour which would have imposed industrial training levy on clubs which were not within the Industrial Training Act 1964.[3]

An illustration of the strict conformity which the courts require is given by an Australian case where the Privy Council held a regulation to be *ultra vires* and void.[4] A statute allowed regulations to be made relating to excavation work, both as to 'the manner of carrying out' such work and as to 'safeguards and measures' to protect workers engaged in it. A regulation requiring tunnels to be 'securely protected and made safe for persons employed therein' was held to be outside the authority of the statute, since it attempted to impose an absolute duty to make tunnels safe, whereas the statute gave power only to prescribe particular methods of work and specific precautions. A worker injured in tunnelling in the Snowy Mountains scheme was thus unable to rely on this regulation in suing for damages.

[1] See *McEldowney v. Forde* [1969] 3 W.L.R. 179 (Lord Guest's remarks at pp. 190–1 as to the absence of precedents are incorrect).

[2] *Powell v. May* [1946] 1 K.B. 330.

[3] *Hotel & Catering Industry Training Board v. Automobile Pty. Ltd.* [1969] 1 W.L.R. 697.

[4] *Utah Construction and Engineering Pty. Ltd. v. Pataky* [1966] A.C. 629.

Constitutional principles

The Bill of Rights 1689, the Act of Settlement 1700 and other primary constitutional statutes are just as subject to repeal or amendment as any others, since constitutional guarantees are inconsistent with the unlimited sovereignty which Parliament possesses. Safeguards like those provided in the constitution of the United States, or in 'entrenched provisions' in some Commonwealth countries, are unknown in this country. But the judges have sometimes treated fundamental rights as exempt from infringement by *delegated* power unless Parliament has expressed itself with unmistakable clarity. A case occurred in 1921 under the Defence of the Realm Regulations, which gave the Food Controller power to make regulations for controlling the sale, purchase, consumption, transport, &c., of food, and to control prices. The Controller gave a dairy company a licence to deal in milk, but on condition that they paid a charge of twopence per gallon, as part of a scheme for regulating prices and controlling distribution. The company expressly agreed to accept this condition, but later refused to pay the charge. It was held by the House of Lords that the condition infringed the famous provision of the Bill of Rights 1689, that no money may be levied to the use of the Crown without consent of Parliament; and that even the company's own written consent could not legalize what the statute made illegal.[1] The argument that the general power to impose controls impliedly included the power to tax was rejected. Lord Justice Atkin said:

The circumstances would be remarkable indeed which would induce the court to believe that the Legislature had sacrificed all the well-known checks and precautions, and, not in express words, but merely by implication, had entrusted a Minister of the Crown with undefined and unlimited powers of imposing charges upon the subject for purposes connected with his department.

In the Second World War the statute itself silenced all such arguments by supplementing its general provision with a battery of specific powers. A somewhat similar case from the earlier war arose in 1920, when a regulation was held invalid because it purported to authorize requisitioning of property without fair

[1] *Attorney-General v. Wilts United Dairies Ltd.* (1921) 38 T.L.R. 781. But contrast *Institute of Patent Agents v. Lockwood* [1894] A.C. 347.

compensation at market value, and without any right to dispute the value in a court of law.[1]

The right of access to the courts is a matter that the courts themselves guard strictly, and that has led to the overthrow of both war-time and peace-time regulations. In 1920 a Defence of the Realm Regulation was held *ultra vires* because, in order to prevent disturbance of munition workers, it provided that no one might sue for possession of a munition worker's house without the permission of the Minister.[2] So extreme a disability, it was held, could only be imposed by express enactment; and it could not really be said to be relevant to the public safety or the defence of the realm. In 1937 a by-law made by the Wheat Commission, which had power to make by-laws for the settlement by arbitration of disputes under the Wheat Act 1932, was invalidated in the House of Lords because it purported to exclude the Arbitration Act 1889 from applying to any such arbitration, and thus it purported to exclude the right to carry a point of law to the High Court.[3] In 1961 a purchase tax regulation was held invalid because it purported to give the Commissioners of Customs and Excise power to determine conclusively what tax was due from a taxpayer, thereby attempting to oust the jurisdiction of the court to determine the matter on appeal.[4]

But in war-time constitutional presumptions have not availed to protect the most fundamental right of all, personal liberty. In the First World War the House of Lords held that the power to make regulations 'for securing the public safety and the defence of the realm' justified a regulation for the compulsory internment of persons of hostile origin or associations.[5] In the Second World War regulations for detention were expressly authorized by the primary legislation. A profound difference of judicial opinion was provoked by the defence regulation actually made, which took power to detain 'if the Secretary of State has reasonable cause to believe any person to be of hostile

---

[1] *Newcastle Breweries v. The King* [1920] 1 K.B. 854.
[2] *Chester v. Bateson* [1920] 1 K.B. 829.
[3] *R. & W. Paul Ltd. v. The Wheat Commission* [1937] A.C. 139.
[4] *Commissioners of Customs and Excise v. Cure and Deeley Ltd.* [1962] 1 Q.B. 340. See below, p. 326.
[5] *R. v. Halliday* [1917] A.C. 260.

origin or associations'. But that question has been discussed elsewhere.[1]

Unreasonableness

Just as with other kinds of administrative action, the courts sometimes allow themselves to pass judgment on its merits.[2] In interpreting statutes it is tempting to make the assumption that Parliament could not have intended powers of delegated legislation to be exercised unreasonably, so that the legality of the regulations becomes dependent upon their content.

A particular case where the courts have applied this assumption is that of local authorities' by-laws. In the leading case, where in fact the court upheld a by-law against singing within fifty yards of a dwelling-house, it was said:

> If, for instance, [by-laws] were found to be partial and unequal in their operation as between different classes; if they were manifestly unjust; if they disclosed bad faith; if they involved such oppressive or gratuitous interference with the rights of those subject to them as could find no justification in the minds of reasonable men, the Court might well say, 'Parliament never intended to give authority to make such rules; they are unreasonable and ultra vires.' But . . . a by-law is not unreasonable merely because particular judges may think that it goes further than is prudent or necessary or convenient. . . .[3]

This rule has been applied so as to invalidate by-laws in various cases, for example where landlords of lodging-houses were required to clean them annually, under penalty, yet would in many cases have no right of access against their lodgers[4]; and where a building by-law required an open space to be left at the rear of every new building, so that in many cases it became impossible to build new extensions to existing buildings.[5] But the court normally construes by-laws benevolently and upholds them if possible.[6]

The same doctrine applies to other rules and regulations as

---

[1] *Liversidge v. Anderson* [1942] A.C. 206; above, p. 87.
[2] See above, p. 70.
[3] *Kruse v. Johnson* [1898] 2 Q.B. 91.
[4] *Arlidge v. Mayor &c. of Islington* [1909] 2 K.B. 127.
[5] *Repton School Governors v. Repton R.D.C.* [1918] 2 K.B. 133.
[6] *Kruse v. Johnson* (above); *Townsend (Builders) Ltd. v. Cinema News and Property Management Ltd.* [1959] 1 W.L.R. 119.

well as to by-laws. It is true that where the power is granted
to a minister responsible to Parliament, the court is less willing
to suppose that Parliament intended his discretion to be limited;
and this attitude is further reinforced if the regulations themselves must be laid before Parliament. On these grounds the
Ministry of Transport's regulations for pedestrian crossings
were upheld in 1943, despite the argument that to give the
right of way to pedestrians was unreasonable during the nightly
war-time blackout.[1] But in a later case a purchase tax regulation made by the Commissioners of Customs and Excise, and
duly laid before Parliament, was held invalid.[2] The Commissioners had power to make regulations 'for any matter for which
provision appears to them to be necessary' for the purpose of
collecting purchase tax. Their regulation provided that where
a proper return was not made they might themselves determine
the tax due and that the amount so determined should be
deemed to be the proper tax payable. This was held *ultra vires*
as an attempt to take arbitrary power to determine a tax
liability which was properly to be determined according to the
Act with a right of appeal to the court, and as an attempt to
oust the court's jurisdiction. The court regarded the regulation
as an arbitrary and unreasonable exercise of the power conferred. This case well shows how even the widest power will
admit judicial control.

Procedural errors

Under the multitude of statutes which empower delegated
legislation by various procedures—some after laying drafts
before Parliament, others requiring later laying before Parliament, others requiring consultation with advisory bodies—
there is plenty of scope for false steps in procedure. It came to
light in 1944 that numerous regulations made under the Fire
Services (Emergency Provisions) Act 1941 had never been laid
before Parliament as the Act required; an Indemnity Act was
passed to prevent this lapse from having any legal consequences, and to validate the regulations.[3] In fact it was by no means
clear that they were invalid, for it is possible that statutory

---

[1] *Sparks v. Edward Ash Ltd.* [1943] 2 K.B. 223.

[2] *Commissioners of Customs and Excise v. Cure and Deeley Ltd.* [1962] 1 Q.B. 340
(Sachs J.). The Crown did not appeal.

[3] National Fire Service Regulations (Indemnity) Act 1944.

requirements of this kind are mere directions, and not mandatory conditions,[1] and do not affect the validity of the regulations themselves. But this point has never come before the courts. In 1954, however, the government were obliged to concede, in an unreported case, that the Post Office had for many years collected charges for wireless transmitting and receiving licences without legal authority, and therefore presumably contrary to the Bill of Rights. The Wireless Telegraphy Act 1904 empowered the Postmaster-General to make regulations for collecting these fees, but no regulations had ever been made. Retrospective legislation was at once enacted by Parliament to cure the default.[2] Whether delegated legislation can itself have retrospective operation is another question on which there is no authority. It is probably right to assume that it cannot, since Parliament can hardly be presumed to intend to confer a power which it uses only most sparingly itself, and which demands every possible constitutional safeguard. Nevertheless retrospective orders are occasionally made.[3]

How far the validity of regulations may be affected by failure to publish them is separately dealt with below.[4]

Sub-delegation

The general rule against sub-delegation of statutory powers has been encountered once already, and has been found to be a question of statutory construction.[5] If Parliament confers power upon A, the evident intention is that it shall be exercised by A and not by B. But where power is conferred upon a minister, it is (as we have seen[6]) taken for granted that his officials may exercise it in his name, since that is the normal way in which executive business is done. This is probably as true of legislative as of administrative powers.[7] Many ministerial regulations, though made in the minister's name, are signed by officials, with or without the minister's official seal.

Delegation to some different authority is another matter.

---

[1] See above, p. 56.
[2] Wireless Telegraphy (Validation of Charges) Act 1954.
[3] An example was reported to the House of Commons by the Select Committee on Statutory Instruments on 17 November 1959: Trustee Savings Banks (Increase of Pensions) Order 1959.
[4] P. 334.   [5] Above, p. 62.   [6] Above, p. 64.
[7] See *Lewisham B.C. v. Roberts* (below, p. 331).

There is no direct judicial authority, but it seems safe to presume that unless Parliament expresses or implies a dispensation, legislative power must be exercised by those to whom it is given, and not by further delegates. But this presumption is subject to circumstances, and may be greatly weakened in time of emergency. Power to make regulations was freely delegated in the First World War, although the Defence of the Realm Act did not authorize it expressly. But no case came before the courts to show whether delegation was lawful. In the Second World War the Emergency Powers (Defence) Act 1939 itself gave express powers to delegate, so that an elaborate pyramid of regulations was constructed, delegated, sub-delegated, sub-sub-delegated, and so on.

Remedies

The commonest method of resisting an invalid regulation or by-law is to plead its invalidity in defence to a prosecution or enforcement proceedings.[1] The court may also grant an injunction, for example where a local authority is threatening demolition of a building[2]; and if unjustified demolition were carried out, an action for damages would lie. Any proceedings against a central government department are subject to the Crown Proceedings Act 1947, as explained in the preceding chapter.

In several cases also the courts have granted declarations to the effect that a by-law or order was invalid.[3] Nor has there been any indication that this remedy will be refused on account of any lack of *locus standi* on the plaintiff's part.[4] The rule that the declaration is a discretionary remedy is a sufficient protection against plaintiffs who are not genuinely concerned.

Certiorari and prohibition apply to 'judicial' rather than legislative action, but the dividing line is far from distinct. It is at least clear that they are not used to challenge such plainly legislative instruments as regulations or by-laws. But mandamus, which has no such limitations, has been used to compel the making of a by-law.[5]

---

[1] As in the purchase tax case, above, p. 326.
[2] As in the *Repton* case, *ibid.*   [3] See above, p. 123.
[4] Zamir, The Declaratory Judgment, 279.
[5] See the *Manchester* case, above, p. 160.

Statutory restriction of judicial control

Just as with administrative powers,[1] Parliament may make delegated legislation virtually judge-proof. Normally this is done by granting very wide powers rather than by clauses restricting the jurisdiction of the courts. 'Modern drafting technique is to use words which do not exclude jurisdiction in terms but positively repose arbitrary power in a named authority.'[2] But, as already observed, it is almost impossible to find language wide enough to exclude judicial control entirely.[3] All subordinate power must have legal limits somewhere.

In the past Parliament has experimented with protective clauses of varying degrees of severity. It has even been enacted that regulations purporting to be made under the Act shall be deemed to be within the powers of the Act, and shall have effect as if enacted by the Act.[4] But such naked attempts to create uncontrolled power are not nowadays acceptable. The formula which has been more used is a simple one, as, for example, in the Emergency Powers Act 1920: 'The regulations so made shall have effect as if enacted in this Act.' But what does this mean? In 1894 a majority of the House of Lords declared that it made the regulations as unquestionable by a court of law as if they were actually incorporated in the Act.[5] Any conflict between the regulations and the Act must, it was said, be solved by interpretation as in any other case of conflicting provisions in the same statute. In other words, the regulations were to be treated as sovereign rather than subordinate legislation and thus as exempt from judicial control. On this view, arbitrary power would reign.

But in 1931 the House found a better solution in a case under the Housing Act 1925, where the Minister of Health had power to confirm a housing scheme and the Act said that his order when made 'shall have effect as if enacted in this Act'. The Minister, it was held, was empowered to confirm only schemes which conformed to the Act; if the scheme itself conflicted with the Act, the order was not an order within the meaning of

---

[1] Above, p. 151.
[2] The purchase tax case (above, p. 326) is the source of this and similar remarks.
[3] *Ibid.*   [4] E.g. Foreign Marriage Act 1892, s. 21 (2).
[5] *Institute of Patent Agents v. Lockwood* [1894] A.C. 347.

the Act, and was not saved by the clause.[1] Although in fact the House upheld the order on its merits, they drew the teeth of the 'as if enacted' clause—which, as the Ministers' Powers Committee recommended, has now fallen into disuse.

These decisions exhibit the same dilemma that has already been pointed out in relation to finality clauses.[2] Such clauses must either be held to make lawful action which ought to be unlawful, or else they must be virtually meaningless. The courts rightly lean to the latter interpretation, which is far the less injurious.

What is legislation?

Although most people assume that they can tell 'legislation' when they see it, it easily merges into 'administration'. A large housing scheme of the kind just mentioned is a typical case. Is the Minister's order legislative or administrative? Probably the only correct answer is that it is both, and that there is an infinite series of gradations between what is plainly legislation and what is plainly administration.[3] Much of the work of administration consists of legislation. Why, then, should they be distinguished? One reason is that it is a general principle that legislative acts should be public, so that all may know the law. Another is that legal rights may depend on the distinction.

Both these problems are illustrated by a case from Blackpool decided in 1947.[4] Under war-time defence regulations, which continued in force after the war, the Minister of Health was empowered to take possession of land for any purpose and to delegate that power, subject to such restrictions as he thought proper. He delegated the power to local authorities by a series of circulars sent out from his department, which contained numerous instructions. Two of these instructions were that there should be no requisitioning of furniture, or of any house which the owner himself wished to occupy. Both these were disregarded in an attempted requisition of the plaintiff's house. The question then was, were the instructions in the circulars legal conditions

---

[1] *The King v. Minister of Health* [1931] A.C. 494. The Minister modified the scheme so as to make it conform to the Act.

[2] Above, p. 149.   [3] See also below, p. 337.

[4] *Blackpool Corporation v. Locker* [1948] 1 K.B. 349. See similarly *Acton B.C. v. Morris* [1953] 1 W.L.R. 1228.

restricting the delegated power, or were they merely administrative directions as to how that power, delegated in all its
plenitude, should in practice be exercised? It was on this that
the legality of the requisition depended. The Court of Appeal
held that the conditions were legislative and therefore had
legal effect, and that the requisition was invalid. But the local
authority and the Ministry had acted on the opposite view: they
had refused to disclose the terms of the circulars, and had even
at first resisted disclosing them to the court on grounds of privilege.[1] Thus they had 'radically misunderstood their own legal
rights and duties', and had refused to let the plaintiff see the very
legislation by which his rights were determined. A judgment
notable for its forceful language, as well as for its awareness of
the wide constitutional implications, was delivered by Lord
Justice Scott, who had been chairman of the Committee on
Ministers' Powers and was inclined to deplore the failure to
implement its Report. He described some of the events as 'an
example of the very worst kind of bureaucracy'. But the root of
the trouble may well have been the difficulty of telling where
legislation began and ended.

In a subsequent case, where power was delegated to a local
authority to requisition a part of one particular house, the Court
of Appeal held the delegation to be an administrative as
opposed to a legislative act, and Lord Justice Scott's classification was criticized.[2] This shows how even judges differ in
their opinion of what is legislation, and how there are only
differences of degree to mark it off from the general run of
administrative activity.

PUBLICATION OF DELEGATED LEGISLATION

The Acts of 1893 and 1946

The maxim that ignorance of the law does not excuse any subject
represents the working hypothesis on which the rule of law rests in
British democracy. . . . But the very justification for that basic
maxim is that the whole of our law, written or unwritten, is accessible to the public—in the sense, of course, that, at any rate, its legal
advisers have access to it, at any moment, as of right.

---

[1] For privilege see above, p. 306.
[2] *Lewisham Borough Council v. Roberts* [1949] 2 K.B. 608.

The theory so stated in the *Blackpool* case [1] is of the greatest importance, but as that case itself showed, it may break down occasionally. It was long ago realized that the first remedial measure demanded by the growing stream of delegated legislation was a systematic scheme for publication and reference. The first statute was the Rules Publication Act 1893, which regulated the publication of *Statutory Rules and Orders*, begun in 1890. The statute now in force is the Statutory Instruments Act 1946, under which the title of the series has been changed to Statutory Instruments.

The Act of 1893 had two different objects. The first was, in the case of rules which had to be laid before Parliament, to give them (with some exceptions) *antecedent* publicity by requiring notice of them to be published and copies to be provided on demand. Any representations made in writing by 'a public body' had then to be considered before the rules were finally made and laid before Parliament. But these safeguards could be evaded on plea of urgency or special reasons, and provisional orders could (and sometimes did) remain in force indefinitely.

The second object was to secure publication of all statutory rules (whether or not to be laid before Parliament) *after* they were made, by requiring them to be sent to the Queen's printer to be numbered, printed and sold. Statutory rules were comprehensively defined as including rules made under any Act of Parliament, by Order in Council, or by any minister or government department. But the Treasury were given power to alter the effect of the definition by regulations, and a number of exceptions were so made for special cases—for example rules of a local and personal nature—and the definition was confined to cases 'of a legislative and not an executive character'. [2] The great bulk of delegated legislation became subject to an orderly system of publication, and this was a great gain. The Ministers' Powers Committee in 1932 made no complaint that delegated legislation was not accessible, and said that the Act had worked well within its sphere. They did, however, suggest widening the provisions for antecedent publicity, and they advocated a new and more comprehensive Act. [3] This eventually came, in time

---

[1] Above, p. 330.
[2] S.R. & O. 1894 No. 734 (Treasury Regulations).
[3] Cmd. 4060 (1932), pp. 62, 66.

to deal with the flood tide of rules and regulations, in the Act of 1946.

The Statutory Instruments Act 1946 came into force in 1948, and has repealed and replaced the Act of 1893. Its definition of Statutory Instrument now covers three categories of 'subordinate legislation' made (or confirmed or approved) under statute:

    (i) Orders in Council;
   (ii) Ministerial powers stated in the statute to be exercisable by statutory instrument; and
  (iii) future rules made under past statutes to which the Act of 1893 applied.

As regards (iii), regulations under the new Act continue the requirement that such rules shall be 'of a legislative and not an executive character'.[1] But as regards (ii), though it applies only to 'legislation', the real test is that it will only apply where Parliament provides, as it now normally does, that 'regulations made under this Act shall be made by statutory instrument'. Parliament has abandoned the attempt to define subordinate legislation by its substance, since this could never achieve precision. It now relies on itself to prescribe when the provisions for publication, &c., shall apply. For statutes made after 1947, therefore, there is a clear-cut but mechanical definition. For statutes made before 1948, the older, vaguer, but more ambitious definition continues. The Act again gives power to control the scope of the old definition by Treasury regulations. And Treasury regulations may exempt any classes of statutory instruments from the requirements of being printed and sold. Exemption has been given to local instruments, and also to instruments regularly printed in some other series. Subject to this, all statutory instruments must be sent to the Queen's printer as soon as made, and must be numbered, printed, and sold. A Reference Committee is empowered to deal with points of difficulty as to numbering, printing, classification, and so on.

Reference to statutory instruments and other delegated legislation on any subject is facilitated by an official index, the Index to Government Orders in Force, published biennially.

[1] S.I. 1947, no. 1.

Sub-delegated legislation

Both the old and the new Acts have been accused of a serious shortcoming, namely, that they do not extend to sub-delegated legislation. A positive opinion was expressed by Lord Justice Scott in the *Blackpool* case in 1947[1]:

They are both expressly limited to such delegated legislation as is made under powers conferred by Act of Parliament, whether on H.M. in Council or on a minister of the Crown. Such primary delegated legislation has now (and had under the Act of 1893) to be printed forthwith by the King's Printer and published as a statutory rule or order, etc.: but for delegated legislation made under powers conferred by a regulation or other legislative instrument not being itself an Act of Parliament, there is no general statutory requirement of publicity in force today. . . . The modern extent of sub-delegated legislation is almost boundless: and it seems to me vital to the whole English theory of the liberty of the subject, that the affected person should be able at any time to ascertain what legislation affecting his rights has been passed under sub-delegated powers.

In another case of 1948 Lord Justice Scott spoke of the unfairness to the public when 'administration is mixed up with sub-delegated legislation and none of the mixture is made public'.[2] But, as to the extent of the statutory definitions, it is not clear that either Act is as limited in its effect as Lord Justice Scott supposed. If the question were fully argued—as in the *Blackpool* case it was not—it might be found that at least some kinds of sub-delegated legislation were included. But since sub-delegated legislation is a product of emergency powers, this problem is unlikely to present itself in normal times.

Effect of non-publication on validity

Another question is whether the validity of rules and regulations is affected by failure to obey the statutory requirements for publication. It may be that these requirements are 'merely directory'—that is to say, that they embody Parliament's directions, but without imposing any penalty for disobedience.[3] In one case a minister was empowered by statute to control the

---

[1] Above, p. 330.
[2] *Jackson, Stansfield & Sons Ltd. v. Butterworth* [1948] 2 All E.R. 558.
[3] See above, p. 57.

use of explosives in mines by order, 'of which notice shall be given in such manner as he may direct', and though he failed to give any notice, his order was upheld on the ground that the condition was directory only.[1] It would seem *a fortiori* that neglect of a general statute requiring publication would be less serious. It was, indeed, held in 1918 that an order made by the Food Controller did not take effect until it was published: *A* had sold 1,000 bags of beans to *B* on 16 May 1917, and on that same day an order was made requisitioning all such beans, but it was not published until the following day; *B* tried to recover his money from *A* but failed, since the order was held to take effect only when it was made known.[2] But the true explanation is probably that the order, as construed by the court, was *intended* to take effect only at that time.

This hypothesis is impliedly supported by a new provision of the Statutory Instruments Act 1946. It requires the Stationery Office to publish lists showing the dates on which they issue statutory instruments, and in any proceedings against any person for offending under such statutory instruments

it shall be a defence to prove that the instrument had not been issued by His Majesty's Stationery Office at the date of the alleged contravention unless it is proved that at that date reasonable steps had been taken for the purpose of bringing the purport of the instrument to the notice of the public, or of persons likely to be affected by it, or of the person charged.[3]

It seems to be assumed that non-publication would not by itself be a sufficient defence, and since the provision deals only with criminal liability, it suggests that non-publication would not affect the validity of a statutory instrument altering civil rights. This was the construction adopted in a case of 1954, where a company were prosecuted for infringing an Iron and Steel Prices Order. The order had been printed, but not the schedules to it, which were extensive and bulky. The judge decided that non-publication of the schedules did not invalidate the order, because the Act made an obvious distinction between the making of the instrument and the issue of it, and the provisions for printing and publication were merely procedural.[4] The

---

[1] *Jones v. Robson* [1901] 1 Q.B. 673.
[2] *Johnson v. Sargant & Sons* [1918] 1 K.B. 101.
[3] S. 3 (2).　　　　[4] *The Queen v. Sheer Metalcraft Ltd.* [1954] 1 Q.B. 586.

making of the instrument was complete, in his opinion, when it was made by the Minister and (if so required by the empowering statute) laid before Parliament. Since the prosecution were able to prove that reasonable steps had been taken for notification by other channels, a conviction followed. The judge's suggestion that validity might depend upon laying before Parliament is in conflict with at least one previous judicial opinion,[1] and it may be that even that requirement is no more than directory. As we have seen, Acts of Indemnity have been used to prevent the question arising.[2]

Laying before Parliament

We have already noticed how the Rules Publication Act 1893 provided for pre-publication of regulations which had to be laid before Parliament, as is commonly required by the statute under which the regulations are made. The Statutory Instruments Act 1946 adopts the same policy but in a different way. It requires the laying to take place before the instrument comes into operation.[3] If, however, it is essential that it should come into operation before it can be laid, it may do so; but a reasoned notification must be sent to both Houses. There will obviously be occasions, especially when Parliament is not sitting, when orders may have to be brought into force urgently. The forty-day period provided by the Act of 1893 has gone, but it gave rise to so many 'provisional orders' ('provisional' merely for the purpose of avoiding it) that the new Act perhaps makes a more realistic compromise.

But even under the new Act it was found inconvenient to make special explanations for every order brought into force at times when Parliament was not sitting. The Laying of Documents (Interpretation) Act 1948 accordingly allowed each House to give its own meaning to 'laying' for the purposes of the Act; the Houses then made standing orders to the effect that delivery of copies to their offices should count as 'laying' at any time when a Parliament was legally in being, even though it was prorogued or adjourned at the time. The safe-

---

[1] *Starey v. Graham* [1899] 1 Q.B. 406 at 412.
[2] Above, p. 326.
[3] S. 4.

guards designed in 1893 have been progressively whittled down as the weight of delegated legislation has grown greater and greater.

The timetable for 'laying' has also been made more u. iiform by the Statutory Instruments Act 1946 in two classes of cases:

(i) instruments which are subject to annulment on an adverse resolution of either House, and
(ii) instruments which must be laid before Parliament in draft, but which may later be made if no hostile resolution is carried.

The first class is much more common than the second. In order to escape from the provisions of numerous Acts which had laid down different timetables, and in order to provide one timetable for the future, it is now provided that instruments of class (i) shall be duly laid and shall be subject to annulment for forty days, and that instruments of class (ii) shall not be made within forty days of being laid. In counting the forty days, no account is taken of periods when Parliament is dissolved or prorogued, or adjourned for more than four days. It will be observed that no provision is made for regulations which expire within a time-limit unless expressly confirmed by Parliament (of which we have already met examples)[1] or for regulations which do not take effect at all unless so confirmed. In those cases the timetable is usually of intrinsic importance to the subject-matter, and is best left as it is.

PRELIMINARY CONSULTATION

Hearing of objections

The principles of natural justice—in particular the rule that objections must be fairly heard before action is taken—do not apply to legislative powers in the way that they apply to administrative powers. Here again the distinction between these powers is of legal importance. But orders for such things as housing and planning schemes, although they may affect numerous people, are for this purpose treated as matters of administration and not of legislation. They are subject to the procedure of preliminary public inquiry under various Acts,

---

[1] Above, pp. 318, 320.

and also to the principles of natural justice, as we have seen.[1] The right to reasoned decisions given by the Tribunals and Inquiries Act 1958 is expressly excluded in the case of rules, orders, or schemes 'of a legislative and not an executive character'.[2] But it may be presumed that the right extends to all orders and schemes of the kind just mentioned.

In the true sphere of delegated legislation, a limited legal duty to consider objections was imposed by the provision of the Rules Publication Act 1893 that the rule-making authority must consider any written representations made within the forty-day period of preliminary publicity. But, as we saw, this proved of little benefit, and was repealed by the Act of 1946. A few statutes however provide for a right to make objection to draft regulations and for a right to a public inquiry in some circumstances. Examples are the Factories Act 1961 and the Offices Shops and Railways Premises Act 1963.[3] Under these Acts certain 'special regulations' must be published in draft and written objections lodged by persons affected must be considered by the Minister. If a majority of persons affected lodge a 'general objection' they are entitled to a public inquiry. But apart from these exceptional cases no-one has a right to a hearing before regulations are made.

In this respect English law has moved in the opposite direction from American law. The Federal Administrative Procedure Act of 1946 gives a right to 'interested persons' to 'participate in the rule-making through submission of written data, views or arguments', and in some cases Congress has prescribed a formal hearing. Hearings preliminary to rule-making have thus become an important part of the administrative process in the United States. But there is often no right to an oral hearing and there is a wide exception where the authority finds 'for good cause' 'that notice and public procedure thereon are impracticable, unnecessary or contrary to the public interest'.

In Britain the practice counts for more than the law. Consultation with interests and organizations likely to be affected by rules and regulations is one of the firmest and most carefully observed conventions. It is not a matter of legal right, any more than it is with Parliament's own legislation. But it is so

---

[1] Above, p. 193.   [2] S. 12 (2).
[3] 4th and 1st Schedules respectively.

well settled a practice that it is most unusual to hear complaint. It may be that consultation which is not subject to statutory procedure is more effective than formal hearing, which may produce legalism and artificiality. The duty to consult is recognized in every sense except the legal one. The Committee on Ministers' Powers were told:

No minister in his senses, with the fear of Parliament before his eyes, would ever think of making regulations without (where practicable) giving the persons who will be affected thereby (or their representatives) an opportunity of saying what they think about the proposal.[1]

But it is for the department to decide whom it will consult, and more attention is likely to be given to official and representative bodies than to individuals. The consultation of local authorities, professional bodies, trade unions, &c., is often on a very wide scale, and may involve reference to dozens of different organizations.

Statutory consultation and advisory bodies

Particular Acts often require particular interests to be consulted. Some provide for schemes of control to be formulated by the persons affected themselves. Another device which is often used is that of an advisory committee or council, which is set up under the Act and which must be consulted. The council will usually be constituted so as to represent various interests, and so as to be independent of ministerial control. And, in its turn, it may often consult other persons. Thus regulations concerning national insurance must be submitted to the National Insurance Advisory Committee, and the Committee must advertise them and consider any objections made to them. The Committee's report must be laid before Parliament by the Minister along with the regulations.[2] Similarly the Home Secretary is required to consult the Police Council or a Police Advisory Board before making certain regulations governing the police[3]; he must consult an advisory committee before making any order for protection of birds[4]; and procedural rules

---

[1] *Minutes of Evidence*, p. 35.
[2] National Insurance Act 1965, s. 108.
[3] Police Act 1964, ss. 45, 46.
[4] Protection of Birds Act 1954, s. 13.

for statutory tribunals may be made only after consultation with the Council on Tribunals.[1] In these cases there is no statutory procedure for consulting other interests such as there is with the National Insurance Advisory Committee. But these councils may consult other people and hear evidence if they wish, and frequently they do so.

Consultation before rule-making, though usually not required by law, is in fact one of the major industries of government. That being so, it is doubtful whether anything would be gained by imposing more general legal obligations and formal procedures. At any rate, no such reform has been demanded.

PARLIAMENTARY SUPERVISION

The trend of the times

One of the features of the twentieth century has been a shift of the constitutional centre of gravity, away from Parliament and towards the executive. Mr. Lloyd George once said: 'Parliament has really no control over the Executive; it is a pure fiction.'[2] Party discipline gives the government a tight control over Parliament in all but the last resort; and the electoral system, tending as it does to eliminate minority parties, normally gives the government a solid basis for its power. But, in addition, the sheer volume of legislation and other governmental work is so great that the parliamentary machine is unequal to it. This is itself one of the principal reasons for delegated legislation. It is also the reason why it is difficult for Parliament to supervise it effectively. To treat the subject of parliamentary control in any detail would take us beyond administrative law. But mention may be made of a few matters of special interest.

'Watch and pray'[3]

One of the commonest statutory requirements is that rules or regulations made under some Act shall be laid before both Houses of Parliament. Parliament thus hopes to keep its eye upon them, and to correct them where necessary. As we have seen, there are a number of different systems: the regulations

---

[1] Tribunals and Inquiries Act 1958, s. 8.
[2] Quoted by Sir Carleton Allen, *Law and Orders*, 3rd ed. p. 161.
[3] Quoted *ibid.*, p. 123.

may merely have to be laid; or they may be subject to negative resolution within forty days; or they may expire unless confirmed by affirmative resolution; or they may have to be laid in draft. Occasionally they do not have to be laid at all, because Parliament has omitted to make any provision.[1] The prescribed procedure corresponds in a general way to the importance of the subject-matter—but only in a general way, for the vagaries in legislative practice have been called by a leading authority 'extraordinary'.[2]

Where the regulations have merely to be laid, there is no special opportunity for control, and the laying does no more than advertise the regulations to members, who may then put questions to ministers. At the other extreme, where an affirmative resolution is necessary, the government must find time for a motion and debate, so that there is full scope for criticism. In the intermediate and commonest case, where the regulations are subject to annulment, the procedure of the House of Commons allows them to be challenged by any member at the end of the day's business. He must move a 'prayer', because the method of annulment is by Order in Council (as provided by the Statutory Instruments Act 1946),[3] and the motion is for a humble prayer to the Crown that the regulations be annulled. Provided that the necessary quorum of forty can be kept in the House, the annulment procedure ensures an opportunity for debate at the instance of any member. But the House could not possibly debate all the annullable regulations laid before it. In 1951, when the Labour government's majority had fallen to 8, there was suddenly a great increase in 'praying'. On many successive nights—for 'praying' is necessarily nocturnal—resolutions were moved against various statutory instruments, as it was alleged, 'for no other reason than the exhaustion of honorable members and Ministers of the Crown'. Although the question here was not exactly that of controlling delegated legislation, the opportunity was taken to ask a Select Committee of the House to consider 'the existing procedures by which the control of this House over delegated legislation is exercised'. The Committee carried out a wide review and considered

---

[1] E.g. regulations for Rent Tribunals under the Furnished Houses (Rent Control) Act 1946, s. 8. The omission is inexplicable.
[2] Sir Carleton Allen, op. cit., p. 130.   [3] S. 5.

many possible reforms—for example, that there should be a Standing Committee to hear 'prayers', and that objectors should be given some sort of formal hearing. But all such ideas were rejected, for various reasons, and the only outcome was a change of procedure to prevent debates on prayers running on far into the night: they must be closed or (in the Speaker's discretion) adjourned at half past eleven. In other respects the House appeared to be satisfied with the machinery of control. The fact that there was not time for everything, or that the procedure might be abused, was the inescapable malady of all Parliament's work.

The Scrutiny Committee

The one successful innovation of importance, which was already part of the machinery with which the Committee of 1953 declared itself satisfied, is the House of Commons' Select Committee on Statutory Instruments, commonly called the Scrutiny Committee. A committee of this kind had been recommended in 1932 by the Ministers' Powers Committee, which thought that it should deal both with Bills proposing new delegated legislation and with all rules and regulations as they were made. But not until 1944 was the Scrutiny Committee appointed, and then only for the second of these purposes. Since then it has been in continuous existence, and has done valuable work contrary to a good deal of expert and official opinion to the effect that its tasks were impracticable, undesirable, and so forth. It is not concerned with policy, but with the manner in which rule-making powers are in fact exercised. Just as with judicial control, the important general questions are often questions of form rather than of substance. This distinction between policy and technique means that the Committee does its work without party strife. Its chairman is normally a member of the Opposition, thus signifying that it exists in order to criticize.

The Scrutiny Committee is required to consider every statutory instrument, rule, order or scheme laid or laid in draft before the House if proceedings may be taken upon it in either House under any statute. The Committee has to decide whether to bring it to the attention of the House on any of the following grounds:

   (i) that it imposes a charge on the public revenues, or imposes or prescribes charges for any licence, consent, or service from any public authority;

   (ii) that it is made under a statute which precludes challenge in the courts;

   (iii) that it appears to make 'some unusual or unexpected use of the powers conferred by the statute';

   (iv) that it purports to have retrospective effect, without statutory authorization;

   (v) that publication or laying before Parliament appear to have been unjustifiably delayed;

   (vi) that notification to the Speaker appears to have been unjustifiably delayed, in cases where the Statutory Instruments Act 1946 requires it[1];

   (vii) 'that for any special reason its form or purport calls for elucidation'.

   (viii) 'that the drafting of it appears to be defective'.

Before reporting an instrument to the House, the Committee must hear the government department's explanations. Since the Committee normally meets fortnightly, this means that, contrary to the proposals of 1932, the report will often not reach the House within the forty-day period, if applicable. The most important result of the Committee's vigilance is not that it brings regulations to debate in the House (though there have been some notable examples of this happening), but that it gives government departments a lively consciousness that critical eyes are kept upon them. The fact that 2 per cent. or less of the instruments scrutinized are reported to the House is in part a measure of the Committee's success in establishing a standard. The Committee makes general reports as well as reports on particular instruments. Its work is another example of the value of a standing body as opposed to periodical inquests by *ad hoc* committees.

   In particular, the Committee has been able to secure more satisfactory explanatory notes, which now accompany statutory instruments as a matter of course and are particularly useful when the instrument is complicated. Obscurities have often been criticized, and also the practices of legislating by reference,

---

[1] Above, p. 336.

sub-delegation on dubious authority, and (occasionally) retro-spective operation. The terms of reference are wide enough (particularly under head (iii)) to enable a point of *ultra vires* to be raised. The Committee has been able to secure consolidation of various scattered regulations, and it helped to provide the impetus for the Statutory Instruments Act 1946. A few regu-lations escape its scrutiny, since statutes sometimes omit to provide for them to be laid. But it covers the greater part of delegated legislation which is of national as opposed to local effect. It may be said to be the one successful result of the efforts of reformers to impose discipline on all this legislative activity.

Scrutiny by the House of Lords

The House of Lords also has its Special Orders Committee, which has been in existence since 1924. But this has a more restricted scope, since it considers only orders and regulations which require an affirmative resolution of the House. The Committee is charged with advising the House whether it can give its approval without special attention, or whether further inquiry should be made before the resolution is moved. The Committee examines departmental representatives before reporting. It has quite often recommended further inquiry, for which the House may appoint a Select Committee. But the class of orders with which it deals is a small one, and it does not keep watch over the general mass of delegated legislation, as does the Scrutiny Committee of the House of Commons.

The Ministers' Powers Committee originally recommended that both Houses should have scrutiny committees with similar terms of reference, but the House of Lords has not followed the lead of the House of Commons. This is perhaps curious, since the supervision of formal and legal proprieties, as opposed to the policy of a measure, is a function which the upper House could well discharge. Such has been the experience in Australia, where an effective Committee on Regulations and Ordinances has been established by the Senate; it was thought that objec-tions to the manner and form of regulations in the House of Representatives would be decided merely on party lines, since the fate of the government might turn upon the vote. In Eng-land this handicap is accepted as inevitable. But it is probably more than counterbalanced by the closer contact of the House of Commons with the work of government departments. The fruits of the Scrutiny Committee's labours are not to be counted in motions carried against the government, but in the improvements in departmental practice which their vigilance has secured. It is to the House of Commons that ministers and officials are most sensitive. Politics play virtually no part in the work of the Committee itself, nor do its reports lose their persuasive force because they face the steam-roller of the ruling majority.

APPENDIX

A. *Smith v. East Elloe Rural District Council*[1]

Although the authority of this case is severely shaken, if not destroyed, by the *Anisminic* case,[2] attention should be drawn to the dangers of the standard form of statutory ouster clause when interpreted without reference to general principles.

The Acquisition of Land (Authorization Procedure) Act 1946,[3] like many others, provides in substance that—

(a) a person aggrieved[4] by a compulsory purchase order may challenge it on the grounds that 'it is not empowered to be granted under this Act' or that 'any requirement of this Act . . . has not been complied with', by applying to the High Court within six weeks of notice of its confirmation; and

(b) subject to (a), a compulsory purchase order 'shall not . . . be questioned in any legal proceedings whatsoever'.

Lords Simonds, Morton and Radcliffe (Lords Reid and Somervell dissenting) held that challenge on the ground of fraud after the six weeks was barred by clause (b). This is the point explained on p. 151.

But Lords Morton, Reid and Somervell (Lord Radcliffe dissenting and Lord Simonds inclining to dissent) also held that fraud was not a ground of challenge which fell within clause (a). Lord Morton held that clause (a) allowed challenge only for violation of the express statutory requirements; Lord Reid held that it did not apply to the whole area of bad faith and unreasonableness described by Lord Greene M.R. in the *Wednesbury* case[5]; and Lord Somervell held that fraud was not a matter of *ultra vires* at all. If the majority opinions on both points are combined (though only Lord Morton supports them both), many kinds of unlawful action are not challengeable *even within*

[1] Above, p. 151. [2] *Ibid.*
[3] 1st sched., para. 16. [4] As to 'person aggrieved' see above, p. 148.
[5] Above, p. 72.

the six weeks. This extraordinary conclusion would allow un-controllable abuse of the statutory power, and is clearly con-trary to principle. The object of the Act is surely to set a severe time limit to judicial control, but not otherwise to restrict it. Thus 'not empowered to be granted' is merely draftsman's language for 'not lawfully made', and comprises all possible kinds of *ultra vires.* Lord Radcliffe's opinion on clause (*a*) there-fore seems correct.[1]

This will all be irrelevant if, as the *Anisminic* case now holds, an ouster clause gives no protection to any act which is in any way *ultra vires.* But for the reasons given on p. 153 it is unlikely that the *Anisminic* case is a final solution. The meaning of clause (*a*) may still therefore be important.

In the *East Elloe* case the House of Lords held unanimously that an action based on bad faith might proceed against the clerk of the council personally, if bad faith could be proved. This action would presumably be for damages for breach of statutory duty,[2] but this was not made clear. No further pro-ceedings were reported.

B. *Judicial control of non-legal acts*

In *R. v. Criminal Injuries Compensation Board*[3] a strong Divi-sional Court held that certiorari might issue to quash a decision of the Board. The Board had rejected the claim of an injured police officer's widow on the ground that a pension award had already compensated her. The Court however agreed with the Board and dismissed the motion for certiorari on the merits.

The curiosity of this case is that the Board has no statutory constitution or power. It distributes compensation to victims of criminal injury from funds voted by Parliament and adminis-tered under a published scheme which was laid before Parlia-ment and approved but not enacted. Legally therefore it merely makes *ex gratia* payments, and no claimant has legal rights.

Lord Parker C.J. said that 'the exact limits of the ancient

---

[1] Lord Denning M.R. expressed this opinion in *Webb v. M.H.L.G.* (above, p. 151), saying also that no clear guidance could be drawn from the conflicting opinions in the *East Elloe* case.

[2] Above, p. 156.

[3] [1967] 2 Q.B. 864.

remedy by way of certiorari have never been and ought not to be specifically defined'. Since the Board was set up in a form which required it to adjudicate claims and clearly required it to act judicially, its awards could be quashed by certiorari like those of other tribunals.

This exploit may be compared with the *Anisminic* case.[1] Neither an express statutory ouster clause nor a non-statutory administrative scheme will now deter the court from intervening. Once again the court shows its determination to preserve the ultimate control of the law, and to circumvent legislative or administrative devices for escaping from it.

The difficulty is to know what 'quashing' can mean when the determination to be quashed is not a determination having legal effect. If certiorari were granted and the Board did nothing further, would the court grant the usual mandamus 'to hear and determine according to law'? Diplock L.J. indeed suggested that the Board possessed legal power. But then the problem is to know how such power can be created without an Act of Parliament. Whatever the correct hypothesis may be, it seems that the court may be prepared to clothe administrative arrangements, if sufficiently formal, with the force of law. This would be an interesting new mode of legislation. Comparison may be made with American decisions holding administrative practices to be binding on government departments: see *Vitarelli v. Seaton*[2] and 81 L.Q.R. at p. 376; and compare *Gonzalez v. Freeman*,[3] where a contractor 'blacklisted' by an American government agency sued successfully.

C. *University discipline and natural justice*

Various attempts, all unsuccessful, have been made by senior and junior members of universities to have disciplinary proceedings invalidated for violation of natural justice. Two Sinhalese cases have already been cited: *Ceylon University v. Fernando*[4]; *Vidyodaya University Council v. Silva*.[5] All the decisions assume that natural justice is in principle applicable.[6] But there are two different foundations on which the right to natural justice may rest.

---

[1] Above, p. 151.
[3] 344 F. 2d 570 (1964).
[5] Above, p. 205.

[2] 359 U.S. 535 (1969).
[4] Above, p. 213.
[6] Contrast p. 200, above.

Where its disciplinary powers are statutory, the university may be regarded as a statutory public authority which by implication is required to observe natural justice like any other such authority. This is administrative law, and all the usual remedies, including certiorari and mandamus, may be available: *King v. University of Saskatchewan.*[1] But the mere fact that the university is established by statute does not necessarily make its powers statutory: see the *Vidyodaya* case (above) and *Fekete v. The Royal Institution for the Advancement of Learning.*[2] The universities of Oxford and Cambridge are ancient universities by prescription, but have statutory powers to make their own rules. Their disciplinary powers, so far as embodied in their own rules, might or might not be held to be statutory.

Where disciplinary powers are not statutory, they may operate by way of contract if there is an implied contract of membership, just as in the case of a trade union or a club. Violation of natural justice will then be a breach of contract leading to the usual remedies of declaration, injunction and damages, as in the cases cited elsewhere.[3] But this is private law, not administrative law, and there is no place for certiorari or mandamus: see *R. v. National Joint Council for Dental Technicians*[4]; the *Vidyodaya* case (above); *R. v. Criminal Injuries Compensation Board*[5]; *Fekete's* case (above).

The court often disclaims jurisdiction in a university's affairs (including the conduct of examinations and the conferring of degrees) on the ground that the proper remedy is appeal to the visitor: see *Thorne v. University of London.* If a university or college has no other visitor, the Crown is visitor and acts through the Lord Chancellor. The visitor's jurisdiction used to be limited to members of the foundation, so that it did not extend (for example) to commoners of a college. But the modern cases do not seem to recognize this restriction. The precise extent of visitatorial jurisdiction is uncertain, and the court may be able to intervene in cases based on statute or contract: see *King v. University of Saskatchewan* (above); *Bell v. University of Auckland.*[6]

---

[1] (1969) 6 D.L.R. (3d) 120.
[2] [1969] B.R. 1 (Quebec), affd (1969) 2 D.L.R. (3d) 129.
[3] Above, p. 175, note 1.   [4] [1953] 1 Q.B. 704.
[5] [1967] 2 Q.B. 864 at 882, 884.   [6] [1969] N.Z.L.R. 1029.

In *R. v. Aston University Senate*[1] (criticized in 85 L.Q.R. 468) two students who had been sent down for failure in examinations applied for certiorari and mandamus. The Divisional Court held that the examiners who had first decided to send them down had not given them a fair hearing, and that later proceedings did not cure this fault (contrast *King v. University of Saskatchewan*, above). But the remedies were refused, since they are not granted 'to those who sleep upon their rights' and the students had taken no action for over seven months. The mystery in this case is how certiorari and mandamus could ever have been the right remedies, since the University of Aston (incorporated by royal charter in 1966) has no statutory powers. The rights of the students could only have been contractual, and certiorari and mandamus are not remedies for breach of contract. Further mysteries are why no mention was made either of the jurisdiction of the visitor or of the six-months time limit for certiorari.

Ceylon University v. Fernando (above) was another case in which the court did not explain whether the right to natural justice was based on statute or contract; but in that case it did not matter, since the remedy sought was a declaration. The English decisions do not seem to observe the distinction between public and private duties. The Canadian decisions observe it clearly.

Mandamus may be granted where a university has an established jurisdiction at common law, as in *Bentley*'s case,[2] and also where a visitor wrongfully refuses to act.

---

[1] [1969] 2 Q.B. 538.   [2] Above, p. 187.

SELECT BIBLIOGRAPHY

I. GENERAL CONSTITUTIONAL LAW

TEXT-BOOKS on constitutional law deal shortly with administrative law, though their treatment must usually be too concise to allow discussion of difficulties. The best general works are WADE (E. C. S.) and PHILLIPS (G. G.), *Constitutional Law*, 8th ed. (by E. C. S. Wade and A. W. Bradley), 1970, HOOD PHILLIPS, *Constitutional Law*, 4th ed., 1967. MITCHELL, *Constitutional Law*, 2nd ed., 1968, pays special attention to administrative law and to Scots law. KEIR and LAWSON, *Cases on Constitutional Law*, 5th ed., 1967, is also helpful, both for cases and commentary.

DICEY's classic, *The Law of the Constitution*, is important, though often misleading for administrative law (see above, p. 7); but the 10th edition, 1959, by E. C. S. WADE has an extensive commentary and also an appendix on *droit administratif* in modern France.

Comments on administrative law will be found in JENNINGS, *The Law and the Constitution*, 5th ed., 1959, and *Principles of Local Government Law*, 3rd ed., 1947 (but not 4th ed., 1960). Practitioners' works are of little use in this field, except for reference. HALSBURY's *Laws of England*, 3rd ed., has no title for administrative law. Its title 'Constitutional Law' deals only with the Crown, while the prerogative writs and orders are disguised under a separate title, 'Crown Proceedings'. Yet crown proceedings (in the sense of the Crown Proceedings Act) are in the title 'Constitutional Law'. These subjects have not yet been given their due place by the legal profession.

2. ADMINISTRATIVE LAW

Two leading works are GRIFFITH and STREET, *Principles of Administrative Law*, 4th ed., 1967, and GARNER, *Administrative Law*, 3rd ed., 1970. The former gives prominence to delegated legislation and public corporations, the latter to local government. Casebooks are YARDLEY, *A Source Book of English Administrative Law*, 2nd ed., 1970; GRIFFITH and STREET, *A Casebook of Administrative Law*, 1964. See also CARR, *Concerning English Administrative Law*, 1941. Important official publications are the *Report of the Committee on Ministers' Powers*, 1932, Cmd. 4060, and the *Report of the Committee on Administrative Tribunals and Enquiries* (the Franks Committee), 1957, Cmnd. 218. The Ombudsman is now the subject of a large literature: see particularly ROWAT (ed.), *The Ombudsman*, 1965, GELLHORN, *Ombudsmen and Others*, 1966, the annual reports of the Parliamentary Commissioner for Administration, the reports of the Select Committee of the House of Commons, and the annual reports of the Ombudsman in New Zealand.

Works available for other Commonwealth countries are—

Australia

BENJAFIELD and WHITMORE, *Principles of Australian Administrative Law*, 3rd ed., 1966.

BRETT and HOGG, *Administrative Law, Cases and Materials*, 1967.

New Zealand

D. E. PATERSON, *An Introduction to Administrative Law in New Zealand*, 1967.

Canada

R.-P. BARBE (ed.), *Droit Administratif Canadien et Québecois*, 1969.

Inquiry into Civil Rights (Ontario Royal Commission: the McRUER Reports). These wide-ranging reports are appearing in a series of volumes.

DUSSAULT, *Le Contrôle Judiciaire de l'Administration au Québec*, 1969.

India

MARKOSE, *Judicial Control of Administrative Action in India*, 1956.

3. JUDICIAL CONTROL AND NATURAL JUSTICE

DE SMITH, *Judicial Review of Administrative Action*, 2nd ed., 1968, is a full-length study of this subject which fills a long-felt want. The work covers the whole subject of *ultra vires*, and also refers to authorities in other English-speaking countries. Natural justice and remedies are also fully treated in this important book, which in fact covers the major part of administrative law.

RUBINSTEIN, *Jurisdiction and Illegality*, 1965, investigates a number of fundamental questions.

ZAMIR, *The Declaratory Judgment*, 1962, is a helpful study of one remedy.

MARSHALL, *Natural Justice*, 1959, is now somewhat out of date, owing to the multitude of later decisions.

4. TRIBUNALS AND INQUIRIES

ROBSON, *Justice and Administrative Law*, 3rd ed., 1951, and ALLEN, *Administrative Jurisdiction*, 1956, were both published before the Franks

Committee's Report. VAN DYK, *Tribunals and Inquiries*, 1965, is useful for reference. Annual reports of the Council on Tribunals have been published from 1960 onwards.

5. CROWN PROCEEDINGS

GLANVILLE WILLIAMS, *Crown Proceedings*, 1948, is recommended. Practitioners' commentaries are BELL, *Crown Proceedings*, 1948, and BICKFORD SMITH, *The Crown Proceedings Act, 1947* (1948). STREET, *Governmental Liability*, 1953, and MITCHELL, *The Contracts of Public Authorities*, 1954, are comparative works covering Britain, the United States and France. WILLIAMS, *Not in the Public Interest*, 1965, discusses crown privilege and official secrecy.

6. DELEGATED LEGISLATION

This daunting subject has been fortunate in its authors, especially SIR CARLETON ALLEN and SIR CECIL CARR. ALLEN, *Law and Orders*, 3rd ed., 1965, is the principal work. SIR CECIL CARR's contributions include *Delegated Legislation* (three lectures), 1921, *Concerning English Administrative Law* (see 2, above), and a chapter in *Parliament, A Survey*, 1952.

INDEX